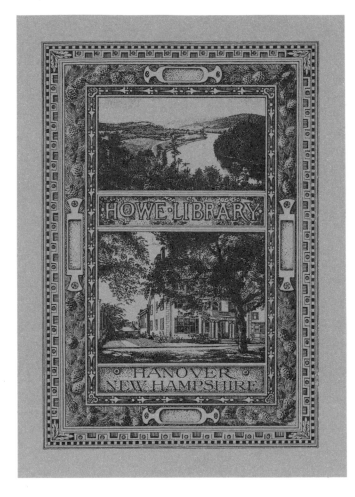

HOWE·LIBRARY

HANOVER
NEW HAMPSHIRE

Also by Annie Somerville

Fields of Greens

everyday greens

everyday Greens

by Annie Somerville

Home Cooking from Greens,
the Celebrated Vegetarian Restaurant

SCRIBNER / New York · London · Toronto · Sydney · Singapore

SCRIBNER
1230 Avenue of the Americas
New York, NY 10020

SCRIBNER and design are trademarks of Macmillan Library Reference USA, Inc.,
used under license by Simon & Schuster, the publisher of this work.

For information about special discounts for bulk purchases,
please contact Simon & Schuster Special Sales:
1-800-456-6798 or business@simonandschuster.com

Illustrations by Mayumi Oda
Designed by Jenny Wunderly
Text set in Minion

Manufactured in the United States of America

1   3   5   7   9   10   8   6   4   2

Library of Congress Cataloging-in-Publication Data
Somerville, Annie.
Everyday Greens : home cooking from Greens, the celebrated vegetarian restaurant / by Annie Somerville.
    p.   cm.
Includes index.
1. Vegetarian cookery. 2. Greens (Restaurant : Fort Mason, Calif.:) I. Title.
TX837.S6825 2003
641.5'636—dc21   2003042452
ISBN 0-7432-1625-3

To my sweetheart, ZRS

Contents

Introduction   *xvii*

Savory Bites 1

Warm Spiced Almonds   *2*

Lotus Root Pickles   *3*

Pickled Daikon Radish   *4*

Crispy Spring Rolls with Spicy Dipping Sauce   *5*

Vietnamese Spring Rolls with Peanut-Hoisin Sauce   *7*

Filo Turnover Samosas   *10*

Hummous   *12*

Guacamole   *13*

Grilled Asparagus   *14*

Grilled Artichokes with Mint   *15*

Quince and Sour Cherry Compote   *16*

TO SPREAD ON BREAD

Garlic Toasts   *17*

Picholine Olive Tapenade   *18*

Artichoke Relish   *19*

Fava Bean Puree   *20*

Warm Cannellini Beans and Wilted Greens   *22*

Grilled Pepper and Fennel Relish with Capers   *23*

Spicy Tomato Jam   *24*

Salads of All Kinds 25

LEAFY GREENS WITH LIVELY VINAIGRETTES

Green Salad with Beets, Fennel, Walnuts, and Ricotta Salata   *28*

Butter Lettuce with Ruby Grapefruit, Avocado, and Grapefruit-Chili Vinaigrette *30*

Butter Lettuce with Blood Oranges, Tangerines, Pistachios, and Citrus-Honey
  Vinaigrette   *32*

Garden Lettuces with Pears, Fennel, Pomegranates, and Pear Vinaigrette   *34*

Bitter Greens with Fuyu Persimmons, Asian Pears, and Pecans   *35*

Romaine Hearts and Watercress with Apples, Beets, Stilton, and Cider Vinaigrette *37*

Romaine Hearts with Sun-Dried Tomatoes, Chunky Sourdough Croutons,
    and Red Wine Vinaigrette   *40*

Wilted Spinach and Escarole Hearts with Portobello Mushrooms and Parmesan   *42*

Wilted Spinach Salad with Pears, Gorgonzola, and Toasted Pecans   *45*

PICK-OF-THE-SEASON SALADS

Asparagus and Beets with Meyer Lemon Vinaigrette   *48*

Panzanella with Artichokes, Olives, and Manchego   *50*

Moroccan Beet Salad   *51*

Simple Artichoke Salad   *53*

Fennel and Parsley Salad with Meyer Lemon   *55*

Corn and Cherry Tomato Salad with Arugula   *56*

Green Beans and Shelling Beans with Cherry Tomatoes   *58*

Couscous Salad with Cherry Tomatoes, Lemon, and Pine Nuts   *60*

White Runner Beans with Champagne Vinaigrette and Tarragon   *61*

Corn and Fire-Roasted Poblano Salad with Cilantro   *63*

Heirloom Tomato Salad with Shaved Manchego   *65*

Tomato Salad with Creamy Blue Cheese Dressing   *66*

Grilled Fig and Endive Salad with Watercress   *68*

Grilled Fingerling Potato Salad with Corn and Cherry Tomatoes   *70*

Yellow Finn Potato Salad with Green Beans and Tarragon   *72*

Roasted Japanese Eggplant Salad with Pine Nuts and Capers   *74*

Farro Salad with Roasted Peppers and Arugula   *75*

Green Papaya Salad   *76*

Lentil Salad with Goat Cheese and Mint   *77*

Grilled Portobello Mushroom and Endive Salad with Shaved Parmesan   *80*

Asian Noodle Salad with Peanut Sauce and Lime   *82*

Soups **85**

Corn Soup with Ginger and Thai Basil   *86*

Chilled Three Beet Soup   *87*

Chilled Cucumber Soup with Yogurt and Mint   *89*

Kabocha Squash Soup with Coconut Milk and Lime Leaves   *90*

Potato, Spring Onion, and Sorrel Soup   *91*

Borlotti Bean Soup with Roasted Garlic and Parmesan Croutons   *93*

Butternut Squash and Chestnut Soup   *95*

Carrot-Parsnip Soup with Orange Crème Fraîche   *97*

Potato, Fennel, and Celery Root Soup 99
Moroccan Chick-Pea Soup 101
Mushroom-Farro Soup 103
Giant Peruvian Lima Bean Soup 105
Curry-Laced Lentil Soup 108
Vegetable Stock 110
Corn Stock 111
Mushroom Stock 112

Sandwiches **113**
Sourdough Baguette with Goat Cheese, Watercress, and Tomatoes 114
Avocado and Tomato Sandwich with Chipotle Aïoli 115
Baguette with Tapenade, Grilled Peppers, and Fontina 117
Grilled Mexican Sandwich with Poblano Chilies and Cheddar 119
Focaccia with Roasted Eggplant, Sun-Dried Tomatoes, and Asiago 120
Fresh Mozzarella Sandwich with Grilled Onions and Wilted Chard 121
Santorini Sandwich on a Rosemary Roll 123
Baguette with Grilled Summer Vegetables, Fromage Blanc, and Basil 125
Portobello Sandwich with Tomatoes, Roasted Onions, and Basil Aïoli 127
Tai's Vietnamese Tofu Sandwich 129

All Wrapped Up: Filo, Tarts, and Tortillas **131**
Filo Purses with Artichokes, Mushrooms, and Asiago 133
Filo Turnovers with Butternut Squash and Gruyère 135
Filo Turnovers Filled with Goat Cheese, Leeks, and Walnuts 137
Artichoke and Spring Onion Tart 139
Corn and Basil Tart 141
Provençal Tartlets 142
Chanterelle Tart with Roasted Garlic Custard 144
Mexican Tartlets with Roasted Winter Vegetables 146
Tart Dough 148
Yeasted Tart Dough 150
Corn Quesadillas 151
Soft Tacos with Grilled Summer Vegetables 152
Soft Tacos with Butternut Squash, Plantain, and Poblano Chilies 154
Roasted Winter Vegetable Enchiladas 156

Pizza 159

Tomato Pizza with Feta, Lemon, and Scallions	161
Mexican Pizza with Corn, Tomatillos, and Chipotle Chilies	162
Roasted Eggplant and Cherry Tomato Pizza with Basil	164
Potato Pizza with Roasted Tomatoes, Olives, and Manchego	165
Pizza with Wilted Greens, Goat Cheese, and Hot Pepper	167
Artichoke and Roasted Shallot Pizza	169
Pizza with Portobello Mushrooms, Spring Onions, and Arugula	171
Pizza Dough	172

Griddle Cakes and Crêpes 173

Corn and Scallion Griddle Cakes	174
Spinach and Feta Griddle Cakes	175
Artichoke Griddle Cakes with Gruyère	177
Butternut Squash Risotto Griddle Cakes	179
Yellow Finn Potato Cakes with Asiago	180
Two Potato Griddle Cakes	182
Potato Gordas	184
Masa Harina Crêpes with Summer Vegetables, Poblano Chilies, and Cheddar	185
Rosemary Crêpes with Goat Cheese and Wilted Greens	187
Buckwheat Crêpes with Winter Vegetables and Caramelized Onions	189
Crêpe Batter	191

Curries, Ragoûts, and Stews 193

Indian Curry with Tamarind and Chilies	194
Red Curry with Summer Vegetables and Thai Spices	196
Vietnamese Yellow Curry	200
Fall Vegetable Ragoût with White Beans	203
Winter Vegetable Ragoût with Portobello Mushrooms	205
Spring Vegetable Tagine	207
Spring Stir-Fry with Peanut Sauce and Thai Basil	210
New Mexican Border Stew	212

Baked in a Casserole 215

Asparagus Bread Pudding	216
Corn Pudding	217
Macaroni and Cheese	218
Potato and Green Garlic Gratin	220

Butternut Squash Gratin *222*

Polenta Gratin with Fire-Roasted Poblano Chilies and Roasted Garlic . . . *223*

Winter Root Vegetable Gratin *225*

Artichoke and Portobello Mushroom Lasagne *227*

Roasted Winter Vegetable Lasagne *229*

Pasta and Risotto **231**

Fusilli Col Bucco with Grilled Tomatoes, Gorgonzola, and Pine Nuts . . . *232*

Linguine with Summer Beans, Gremolata, and Olives *234*

Papparadelle with Spring Vegetables and Lemon Cream *236*

Spinach Tagliarini with Corn, Cherry Tomatoes, and Basil *238*

Pasta and White Beans with Roasted Garlic, Rainbow Chard, and Olives . *239*

Orecchiette with Broccoli Rabe, Almonds, and Manchego *241*

Linguine with Arugula, Sun-Dried Tomatoes, and Ricotta Salata *243*

Penne with Roasted Butternut Squash, Brown Butter, and Sage *244*

Udon with Miso, Shiitake Mushrooms, and Bok Choy *246*

Risotto with Asparagus, Morels, and Parmigiano-Reggiano *249*

Summer Risotto with Tomatoes, Mascarpone, and Basil *251*

Risotto with Roasted Butternut Squash and Kale *253*

Roasted and Stuffed Vegetables **255**

Roasted Butternut Squash Rounds with Sage Leaves *256*

Glazed Cipollini Onions *257*

Crisp Sliced Potatoes with Garlic and Fresh Thyme *258*

Gingered Yams *259*

Roasted Portobello Mushrooms *260*

Roasted Tomatoes *261*

Mashed Yellow Finn Potatoes *262*

Roasted Portobello Mushrooms Filled with Winter Vegetables and Fontina *263*

Anaheim Chilies Filled with Corn, Cheddar, and Cilantro *265*

Gypsy Peppers Filled with Fromage Blanc and Fines Herbes *267*

Artichokes Stuffed with Garlic Bread Crumbs, Lemon, and Pine Nuts . . . *269*

Warm Beans and Grains **271**

Spicy Rattlesnake Beans *272*

Warm White Beans *273*

Braised French Lentils *275*

Basmati Rice with Pumpkin Seeds *276*

Jasmine Rice with Cashews … 277
Coconut Jasmine Rice … 278
Almond-Cherry Couscous … 279
Polenta … 280
Crisp Polenta Triangles with Gorgonzola Cream, Walnuts, and Basil … 281

Salsas and Sauces ……………………………………**283**
Cucumber Raita … 284
Avocado-Mango Salsa … 285
Corn and Tomatillo Salsa … 286
Fire-Roasted Salsa … 287
Salsa Negra … 288
Tomatillo Sauce … 289
Roasted Pepper Sauce … 290
Grilled Tomato, Garlic, and Basil Sauce … 292
Charmoula … 293
Mushroom-Sherry Sauce … 294
Tomato-Zinfandel Sauce … 295
Meyer Lemon Beurre Blanc … 296
Herb Cream … 297

A Few of Our Favorite Greens …………………**299**
Broccoli Rabe with Hot Pepper … 300
Dinosaur Kale with Toasted Almonds … 301
Rainbow Chard with Pumpkin Seeds … 302
Sautéed Winter Greens … 304
Spicy Asian Greens … 305

Desserts and Pastries ……………………………**307**
Ginger Cookies … 308
Almond Macaroons … 309
Candied Ginger Shortbread … 310
Debbie's Pecan Brownies … 312
Raspberry-Plum Cobbler … 313
Shortcake … 314
Nectarine-Blackberry Shortcake … 315
Ginger Crunch Cake with Poached Pears … 316

Almond Brown Butter Cake with Plums 318

Nectarine-Almond Upside-Down Cake 320

Poached Pears 322

Poached Sour Cherries 323

Rhubarb Tartlets with Almond Streusel 324

Apricot Lattice Tart 326

Apple-Quince Turnovers 328

Cream Cheese Dough 331

Fromage Blanc Cheesecake with Pistachio Crust 332

Triple Chocolate Angel Food Cake 333

Chocolate Mousse with Filo Crisps 335

Chocolate-Rum Steamed Pudding 337

Chocolate-Chestnut Mousse Cakes 338

Basmati Rice Pudding with Mascarpone 339

Cranberry Compote with Tangerines 341

Bittersweet Chocolate Sauce 342

Rose Geranium Ice Cream 343

Toasted Almond Ice Cream 344

Plum Sorbet 345

Blackberry Sorbet 346

Blueberry-Orange Bread 347

Currant-Pecan Scones 348

Maple-Pecan Spice Muffins 349

The Kitchen Cupboard 351

Wines with Greens 351

Oils in the Greens Kitchen 352

Some Outstanding Locally Made Cheeses 354

The Asian Pantry 358

The Dessert Pantry 363

Kitchen Tool Box 369

Worm Composting 371

Acknowledgments 375

Index 377

Introduction

It's been nearly twenty-five years since we first opened our doors here in historic Fort Mason, right on the water's edge, facing the Golden Gate and the glorious headlands of Marin County. That expansive view out to the west reflects the richness of life and the extraordinary environment of San Francisco and the Bay Area—the people, the place, the culture, and of course, the food. This fertile piece of paradise produces a wonderful way of life for gardeners and farmers, home cooks and chefs, and anyone who loves fine, fresh ingredients and delicious food.

Our approach to cooking has always been a celebration of ingredients—fresh, locally grown organic produce, great cheeses, eggs, and dairy products, oils, nuts, and just about anything we can get our hands on that isn't meat, fish, or fowl. Yes, we've always included tofu, it's right up there on our list of favorites, but we don't think of it as a substitute—it's just one of the many ingredients we love to use. We've been fortunate from the very beginning, working closely with local organic growers and purveyors to bring the finest and freshest ingredients to Greens each day. Our special connection to Green Gulch, Zen Center's organic farm in Marin County, just 17 miles across the Golden Gate, remains constant and strong. The Green Gulch farmers provide us with tender lettuces and bitter greens, potatoes of all sizes, shapes and colors, fresh herbs, winter squash, gigantic heads of cabbage, and generous bunches of chard and kale—all grown in that incredible soil they've been cultivating for over 30 years. In exchange, we send them our kitchen scraps, which they turn into compost to feed the soil. It's a cool, coastal climate there, so the warm weather crops come to us from the inland areas and microclimates near the coast that are sheltered from the wind and the fog.

Our local farmers' markets are hives of bustling activity—they're spontaneous and alive and full of surprises, a sensual liberation from supermarket shopping and the intensity of our tightly organized lives. People of all ages and walks of life turn out to shop, taste, and chat with the growers, purveyors, and maybe best of all, each other—informally and passionately—in the spirit of fun, pleasure, and inquiry. The market is the nerve center of the Bay Area food scene, which provides us with everything from freshly cropped walnuts to pomegranate juice—it's the ultimate source of our inspiration. If it's out there in the marketplace, we'll find a place for it on the menu.

These recipes are an expression of the everyday cooking of Greens—dishes you'll find any day of the week on our menu—spicy curries and rustic ragoûts, soups, salads, savory pastries, and extravagant desserts. There's a wide range of dishes here, representing simplicity, complexity, and everything in between. Many of the recipes can be made at a moment's notice, while others require advance preparation and a good bit of time. There are plenty of tips and make-ahead steps that are helpful to cooks of all levels of experience. Yes, there are sub-recipes—soup stocks and all—the bane of restaurant cookbooks, but without them, the dishes wouldn't be true to the unique taste and style we've developed over the many years at Greens. Besides, many of the sub-recipes are delicious all by themselves, so if you never get to the main dish, that's okay.

We've adapted our recipes for the home kitchen — testing them again and again — simplifying the ingredients and shortening the steps until we were completely satisfied with each and every dish. We'd set up shop each day, cooking, talking, eating, and jotting down notes, adjusting and revising every step of the way. When we'd get to a tough spot, we'd call in the experts, our longtime Greens chefs, to help us get it right, so we could say with confidence, "That's it, we're there." Neighbors, family, and friends would stop by to taste and snack and give us their honest opinions. At the end of the day, the favorite dishes were always the first to disappear.

If you think you need a sleek, designer kitchen to make these recipes, that's not the case. The test kitchen is in a charming, old San Francisco flat here in North Beach — a spacious, airy room with a porcelain sink, a faithful antique O'Keefe and Meritt gas stove, a butcherblock table, and two sets of wooden shelves recycled from the Tassajara Bread Bakery counter at Greens. We kept it open, uncluttered, and stocked simply with the minimalist tools we needed for testing recipes and it worked beautifully. It was a magical scene both inside and out — from the clang of cable cars at the end of the street, to the raucous banter of the wild parrots flying overhead each morning on their way from the trees of upper Fort Mason, just above Greens, to their perch on Telegraph Hill.

Wave after wave of change has washed over Greens since we first opened in 1979. At first glance, we don't appear to have changed much at all, but we have. The interior remains much the same as it did that first day — open and light and full of fresh air. The simplicity of the dining room speaks for the stunning natural beauty all around us. The slow, steady transformation of the Tassajara Bread Bakery counter to our bustling take-out counter, Greens to Go, is the most noticeable difference and it's a good one. It offers a new, informal entry to Greens and another great way to greet and serve customers and friends in this very public place. It's amazing how many people feel they own a piece of Greens; whether they're residents of Fort Mason or the National Park, artists or teachers in for a class, long-time customers, or bicyclists and walkers who drop in for coffee and pastry or a late afternoon snack while they're on their way to the bridge or out for a stroll along the Marina Green.

We've adapted our menu endlessly over the years, taking in the wealth of fantastic ingredients and new ideas that come our way. The flavors of Southeast Asia, particularly Vietnam and Thailand, have had a profound and delicious influence in our kitchen in recent years. Green Papaya Salad, fresh spring rolls, crunchy pickles, soups, and curries made with coconut milk, lemongrass, ginger, galangal, lime leaves, cilantro, and Thai basil are among our favorite dishes. They're an exciting addition to our repertoire, a melting pot of the great cuisines of the world—Italy, France, India, Mexico, North Africa, Asia, and of course, America.

It's always been our goal to prepare great food that's accessible to our guests, vegetarians and nonvegetarians alike. But you'll have to look hard to find the word *vegetarian* mentioned anywhere at Greens—that too has been our philosophy from the beginning.

There's a spirit and continuity that runs through the restaurant—it's a vigorous and lively place, rich with stories of the Zen Center and the Zen students who opened Greens and contributed so much in the early years. I've always felt that Zen practice is excellent training for work at Greens, like all restaurants, where anything can and will happen anytime, any day. It's a wonderful place to practice *everyday mind,* the Buddhist teaching of bringing awareness and acceptance to every moment of everyday life.

Generations of dedicated staff, customers, and friends have shaped the restaurant and made it the special place it is today. There's always more work to do and changes to be made—that's part of the beauty and challenge of life here at Greens. We plan to keep working away, cooking up great food and welcoming and serving our guests—hopefully, for the next hundred years.

Savory Bites

Warm Spiced Almonds

Make these spicy almonds for a tasty snack or a little bite before a meal. There's just the right amount of spice and heat here—toasted cumin, paprika, and cayenne—and very little oil. If you don't have yellow mustard powder, add an extra pinch of cayenne. They are best served warm.

MAKES 1 CUP

6 ounces whole almonds, about 1 cup

1 teaspoon olive oil or vegetable oil

¾ teaspoon cumin seeds, toasted and ground (page 214)

½ teaspoon paprika

½ teaspoon salt

Cayenne pepper and yellow mustard powder

Preheat the oven to 350°F.

In a small bowl toss the almonds with the oil, cumin, paprika, salt, and 2 pinches each of cayenne and mustard powder. For spicier nuts, add another pinch of cayenne. Roast them on a baking sheet until toasted and fragrant, 10 to 12 minutes. Serve warm or cool and store in an airtight container.

TIP: These keep exceptionally well, so make them ahead of time. If they lose their crispness, put them in a 350°F oven for about 5 minutes.

Lotus Root Pickles

You may never have seen a lotus root or thought about buying one, but they're usually at Asian markets. They're very exotic looking with their smooth, cream-colored skin and beautiful open pattern inside.

The crunchy pickles get better as they sit, so make them a day ahead. They'll keep for weeks in a sealed container in the refrigerator. We serve them with Crispy Spring Rolls and rice noodles cupped in crisp leaves of butter lettuce, or alongside Pickled Daikon Radish.

MAKES ABOUT 1 QUART

10 cups cold water

Juice of 1 lemon

2 medium, firm, fresh lotus roots, about 1 pound

1 cup rice vinegar

¼ cup hot water

½ cup sugar

1 teaspoon tamari or soy sauce

Pinch of salt

Pinch of red pepper flakes

Combine the cold water and the lemon juice in a large nonreactive pot. Trim the ends off the lotus root and use a vegetable peeler to remove the skin. Cut diagonally into ⅛-inch slices and add to the pot. Bring to a boil, lower the heat, and simmer until tender, about 10 minutes.

Combine the vinegar, hot water, sugar, tamari, salt, and red pepper flakes in a large bowl and whisk together. Drain the lotus root and toss with the vinegar mixture. Cool and refrigerate for at least 1 hour before serving.

TIP: You can slice the lotus roots ahead of time, even the day before. Just be sure to cover them with the lemon water right away to keep them from discoloring.

3

Pickled Daikon Radish

These crisp radish pickles give off a big stink when you cook them but don't be put off—they're incredibly tasty. A little tamari gives this pure white radish a warm, tawny color. They're best made a day ahead and keep in the refrigerator for 2 to 3 weeks. Just be sure to store them in an airtight container. Serve with Crispy Spring Rolls.

MAKES ABOUT 1 QUART

1 pound daikon radish, peeled and thinly sliced on a slight diagonal

¼ red onion, cut into thin wedges

1 cup rice vinegar

2 teaspoons tamari or soy sauce

1 cup sugar

4 thin coins of fresh ginger

Place the daikon and onion in a large bowl. Combine the remaining ingredients in a small saucepan; bring to a boil and pour over the vegetables. Let cool, cover, and refrigerate for at least an hour before serving.

4

Crispy Spring Rolls with Spicy Dipping Sauce

These crunchy, fried spring rolls are filled with traditional ingredients—bean threads, taro root, scallions, fresh ginger, and black fungus, all available in Asian markets. The fresh, clean taste of the Spicy Dipping Sauce goes perfectly with the flavors and textures here. Serve with Lotus Root Pickles for a memorable appetizer.

SERVES 4 TO 6; MAKES 16 ROLLS

Spicy Dipping Sauce (recipe follows)

1 individual package bean thread noodles (rice vermicelli), about 1½ ounces

¼ ounce black fungus

½ tablespoon toasted sesame oil

½ pound firm tofu, cut into ½-inch-thick slices, brushed with 2 tablespoons of tamari or soy sauce

Vegetable oil for frying

Salt and pepper

½ pound taro root, peeled and grated, about 1 cup

1 medium carrot, peeled and grated, about ½ cup

2 or 3 scallions, both green and white parts, cut on the diagonal, about ⅓ cup

½ teaspoon minced garlic

½ tablespoon grated fresh ginger

½ cup chopped cilantro

½ teaspoon salt

Pinch of cayenne pepper

Sixteen 9-inch-square egg roll wrappers, about 1 pound, separated and placed under a damp towel

1 large egg, beaten

Make the Spicy Dipping Sauce and set aside.

Bring a small pot of water to a boil. Place the bean thread noodles and fungus in two small bowls. Pour the water over and set aside to soak, allowing 3 to 4 minutes for the noodles and about 15 minutes for the fungus. Rinse the noodles under cold water, drain, and shake off the excess moisture. Roughly chop them, place in a medium-size bowl, and toss with the sesame oil. Drain the fungus and slice into thin threads. You should have about ½ cup; toss it into the noodles.

Pour ½ inch of oil in a skillet and heat until just below the point of smoking, when the first wisp of vapor appears. Fry the tofu until crisp on the outside, allowing about 3 minutes per side. Drain on paper towels and sprinkle with salt and pepper. When cool enough to handle, thinly slice and add to the noodle mixture. Add the taro, carrots, scallions, garlic, ginger, cilantro, salt, and cayenne to the noodle mixture. Gently toss together.

Lay a few of the wrappers on a work surface and brush the top edge of each with the egg. Spread ¼ cup of the filling just below the center of each wrapper. Roll the wrappers snugly over the filling, folding in the ends as you go. Fill and roll the remaining wrappers in the same way.

Fill the skillet with fresh oil and heat to 350°F. Fry the egg rolls, a few at a time, turning them as needed, until crisp and golden, about 10 minutes. Drain on paper towels, and keep in a warm oven (250°F) while you fry the rest.

Spicy Dipping Sauce: This simple, refreshing sauce is great to have on hand. Make a double recipe and toss with cold skinny noodles—Asian or Italian—Carrot-Daikon Radish Pickles, and chopped cilantro for a light summer supper. For a spicier sauce add an extra pinch or two of red pepper flakes.

MAKES ABOUT 1 CUP

½ cup hot water
¼ cup sugar
¼ cup tamari or soy sauce
3 tablespoons fresh lime juice
1 tablespoon rice vinegar
Pinch of red pepper flakes
Pinch of salt

Combine everything in a small bowl and whisk until the sugar is dissolved. Set aside to cool.

MAKE-AHEAD TIP: Make the filling in advance and roll the spring rolls ahead of time. Once rolled, you can cover them and set aside for a couple of hours until you're ready to fry them. They keep beautifully in a warm oven (250°F), so fry them a little ahead of time if you need to.

VARIATION: If taro root isn't available, you can use thinly sliced bamboo shoots instead.

Vietnamese Spring Rolls with Peanut-Hoisin Sauce

These fresh spring rolls are irresistible in every way. Whole mint leaves, cilantro, fried shallots, and Hoisin sauce spark up the flavors of the crisp vegetable filling. We like the mild heat of jalapeño chilies here, but you can use serrano or fiery Thai bird chilies instead. You'll find the key ingredients at Southeast Asian markets—rice wrappers, Hoisin sauce, and sambal. If you haven't worked with rice wrappers before, they're a bit of an adventure, but simple to master. Be sure to read the tips.

SERVES 4 TO 6

Vegetable oil for frying

14 ounces firm tofu, cut into ½-inch-thick slices, brushed with 2 tablespoons tamari or soy sauce

Salt and pepper

1 large shallot, peeled and sliced, about ¼ cup

1 teaspoon vegetable oil

1 medium carrot, peeled and cut into matchsticks, about 1½ cups

½ small jicama, peeled and cut into matchsticks, about 1½ cups

1 medium red pepper, cut into matchsticks, about 1½ cups

2 or 3 jalapeño chilies, seeded and thinly sliced, about ⅓ cup

2 scallions, both green and white parts, thinly sliced on the diagonal, about ½ cup

½ tablespoon Hoisin sauce

Sixteen 9-inch round rice wrappers

1 or 2 heads butter lettuce, leaves separated and washed

1 bunch mint, leaves only

1 bunch cilantro, small sprigs only

Peanut-Hoisin Sauce (recipe follows)

Pour ½ inch of oil in a skillet and heat until just below the point of smoking, when the first wisp of vapor appears. Fry the tofu until crisp on the outside, allowing about 3 minutes per side. Drain on paper towels and sprinkle with salt and pepper. When cool enough to handle, thinly slice and set aside.

Return the pan to the heat, add the shallots and fry until crisp and golden. Drain on a paper towel and sprinkle with salt and pepper. Finely chop and set aside.

Heat the vegetable oil in a large sauté pan and add the carrot, jicama, peppers, and ¼ teaspoon salt and cook over high heat about 1 minute, stirring constantly. Add the chilies and a spoonful of water to keep the vegetables from sticking to the pan. Cook until the vegetables are just tender, about 2 minutes. Transfer to a bowl and mix in the scallions, shallots, and Hoisin sauce.

Lay 2 wrappers side by side on a damp kitchen or paper towel and spray with water. Cover with a damp towel and repeat until you have a pile of 6 wrappers softening. Gently turn the pile of wrappers over so the first ones are now on top.

Place the first wrapper on the work surface and lay 1 or 2 lettuce leaves on top. Spread ¼ cup of the vegetable mixture across the center, add 3 or 4 tofu slices, and top with a few mint leaves and cilantro sprigs. Roll the wrapper snugly but gently over the filling, tucking in the ends as you go, finishing with the seam side down. Roll the remaining wrappers in the same way.

The rolls can be made several hours in advance, rolled in plastic wrap, and refrigerated. Before serving, cut each roll in half on a slight diagonal and serve with Peanut-Hoisin Sauce.

RICE WRAPPER TIPS: Relax, be patient, and don't expect to roll perfect spring rolls the first time. Have on hand: a spray bottle of water to moisten the wrappers and paper towels or a stack of clean, lightweight kitchen towels to layer between them, which will keep them moist and supple. Once they're sprayed, they soften and then they can be rolled. It takes a few tries before you can fill and roll them without tearing them. If the wrapper tears, just remove the filling and start over with a fresh wrapper or simply roll it into a second wrapper. If you wrap them too tight, they're sure to tear. Too loose and they'll be floppy, but better floppy than none at all. Be sure to assemble all the ingredients and have everything ready so the rolls go together smoothly.

Peanut-Hoisin Sauce: This intensely flavored sauce is salty and sweet—perfect for dipping spring rolls. We enliven Hoisin sauce with fried shallots, toasted peanuts, and sambal. It keeps for weeks in the refrigerator, minus the peanuts. If you're making it in advance, add the toasted peanuts right before serving.

MAKES ABOUT 1 CUP

2 tablespoons vegetable oil
1 large shallot, thinly sliced, about 1/4 cup

Salt and pepper
½ cup Hoisin sauce
⅓ cup water
½ teaspoon rice vinegar
¼ cup peanuts, toasted (page 46) and chopped
1 teaspoon sambal, or to taste

Heat the oil in a small sauté pan and add the shallots and a pinch of salt. Cook over medium-high heat until crisp, about 2 minutes. Drain on a paper towel and sprinkle with salt and pepper. Finely chop and transfer to a small bowl. Add all the remaining ingredients except the sambal, then season to taste with sambal.

Serving suggestion: Arrange the spring rolls on a platter, spoon a little of the Peanut-Hoisin Sauce over each of them, and sprinkle toasted peanuts over. Garnish with big sprigs of cilantro and mint.

MAKE-AHEAD TIP: Prepare the vegetables and make the filling a few hours ahead of time. You can also fry the tofu and the shallots in advance. The Peanut-Hoisin Sauce can be made well in advance—you can always add the peanuts to the sauce at the last minute.

VARIATION: Substitute whole Thai basil leaves for the mint and cilantro. You can also try Spicy Dipping Sauce (page 6) instead of Peanut-Hoisin Sauce.

Filo Turnover Samosas

A favorite customer introduced these Indian turnovers to us during a family celebration held at Greens. All the traditional seasonings for samosas are here—lemon, ginger, fresh chilies, cilantro, and peas—minus the samosa dough. The spicy potato filling is quick to prepare and keeps well, so you can make it a day in advance. Just add the cilantro at the last minute, before you roll the turnovers. Serve with Spicy Tomato Jam and cooling Cucumber Raita.

MAKES 18 BITE-SIZE TURNOVERS

1 pound Yellow Finn potatoes, cut into ½-inch dice, about 3 cups

3 tablespoons vegetable or olive oil

Salt and pepper

1 large yellow onion, diced, about 2 cups

1 tablespoon minced garlic

1 tablespoon grated fresh ginger

2 jalapeño chilies, seeded and finely chopped

2 teaspoons cumin seeds, toasted (page 214) and ground

2 teaspoons coriander seeds, toasted (page 214) and ground

½ cup peas, fresh or frozen

½ cup water

1 tablespoon fresh lemon juice

2 to 3 tablespoons chopped cilantro

9 sheets frozen filo dough, thawed in the refrigerator overnight

¼ cup unsalted butter, melted and kept warm

Preheat the oven to 400°F.

Toss the potatoes in a baking dish with 1½ tablespoons of the oil, ½ teaspoon of salt, and a pinch of pepper. Roast until just tender, about 20 minutes. Remove from the oven. Lower the heat to 375°F.

Heat the remaining oil in a large sauté pan and add the onions, ¼ teaspoon salt, and a pinch of pepper. Sauté over medium heat until the onions begin to soften, 3 to 4 minutes. Add the garlic, ginger, jalapeños, cumin, and coriander and cook 1 minute more. Stir in the peas, the potatoes, and the water. Lower the heat, cover the pan, and cook until the peas are tender, 3 to 4 minutes. Transfer to a bowl. When cool, season with the lemon juice, cilantro, and salt and pepper to taste.

To assemble the turnovers, lay the filo sheets on a clean work surface and cover with a damp cloth.

Lay a single sheet of filo out and brush it lightly with butter. Place two more sheets on top and brush with butter. Cut the sheets crosswise into 6 strips.

Place a heaping tablespoon of filling at the end of each strip, and then fold over at a 45-degree angle to form a triangle. As you roll the turnovers, think of folding a flag. Roll them loosely, so the filling will have room to expand during baking. Keep folding at an angle until you reach the end of the strip, trimming any excess filo. Make the rest of the turnovers in the same way, brush them with butter, and place on a parchment-lined baking sheet. The turnovers can be refrigerated or frozen at this point for later baking.

Bake until golden and crisp, about 15 minutes.

Hummous

We've served this spicy chick-pea puree since the day Greens opened and it's still a favorite. Chick-peas take forever to cook, but they're worth every minute. They're exceptionally smooth and creamy, particularly if pureed while still warm. If you can find roasted or toasted tahini in the natural foods store, buy it and use it here. It is much tastier than the usual raw variety.

MAKES 3 CUPS

1 cup chick-peas, about 6 ounces, sorted and soaked overnight

8 cups cold water

¼ cup roasted sesame tahini

¼ cup olive oil

1 teaspoon minced garlic

1 teaspoon cumin seeds, toasted (page 214) and ground

¾ teaspoon salt

2½ or 3 tablespoons fresh lemon juice

Cayenne pepper

Drain and rinse the chick-peas. Place them in a large saucepan with the water and bring to a boil. Lower the heat and simmer until completely tender, about 1½ hours. Drain the chick-peas and reserve ½ cup of the cooking liquid.

Combine the chick-peas, tahini, oil, garlic, cumin, salt, 2½ tablespoons of the lemon juice, and a pinch of cayenne in the bowl of a food processor. Pulse until completely smooth, adding the cooking liquid as needed to thin. Adjust the seasoning with salt, lemon juice, and cayenne to taste.

TIP: You can always cook the chick-peas the day before and make the hummous the following day. Just be sure to keep the chick-peas in their cooking liquid until you are ready to puree them. They keep for 2 to 3 days in the refrigerator in an airtight container.

Guacamole

This by-now classic spread is always on our menu, usually as part of a platter of Mexican food. But it's also great by itself, with tortilla chips or vegetable dippers such as spears of jicama. Although everyone else insists you must make guacamole at the last minute, that's not practical in a restaurant, and we make it a bit ahead of time—it will keep perfectly for at least an hour or so, as long as the plastic wrap is pressed directly against the surface of the guacamole.

MAKES ABOUT 1 CUP

2 or 3 medium avocados
1½ or 2 tablespoons lime juice
½ teaspoon cumin, toasted (page 214) and ground
Salt and cayenne pepper
2 tablespoons chopped cilantro

Slice the avocados in half, remove the seeds, scoop the flesh from the skin, and place in a small bowl. Mash the avocados with a fork until mostly smooth (there will still be a few chunks). Stir in 1½ tablespoons of lime juice, the cumin, ½ teaspoon salt, and a few pinches of cayenne. Press a piece of plastic wrap flush over the guacamole's surface and refrigerate until ready to serve. Stir in the cilantro, the additional lime juice (if needed), and add salt and cayenne to taste.

VARIATIONS

Stir in ½ small red onion, finely diced and pickled, before serving.

Add 1½ or 2 teaspoons Chipotle Puree (page 163) for a smoky guacamole with a little more kick.

Grilled Asparagus

Asparagus has its own special place on the menu each spring. We grill big, plump spears of this beautiful vegetable over coals and feature it in any number of ways. Here are a few of our favorites: Heap the spears on a platter with sprigs of watercress all around, drizzle with Meyer Lemon Vinaigrette, followed with shavings of pecorino pepato cheese; or arrange the spears loosely on individual plates, drizzle with Champagne Mustard Vinaigrette, sprinkle with Garlic Bread Crumbs, and Hard-Cooked Eggs. For a fine antipasto, serve it alongside Farro Salad with Roasted Peppers and Arugula, with grilled bread, Mount Tam triple cream cheese, and olives.

SERVES 6 TO 8

2 pounds thick asparagus, tough stem ends removed
Garlic Oil (see box)
Salt and pepper

Prepare the grill.

Bring a large pot of water to a boil and salt lightly. Drop in the asparagus, lower the heat, and simmer until just tender, 2 to 3 minutes. Drain, rinse under cold water, and place on a clean kitchen towel to dry. Brush the asparagus with garlic oil and sprinkle lightly with salt and pepper. Grill over medium coals, turning until evenly marked.

Garlic Oil

We use this garlic-infused oil to brush on bread before toasting, vegetables before roasting, and just about everything we grill. We also brush it over rolled pizza dough to protect the crust from moist toppings and for an extra bit of garlic flavor.

To make, mince a few garlic cloves, and cover with extra-virgin olive oil. You can use it right away or let it steep for 30 minutes to create more intense garlic flavor. We add 1 tablespoon minced garlic to every ½ cup oil, but it's up to you—use as little or as much garlic as you like. Strain out the garlic and store the oil in a tightly sealed container in the refrigerator.

Grilled Artichokes with Mint

Grilling artichokes over coals brings out the best of their distinctive flavor. We cook them in a lemon marinade until they're tender, then grill them just long enough to heat through. To save some time, you can cook the artichokes a day or two in advance and refrigerate them in their marinade until you're ready to grill.

SERVES 4

Juice of 1 lemon
4 large artichokes, about 2 pounds
Artichoke Marinade (page 53)
Garlic Oil (page 14)
Salt and pepper
1 tablespoon chopped mint, about 15 leaves

Prepare the grill.

Fill a large bowl with water and add the lemon juice. Trim off the artichoke tops, the base of the stems, and peel away the thorny outer leaves. Cut the artichokes in half from tip to base and use a small spoon to scoop out the choke. Drop the prepared artichokes in the lemon water and set aside.

Make the Artichoke Marinade and cook the artichokes as directed.

Drain the artichokes, brush generously with garlic oil, and season with salt and pepper. Place them on the grill, cut side down, and cook over medium coals until marked, then turn and grill the other side. Sprinkle with the mint just before serving.

15

Quince and Sour Cherry Compote

This lovely fall compote is a great way to use quince, especially if you've never tried it before. Once the quince are peeled and cored, the compote comes together easily. The quince turns a beautiful rosy hue, a sure sign that it's cooked all the way through. The compote keeps well in a sealed container for up to a week. Just bring it to room temperature or warm it and thin with apple juice as needed. Quince is filled with pectin, so the compote will thicken as it sits. Serve it with Yellow Finn Potato Cakes or fold it into Buckwheat Crêpes with a spoonful of Crème Fraîche.

MAKES ABOUT 3 CUPS

2 cups unfiltered apple juice
3 tablespoons sugar
3 thin coins of fresh ginger
3 large quince, about 1½ pounds, peeled, cored, and chopped into ¾-inch cubes
Pinch of salt
1½ ounces dried tart cherries, about ⅓ cup

Combine the apple juice, sugar, and ginger in a medium-size saucepan and bring to a boil. Add the quince and salt and return to a boil. Lower the heat and simmer gently until the quince are tender but still hold their shape, about 20 minutes.

Add the cherries and cook 5 minutes more. Set aside to cool. The compote will be very juicy, but as it cools the fruit will soak up most of the poaching liquid. Remove the ginger and serve warm or at room temperature.

Garlic Toasts

MAKES ABOUT 16 CROUTONS

½ baguette, thinly sliced on a slight diagonal
Garlic Oil (page 14)

Preheat the oven to 375°F.

Brush the baguette slices lightly with garlic oil and place on a baking sheet. Bake until golden and crisp, 8 to 10 minutes.

Garlic Croutons

If you're wondering what to do with half a loaf of leftover bread, croutons are the answer. These crunchy bites of toasted bread are great for dressing up a salad.

We prepare the croutons in a couple of ways, depending on the type of salad we're making and the size and shape of the bread. For big loaves of French or Italian bread, cut large cubes and toss with garlic oil. As for baguettes, thinly slice and brush with the oil. Day-old bread is always best.

Preheat the oven to 375°F. Prepare the bread and brush or toss with garlic oil. Toast on a baking sheet until golden and crisp, 8 to 12 minutes, depending on the size of the bread.

For an irresistible variation, sprinkle with grated Parmesan halfway through baking. You can also toss or sprinkle the croutons with fresh herbs. Cool and store in an airtight container; they'll keep for a least a week. After that, you'll need to put them in a 350°F oven for a few minutes until crisp. Cool before using.

Picholine Olive Tapenade

Picholine olives make an exceptional tapenade. These French green olives with the pointed tips are rich without being too salty. Because they're not as ripe as black olives, they're a bit crunchy and make tapenade that's lighter than the standard black olive one. You can always use another variety of green or black olive instead, but don't buy pitted olives. Once the pit is removed, there goes the flavor. If you don't have a small food processor, just chop the tapenade by hand.

SERVES 4 TO 6; MAKES ABOUT 1 CUP

Garlic Toasts (page 17)

¼ small red onion, finely diced, about ¼ cup

1 tablespoon Champagne vinegar

6 ounces Picholine or green or black olives, pitted, about 1 cup

1½ tablespoons coarsely chopped flat-leaf parsley

1 tablespoon extra-virgin olive oil

Pinch of black pepper

Make the Garlic Toasts.

Bring a small pot of water to a boil and drop in the onion for 15 seconds. Drain, toss with the vinegar, and set aside to cool.

Place the olives in the bowl of a small food processor and pulse briefly. Add the remaining ingredients, including the onion and vinegar, and pulse until just combined. Spread the tapenade on the croutons and serve.

VARIATION: Try adding diced fennel instead of the red onions. Sauté the fennel in a little olive oil with a pinch of salt and pepper just long enough to soften it.

Artichoke Relish

The fresh flavors of this classic relish are irresistible—artichokes, lemon, parsley, and a splash of fruity olive oil. The relish is so intense that a little goes a long way.

Use leftover Simple Artichoke Salad and make ahead for a party. Serve in a trio of crostini with Picholine Olive Tapenade and chèvre or fromage blanc sprinkled with chopped chives.

SERVES 4 TO 6; MAKES ABOUT 1 CUP

Garlic Toasts (page 17)

Simple Artichoke Salad (page 53), finely chopped, about 1 cup

1 tablespoon chopped flat-leaf parsley

½ teaspoon fresh lemon juice

Salt and pepper

Extra-virgin olive oil (optional)

Make the Garlic Toasts and the Simple Artichoke Salad.

Toss the artichokes, parsley, and lemon juice in a small bowl and season to taste with salt and pepper. Add a splash of olive oil if, using.

Spread the relish on the toasts.

Fava Bean Puree

This simple make-ahead spring dish has a flavor that's out of this world. It takes time to shell the fava beans, but you can do it the day before. We blanch the favas, slip them out of their skins, sauté them in fruity olive oil, and then give them a quick puree. Add a splash of lemon and it's ready to spread on crisp, toasted bread.

MAKES ABOUT 1 CUP

Garlic Toasts (page 17)
2 pounds fava beans, shelled
1½ tablespoons extra-virgin olive oil
Salt and pepper
Fresh lemon juice

Make the Garlic Toasts.

Bring a small pot of water to a boil and salt lightly. Drop in the beans and cook until bright green, 1 or 2 minutes. Drain and rinse under cold water. Open the skin along the seam with your thumbnail and slip the beans out of their skins.

Heat the oil in a small saucepan and add the beans and a pinch each of salt and pepper. Cook over medium-low heat until tender, about 4 minutes, adding a little water to keep them moist. Transfer to a small food processor and puree until smooth. Season with a few drops of lemon juice and salt and pepper to taste.

Fava Beans

These funny-looking beans thrive in the warmth of early spring and the cool, foggy weather out on the coast all summer long. Don't be put off by the humble appearance of this ancient legume—there's a delicate treasure inside every pod. Fava beans take some time to prepare, but they're worth every minute, especially when they're slow-simmered in olive oil or tossed into pasta with Meyer lemon, asparagus, and spring peas. Straight off the vine, they're tender and incredibly sweet. You can even eat the littlest ones right in their skin. As they grow past their prime, their sugar turns to starch and they begin to develop a sprout—they're not nearly as tasty. So catch them while they're young and sweet.

Bring a pot of water to a boil and salt lightly. Remove the fava beans from the pods and discard the pods. (Along with skins, these are a great addition to your compost pile or worm bin, page 371.) Drop them into the water for a minute or two, then drain, and rinse under cold water. Use your thumbnail to slip them out of their skins and prepare as directed. You can shell the fava beans a day in advance and blanch and slip them out of their skins a few hours ahead of time.

Warm Cannellini Beans and Wilted Greens

Just about any variety of big, starchy white beans will do to make these rustic, satisfying crostini. Leftover Warm White Beans are perfect here (use 1½ cups). As for the greens, we use chard, but kale and broccoli rabe are equally delicious.

SERVES 6 TO 8

Garlic Toasts (page 17)

3 ounces dried cannellini, emergo, or white runner beans, about ½ cup, sorted and soaked overnight

6 cups water

1½ teaspoons minced garlic

1 bay leaf

2 fresh sage leaves

3 tablespoons extra-virgin olive oil

Salt and pepper

1 bunch of chard, stems removed, cut into thick ribbons, 6 to 8 cups

1 or 2 tablespoons sherry vinegar

Make the Garlic Toasts.

Drain the beans and rinse well. Place in a saucepan with the water, ½ teaspoon garlic, bay leaf, and sage. Bring to a boil, lower the heat, and simmer, uncovered, until completely tender, about 1½ hours. There should be some broth in the pan, just enough to cover the beans. Remove the bay leaf and sage; season the beans with 1 tablespoon oil, ¼ teaspoon salt, and a pinch of pepper. Use a fork or potato masher to mash the beans. If they're too thin, return the pan to the heat and cook over low heat for a minute or two until thick enough to spread, stirring to keep them from sticking to the pan. Keep the beans warm.

Heat the remaining oil in a large sauté pan over medium heat and add the greens, the remaining garlic, 2 pinches of salt, and a pinch of pepper. Cook until the greens are completely wilted, 2 to 3 minutes, using metal tongs to toss them. Season with 1 tablespoon of the vinegar and salt and pepper to taste. Add more vinegar if needed.

Spread the beans on the toasts and top with the wilted greens.

TIPS: Unless the kale or broccoli rabe is young and tender, parboil it before you sauté it—drop it in boiling water for a couple of minutes and drain before cooking.

Grilled Pepper and Fennel Relish with Capers

Make this delectable relish in the early fall, when peppers are at their best and fennel is coming into season. It's a perfect appetizer, spooned over grilled or toasted bread, or served as a small salad with creamy fresh cheese, rustic croutons, and caperberries or olives. Just chop the vegetables coarsely if you're making a salad instead of the relish.

MAKES 1½ CUPS

1 medium red or yellow pepper, cut into wide strips

1 medium fennel bulb, base and top trimmed, sliced down through the top of the bulb in ¼-inch slices

1 medium red onion, peeled and sliced into ½-inch-thick rings

Garlic Oil (page 14)

Salt and pepper

2 tablespoons chopped flat-leaf parsley

1 heaping tablespoon capers, rinsed

Balsamic vinegar

½ tablespoon extra-virgin olive oil

Prepare the grill.

Brush the vegetables with garlic oil and sprinkle generously with salt and pepper. Place the vegetables on the grill with the peppers skin side down and grill until marked. Turn over and grill the other side until tender and cooked through. When the vegetables are cool, finely chop and place in a bowl. Toss in the parsley, capers, ½ tablespoon vinegar, and oil. Season to taste with salt and pepper and a splash of vinegar, if needed. Set aside for 30 minutes to allow the flavors to develop.

TIP: If you're short on time, roast the vegetables instead of grilling them. The relish will still be delicious, but without the smoky flavor. Prepare the vegetables as directed and roast on a baking sheet at 400°F for 10 minutes. Use a spatula to turn them over and roast until tender, about 10 minutes more.

VARIATION: For added sweet pepper flavor and contrasting color, include an extra red or yellow pepper. Chopped basil is a mouthwatering addition.

Spicy Tomato Jam

This piquant Mediterranean chutney—our version of Joyce Goldstein's recipe—always sells out. We stew cherry tomatoes—big ones are fine here—with lots of fresh ginger, lemon, sugar, and warm spices until they caramelize. Serve alongside Hummous, Lentil Salad with Goat Cheese and Mint, and warm pita bread. The jam keeps for weeks in the refrigerator, so make a double recipe— it's good to have on hand.

MAKES ABOUT 2 CUPS

1 pound ripe, cherry tomatoes, about 3 cups

6 tablespoons sugar

6 tablespoons light brown sugar, packed

2 tablespoons grated fresh ginger

½ lemon, sliced in thin half-moons

½ teaspoon ground cinnamon

½ teaspoon cumin seeds, toasted (page 214) and ground

½ teaspoon ground cloves

2 tablespoons unfiltered cider vinegar

Salt and cayenne pepper

Combine the tomatoes, sugars, ginger, lemon, spices, and 1½ tablespoons of the vinegar in a medium-size, heavy-bottomed saucepan. Add a pinch each of salt and cayenne and cook over medium-high heat, stirring often, until the tomatoes cook down to a jam and the sugars are bubbly and caramelized, about 30 minutes. Set aside to cool. If it's too sweet, adjust the seasoning with up to ½ tablespoon of the vinegar.

Salads of All Kinds

Making Salads Simple

Salads have been a mainstay on our menu since the earliest days of Greens. Our mild Mediterranean climate—and all the microclimates within it—and the fertile growing grounds of this northern California paradise conspire to produce a stunning array of delicious salad greens. You name it and we can grow it here. With all the European seeds coming into the marketplace, it's an exciting time to feast on salads of tender and bitter greens. Life is busy for all of us, so here are a few tips for making salads simply.

MAKE THE MOST OF YOUR SALAD SPINNER: First of all, if you don't have one, get yourself a salad spinner. It's great for washing fruits, vegetables, and savory greens. You can store the greens in it and refrigerate them; in effect this is a mini-greenhouse, a great way of keeping greens fresh and crisp. The basket pinch-hits as an extra colander, and there's no more effortless way to dry greens. Prepare the greens and wash and dry them in the salad spinner. Instead of transferring them to a salad bowl or another container, simply store the washed greens in the spinner. Pour the extra water out of the bottom, cover, and refrigerate until you're ready to make the salad.

MAKE-AHEAD STEPS: Wash the salad greens and spin dry a few hours ahead of time. If the vibrant lettuces you bought at the market this morning have lost their pep, try refreshing them in a sink full of cold water. You can even use your salad spinner here—give the lettuces a soaking right inside the spinner, then drain and spin dry. They'll usually come right back. Toast nuts or croutons a day or two in advance and store in an airtight container. You can prepare fruits and vegetables ahead of time as long as they hold their texture and keep their color. Avoid tossing green vegetables with vinaigrette until just before serving, so they keep their bright green color. Apples, pears, and avocados are best left to the last minute to avoid discoloring.

Crumble or grate cheeses in advance and refrigerate them in a small sealed container. Shave aged cheeses over the salad right after tossing.

VINAIGRETTES DEMYSTIFIED: I've tasted my share of vinaigrettes over the years and have a deep respect for acidity and the delicate balance between bland and overly sharp vinaigrettes. If you don't know a thing about making vinaigrette, start with a simple recipe or two, follow them religiously, and don't stray from the formula until you're completely at ease making them. The number one rule: Start with the vinegar and the seasonings, then slowly whisk in the oil. You can always adjust the oil by adding a little more of it, but once the balance of flavor is lost to too much oil, it's hard to regain it. Be sure to taste as you go—for some reason, you can make the exact same vinaigrette two days running and they turn out tasting slightly different. But you can always taste your way to the right balance since you haven't added an overwhelming amount of a single ingredient.

THE BASICS: A vinaigrette is only as flavorful as the oil and vinegar you use and as fresh as the citrus juice and minced zest. Stock your pantry with a few good oils and vinegars, sea salt, a pepper mill, and high-quality stone-ground and Dijon mustard. In addition to its tart complexity, the starch and solids in the fresh mustard help to emulsify the vinaigrette and keep it blended. And don't forget minced garlic and shallots—both have delicious flavor.

Most vinaigrettes—with the exception of citrus, which lose their sparkling, fresh flavors after a few hours—can be made days ahead of time and refrigerated in an airtight container. If you know you won't be using the vinaigrette within a few days, strain out any onion-garlic elements so they won't overpower it. Without them, the vinaigrette will keep for weeks.

FRESH CITRUS JUICE AND ZEST: Vinaigrettes made with fresh citrus juice and minced citrus zest add zesty, fresh flavor to salads of tossed greens, crisp vegetables, beans, and grains. We complement the citrus juice with a light-tasting vinegar— Champagne vinegar, rice vinegar, or a splash of sherry vinegar—to draw out its flavor. To intensify the flavor of citrus, toss additional minced zest right into marinated salads.

MAKING SIMPLE FRUIT VINEGARS: We make fruit vinegars on the spot by pureeing or mashing fresh fruit, usually apples and pears, into a crisp, light-tasting vinegar and let it sit for up to an hour before making the vinaigrette. Apple cider, pear, or Champagne, or another high-quality white vinegar is a great choice here.

REFRESHING LEFTOVER VINAIGRETTES: After a few days, the fresh herbs, shallots, or garlic in an herb vinaigrette grow tired and should be strained and discarded. Chop a fresh round of herbs and whisk them into the vinaigrette along with a splash of vinegar. Taste it; you may need to add a pinch or two of salt. The garlic or shallot flavor will still be there as a subtle background flavor.

Green Salad with Beets, Fennel, Walnuts, and Ricotta Salata

We make this salad in the fall and winter, when crisp bulbs of fennel and gigantic bunches of deep red beets are side by side in the market bins. Tender leaves of butter lettuce are tossed with sprigs of flat-leaf parsley, slivers of thinly sliced fennel, toasted walnuts, and ricotta salata—a firm, salty sheep's milk cheese that goes beautifully with beets and citrus. To keep the beets from coloring the greens, tuck them into the leaves just before serving. We add a little orange juice to the Sherry-Walnut Vinaigrette to brighten all the flavors. If ricotta salata isn't available, try crumbled feta or aged goat cheese instead.

SERVES 4 TO 6

Sherry-Walnut Vinaigrette (recipe follows)

2 medium beets, about ½ pound, roasted, peeled, and cut into wedges (page 29)

Salt and pepper

2 heads of butter lettuce, about 10 cups inner leaves and trimmed outer leaves

1 cup flat-leaf parsley, small sprigs and leaves

½ fennel bulb, core and stalks removed and sliced thin crosswise

⅓ cup walnut pieces, toasted (page 46) and coarsely chopped

1½ to 2 ounces ricotta salata cheese, 2 to 3 tablespoons

Make the vinaigrette.

Place the cut beets in a small bowl, toss with 1½ tablespoons of the vinaigrette, and sprinkle with a pinch of salt and pepper.

Wash and dry the lettuce and parsley. Combine the greens, fennel, walnuts, and half the cheese in a large bowl; gently toss with the vinaigrette.

Separate the salad onto individual plates, tucking the beets between the leaves, and sprinkle with freshly ground black pepper and the remaining cheese.

Sherry-Walnut Vinaigrette

MAKES ABOUT ½ CUP

1 tablespoon fresh orange juice

1½ tablespoons sherry vinegar

¼ teaspoon salt

3 tablespoons olive oil

2 tablespoons walnut oil

Whisk everything but the oils together in a small bowl. Slowly pour in the oils, whisking until emulsified.

Beets

These colorful gems—golden, Chioggia, and red—are wonderful in salads and antipasto platters. Tossed with vinaigrette, crumbled ricotta salata, and a handful of tender greens, they're a feast for the senses. We also combine all three types of beets for a gorgeous chilled soup and finish it with a spoonful of crème fraîche or mascarpone.

Golden and rosy-hued Chioggias hold on to their distinctive color, but red beets should be added to dishes at the last minute to keep their color from running. Their flavor varies according to the variety, but big, old red beets—the more common of the bunch—are often the sweetest. If the tops are fresh, save them. These greens are delicious sautéed with rainbow chard or dinosaur kale or on their own.

Preheat the oven to 400°F. Trim off the greens and reserve for another use. Rinse the beets under cold water and place in a small baking dish with ¼ inch water. Cover and roast until tender, about 35 to 40 minutes, depending on their size. When you test for doneness with a paring knife or skewer, there should be no resistance. If there is, they'll be difficult to peel. Cool and peel, then slice or cut them into wedges, or as directed in the recipe. To make the peeling easier, set up a small bowl of water and wet your fingertips. Then use your moistened fingers to slip the skins off the beets. If you're using more than one color of beet, just be sure to peel the red ones last.

29

Butter Lettuce with Ruby Grapefruit, Avocado, and Grapefruit-Chili Vinaigrette

With its stellar cast of ingredients, this sparkling salad is sure to brighten a gray winter day. Crunchy toasted pumpkin seeds are the perfect accent for the juicy, plump sections of ruby grapefruit, rich avocado, and the bold vinaigrette.

We puree the Grapefruit-Chili Vinaigrette with whole grapefruit sections and a red jalapeño to give it body, a warm, rosy color, and heat. If red jalapeños aren't available, you can always use green. Be sure to taste the chili first; you never know how mild or hot it will be.

SERVES 4 TO 6

2 heads of butter lettuce, about 10 cups inner leaves and trimmed outer leaves
2 large ruby grapefruit
Grapefruit-Chili Vinaigrette (recipe follows)
1 avocado, peeled and sliced ¼ inch thick on a slight diagonal
Salt and pepper
1½ tablespoons pumpkin seeds, toasted (page 46)

Wash and dry the lettuce.

Using a zester, remove enough zest from one of the grapefruit to make 1 teaspoon minced zest; set aside. With a sharp knife, trim the peel and white pith from the grapefruit. Hold the grapefruit over a bowl to catch the juice for the vinaigrette, and cut each section loose from the membranes that hold it. Reserve ⅓ cup of the sections for the vinaigrette. Make the vinaigrette.

Place the avocado in a small bowl and toss with 1 to 2 tablespoons of the vinaigrette and sprinkle with a little salt and pepper.

Combine the lettuce, grapefruit sections, and 1 tablespoon of the pumpkin seeds in a large bowl. Gently toss with the vinaigrette and divide onto four chilled plates. Tuck the avocado slices in between the leaves, garnish with the remaining pumpkin seeds, and serve.

Grapefruit-Chili Vinaigrette

MAKES ABOUT ½ CUP

⅓ cup grapefruit sections

1 tablespoon fresh grapefruit juice

½ tablespoon Champagne vinegar

1 red or green jalapeño chili, seeded and coarsely chopped

¼ teaspoon salt

3 tablespoons olive oil

1 teaspoon minced grapefruit zest

Combine everything but the zest in a blender, puree until smooth, then whisk in the zest.

VARIATION: Cara cara oranges, with their creamy color and light acidity, would be stunning in place of the ruby grapefruit. Navel oranges are also delicious.

Butter Lettuce with Blood Oranges, Tangerines, Pistachios, and Citrus-Honey Vinaigrette

We serve this gorgeous winter salad when freshly picked oranges and tangerines of all kinds fill the markets. Tender leaves of butter lettuce catch rounds of juicy, sweet tangerines, crimson blood oranges, and the vinaigrette. If blood oranges aren't available, use navel oranges in their place. Toasted pistachios add a festive touch, but pecans are equally delicious. Thinly sliced kumquats are also a lovely addition; just remove any seeds and marinate in a little of the vinaigrette to soften their acidity before tossing them with the salad.

SERVES 4 TO 6

2 or 3 tangerines

2 blood oranges

Citrus-Honey Vinaigrette (recipe follows)

2 large heads of butter lettuce, about 12 cups inner leaves and trimmed outer leaves

2 to 3 tablespoons pistachios, toasted (page 46) and coarsely chopped

Mince the zest of one tangerine, about ½ teaspoon, and place in a small bowl. Squeeze the juice from ½ tangerine and ½ blood orange; you'll need 1 tablespoon of each. Combine the juice with the zest and make the vinaigrette.

Use a sharp knife to remove the peel and white pith of the remaining citrus. Slice the tangerine in ¼-inch-thick rounds and the blood orange in half-moons of the same thickness; set aside.

Wash and dry the lettuce, cover with a damp towel, and refrigerate.

Combine the lettuce, citrus, and pistachios in a large bowl; gently toss with the vinaigrette.

Citrus-Honey Vinaigrette

MAKES ABOUT ⅓ CUP

½ teaspoon tangerine zest, minced

1 tablespoon fresh blood orange juice

1 tablespoon fresh tangerine juice

1 tablespoon Champagne vinegar

1 teaspoon honey

¼ teaspoon salt

3 tablespoons olive oil

Combine everything but the oil together in a small bowl; gradually whisk in the oil until emulsified.

Garden Lettuces with Pears, Fennel, Pomegranates, and Pear Vinaigrette

Any combination of greens works in this fall salad—just be sure to include arugula; its flavor is exceptional with juicy, ripe pears and the crisp, fresh taste of fennel.

SERVES 4 TO 6

2 large heads of lettuce, about 10 cups of leaves

A large handful of arugula

Pear Vinaigrette (recipe follows)

½ large fennel bulb, cored, and thinly sliced crosswise

1 ripe pear, such as Comice or Bartlett

¼ cup pomegranate seeds

Wash and dry the greens; cover with a damp towel and refrigerate.

Make the vinaigrette.

Place the greens and fennel in a large bowl.

When you're ready to serve the salad, cut the pear in half; trim away the core and slice lengthwise. Add the pear to the salad and gently toss with the vinaigrette. Arrange on individual plates and sprinkle with the pomegranate seeds.

Pear Vinaigrette

MAKES ABOUT ⅓ CUP

½ medium pear, peeled, cored, and chopped

3 tablespoons pear vinegar (see Tip)

¼ teaspoon salt

3 tablespoons olive oil

Place the pear in a blender with the vinegar and salt; puree, then drizzle in the oil, blending until emulsified.

TIP: We use a delicious pear vinegar from Western Shore Orchard in Hood, California, made with pear juice, white wine vinegar, and a slice of Bartlett pear in the bottle. If pear vinegar isn't available in your local specialty market, substitute 2 tablespoons unfiltered apple cider vinegar and 1 tablespoon unfiltered apple juice in its place.

Bitter Greens with Fuyu Persimmons, Asian Pears, and Pecans

Crisp Asian pear, vibrantly colored Fuyu persimmon, and toasted pecans are tossed together with seasonal greens and Tangerine-Sherry Vinaigrette to make this outstanding fall salad. The tender inner leaves of escarole, peppery watercress, and bitter radicchio contrast beautifully with the sweetness of the fruit and the sharp vinaigrette. Be sure the Fuyu persimmons are firm to the touch when you buy them. If Asian pears are unavailable, use a firm, ripe pear instead. To dress up the salad, sprinkle jewel-like pomegranate seeds over the tossed salad just before serving.

SERVES 4 TO 6

1 large head of escarole, about 6 cups of inner leaves

½ small head of radicchio, about 3 cups of leaves

1 small bunch of watercress, about 3 cups of sprigs

Tangerine-Sherry Vinaigrette (recipe follows)

1 medium Asian pear

1 medium Fuyu persimmon

¼ cup pecan pieces, toasted (page 46) and coarsely chopped

Cut or tear the leaves of escarole and radicchio into large pieces. Wash and dry the greens; cover with a damp towel and refrigerate.

Make the vinaigrette.

Cut the pear in half, trim away the core, and slice crosswise. Cut the persimmon in half and slice crosswise into thin half-moons.

Combine the greens, sliced fruit, and pecans in a large bowl; gently toss with the vinaigrette.

Tangerine-Sherry Vinaigrette

MAKES ABOUT ½ CUP

½ teaspoon minced tangerine zest

2 tablespoons fresh tangerine juice

1 tablespoon sherry vinegar

¼ teaspoon salt
¼ cup olive oil

Whisk everything but the oil together in a small bowl. Slowly pour in the oil, whisking until emulsified.

The Two Persimmons

Sometimes in late autumn, you'll see a persimmon tree that's dropped all its leaves—its bare, outstretched limbs dangling with vibrant orange fruit. It's an unforgettable image.

Persimmons come in two distinctly different varieties: Hachiya and Fuyu. Hachiya, the large, heart-shaped variety, is used for baking. It's the key ingredient in persimmon pudding and makes delicious soft spice cookies, quick breads, and homey cakes. A word to the wise: Hachiyas must be soft and squishy to the touch, or their astringent flesh is inedible. They are so beautiful that we plan ahead, buying them a couple of weeks early to let them ripen in a bowl where we can see them. If you're short on time, pop them in the freezer and they'll soften right away. And freezing is a great way to keep them.

Fuyu persimmons have an endearing squat shape, which resembles a funny-looking apple. Unlike Hachiyas, they're firm and crisp at their very best. They're delicious sliced and tossed into salads or served simply with warm, toasted almonds and a wedge of locally made artisan cheese. You'll know they're near the end of their season when their small seeds grow large and there's actually more seed than fruit. Time to give the Fuyus a rest and move on to the winter crop of citrus.

Romaine Hearts and Watercress with Apples, Beets, Stilton, and Cider Vinaigrette

We feature this beautiful salad in the late summer, when the first Gravenstein apples—a juicy, crisp Sonoma County variety—appear in the farmers' markets. Their season is short, so we quickly move on to Sierra Beauties, Fujis, Black Jonathans, and Galas in the fall. Stilton is our choice of cheese here, but Maytag, Roquefort, or any tangy blue cheese will do. Roast the beets ahead of time and the salad comes together quickly.

SERVES 4 TO 6

2 heads of romaine, about 8 cups of inner leaves

1 large bunch of watercress, about 2 cups sprigs

⅓ head of frisée, about 2 cups leaves

1 crisp, flavorful apple

Cider Vinaigrette (recipe follows)

2 large beets, about ½ pound, roasted, peeled, and cut into wedges (page 29)

Salt and pepper

2 ounces Stilton cheese, crumbled, about ¼ cup

Cut or tear the romaine leaves into large pieces, keeping the smaller leaves whole. Wash and dry the greens; cover with a damp towel and refrigerate.

Cut the apple into quarters and remove the core. Set aside one-quarter for the vinaigrette and thinly slice the rest.

Make the vinaigrette.

Toss the beets in a small bowl with 1 tablespoon of the vinaigrette, sprinkle with ¼ teaspoon salt, and a pinch of pepper.

Place the greens, apple slices, and half the cheese in a large bowl; toss gently with the remaining vinaigrette.

Separate the salad onto plates, tucking the beets between the leaves, and sprinkle the top with the remaining cheese.

Cider Vinaigrette: We add a quarter of an apple to this blended vinaigrette to thicken it, so it coats the leaves of romaine nicely. A little apple juice smoothes the tart taste of the cider vinegar to balance the flavors. Be sure to use unfiltered cider vinegar, available in natural food stores and specialty markets, because it's so much tastier.

MAKES ABOUT ½ CUP

¼ apple, cored, peeled, and chopped

2 tablespoons unfiltered apple cider vinegar

2 tablespoons unfiltered apple juice

¼ teaspoon salt

¼ cup olive oil

Place the apple in a blender and add the vinegar, apple juice, and salt; puree and add the oil until emulsified.

A Few of Our Favorite California Apples

While cold storage apples may be available all year, they've lost much of their flavor and texture. That's why in apple season—a relatively short period that begins in late summer here and runs through the fall—we go wild for apples. First up are Gravensteins, which hit the farmers' markets in late July. This crisp, tart old-fashioned apple is great for salads. Gravensteins—once grown all over Sonoma County—are now a specialty apple, a symbol of days gone by. When apple season is in full swing, heirloom varieties come our way, one right after the other. Catch them when the new crop is in. Here are the shining stars of our autumn menu.

ARKANSAS BLACK

This firm, sweet apple is so deeply red it's almost black. It's a late season apple, ideal for cooking, tossing in a salad, or eating out of hand.

BLACK JONATHAN

This early season apple—grown locally in Sonoma and Sebastopol—is named for its deep, dark red skin. It's delicious fresh or cooked and because of its color, makes a lovely rosy applesauce.

FUJI

If you like a snappy, sweet apple, Fuji's the one for you. Originally from Japan and prized for their unblemished skin, they're now grown locally and in eastern Washington, along the fertile, rolling shores of Lake Chelan. They're excellent for salads and snacks.

GALA

This crisp, sweet-tart apple with the blushing rosy skin, originally from New Zealand, is also grown locally in Sonoma. Pass by late-season Galas, which have lost their hue along with most of their taste.

GRANNY SMITH

These bright green apples with an unmistakable tart flavor are a favorite for pies and *Tarte Tatin*. Their firm, juicy flesh holds up well in the heat of the oven. The skin tends to be tough, so we always peel before baking. They're also great for snacking. Granny Smiths are available all year long and they're the exception to the rule: They store well.

NORTHERN SPY

These tart, firm apples with the mysterious name make a quick appearance every year in our specialty markets—now you see them, now you don't. Grab them when you do; they're delicious for pies and baking.

PIPPIN

This small, green, early-season tart apple with a golden crown breaks down quickly, so it's ideal for applesauce. Their skin should be smooth and firm, a sure sign of freshness.

SIERRA BEAUTY

This late season Rome Beauty apple—named for the spectacular beauty of the Sierra Nevada—has incredible flavor balanced between tart and sweet. The texture is perfectly crisp. It's delicious tossed into a wilted cabbage salad and makes a luscious pink applesauce.

Romaine Hearts with Sun-Dried Tomatoes, Chunky Sourdough Croutons, and Red Wine Vinaigrette

Crisp leaves of romaine, chunky croutons, and wedges of hard-cooked eggs work beautifully together in this favorite winter salad. The bold vinaigrette sets off all the flavors. We include a handful of young dandelion greens when they're available, but you can also use mizuna or red mustard greens instead. The croutons can be made ahead of time; just be sure to store them in an airtight container.

SERVES 4 TO 6

4 hard-cooked eggs, peeled (see box)

8 thick slices of sourdough bread, cut into ¾-inch cubes, about 2 cups

Garlic Oil (page 14)

2 heads of romaine lettuce, about 10 cups inner leaves

A large handful of mizuna, red mustard, or young dandelion greens, about 2 cups

Red Wine Vinaigrette (recipe follows)

6 or 7 oil-packed, sun-dried tomato halves, thinly sliced, about ⅓ cup

16 to 20 Gaeta olives, pitted and coarsely chopped, about ⅓ cup

Salt and pepper

Preheat the oven to 375°F. Make the hard-cooked eggs and set aside to cool.

Toss the bread with a little garlic oil, place on a baking sheet, and bake until golden and crunchy, about 10 minutes. Set aside to cool.

Cut or tear the romaine leaves into large pieces. Wash and dry the greens; cover with a damp towel and refrigerate.

Make the vinaigrette.

Toss the greens in a large bowl with the sun-dried tomatoes, olives, and the croutons. Cut the eggs into quarters, brush with a little of the vinaigrette, sprinkle with salt and pepper, and set aside.

Toss the salad with the vinaigrette and arrange on individual plates, tucking the hard-cooked eggs between the leaves. Sprinkle with pepper and serve.

Red Wine Vinaigrette

3 tablespoons red wine vinegar

½ tablespoon Dijon mustard

¼ teaspoon minced garlic

¼ teaspoon salt

6 tablespoons extra-virgin olive oil

Whisk everything but the oil together in a small bowl; slowly add the oil, whisking constantly, until emulsified.

Hard-Cooked Eggs

This tried-and-true method makes perfect eggs every time. They're slightly soft in the center, just the way we like them, with no gray rings around the yolks from overcooking. We use very fresh, organic eggs and cook them every day for egg salad sandwiches at our take-out counter, Greens to Go. They're also delicious cut into quarters and tucked into a salad of crisp romaine leaves or chopped and sprinkled over Grilled Asparagus (page 14) with Garlic Bread Crumbs (page 219).

Place several large eggs in a small saucepan just big enough to hold them, cover with cold water, and bring to a boil. As soon as the water comes to a boil, remove from the heat, cover the pan, and set aside for 10 minutes. Drain and rinse until cool, then peel.

TIP: If the eggs are difficult to peel, peel them in a bowl of water to loosen the membrane and remove any tiny pieces of shell.

Wilted Spinach and Escarole Hearts with Portobello Mushrooms and Parmesan

Roasted portobello mushroom juices mingle with hot olive oil, balsamic vinegar, and freshly grated Parmesan cheese to make this wilted spinach salad a year-round favorite. Add a smoky element by grilling the portobello mushrooms over coals instead of roasting them. For a simple variation, substitute chunky garlic croutons for the pine nuts—the crisp, toasted bread picks up all the delectable flavors. Have all your ingredients ready ahead of time, so the salad is easily put together.

SERVES 4

Roasted Portobello Mushrooms (page 260), thinly sliced, about 1½ cups

½ medium red onion, thinly sliced, about ½ cup

1 or 2 bunches of spinach, about 12 cups leaves

A handful of tender escarole leaves, 2 to 3 cups

3 tablespoons balsamic vinegar

½ teaspoon minced garlic

½ teaspoon salt

Pepper

½ pint ripe, little cherry tomatoes

2 tablespoons pine nuts, toasted (page 46)

1 tablespoon chopped fresh mint (optional)

¼ cup extra-virgin olive oil

1 ounce Parmesan cheese, grated, about ⅓ cup

Make the Roasted Portobello Mushrooms and set aside.

Cover the onions with cold water and set aside for 10 to 15 minutes.

Discard the bruised outer leaves of the spinach and trim off the stems, keeping the leaves whole. Trim the base of the escarole and discard the outer leaves; cut or tear the light green inner leaves into large pieces. Wash and dry the greens.

Drain the onions and give them a good shake to remove the excess water. Combine the vinegar, garlic, salt, and a pinch of pepper in a large bowl. Add the greens, tomatoes, onions, mushrooms, pine nuts, and mint, if using. Heat the oil in a small skillet until just below the point of smoking, when the first wisp of vapor appears. Pour it over the salad, using metal tongs to toss, sprinkling in the Parmesan as you go. Serve immediately.

Bitter Greens

Bitter greens aren't for everyone, but we've grown to love everything about them. They dress up our fall and winter salads—and just in time—when tender lettuces are few and far between. Our cool, coastal weather is ideal for growing these distinctive members of the endive family, so they're available year-round. They're delicious wilted in brown butter with plump currants and toasted pine nuts, or just finished with a splash of sherry vinegar and simply savored. If you've been wondering what to do with them, take a chance, and give these extraordinary greens a try.

CURLY ENDIVE

This sturdy endive with curly outer leaves has a strong bitter flavor. It's delicious paired with wilted spinach and escarole or tossed with a warm potato salad. *Frisée* is frilly, with open leaves and tender hearts; it's also a bit milder. Just give the prepared leaves a fluff—they'll become surprisingly light and airy. This bitter green gives wonderful body to salads.

ESCAROLE

The broad, light green leaves of this voluptuous endive are delicious any way you prepare them—wilted for a pizza, tossed into a salad, or simmered in a rustic soup. Pull away the tough outer leaves and you'll find tender inner leaves and a pale heart in the center.

RADICCHIO

Once an exclusive Italian import, this gorgeous ruddy-faced member of the endive family is now grown locally and often organically. Radicchio must be here to stay, now that it's a fashion color. Here are a few of our favorite radicchios.

43

TREVISO

This elegant variety looks like a slender head of romaine with pale ribs and crimson leaves. We love to toss it in salads.

CASTELFRANCO

This stunning radicchio comes in light, open heads with pale green leaves speckled with magenta. Tossed with butter lettuce or escarole and winter citrus, it makes a beautiful salad.

ROSSA DE VERONA

The most familiar of all, this variety looks like a small magenta cabbage with white ribs and veins. The compact heads are dense and voluminous—it's great for salads, sautéing, and grilling.

ENDIVE

The smooth tapered heads of this elegant chicory are wonderful for grilling, braising, and slivered for salads. No longer an extravagant European import, beautiful red and white endive is now grown here in the Delta. *Endigia* is new on the scene—it looks just like red endive with frilly edged leaves; imagine endive with a radicchio grandparent on one side.

DANDELION GREENS

These pungent weeds with the slender, spiky leaves can be pretty spicy. When they're young, we toss them with butter lettuce, romaine hearts, or into a wilted spinach salad. The big, hot ones are delicious sautéed with chard or kale. Little red dandelion greens—with red ribs and veins—are a hot ticket item in our kitchen. If you see them, grab them.

Wilted Spinach Salad with Pears, Gorgonzola, and Toasted Pecans

Ripe pears and creamy Gorgonzola are the surprise ingredients of this outstanding wilted spinach salad. It's great for holidays and special occasions or a casual fall supper with Butternut Squash and Chestnut Soup and good, crusty rustic bread. Use savoy spinach if you can find it—the sturdy, crinkly leaves hold up well to the heat of the olive oil and trap bits of crumbled Gorgonzola as the salad is tossed together.

SERVES 4 TO 6

2 ripe, flavorful pears: French Butter, Comice, or Bartlett

2 tablespoons pear or unfiltered apple cider vinegar

1 shallot, thinly sliced, about ⅓ cup

1 tablespoon sherry vinegar

1 large bunch of spinach, about 12 cups leaves

2 handfuls of frisée hearts, about 3 cups

¼ teaspoon salt

Pepper

¼ cup pecan pieces, toasted (page 46)

3 ounces Gorgonzola, crumbled, about 6 tablespoons

¼ cup extra-virgin olive oil

Cut one of the pears in half. Peel and core one half (you won't be using the other half). Mash the peeled pear in a large bowl, pour the vinegar over it, and set aside for 30 minutes.

Bring a small pot of water to a boil and drop in the shallots for 20 seconds. Drain and toss with the sherry vinegar. Set aside.

Discard the bruised outer leaves of the spinach and trim off the stems, keeping the leaves whole. Trim the base of the frisée hearts. Wash and dry the greens.

Stir the shallots, salt, and a pinch of pepper into the pear or apple cider vinegar. Thinly slice and core the remaining pear. Add the greens, pecans, sliced pear, and two-thirds of the Gorgonzola, saving the rest to crumble over the salad. Heat the oil in a small skillet until just below the point of smoking, when the first wisp of vapor appears. Pour it over the salad and toss with a pair of metal tongs to coat and wilt the leaves. Sprinkle the reserved Gorgonzola over the salad and serve.

Toasting Nuts and Seeds

This basic preparation is almost second nature in our kitchen. We do most of our toasting in the oven—almonds, walnuts, pine nuts, pecans, hazelnuts, peanuts, and pumpkin seeds—but a small, dry skillet on the stove works well for small quantities of pine nuts, pumpkin seeds, and sesame seeds. Whether you toast them in the oven or on the stovetop, the key is to catch them at that perfect moment when they smell intensely nutty—and it's just a moment, sometimes two—before they start to burn. We've lost countless trays of nuts and seeds to that point of no return, so if you're absent-minded, set a kitchen timer and keep it within earshot.

Whether you use the oven or stovetop method, be sure to use a baking dish, pan, or skillet that's not too large; otherwise, the exposed surface will attract the heat unevenly and the nuts or seeds on the outer edge will tend to burn. Don't be in a hurry; nuts and seeds prefer to be lavished with attention and roasted at moderate heat. If they've gone a little too far and start to turn too dark and burn, it's not too late to save them if you're quick: Just transfer them to a cool surface and give them a shake to spread and cool them down.

In the oven: Toast in an ovenproof dish or on a rimmed baking sheet in a preheated 350°F oven until they smell nutty and begin to turn golden, 8 to 10 minutes, depending on the nut or seed. Give them a shake after 4 to 5 minutes, to redistribute them and keep their color even. Pine nuts brown quickly, while almonds take longer; you'll know by their lovely aroma and warm golden color, inside and out. Peanuts are the slowest of all, basking in the heat for up to 12 minutes. Toasted hazelnuts need to be peeled right away, so wrap them in a dishtowel and rub the towel between your hands to loosen the skins.

In a small skillet: Use a heavy-bottomed skillet—the little French ones or cast-iron skillets are ideal conductors of heat. Don't be tempted to walk away while toasting nuts or seeds on the stovetop. Toast them over very low heat, shaking the pan as needed, until they're golden and smell nutty. (This is best done over a gas burner; electric heat is difficult, but not impossible, to control.) Sesame seeds take a minute or two, while pine nuts and pumpkin seeds can take up to 5 minutes.

Chopping and grinding: Chop nuts by hand or in a food processor, pulsing and watching carefully to be sure they don't turn into nut butter. Seeds are best ground in a clean coffee grinder.

STORAGE: Nuts and seeds can be toasted in advance; just allow them to cool down completely before storing in an airtight container in the refrigerator. Though they're best served right away, you can toast them up to a few days ahead of time. To refresh them, toast on the stovetop or in the oven at 350°F for a few minutes; it makes a big difference in their flavor.

Asparagus and Beets with Meyer Lemon Vinaigrette

This spring salad is full of color and flavor. You can make it the day before—just be sure to add the asparagus right before serving, so it stays bright green. If Meyer lemons aren't available, use regular lemons or make Tangerine-Shallot Vinaigrette instead.

SERVES 4 TO 6

½ pound medium beets, preferably Chioggia or golden, scrubbed and trimmed

Meyer Lemon Vinaigrette (recipe follows)

Salt and pepper

1 pound asparagus, tough stem ends removed, cut into 2-inch lengths on the diagonal

Preheat the oven to 400°F.

Place the beets in a small baking dish with ¼ inch water. Cover the dish and roast until tender when pierced with a skewer or paring knife, 35 to 40 minutes, depending on their size. While the beets are roasting, make the vinaigrette. When the beets are cool enough to handle, peel and cut in wedges. Place them in a serving bowl and toss with the vinaigrette.

Bring a small pot of water to a boil and salt lightly. Drop in the asparagus and cook for 2 minutes, until tender, but still bright green. Drain the asparagus and rinse under cold water. Give them a good shake to remove the excess water, and let dry on a kitchen towel. Just before serving, toss the asparagus with the beets and season to taste with salt and pepper.

Meyer Lemon Vinaigrette

MAKES ABOUT ½ CUP

1 teaspoon minced Meyer lemon zest
2 tablespoons Meyer lemon juice
1 tablespoon Champagne vinegar
¼ teaspoon salt
6 tablespoons extra-virgin olive oil

Whisk everything but the oil together in a small bowl. Slowly pour the oil in, whisking until emulsified.

TIP: Since this recipe calls for just a half pound of beets, it's a good idea to roast some extras, so they'll be ready when you need them. They keep well for two to three days in the refrigerator.

Panzanella with Artichokes, Olives, and Manchego

This sumptuous bread salad is a great make-ahead dish for a picnic or party. Use a good, sturdy rustic bread such as day-old levain, ciabatta, or sourdough Italian. The lightly toasted cubes of bread soak up the sharp red wine vinaigrette, while succulent roasted peppers and their juices keep everything moist. A big handful of arugula, tossed in at the last minute, adds freshness.

SERVES 6 TO 8

Simple Artichoke Salad (page 53), about 3 cups, quartered

1 pound loaf of rustic bread, crust removed, cut into ¾-inch cubes, about 12 cups

Garlic Oil (page 14)

Salt and pepper

2 tablespoons red wine vinegar

2 tablespoons sherry vinegar

½ cup extra-virgin olive oil

1 each large red and yellow pepper, roasted (page 291), peeled, and cut into thick strips, about ½ cup

24 Gaeta olives, pitted and coarsely chopped, about ½ cup

A large handful of arugula

2 ounces Manchego cheese, grated, about ½ cup

Preheat the oven to 350°F.

Make the Simple Artichoke Salad and set aside.

Toss the bread cubes with garlic oil and a little salt and pepper. Place on a baking sheet and bake until lightly browned and just crisp on the outside, about 10 minutes.

Combine the vinegars, ¼ teaspoon salt, and a pinch of pepper in a small bowl and slowly whisk in the oil. Toss the bread cubes, peppers, olives, and vinaigrette together in a large bowl. Set aside to marinate for 5 to 10 minutes. Just before serving, toss in the arugula and cheese and adjust the seasoning with salt and pepper.

VARIATIONS: This is a great place to use jarred or canned piquillo peppers if you can find them. These spicy little roasted peppers from Spain are a delicious substitute for the usual roasted peppers. Manchego is the perfect cheese for this dish, but you can use freshly grated Parmesan, dry jack, or aged goat cheese instead.

Moroccan Beet Salad

This spicy beet salad is especially delicious with Lentil Salad with Goat Cheese and Mint, Grilled Artichokes, and tasty black olives. Dress the warm beets with the Moroccan Vinaigrette ahead of time, so the earthy flavor of toasted cumin and coriander seeds develops. For a simple variation, toss in small sprigs of cilantro just before serving.

SERVES 4 TO 6

1 pound medium Chioggia or golden beets, scrubbed and trimmed
Moroccan Vinaigrette (recipe follows)
Champagne vinegar
Salt

Preheat the oven to 400°F.

Place the beets in a small baking dish with ¼ inch water. Cover the dish and roast until tender when pierced with a skewer or paring knife, 35 to 40 minutes, depending on their size. While the beets are roasting, make the vinaigrette. When the beets are cool enough to handle, peel and cut them in wedges. Place them in a serving bowl and toss with the vinaigrette.

Season to taste with a splash of vinegar and a pinch of salt if needed.

Moroccan Vinaigrette

MAKES ABOUT ⅓ CUP

2 tablespoons fresh orange juice
1 tablespoon Champagne vinegar
¼ teaspoon cumin seeds, toasted (page 214) and ground
¼ teaspoon coriander seeds, toasted (page 214) and ground
¼ teaspoon salt
3 tablespoons extra-virgin olive oil
Cayenne pepper

Combine the orange juice, vinegar, spices, and salt in a small bowl. Slowly whisk in the oil until emulsified. Add a pinch of cayenne pepper to taste.

Beets with Tangerine-Shallot Vinaigrette: This lively salad is a mainstay of our fall and winter appetizer menu. We serve it with Yellow Finn Potato Cakes or alongside White Runner Beans with Champagne Vinaigrette and Tarragon as part of an antipasto. The tangerines work exceptionally well with beets. If they're not available, you can always use oranges instead.

Prepare the beets as described on page 51 and toss with the Tangerine-Shallot Vinaigrette.

Tangerine-Shallot Vinaigrette

MAKES ABOUT ⅓ CUP

2 teaspoons minced tangerine zest

2 tablespoons fresh tangerine juice

1 tablespoon Champagne vinegar

1 small shallot, thinly sliced, about 1 tablespoon

¼ teaspoon salt

3 tablespoons olive oil

Combine everything but the olive oil in a small bowl. Slowly whisk in the oil until emulsified.

Simple Artichoke Salad

We feature artichokes of all sizes in all kinds of dishes, but for this classic salad we like to use the little ones. Because they're small, there's no choke inside, so trimming them is surprisingly easy. You can use the larger ones as well; just be sure to trim away the outer leaves and scoop out the choke.

Serve them alongside Farro Salad with Roasted Peppers and Arugula, or simply with marinated olives. Save your leftovers and chop them with flat-leaf parsley for a quick relish or spread on toasted bread for crostini. Tossed with Parmesan cheese and thyme, the relish becomes a filo turnover filling.

SERVES 4 TO 6

2 pounds small artichokes, trimmed or 4 large artichokes (page 178)

Artichoke Marinade (recipe follows)

½ tablespoon extra-virgin olive oil

½ teaspoon minced garlic

½ teaspoon minced lemon zest

Salt and pepper

Prepare the artichokes.

Make the Artichoke Marinade and cook the artichokes as directed. Drain and toss with the oil, garlic, zest, ¼ teaspoon salt, and a pinch of pepper.

Artichoke Marinade

ENOUGH FOR 2 POUNDS OF ARTICHOKES

2½ cups water

¼ cup extra-virgin olive oil

¼ cup white wine

3 tablespoons fresh lemon juice

1 tablespoon Champagne vinegar

2 garlic cloves, smashed with the flat side of a knife, skin left on

3 fresh thyme sprigs

1 bay leaf

¾ teaspoon salt

Pinch of pepper

Combine the ingredients in a wide, nonreactive pan and bring to a boil. Drop in the artichokes (cut side down if you're using large artichokes). Cover the surface with parchment paper or an inverted plate to keep the artichokes submerged so they cook evenly. Bring the liquid back to a boil, lower the heat, and simmer until just tender, 10 to 12 minutes, depending on their size. Check for doneness by inserting a skewer or paring knife into the base. Drain the artichokes and proceed with the recipe as directed.

Fennel and Parsley Salad with Meyer Lemon

This simple, refreshing salad is a great way to begin a meal. Meyer lemons add their distinctive fragrance and flavor, but if they're not available, just use regular lemons, tangerines, or oranges. Don't hold back on the parsley—the dark green sprigs taste great with thinly sliced fennel.

SERVES 4 TO 6

2 large fennel bulbs

½ bunch flat-leaf parsley, about 1 cup small sprigs and leaves

2 teaspoons minced Meyer lemon zest

Salt and pepper

2 tablespoons extra-virgin olive oil

2 tablespoons Meyer lemon juice

Cut the fennel in half from top to bottom, cut out the core, and remove any bruised outer leaves. Use a mandoline, vegetable slicer, or sharp knife to slice the fennel crosswise, as thin as possible. Transfer the fennel to a medium-size bowl and toss with the parsley, lemon zest, ¼ teaspoon salt, a pinch of pepper, and the oil. Add the lemon juice, toss again, and season to taste with salt and pepper.

VARIATION: Shave Manchego, Parmesan, or aged goat cheese over the salad and serve nestled in a bed of tender greens—nutty arugula, mâche, or peppery sprigs of watercress are just a few of the possibilities.

55

Corn and Cherry Tomato Salad with Arugula

Make this quick summer salad when both corn and cherry tomatoes are abundant. Use the sweetest, ripest cherry tomatoes you can find. Cut them in half, even though they're little, so their juices mingle with the corn and peppery arugula. This is a great make-ahead dish for a picnic or light supper. Serve it simply with toasted bread and goat cheese.

SERVES 4 TO 6

1 tablespoon olive oil

1 large shallot, diced, about ¼ cup

Salt and pepper

4 ears corn, shaved, about 4 cups kernels

¼ cup water

Champagne vinegar

½ pint ripe, little cherry tomatoes, cut in half

A large handful of arugula

Heat the oil in a large sauté pan and add the shallots, ¼ teaspoon salt, and a pinch of pepper. Sauté over medium heat until the shallots begin to soften, about 2 minutes. Add the corn and sauté for 1 minute. Add the water, lower the heat, and cover the pan. Simmer until the corn is tender, about 3 to 4 minutes. Transfer to a bowl and season with 1 tablespoon of the vinegar and ¼ teaspoon salt. Set aside to cool.

Toss in the cherry tomatoes and arugula just before serving and adjust the seasoning with salt, pepper, and a splash of vinegar, if needed.

VARIATION: Substitute leftover grilled or roasted peppers for the cherry tomatoes. Quickly dice the peppers and don't mind the little flecks of skin—they add a rustic touch to the salad. In place of the shallot and arugula, use scallions and thinly sliced basil.

Cherry Tomatoes

Of all the cherry tomatoes available here in this cook's paradise—a wild array of colors, shapes, and sizes—little Sweet 100 and Sungold varieties are always our first pick. These bite-size red and golden gems are bursting with sweet, concentrated flavor. Here are a few of their accomplishments in our kitchen: Tossed with a salad of romaine hearts, freshly grated Parmesan, and a sharp Champagne-caper vinaigrette; scattered over a roasted eggplant pizza; and sprinkled over a late-harvest heirloom tomato salad, they're the last bite of sunny summer to savor as the days grow shorter.

Of course, we enjoy other specialty varieties: Red and yellow pear and variegated green grapes are among our favorites. With their exceptional flavor and unique shapes and colors, they're a stunning addition to pastas, fresh salsas, and salads. And special recognition goes to Early Girls: These small, intensely flavored tomatoes are so juicy and sweet. While they may look like commercially grown cherry tomatoes, they don't taste that way at all. In winter, however, it's worth looking for the organic cherry tomatoes grown in Baja California and widely available at markets. These are reminiscent of the real thing, and a great treat on a cold winter day.

Green Beans and Shelling Beans with Cherry Tomatoes

Young shelling beans—available at farmers' markets throughout the summer months—are the big deal here, cooked until completely tender and dressed warm, so they soak up the sharp Champagne Vinaigrette. You can use different varieties of beans; just be sure to cook them separately, as the cooking time will vary with their size.

SERVES 4

Champagne Vinaigrette (recipe follows)

½ pound shelling beans: cranberry, cannellini, or flageolet, shelled, about ¾ cup beans

½ pound fresh summer beans: yellow wax or Blue Lake green beans, green or yellow Romano, stem ends trimmed and cut in half on the diagonal

½ cup ripe, little cherry tomatoes, cut in half

2 tablespoons chopped flat-leaf parsley or ½ teaspoon chopped fresh oregano

Salt and pepper

Champagne vinegar

Make the vinaigrette and set aside.

Bring a small pot of water to a boil and drop in the shelling beans. Lower the heat to a gentle boil and cook until completely tender, about 12 to 15 minutes. Taste the beans to be sure they're ready before you drain them. Drain and toss in a large bowl with half of the vinaigrette and sprinkle lightly with salt and pepper. Set aside to cool.

Bring a medium-size pot of water to a boil and salt lightly. Cook the fresh beans separately, allowing 2 to 3 minutes for green beans, 4 to 6 minutes for yellow wax, and 6 to 8 minutes for large Romano beans. Scoop them from the water with a strainer; rinse under cold water and drain. Toss the fresh beans into the shelling beans along with the remaining vinaigrette and the herbs.

Just before serving, add the tomatoes and parsley or oregano and season to taste with salt, pepper, and a splash of vinegar, if needed.

Champagne Vinaigrette

2 tablespoons Champagne vinegar

½ tablespoon Dijon mustard

½ teaspoon salt

Pinch of pepper

¼ cup extra-virgin olive oil

Combine everything but the oil in a small bowl. Gradually whisk in the oil until emulsified.

TIP: If shelling beans aren't available, just make the salad without them and increase the cherry tomatoes to 1 cup.

Shelling Beans

If you're confused about shelling beans (sometimes called shelly beans), just think of them as beans still in the pod, in a state halfway between fresh and dried. Unlike dried beans, which are starchy, shelling beans are tender and creamy. You'll find them in their beautiful pods at farmers' markets throughout the summer and early fall. Speckled cranberry beans, tongues of fire, pale green flageolets, purple crowder, black-eyed peas, and Italian butter beans are a few of the varieties that come our way. Toss them with haricots verts, yellow wax beans, and a sharp vinaigrette for a light summer salad or sauté them with big green and yellow Romano beans, olive oil, and garlic for a satisfying side dish. If you're cooking more than one kind of bean, cook them separately; the cooking time varies with each variety.

Shell the beans and bring a pot of water to a boil. Drop the beans into the water and lower the heat to a gentle boil. Cook until plump and tender, 12 to 15 minutes. Drain and toss immediately with a little extra-virgin olive oil, vinegar of your choice, and salt and pepper. Or you can toss them right away with a vinaigrette; just be sure to season them while they're warm.

Couscous Salad with Cherry Tomatoes, Lemon, and Pine Nuts

Crunchy bites of toasted pine nuts contrast with juicy cherry tomatoes and the fresh taste of parsley and mint in this lemony, lively salad. We use a flat bottom dish to prepare the couscous, so the individual grains absorb the hot dressing evenly. Make this for a picnic or party—have the couscous ready in advance, and just toss in the cherry tomatoes, pine nuts, and herbs right before serving.

SERVES 4

1 cup instant couscous

1 teaspoon minced lemon zest

1 cup water

2 tablespoons fresh lemon juice

1 tablespoon Champagne vinegar

3 tablespoons olive oil

¾ teaspoon salt

Pinch of pepper

3 tablespoons pine nuts, toasted (page 46)

1 scallion, both white and green parts, thinly sliced on the diagonal

1 cup ripe, little cherry tomatoes, cut in half

2 tablespoons chopped flat-leaf parsley

2 tablespoons chopped fresh mint

Pour the couscous grains into a small baking dish. Set the lemon zest aside to toss with the salad later. Combine the water, lemon juice, vinegar, olive oil, salt, and pepper in a small saucepan. Bring to a boil, pour over the couscous, and give it a quick stir. Cover the dish and set aside for 20 minutes.

When the couscous is ready, gently fluff it with a fork to separate the grains. Transfer to a serving bowl and toss with the reserved lemon zest and the remaining ingredients.

White Runner Beans with Champagne Vinaigrette and Tarragon

Large, starchy white runner beans are our choice for this versatile, year-round salad. Allow plenty of time and cook the beans gently, so they hold their shape when tossed with the vinaigrette—they really take on the sharp flavor of Dijon mustard and the anise taste of tarragon. If white runner beans aren't available, use cannellini, white emergo, or smaller white beans instead. Dark, speckled scarlet runner beans also make a beautiful salad.

SERVES 4 TO 6

1½ cups white runner beans, about 9 ounces, sorted and soaked overnight

8 cups cold water

1 bay leaf

Champagne Mustard Vinaigrette (recipe follows)

¼ large red onion, finely diced, about ½ cup

1 tablespoon Champagne vinegar

Salt and pepper

1 tablespoon chopped fresh tarragon

Drain and rinse the beans. Place them in a large saucepan with the water and bay leaf and bring to a boil. Lower the heat and simmer until they're tender but still hold their shape, about 1½ hours.

Make the vinaigrette and set aside.

Bring a small pot of water to a boil and drop in the onion for 20 seconds. Drain and toss in a small bowl with the vinegar.

Drain the beans, discard the bay leaf, and toss immediately with the vinaigrette. Add the onions and season to taste with salt and pepper. Marinate for 30 minutes to an hour, stirring occasionally as the salad cools. Just before serving, add the tarragon and adjust the seasoning with salt and pepper.

Champagne Mustard Vinaigrette

MAKES ABOUT ½ CUP

3 tablespoons Champagne vinegar

1 teaspoon Dijon mustard

¾ teaspoon salt

¼ teaspoon pepper

½ teaspoon minced garlic

6 tablespoons extra-virgin olive oil

Whisk everything but the oil together in a small bowl. Slowly pour in the oil, whisking constantly until emulsified.

Corn and Fire-Roasted Poblano Salad with Cilantro

We feature this zesty summer salad with quesadillas, Guacamole, and Fire-Roasted Salsa. The combination couldn't be better. Be sure to taste the roasted chilies before adding them to the salad; though usually mild, they can be surprisingly fiery.

SERVES 4 TO 6

½ medium red onion, diced, about ½ cup

1 tablespoon Champagne or rice vinegar

1 tablespoon olive oil

4 ears of corn, shaved, about 4 cups kernels

Salt

¼ cup water

Fire-Roasted Poblano Chilies (page 64), peeled, seeded, and diced, about ½ cup

4 teaspoons fresh lime juice

Cayenne pepper

3 tablespoons coarsely chopped cilantro

Bring a small pot of water to a boil and drop in the onions for 20 seconds. Drain and toss with the vinegar.

Heat the oil in a large sauté pan. Add the corn, ¼ teaspoon salt, and sauté over medium heat for about 1 minute. Add the water, lower the heat, and cover the pan. Simmer, covered, until the corn is tender, about 5 minutes.

Transfer to a bowl and toss with the chilies, onions, lime juice, ¼ teaspoon salt, and a pinch of cayenne. Set aside to cool.

Just before serving, add the cilantro and season to taste with salt and cayenne.

TIP: To make this salad even easier, you can prepare the separate elements ahead of time and combine them at the last minute. The poblano chilies keep well for several days in the refrigerator or can be frozen and defrosted just before using.

Fire-Roasted Poblano Chilies

The flavor of these tapered, dark green chilies is unmistakable. We grill them over an open flame until their skins are charred and their enticing aroma fills the Greens kitchen. They're quick to grill and easy to peel. Once peeled and chopped, we add them to scrambled eggs, soft tacos, and enchilada fillings. They keep well in the refrigerator for up to a few days; so grill an extra chili or two to have on hand for last-minute quesadillas.

MAKES ABOUT ½ CUP

2 Poblano chilies, about ½ pound
Vegetable oil or olive oil

Rub the chilies lightly with oil and place them on a stovetop grill or directly over an open flame. Grill over medium-high heat and turn, using metal tongs, until the skins are evenly blistered and charred. Remove from the heat, transfer to a bowl, and cover with a plate or a lid; they'll steam as they cool.

When the chilies are cool, peel them, removing as much of the charred skin as you can. Make a lengthwise slit in each chili and remove the stem and seeds. (If you're planning to stuff them, leave the stems in place and carefully peel around them.) Once peeled, dice or slice them, according to the recipe. You should have about ½ cup. The roasted, peeled chilies will keep well in the freezer for months; just pop them in a plastic freezer bag.

STOVETOP GRILLING: The stovetop grill called El Asador is particularly helpful here; you can use it over a gas flame, or even an electric burner to grill two or three chilies at a time. This inexpensive grill is essential in my home kitchen.

STEAMING: This simple step is the key to easy peeling. Place the grilled chilies in a bowl or pot and cover it—or seal them in a plastic bag. As the chilies steam, the flesh will pull away from the skin. Once cool, the skins slip off easily.

PEELING: Bits of charred skin are okay. You can dip your fingers in water and use them to loosen the skins, but don't be tempted to dip the chilies in water or peel them under the running faucet—you'll lose their delicious flavor.

Heirloom Tomato Salad with Shaved Manchego

This is the ultimate summer salad, featuring the best of the season—juicy, ripe tomatoes of all sizes, shapes, and colors, dressed with tangy Caper Vinaigrette and shavings of Manchego cheese. A handful of tender greens add their fresh, distinctive flavor.

SERVES 4 TO 6

2 tablespoons Champagne vinegar

2 tablespoons capers, drained and rinsed

½ tablespoon Dijon mustard

¼ cup extra-virgin olive oil

Salt and pepper

Two large handfuls of tender greens: watercress, arugula, mâche, or small lettuces, about 4 cups leaves

1 pound ripe tomatoes, preferably heirloom, cut into ¼-inch-thick slices and half-moons

½ pint ripe, little cherry tomatoes

A wedge of Manchego cheese

Place the vinegar, capers, mustard, oil, ¼ teaspoon salt, and a pinch of pepper in a blender and puree until smooth, about 1 minute.

Place a handful of greens on each plate and layer the tomatoes on top. Scatter the cherry tomatoes over, sprinkle lightly with salt and pepper, and pour the dressing over the tomatoes and greens. Use a vegetable peeler to shave several thin sheets of the cheese over the salads.

Tomato Salad with Creamy Blue Cheese Dressing

An extravagant array of ripe heirloom tomatoes—cut in thick slices to show off their exotic shades of deep red, green zebra stripes, and pale gold—are drizzled with a creamy blue cheese dressing and served on a bed of arugula leaves. We like to use Bleu d'Auvergne or Point Reyes Original Blue for the dressing, but you can use Maytag, Roquefort, or any high-quality blue cheese. Double the recipe for the dressing and save half of it to toss with crisp leaves of romaine and wedges of tomato.

SERVES 4 TO 6

¼ cup buttermilk

2 tablespoons heavy cream

2 ounces tangy blue cheese, crumbled, about ¼ cup

1 tablespoon Champagne vinegar

1 tablespoon extra-virgin olive oil

Salt and pepper

½ tablespoon chopped flat-leaf parsley

2 ounces arugula, about 4 cups leaves

1 pound ripe tomatoes, preferably heirloom, cut into thick slices or half-moons

½ pint ripe, little cherry tomatoes

Puree the buttermilk, cream, half of the cheese, vinegar, oil, ¼ teaspoon salt, and a pinch of pepper in a blender until smooth, about 1 minute. Transfer to a small bowl and stir in the parsley.

Place a handful of arugula on each plate, layer the tomatoes over it and sprinkle lightly with salt and pepper. Sprinkle on the cherry tomatoes and pour the dressing over. Crumble the remaining cheese on top and serve.

Creamy Roasted Garlic Dressing:
The soft, smooth taste of roasted garlic works with tangy buttermilk in this unusual dressing. Sharp sherry vinegar heightens the flavors.

2 tablespoons Roasted Garlic Puree (page 145)
¼ cup buttermilk
1 tablespoon sherry vinegar
Salt and pepper

Blend the garlic puree, buttermilk, vinegar, ¼ teaspoon salt, and a pinch of pepper in a blender until smooth.

Grilled Fig and Endive Salad with Watercress

For this salad, we start with the ripest figs we can find and grill them slowly until their soft, inner flesh is bubbly and jamlike. The heat of the coals brings out their succulent sweetness and softens the slightly bitter flavor of the endive. For an exceptionally beautiful salad, combine a variety of figs—Black Mission, Kadota, or green Adriatic, which have exotic, deep purple insides.

If you've been wondering what to do with your fine, aged balsamic, this is the place to use it. The salad is also delicious with shaved Manchego, Pecorino, or aged goat cheese.

SERVES 4

2 heads of Belgian endive
Extra-virgin olive oil
Salt and pepper
6 to 8 ripe, fresh figs
A handful of small watercress sprigs, washed and dried
½ tablespoon balsamic vinegar

Prepare the grill.

Trim the ends of the endive, remove any bruised outer leaves, and cut in half lengthwise. Brush lightly with olive oil and sprinkle with salt and pepper. Cut the figs in half, leaving the stem end on, and brush with olive oil.

Place the figs and endive on the grill over medium coals, face side down. Grill the figs for a minute or two, turn them over, and grill the other side. When the figs are soft, move them to a cool spot on the grill. Turn the endive when they begin to soften, 2 to 3 minutes, and grill until wilted and completely tender. Remove the figs and endive from the grill. Cut the endive in half lengthwise and sprinkle with salt and pepper.

Place the watercress on a platter and loosely arrange the figs and endive over, fanning the endive slightly. Drizzle lightly with olive oil and the vinegar and serve.

A Cress Primer

We feature these peppery greens in many ways—tucked into grilled figs and melon, tossed with beets and fresh summer beans, or as a bright green puree for a creamy potato-watercress soup. Our favorite cresses are grown organically by Sausalito Springs in Sonoma County and Star Route Farms in Bolinas. Like all tender greens, they're perishable, so buy them in small quantities. Or grow your own cress from seed or cuttings—a few sprigs of watercress left in a glass of water will sprout.

WATERCRESS

This elegant French watercress with little round leaves comes to us in Ziploc bags packed with a little water to keep it fresh. It's really alive; you can tell by the tiny white root hairs on the stems. When it's in bloom, its delicate white flowers are stunning. Unlike the greenhouse varieties, it's grown outside in lots of water and exposed to the wind and the rain. It's harvested young, while its leaves and stems are small and tender, but if allowed to keep growing, it will grow large like the supermarket variety. Its strong, peppery flavor is full of character and grows stronger in the heat. Its botanical name is *nasturtium officinale,* but it's quite different from the common nasturtium. In Latin, nasturtium means, "to twist your nose," just what you'll do when you bite into those peppery leaves.

CURLY CRESS

This frilly cress with light green leaves, also known as garden cress, pepper cress, or pepper grass, is prized in the Middle East for its perfumy flavor. A little goes a long way. You'll find it at farmers' markets and specialty food stores. This pungent cress is grown in soil, not in water.

ANCHO CRESS

This slender cress has long, single stems and wide, flat leaves—ancho means wide in Spanish—and a lot of flavor. Also known as Upland or Winter Cress, you'll find it at specialty food stores and farmers' markets. Ancho cress is usually grown in soil, not in water. It's also available at specialty markets with the roots still attached and labeled "living watercress." Living watercress is grown hydroponically (in water, not soil) in a greenhouse.

Grilled Fingerling Potato Salad with Corn and Cherry Tomatoes

Crisp potatoes and rings of red onions are tossed hot off the grill with tender kernels of corn, cherry tomatoes, and spicy Jalapeño-Lime Vinaigrette. We use Rosefirs and Russian Bananas here— fingerling potatoes grown for us at Green Gulch Farm—but any variety of potato will do. For added smoky flavor, we throw the jalapeños for the vinaigrette right on the grill. If you don't have time to light up an outdoor grill, just roast the potatoes and grill the onions and jalapeños on a stovetop grill instead.

SERVES 4 TO 6

1½ pounds fingerling potatoes

Garlic Oil (page 14)

Salt and pepper

1 ear of corn, shaved, about 1 cup kernels

1 large red onion, peeled and sliced into ½-inch-thick rings

2 or 3 jalapeño chilies (for the vinaigrette)

Jalapeño-Lime Vinaigrette (recipe follows)

½ pint ripe, little cherry tomatoes, cut in half

¼ cup chopped cilantro

Preheat the oven to 400°F.

Prepare the grill.

Toss the potatoes in a baking dish with 1½ tablespoons of garlic oil, ½ teaspoon salt, and a pinch of pepper. Cover and roast until tender, about 30 minutes. When the potatoes are cool enough to handle, slice them in half on the diagonal.

While the potatoes are roasting, heat ½ tablespoon garlic oil in a small sauté pan. Add the corn and ¼ teaspoon salt and cook over medium heat for 1 minute. Add a little water, lower the heat, cover the pan, and cook until tender, 2 to 3 minutes. Set aside.

Brush the potatoes, onions, and chilies lightly with garlic oil and sprinkle with salt and pepper. Grill the potatoes until they're evenly marked, 4 to 5 minutes. Grill the onions until softened and evenly marked, about 3 minutes on each side. Grill the chilies until the skin is charred and blistered, about 2 minutes. Place the chilies in a covered bowl to steam for about 5 minutes.

Make the vinaigrette.

Coarsely chop the onion and place in a large bowl with the potatoes, corn, cherry tomatoes, and cilantro. Toss with the vinaigrette and season to taste with salt and pepper.

Jalapeño-Lime Vinaigrette

MAKES ABOUT ⅔ CUP

2 or 3 grilled jalapeño chilies, peeled and seeded
2 tablespoons fresh lime juice
1 tablespoon Champagne vinegar
¼ cup olive oil
¼ teaspoon salt
A pinch of cayenne pepper

Combine everything but the cayenne in a blender and blend until smooth. Season to taste with cayenne.

TIP: When corn is exceptionally sweet and tender, you can toss the shaved kernels right into the salad without sautéing them. You can also grill the corn on the cob—along with the potatoes, onions, and chilies—and then cut off the kernels.

Yellow Finn Potato Salad with Green Beans and Tarragon

Buttery, rich Yellow Finn potatoes, crisp green beans, and fresh tarragon are tossed with a bold mustard vinaigrette in this addictive potato salad. You can combine a variety of potatoes here if you like— little reds, fingerlings, Yukon Golds, or large potatoes cut into chunks if little ones aren't available. Just be sure to toss the warm potatoes gently with the vinaigrette, so they keep their shape.

SERVES 4 TO 6

2 pounds small Yellow Finn potatoes

Garlic Oil (page 14)

Salt and pepper

Red Wine Mustard Vinaigrette (recipe follows)

½ medium red onion, diced, about ½ cup

Red wine vinegar

¼ pound Blue Lake green beans, cut in half on the diagonal, about 1 cup

1½ tablespoons capers, drained and rinsed

½ tablespoon coarsely chopped fresh tarragon

Preheat the oven to 400° F.

Toss the potatoes in a baking dish with a little garlic oil and sprinkle with salt and pepper. Cover and roast until tender, 35 to 40 minutes. Set aside.

Make the vinaigrette.

Bring a pot of water to a boil and salt lightly. Place the onions in a small bowl and scoop a little water out of the pot, just enough to cover them. Let the onions soak for 30 seconds, drain, and toss with ½ tablespoon of the vinegar. Drop the green beans into the boiling water and cook until just tender, 2 to 3 minutes. Drain and rinse under cold water to keep them crisp and bright green. Give them a good shake to remove the excess water.

When the potatoes are cool enough to handle, cut them into halves or quarters. Toss the warm potatoes in a large bowl with the onions, capers, tarragon, and the vinaigrette. Add the green beans just before serving (so they won't discolor), and adjust the seasoning with salt, pepper, and a splash of vinegar, if needed.

Red Wine Mustard Vinaigrette

MAKES ABOUT ½ CUP

3 tablespoons red wine vinegar

½ tablespoon Dijon or stone ground mustard

¼ teaspoon minced garlic

¼ teaspoon salt

6 tablespoons extra-virgin olive oil

Whisk everything but the oil together in a small bowl. Slowly pour in the oil, whisking until emulsified.

Purple Potato Salad: *This simple variation makes an exotic-looking pale blue salad with slivers of celery and parsley for added crunch and freshness. Use purple potatoes, substitute 1 cup celery, sliced thinly on the diagonal, for the green beans, and 2 to 3 tablespoons coarsely chopped flat-leaf parsley for the tarragon.*

Purple Potatoes

Purple potatoes come to us in a stunning array of colors—from deep Purple Peruvians to pinkish Huckleberries and All Blue, which as their name hints are closer to blue than purple. Delightful in potato salads, they're delicious roasted or grilled, combined with contrasting Yellow Finns or fingerlings and served on their own or alongside a savory tart or filo.

This ancient variety of potato really does come from Peru. With their creamy flavor and texture, purple potatoes are ideal for roasting. Though their color lightens a bit, they retain their intense purple and hold true to their name.

Roasted Japanese Eggplant Salad with Pine Nuts and Capers

The rustic flavors of this exceptionally good summer salad bring out all the complexity of the roasted eggplant. Crunchy, toasted pine nuts and fragrant basil balance the little bites of pungent capers, while balsamic and red wine vinegars add both sweetness and intensity. This recipe is similar to caponata, *but the eggplant is roasted— not fried— so it is lighter and much easier to prepare. We use slender, firm Japanese eggplant here; it holds its texture when roasted and absorbs far less oil than traditional globe eggplant. This is a great dish for a party; serve it with croutons, olives, and Marinated Fresh Mozzarella.*

SERVES 6 TO 8

2 pounds Japanese eggplant, sliced ½ inch thick on the diagonal

3 tablespoons extra-virgin olive oil

½ tablespoon minced garlic

Salt and pepper

¼ large red onion, finely diced, about ½ cup

Red wine vinegar

2 tablespoons capers, drained and rinsed

2 tablespoons pine nuts, toasted (page 46)

20 large basil leaves, stacked and sliced into thin ribbons, about ¼ cup

3 tablespoons balsamic vinegar

Sugar (optional)

Preheat the oven to 375°F.

Toss the eggplant in a large bowl with the oil, garlic, ¼ teaspoon salt, and a few pinches of pepper. Lay the slices in a single layer on baking sheets and roast for 10 minutes. Rotate the pans, and cook until tender, about 10 minutes more. When the eggplant is cool enough to handle, slice it into ¼-inch thick diagonal strips.

Bring a small pot of water to a boil and drop in the onions for 20 seconds. Drain and toss with 1 tablespoon red wine vinegar.

Combine the eggplant, capers, pine nuts, basil, and onions in a large bowl. Toss gently with the balsamic vinegar and set aside to marinate for 30 minutes. Season to taste with salt, pepper, and a splash of red wine vinegar, if needed. If the salad is tart, add a pinch or two of sugar.

Farro Salad with Roasted Peppers and Arugula

Farro, a unique, old world grain from Tuscany, has a nutty, complex taste and chewy texture that's perfect for marinated salads. We toss the warm farro with the sharp Red Wine Vinaigrette so the tender, plump grains soak up every bit of flavor. You can make this salad a few hours ahead of time, then just toss in the arugula at the last minute.

SERVES 6

1 cup farro, about 6 ounces
Red Wine Vinaigrette (recipe follows)
1 each red and yellow pepper, roasted (page 291), peeled, and diced, about ½ cup
A generous handful of arugula
Salt and pepper

Place the farro in a large pot of lightly salted water. Bring to a boil, lower the heat, and simmer until the grains are tender, 15 to 20 minutes.

Make the vinaigrette.

Drain and toss the warm farro with the vinaigrette and peppers; set aside to cool. Just before serving, toss in the arugula and season with salt and pepper to taste.

Red Wine Vinaigrette

MAKES ABOUT ½ CUP

3 tablespoons red wine vinegar
½ teaspoon salt
Pinch of pepper
¼ cup extra-virgin olive oil

Whisk everything but the oil together in a small bowl. Slowly pour the oil in, whisking until emulsified.

VARIATION: For an equally delicious salad, substitute little cherry tomato halves and basil for the peppers and arugula.

Green Papaya Salad

If you have a Southeast Asian market nearby, you're sure to find green papaya there. Tossed with roasted peanuts, Thai basil, and a spicy lime dressing, the green papaya— which has a unique, crunchy texture but little flavor of its own— takes on all the other addictive flavors in this refreshing salad.

SERVES 6 TO 8

Vegetable oil for frying

½ pound firm tofu, cut into ½-inch-thick slices

Salt and pepper

1 tablespoon rice vinegar

¼ cup fresh lime juice

½ cup sugar

2 tablespoons hot water

2 tablespoons tamari or soy sauce

½ teaspoon sambal, or to taste

1 large green papaya, about 2 pounds

½ small red onion, peeled and thinly sliced lengthwise, about 1 cup

20 to 30 Thai basil leaves, bundled and thinly sliced, about ¼ cup

½ cup unsalted peanuts, roasted and coarsely chopped (page 46)

1 head of butter lettuce, whole leaves separated, washed and dried

Pour enough oil in a small sauté pan to measure ¼ inch deep and heat until just below the point of smoking, when the first wisp of vapor appears. Fry the tofu until golden and crisp, 3 to 4 minutes per side. Drain on paper towels. Slice the tofu into long thin strips and season with salt and pepper.

Make the dressing: In a small bowl whisk together the vinegar, lime juice, sugar, and hot water. Once the sugar has dissolved, add the tamari, 1 teaspoon salt, and the sambal.

Cut the ends off the papaya, cut in half lengthwise, and scoop out the seeds. Lay the fruit cut side down on a cutting board, trim off the skin, and cut in half crosswise. Using a mandoline or vegetable slicer, julienne into long thin strips. You should have about 6 cups. Place the papaya in a large bowl with the onions, basil, half of the tofu, and half of the peanuts. Toss with half of the dressing and set aside to marinate for 15 minutes.

Arrange two butter lettuce leaves on each plate to form a bowl and scoop ½ to ¾ cup salad in the hollow. Lay several tofu strips on top of each salad and spoon the remaining dressing over, dividing it evenly. Sprinkle the remaining peanuts over and serve.

Lentil Salad with Goat Cheese and Mint

Little green lentils are the key ingredient that make this classic salad such a hit. Unlike the larger lentils we use for soups and Indian dishes, the small green variety holds its shape when cooked. Toss the warm lentils right away with the Lemon Vinaigrette, so they absorb all the flavors. Serve with Simple Artichoke Salad and Spicy Tomato Jam for a trio of make-ahead appetizers. It's also delicious with crumbled feta or ricotta salata cheese.

SERVES 4 TO 6

1½ cups small green lentils, about 11 ounces

6 cups cold water

1 bay leaf

½ medium red onion, finely diced, about ½ cup

Champagne vinegar

Lemon Vinaigrette (recipe follows)

1 medium carrot, peeled and finely diced, about ½ cup

½ fennel bulb, finely diced, about ½ cup

3 tablespoons chopped fresh mint

Salt and pepper

3 ounces creamy goat cheese, about ½ cup

Rinse the lentils and place them in a large saucepan with the water and bay leaf and bring to a boil. Lower the heat and simmer until tender, about 20 minutes.

While the lentils are cooking, bring a small pot of water to a boil. Drop in the onions for 20 seconds, drain, and toss with 1 tablespoon Champagne vinegar.

Make the vinaigrette.

Drain and toss the warm lentils in a large bowl with the vegetables and the vinaigrette. Set aside to marinate for 30 minutes, stirring occasionally as the salad cools. Add the mint and season with salt, pepper, and a splash of Champagne vinegar, if needed. Remove the bay leaf. Crumble the goat cheese over the salad and serve.

Lemon Vinaigrette

MAKES ABOUT ½ CUP

½ tablespoon minced lemon zest

3 tablespoons fresh lemon juice

½ teaspoon minced garlic

2 tablespoons Champagne vinegar

1 teaspoon salt

¼ cup extra-virgin olive oil

Whisk everything but the oil together in a small bowl. Slowly pour the oil in, whisking constantly until emulsified.

Lentils

These legumes come in all varieties and colors and we use them in all kinds of ways—braised with red wine for an elegant side dish, gently simmered for a Mediterranean salad, and stewed with aromatic spices for an exotic soup or dal. Lentils are the convenience food of the bean world: There's no soaking involved and they cook quickly, so you can start them from scratch and enjoy within an hour.

It's hard to go wrong with lentils, but we've included a few tips just in case: Sort through them carefully and look for hidden small stones and debris, which look just like lentils. Cook them in water with a bay leaf and fresh herbs or spices, depending on the dish you're making. Lentils are less sensitive to salt than other beans (salt toughens the skins and slows down the cooking time of big beans), but we still cook them in unsalted water. There's no need for stock here; like all other beans, they make their own delicious broth as they cook and break down.

BROWN LENTILS

This common variety ranges in color from mottled khaki to reddish brown. They're available in supermarkets and natural food stores, often found in bulk bins, along with a stunning array of beans and whole grains. These thrifty lentils may be commoners, but they cook beautifully and make delicious soups and purees.

RED CHIEF LENTILS

These gorgeous lentils are widely used in Indian cooking. They break down quickly, so they're great for smooth, pureed soups and dal. You'll find them in natural food stores and Indian markets. Don't buy them for their beautiful coral color—they fade to yellow when cooked.

YELLOW LENTILS

Another staple of the Indian kitchen, they're commonly known as pulse, the British and East Indian name for lentils.

FRENCH GREEN LENTILS

Also known as *lentilles du Puy,* these little green lentils have always been a staple in our kitchen. They're now grown all over the world and organically here in the United States, but a true *lentil du Puy* can only be grown in France. They hold their shape when cooked, so they're great for braising and marinated salads—we always dress them warm. Toss them into pasta with ribbons of chard, hot pepper flakes, and crumbled ricotta salata or goat cheese for a rustic winter meal.

BLACK BELUGA LENTILS

These tiny black lentils, available in natural food stores and specialty markets, are named for the caviar they so strongly resemble. Like French green lentils, they have a nutty flavor and hold their shape when cooked; we use them interchangeably.

PARDINA LENTILS

This tiny brown variety is organically grown in Spain and can be used in place of Black Beluga and French green lentils.

WHITE LENTILS

Also known as albinos, these creamy-textured lentils are really just lentils with their outer coat removed, to reveal the light color inside. They're great for braising, though their delicate color darkens as they cook.

Grilled Portobello Mushroom and Endive Salad with Shaved Parmesan

This simple, elegant salad is a great way to begin a fall or winter meal. We grill the endive until completely tender, so their bitterness disappears and their delicious underlying sweetness emerges. Be sure the coals are not too hot and don't be in a hurry; give the endive the time to cook all the way through and you'll be rewarded as their crisp, firm texture turns surprisingly soft and supple. Grill a few extra endive while you're at it to inspire an upcoming meal— spread them over pizza dough with sautéed greens, black olives, and tangy feta cheese, chop and toss them into a salad, or savor them simply on their own.

The smoky portobello mushrooms pick up the complexity of flavors— balsamic vinegar, fruity olive oil, and shavings of Parmesan cheese. When wild porcini mushrooms appear each year in late autumn— just as they do in Italy— we celebrate their arrival by featuring them here in place of the portobellos.

SERVES 4

1 pound portobello mushrooms, 3 to 4 caps, stems removed
2 heads of Belgian endive, cut in half lengthwise
Garlic Oil (page 14)
Salt and pepper
2 tablespoons balsamic vinegar
⅓ cup extra-virgin olive oil
2 handfuls of tender greens: watercress, arugula, or mâche
Wedge of Parmesan cheese

Prepare the grill.

Brush the mushrooms and endive with garlic oil and sprinkle with salt and pepper. Place the endive on the grill, face side down, and the mushrooms gill side up. When the endive begin to soften, turn them over and grill the other side until wilted and completely tender. When the mushrooms begin to release their juices, turn them over, and grill them until cooked through.

Move the vegetables to a cool side of the grill. Combine the vinegar and a couple of pinches salt in a small bowl and whisk in the oil until emulsified.

Thinly slice the mushrooms on the diagonal and sprinkle with salt and pepper. Loosely arrange the greens on a platter and place the endive on top, fanning them slightly. Lay the mushrooms on top and pour the vinaigrette over. Use a vegetable peeler to shave curls of Parmesan cheese over the salad just before serving.

Salt

This elemental ingredient is so common we take it for granted, but it performs miracles on virtually every dish we make, drawing out flavors and bringing them to life. We've used fine sea salt since the day we opened our doors and we still stand firmly behind it. Though kosher salt is the choice of many chefs and home cooks, sea salt is our first choice.

I once asked our dear friend Barbara Tropp (who included a salt tasting in a Chinese cooking class she once taught in the early days at Greens) if we should switch from sea salt to kosher. In her inimitable wisdom, she asked the right questions, "Does it work for you? If it does, why would you change?" I've never asked the question again.

81

Asian Noodle Salad with Peanut Sauce and Lime

This peanut noodle salad is an all-time favorite at Greens to Go. It's not only highly portable, but it sits well on a buffet table for hours. A sprinkling of Spicy Peanuts is a perfect finishing touch.

SERVES 6 TO 8

Peanut-Ginger Sauce (recipe follows)

Spicy Peanuts (recipe follows), coarsely chopped, about ¾ cup

Vegetable oil for frying

½ pound firm tofu, cut into ½-inch-thick slices

Salt and pepper

1 large carrot, peeled, thinly sliced on the diagonal and cut into matchsticks, about 1 cup

1 pound dried linguine

¼-pound piece of daikon radish, peeled, thinly sliced on the diagonal and cut into match-
    sticks, about 1 cup

3 or 4 scallions, both white and green parts, sliced on the diagonal, about ½ cup

½ ounce fresh ginger, thinly sliced and cut into thin matchsticks, about ¼ cup

⅓ cup coarsely chopped cilantro

Juice of 1 lime

Hot pepper flakes

Sprigs of cilantro for garnish

Make the Peanut-Ginger Sauce and the Spicy Peanuts.

Bring a large pot of water to a boil and salt lightly.

Pour a thin layer of oil (about ¼ inch deep) into a sauté pan and heat until just below the point of smoking, when the first wisp of vapor appears. Fry the tofu until golden and crisp, 3 to 4 minutes per side. Place the tofu on paper towels to drain and sprinkle lightly with salt and pepper. When cool enough to handle, cut into thin strips. Toss in a small bowl with ¼ cup of the Peanut-Ginger Sauce and set aside.

Place the carrots in a small bowl and pour 1 cup of the boiling water over. Allow to sit for 1 minute, drain, and set aside. Cook the pasta in the boiling water until just tender, about 10 minutes. Drain in a colander, rinse under cold water, and shake off the excess moisture.

Place the pasta in a large bowl along with the tofu, carrots, daikon, scallions, ginger, cilantro, and half of the Spicy Peanuts. Add the Peanut-Ginger Sauce, the lime juice, ½ teaspoon salt, and a pinch of pepper flakes; gently toss to coat the noodles. Add pepper flakes to taste. Sprinkle the remaining peanuts over the salad and garnish with the sprigs of cilantro.

TIP: We use dried linguine here; because it's made with hard wheat, it holds its texture for hours and even overnight. You can also use dried udon noodles, available in the Asian section of grocery stores. Fresh Shanghai or Chinese noodles are also delicious, but they don't have the staying power of dried pasta and quickly break down when tossed with the acidic Peanut-Ginger Sauce. If you use them, be sure to serve the salad right away.

MAKE-AHEAD TIP: This salad goes together in a snap if you do some preparation in advance. You can make the Peanut-Ginger Sauce ahead of time. Cook the pasta the day before and toss with a little oil to keep the noodles from sticking together. Combine everything but the Peanut-Ginger Sauce, lime juice, cilantro, tofu, and Spicy Peanuts a few hours before serving and refrigerate. Toss the salad at the last minute with the remaining ingredients and garnish with the Spicy Peanuts. You can also toss half of the tofu into the salad and sprinkle the rest over the top.

Peanut-Ginger Sauce: This sauce is packed with big flavors. It keeps for weeks in the refrigerator. If you're making it more than a day or two ahead of time, add the fresh ginger right before serving.

MAKES ABOUT 2 CUPS
½ cup smooth, natural peanut butter
½ cup light brown sugar, packed
½ cup peanut oil
⅓ cup rice vinegar
¼ cup tamari or soy sauce
¼ cup water
1 tablespoon grated fresh ginger
¼ teaspoon salt
Pinch of cayenne pepper

Puree everything in a blender until smooth.

Spicy Peanuts: These nuts add spice and crunch to Asian noodle dishes and are also great all on their own. Serve them with Lotus Root Pickles and Pickled Daikon Radish for a trio of condiments. They keep well in an airtight container, so make a double recipe. They're great to have on hand.

MAKES 1 CUP

1 cup raw peanuts

½ teaspoon peanut oil

¼ teaspoon paprika

¼ teaspoon cayenne pepper

¼ teaspoon salt

Preheat the oven to 325°F. Toss everything together in a small bowl. Roast on a baking sheet for about 10 minutes, until the mixture smells nutty. Set aside to cool.

Soups

Corn Soup with Ginger and Thai Basil

Make this spicy corn soup when corn and peppers are brimming from the bins at the farmers' market. The heat of fresh ginger and chilies really stands out against the creamy pureed corn and potatoes. Sweet red peppers and jalapeños lend a beautiful, rosy hue. You can use green or opal basil— or a combination of the two— if Thai basil isn't available. For a spicier soup, add another chile or a pinch of cayenne.

MAKES ABOUT 2 QUARTS

Corn Stock (page 111), about 7 cups

1½ tablespoons olive oil

1 large yellow onion, diced, about 2 cups

½ tablespoon minced garlic

1½ tablespoons grated fresh ginger

Salt and pepper

6 ears of corn, shaved, about 6 cups

1 large potato, peeled and diced, about 2 cups

1 medium red pepper, diced, about 1 cup

1 or 2 red jalapeño chilies, seeded and minced

10 to 15 Thai basil leaves, bundled and thinly sliced, about 2 tablespoons

Make the Corn Stock and keep it warm over low heat.

Heat 1 tablespoon of the oil in a soup pot and add the onions, garlic, ginger, ¼ teaspoon salt, and a pinch of pepper. Sauté over medium heat until they begin to soften, about 3 minutes. Add the corn, potatoes, and 5 cups of the stock. Lower the heat, cover the pan, and simmer until the potato is tender, about 10 minutes. Reserve 3 cups of the corn-potato mixture and set aside. Place the rest of the mixture in a blender and puree until smooth, adding stock as needed. Pass through a food mill and return to the pot over low heat.

Heat the remaining oil in a small sauté pan and add the peppers, chilies, and ¼ teaspoon salt. Sauté over medium heat until soft, about 3 minutes, adding a little stock if needed to keep them from sticking to the pan. Add to the puree along with the reserved corn-potato mixture and stock to thin, if needed. Cook over medium-low heat for 10 minutes and season with salt and pepper to taste.

Sprinkle a little basil over each serving.

Chilled Three Beet Soup

This gorgeous soup is the place to use those beautiful, big bunches of beets you couldn't resist at the market. We use three colors of beets here— golden, Chioggia, and red— each in its own third of the soup bowl. The red beets will color the others, so be sure to peel and puree them last. If red beets are all that's available, this favorite chilled soup will still be a hit. For an elegant touch, we finish each serving with a spoonful of crème fraîche and a sprinkling of Orange Zest Threads.

MAKES ABOUT 2 QUARTS

1 pound medium Chioggia beets, scrubbed and trimmed

1 pound medium golden beets, scrubbed and trimmed

1 pound medium red beets, well scrubbed and trimmed

Orange Zest Threads (recipe follows)

1½ tablespoons olive oil

1 large yellow onion, chopped, about 2 cups

Salt and pepper

½ tablespoon minced garlic

1½ cups fresh orange juice

3 cups water

Crème Fraîche (page 98)

2 to 3 tablespoons chives, cut into ½-inch lengths (optional)

Preheat the oven to 400°F.

Place the beets, according to color, into three separate baking dishes. Pour a little water in the bottom of each dish. Cover and roast until tender, 35 to 40 minutes, depending on their size. Test for doneness with a paring knife or skewer. Set them aside until they're cool enough to peel.

Make the Orange Zest Threads.

Heat the oil in a small sauté pan and add the onions, ¼ teaspoon salt, and a pinch of pepper. Sauté over medium heat until soft, about 5 minutes. Add the garlic and cook 1 minute more. Transfer to a bowl.

Peel and cut the beets into large chunks, keeping them separate by color. Be sure to peel the red beets last, so they don't discolor the others. Starting with the lightest color, place the first batch of beets in the blender, along with one-third of the onions, ½ cup orange juice, 1 cup water, ½ teaspoon salt, and a pinch of pepper. Puree until smooth, adding a little water if needed to thin the puree. Transfer to a container and chill. Puree the next color in the same way with half the remaining ingredients and chill in a separate container, leaving the red beets for last. Refrigerate for at least 30 minutes and season to taste with salt and pepper.

To serve, ladle the thickest puree first into a shallow soup bowl along the left side. Ladle the other two purees carefully, one after the other, side by side. Garnish with a spoonful of crème fraîche and a sprinkling of Orange Zest Threads and chives, if you're using them.

Orange Zest Threads

1 large orange

Use a zester to remove the threads from the orange, keeping the strips as long as possible. Bring a small pot of water to a boil and drop in the threads for 10 seconds. Drain and rinse.

Chilled Cucumber Soup with Yogurt and Mint

We know we're in luck when the blanket of cool, moist marine air that covers San Francisco all summer long clears for a few glorious days of warmth and sunshine. That's when this refreshing chilled soup appears on the menu. We use the long European cucumbers (also known as hothouse) here. Their flesh is denser than that of ordinary varieties, so their flavor is more concentrated and they have fewer seeds. Be sure to select a high quality, whole milk yogurt— we use organic yogurt from Straus Family Creamery in West Marin. This is a great place to use your garden mint.

MAKES ABOUT 2 QUARTS

½ medium red onion, small dice, about 1 cup

1 tablespoon Champagne vinegar

2 pounds European cucumbers, peeled and seeded

Salt and pepper

½ pound seedless green grapes, about 1½ cups loose

1 cup plain yogurt

¼ cup coarsely chopped fresh mint

6 to 8 mint leaves, bundled and thinly sliced for garnish

Bring a small pot of water to a boil. Drop in the onions for 20 seconds, drain and toss in a small bowl with the vinegar. Set aside.

Finely dice half of the cucumber, season with a pinch of salt and pepper, and set aside. Coarsely chop the remaining cucumber and place in a blender. Add the grapes, yogurt, chopped mint, ½ teaspoon salt, and a pinch of pepper and puree until completely smooth, about 5 minutes. Transfer to a large container, stir in the diced cucumbers and onions, and chill for 30 minutes. Season to taste with salt and pepper. Serve in chilled bowls and garnish each serving with a little mint.

Kabocha Squash Soup with Coconut Milk and Lime Leaves

This soup is well worth the trip to an Asian market to find the ingredients. With its thick skin and firm, dense flesh, kabocha squash was born to be roasted. It soaks up the rich, exotic flavors of coconut milk, lime leaves, lemongrass, and Thai basil, which adds a spicy touch; if you can't find it, use regular basil or cilantro instead. If kabocha squash isn't available use red kuri, butternut, or another winter squash instead.

MAKES ABOUT 2 QUARTS

Vegetable Stock (page 110), 5 cups

1 medium kabocha squash, about 3½ pounds, cut in half, seeds removed

1 tablespoon vegetable oil or olive oil

1 large yellow onion, chopped, about 2 cups

Salt and pepper

1 tablespoon minced garlic

3 stalks lemongrass, tough tops and outer leaves removed, finely chopped, about ⅓ cup

¼ cup grated fresh ginger

1 or 2 kaffir lime leaves

One 14-ounce can unsweetened coconut milk

10 to 15 Thai basil leaves, bundled and cut into thin ribbons, about 2 tablespoons

Preheat the oven to 400°F.

Make the Vegetable Stock and keep it warm over low heat.

Place the squash, cut side down, in a baking dish with a little water. Cover and roast until tender, 30 to 35 minutes. When the squash is cool enough to handle, scoop it out of the skin. You should have about 4 cups.

Heat the oil in a soup pot and add the onions, ½ teaspoon salt, and a pinch of pepper and cook until they begin to soften, about 3 minutes. Add the garlic, lemongrass, and ginger and cook for 2 minutes. Add the squash, the stock, and the lime leaf and bring to a boil. Lower the heat and simmer, uncovered, about 30 minutes.

Remove the lime leaf and puree the squash mixture in a blender until smooth. Pass through a food mill and return to the pot over medium-low heat. Add the coconut milk and cook for 5 to 10 minutes. Adjust the seasoning with salt and pepper to taste. Garnish each serving with Thai basil.

Potato, Spring Onion, and Sorrel Soup

If you love the lemony taste of French sorrel, here's a perfect place to use it. The bright green leaves melt into the smooth potato base and quickly turn color; it may not be pretty, but the unmistakable tangy flavor is delicious. French sorrel is available at farmers' markets, but the most reliable source is your very own garden bed. This hearty, vigorous plant grows like crazy, so keep it in check. If spring onions aren't available, you can always use leeks or yellow onions in their place.

MAKES ABOUT 2 QUARTS

Vegetable Stock (page 110), 7 to 8 cups

3 pounds Yellow Finn potatoes, peeled

Salt and pepper

1 tablespoon olive oil

1 tablespoon unsalted butter

1 bunch spring onions, about ½ pound, sliced, including the firm part of the green, about 3 cups

1 tablespoon minced garlic

½ cup white wine

⅓ cup heavy cream

¼ pound sorrel, stems removed and leaves bundled and thinly sliced, about 2 cups

Grated Gruyère cheese

2 to 3 tablespoons chopped flat-leaf parsley

Make the Vegetable Stock and keep it warm over low heat.

Dice enough of the potatoes into ½-inch cubes to make 2 cups and set aside. Slice the remaining potatoes and place them in a soup pot, along with 6 cups of the stock, ½ teaspoon salt, and a pinch of pepper. Bring to a boil, lower the heat, and cook over medium heat until the potatoes begin to break apart, about 30 minutes. Pass through a food mill or quickly puree in a blender and return to the pot over low heat.

Heat the oil and butter in a large sauté pan and add the onions, ¼ teaspoon salt, and a pinch of pepper and cook over medium heat until soft and translucent, about 5 minutes. Add the garlic and cook 1 minute more. Pour in the wine and cook until the pan is nearly dry, about 3 minutes.

Stir in the diced potatoes, 1 cup of the stock, ¼ teaspoon salt, and a pinch of pepper.

Cover the pan and simmer until the potatoes are tender, about 10 minutes. Add to the potato puree, adding stock, if needed, to thin. Stir in the cream and the sorrel and cook over low heat for 5 minutes. Season to taste with salt and pepper. Garnish each serving with a spoonful of Gruyère and a sprinkling of parsley.

VARIATION: If sorrel isn't available, use thinly sliced spinach instead, but the tart sorrel flavor will be missed. You can also try thin ribbons of chard or kale, but allow extra time to cook the greens, particularly if using kale.

Borlotti Bean Soup with Roasted Garlic and Parmesan Croutons

Borlotti beans— also known as dried cranberry beans— have an exceptionally meaty flavor and a smooth, creamy texture that's out of this world. You'll find them in specialty food stores. Vegetable Stock is an essential ingredient here, building depth and richness into the beans, as they slowly simmer with fresh herbs and a bay leaf. This hearty, rustic soup is even better the next day.

MAKES ABOUT 2 QUARTS

Vegetable Stock (page 110), 8 cups

¾ pound borlotti beans, about 2 cups, sorted and soaked overnight

1 bay leaf

2 fresh thyme sprigs

2 fresh oregano sprigs

3 fresh sage leaves

2 tablespoons extra-virgin olive oil

1 large yellow onion, chopped, about 2 cups

Salt and pepper

2 teaspoons dried oregano, toasted (page 214)

½ tablespoon minced garlic

⅓ cup red wine

1 medium carrot, peeled and diced, about 1 cup

1 medium red pepper, diced, about 1 cup

Parmesan Croutons (recipe follows)

Roasted Garlic Puree (page 145), about ⅓ cup

Make the Vegetable Stock.

Drain the beans and rinse them well. Combine 6 cups of the stock, the beans, bay leaf, and the fresh herbs in a soup pot and bring to a boil. Lower the heat and simmer, uncovered, until completely tender, about 1½ hours.

While the beans are cooking, heat the oil in a large sauté pan and add the onions, ¼ teaspoon salt, and a pinch of pepper. Cook over medium heat for about 3 minutes; add the dried oregano and the minced garlic and cook 1 minute more. Pour in the wine and cook until the pan is nearly dry, about 3 minutes. Add the carrots and peppers and cook until tender, adding stock as needed to keep them from sticking to the pan.

93

soups

Make the Parmesan Croutons and the Roasted Garlic Puree.

Remove the bay leaf and herbs from the beans. Combine the Roasted Garlic Puree, 2 cups of the beans and their broth, and 1 cup of the stock in a blender and puree until smooth. Return to the pot, add the carrot and pepper mixture, and simmer over low heat for 15 minutes. If the soup is thick, add a little stock to thin it and season to taste with salt and pepper before serving.

Parmesan Croutons

¼ baguette, thinly sliced on the diagonal
Extra-virgin olive oil
½ ounce Parmesan cheese, grated, 2 to 3 tablespoons

Preheat the oven to 375°F. Brush the baguette slices lightly with oil and toast on a baking sheet for 5 minutes. Sprinkle on the cheese and bake until lightly browned and crisp, about 8 minutes.

VARIATION: Roasted Tomatoes (page 261) add another layer of richness to the soup. Coarsely chop 1 or 2 cups and stir into the soup a few minutes before serving, just long enough to heat through. Instead of the Parmesan Croutons, garnish each serving with a drizzle of extra-virgin olive oil and a sprinkling of fresh herbs. Grated Parmesan, Pecorino, or Asiago cheese is also a tasty, last-minute addition.

Butternut Squash and Chestnut Soup

Butternut squash and chestnuts are made for each other and this simple, elegant soup is a great example of their affinity. We use vacuum-packed chestnuts imported from France, but you can also use canned chestnuts— both are available in specialty food stores. Either way, the rich Chestnut Puree blends right into the silky butternut squash, adding depth and earthy flavor. For a lovely autumn supper, serve with crusty rustic bread and Romaine Hearts and Watercress with Apples, Beets, Stilton, and Cider Vinaigrette.

MAKES ABOUT 2 QUARTS

Vegetable Stock (page 110), 6 to 7 cups

1 medium butternut squash, about 2½ pounds, chopped, 6 cups

1 tablespoon olive oil

1 tablespoon unsalted butter

1 large yellow onion, coarsely chopped, about 2 cups

Salt and pepper

2 teaspoons minced garlic

¼ cup white wine

Chestnut Puree (recipe follows)

10 fresh sage leaves, stacked and thinly sliced, about 2 teaspoons

Make the Vegetable Stock and keep it warm over low heat.

Place the squash and 5 cups of stock in a soup pot. Bring to a boil, lower the heat, and simmer until the squash is tender and starting to break apart, about 30 minutes.

Heat the oil and butter in a sauté pan and add the onion, ¼ teaspoon salt, and a pinch of pepper. Cook over medium heat until the onions soften, about 5 minutes. Add the garlic and cook 1 minute more. Pour in the wine and cook until the pan is nearly dry, about 3 minutes.

Make the Chestnut Puree and reserve ½ cup for the garnish. Add the remaining puree to the squash, along with the onions and a pinch of salt. Cook together over low heat for 15 to 20 minutes. Place in a blender and puree until smooth, adding stock as needed. Adjust the seasoning with salt and pepper. Garnish each serving with a swirl of the reserved Chestnut Puree and sprinkle with the sage.

Chestnut Puree: If you're lucky enough to find vacuum-packed chestnuts, use them
here. Their flavor is exceptional. The puree will thicken as it sits, so if it's too thick to swirl, thin
it with a little stock, water, or liquid from the canned chestnuts, if using.

MAKES ABOUT 2 CUPS

½ pound vacuum-packed whole chestnuts, about 1½ cups, or 10 ounces canned whole
    chestnuts, packed in water, drained and liquid reserved

1 cup Vegetable Stock or water

Salt and pepper

If using vacuum-packed chestnuts, place them in a small saucepan with the stock or water
and bring to a boil. Lower the heat, cover the pan, and simmer until soft, about 20 minutes.
Puree in a food processor or blender until smooth, adding stock or water as needed to thin,
and season to taste with salt and pepper.

    If you're using canned chestnuts, they won't need to be cooked. Combine the chestnuts
with ¾ cup of their liquid in a small food processor or blender and puree until smooth. (Save
the remaining liquid to add to the puree if it needs to be thinned.) Season with salt and pepper to taste. Makes about 1½ cups.

Carrot-Parsnip Soup
with Orange Crème Fraîche

Toasted coriander seeds elicit the sweetness of the carrots and the earthy taste of the parsnip in this satisfying, smooth puree. Be careful with the parsnip; if you use too much, its strong root flavor will overpower the carrots. A little potato binds the soup and gives it a creamy texture, but you can always add a spoonful of cream to take it over the top. A swirl of Orange Crème Fraîche is a perfect finish.

MAKES ABOUT 2½ QUARTS

Vegetable Stock (page 110), 7 to 8 cups

1 tablespoon olive oil

1 tablespoon unsalted butter

1 large yellow onion, chopped, about 2 cups

Salt and pepper

1 tablespoon minced garlic

¼ cup white wine

1½ tablespoons coriander seeds, toasted and ground (page 214)

1½ pounds carrots, coarsely chopped, about 4 cups

1 medium parsnip, about ½ pound, peeled and coarsely chopped, 1½ cups

1 medium potato, peeled and coarsely chopped, about 1 cup

Orange Crème Fraîche (recipe follows)

Make the Vegetable Stock and keep it warm over low heat.

Heat the oil and butter in a large soup pot and add the onions, ¼ teaspoon salt, and a pinch of pepper. Cook over medium heat until the onions are soft, about 5 minutes. Add the garlic and cook 1 minute more. Add the wine and cook until the pan is nearly dry, about 3 minutes. Stir in the coriander, followed by the carrots, parsnips, potatoes, ¼ teaspoon salt, and a pinch of pepper. Add 5 cups of stock and simmer, uncovered, until the vegetables are tender, 35 to 40 minutes.

Make the Orange Crème Fraîche.

Puree the soup in a blender until smooth, adding a little stock if needed to each batch, then pass it through a food mill, and return to the pot over low heat. Add stock to thin to desired consistency and season to taste with salt and pepper. Garnish each serving with a swirl of Orange Crème Fraîche.

Orange Crème Fraîche: *For a different effect, try tangerine juice and zest in the Crème Fraîche instead of orange.*

MAKES ABOUT ½ CUP

¼ teaspoon minced orange zest

2 tablespoons fresh orange juice

½ cup Crème Fraîche (see box)

Whisk together in a small bowl.

Crème Fraîche

The way it's traditionally made in France, this fresh cultured cream is the true sour cream. With a tangy flavor and smooth, silky texture, it's wonderful in sauces, pastas, and stews. Just a spoonful is all that's needed to elevate a rustic potato soup to elegant status. Seasoned with sugar and vanilla bean, it's a transcendent sauce for Poached Pears or Poached Sour Cherries. You can even add a little citrus juice and minced zest; unlike sour cream, it doesn't curdle when you add it to acidic ingredients.

We've always made our own crème fraîche, but it is now available in specialty markets. The cowgirls at Cowgirl Creamery in Point Reyes Station in West Marin make their crème fraîche with Straus organic cream; its flavor is exceptional. Unlike yogurt, which requires a constant temperature to thicken, crème fraîche isn't temperamental at all. It's very easy to make—you just need 24 to 36 hours for it to thicken.

To make 2 cups of crème fraîche, pour 1 pint heavy cream into a jar or plastic container, add 1 tablespoon buttermilk, and whisk together. Set the container in a warm place in the kitchen (on top of the refrigerator is a good spot) and place a lid on top, but leave it ajar to help the culture grow. The cream will thicken after 24 hours and you can use it at this point, but we like to let it sit for another 12 hours; that's when the flavor really develops. Cover and refrigerate. It will keep for a couple of weeks in the refrigerator. Reserve 2 tablespoons crème fraîche to make your next batch. Then, go back to buttermilk for the third batch. Alternate the crème fraîche starter with buttermilk every other time to keep the culture fresh.

Potato, Fennel, and Celery Root Soup

The licorice taste of fennel— both the fresh bulbs and toasted seeds— makes this earthy winter soup sing. Little bites of fennel, potato, and leeks punctuate the smooth celery root and creamy Yellow Finn potatoes. We garnish the soup with aged Gruyère, but a spoonful of mascarpone or Orange Crème Fraîche is also good. Sprinkle a few feathery fennel sprigs on top if they're fresh.

MAKES ABOUT 2 QUARTS

Vegetable Stock (page 110), 7 to 8 cups

1½ pounds Yellow Finn or Yukon Gold potatoes, peeled

2 to 3 medium fennel bulbs, ends trimmed, outer leaves removed, halved and cored

1 large celery root, about 1 pound, peeled, quartered, and sliced, about 4 cups

1 bay leaf

Salt and pepper

1 tablespoon olive oil

1 tablespoon unsalted butter

2 leeks, white parts only, cut in half lengthwise, sliced and washed, about 2 cups

1 tablespoon minced garlic

½ teaspoon fennel seeds, toasted and ground (page 214)

½ cup white wine

⅓ cup heavy cream

Grated Gruyère cheese

2 tablespoons chopped fennel tops, chervil, or flat-leaf parsley

Make the Vegetable Stock and keep it warm over low heat.

Dice enough of the potatoes and the fennel to make 1 cup each and set aside. Slice the remaining potatoes and fennel and transfer to a soup pot, along with the celery root and 6 cups of stock. Add the bay leaf, ½ teaspoon salt, and a pinch of pepper and bring to a boil. Lower the heat and simmer until the vegetables are tender and begin to break apart, about 30 minutes. Remove the bay leaf, pass the soup through a food mill or quickly puree in a blender, and return to the pot over low heat.

While the vegetables are cooking, heat the oil and butter in a large sauté pan over medium heat. Add the leeks, ½ teaspoon salt, and a pinch of pepper and sauté until soft, about

3 minutes. Add the garlic and ground fennel seeds and cook for 1 minute. Pour in the wine and cook until the pan is nearly dry, about 3 minutes.

Add the diced potatoes and fennel, 1 cup of stock, cover the pan, and simmer until the vegetables are tender, about 8 minutes. Add to the potato-celery root puree, adding stock if needed to thin the soup. Add the cream and season to taste with salt and pepper. Garnish each serving with a spoonful of Gruyère and sprinkle with the fennel tops or herbs.

TIP: A food mill is indispensable here; it smoothes the texture of the potato and celery root base. If you don't have a food mill, you can also use a blender or food processor to puree the soup, but do it quickly. Otherwise, the starch in the potatoes will make the soup gummy.

RESTAURANT TIP: You can peel and slice the celery root up to a day ahead of time, but be sure to cover it with lemon water to keep it from discoloring.

Moroccan Chick-Pea Soup

This simple soup is filled with warm Mediterranean spices and a bit of heat, just enough to take the chill off a cool, windy San Francisco day. It's worth every minute it takes to cook the chick-peas; they make their own fragrant broth as they slowly simmer with cinnamon, fresh ginger, and a bay leaf. A sprinkling of cilantro adds a lively touch.

MAKES ABOUT 2 QUARTS

¾ cup chick-peas, about 5 ounces, sorted and soaked overnight

8 cups cold water

One 3-inch cinnamon stick

1 bay leaf

3 thin coins of fresh ginger

Spice Mixture (recipe follows)

1½ tablespoons extra-virgin olive oil

1 large yellow onion, chopped, about 2 cups

Salt and pepper

1 tablespoon minced garlic

1½ tablespoons grated fresh ginger

½ cup red wine

1 medium carrot, peeled and diced, about ¾ cup

2 celery ribs, diced, about ¾ cup

1 medium zucchini, diced, about 1 cup

One 14½-ounce can tomatoes, chopped, including the juice

2 to 3 tablespoons chopped cilantro

Drain and rinse the chick-peas. Place them in a soup pot with the water, cinnamon stick, bay leaf, and ginger coins. Bring to a boil, lower the heat and simmer, uncovered, until completely tender, about 1½ hours. (Keep the chick-peas in their broth.) Meanwhile, make the Spice Mixture.

While the chick-peas are cooking, heat the oil in a large sauté pan and add the onions, ¼ teaspoon salt, and a pinch of pepper. Cook over medium heat until they begin to soften, 3 to 4 minutes. Add the garlic, grated ginger, and Spice Mixture and cook until completely soft, about 3 minutes. Add the wine and cook until the pan is nearly dry, about 3 minutes. Stir in the carrots, celery, and zucchini, ¼ teaspoon salt, and a pinch of pepper and cook until tender, 3 to 4 minutes. Add the tomatoes and simmer for 5 minutes.

Remove the cinnamon, bay leaf, and ginger coins from the chick-peas. Add the vegetable mixture and simmer for 15 to 20 minutes. Adjust the seasoning with salt and pepper and add the cilantro just before serving.

Spice Mixture

½ tablespoon cumin seeds
½ tablespoon coriander seeds
¼ teaspoon mustard seeds
¼ teaspoon ground cinnamon
¼ teaspoon powdered turmeric
Pinch of cayenne pepper

Toast the cumin and coriander seeds together in a small skillet over medium heat until fragrant, 1 to 2 minutes. Grind them in a spice grinder. Toast the mustard seeds over medium heat in the skillet until they begin to pop. Combine the spices in a small bowl and set aside.

TIP: You can toast the spice mixture and cook the chick-peas a day ahead of time. Just be sure to remove the cinnamon, bay leaf, and ginger coins once they're cool.

Mushroom-Farro Soup

This hearty soup is similar to the classic mushroom barley, but with an unusual twist. Instead of barley, we use farro, a unique heirloom grain from Tuscany. We cook the farro in Mushroom Stock with dried porcini and sherry for added richness. It's well worth the trip to your local specialty market for farro, but if it isn't available, you can use barley instead.

SERVES 4 TO 6

Mushroom Stock (page 112), about 6 cups

½ ounce dried porcini mushrooms, soaked in ½ cup hot water for about 10 minutes

2½ tablespoons olive oil

1 large yellow onion, chopped, about 2 cups

Salt and pepper

2 tablespoons minced garlic

1 medium carrot, peeled and diced, about 1 cup

2 celery ribs, diced, about 1 cup

½ cup sherry

½ cup farro

1 bay leaf

1½ pounds Crimini or white mushrooms, sliced, about 8 cups

1 tablespoon unsalted butter

1 to 2 tablespoons chopped fresh herbs: flat-leaf parsley, chives, oregano or marjoram, and thyme

Make the Mushroom Stock and keep it warm over low heat.

Pour the porcini through a fine sieve and save the liquid to use later. Finely chop the porcini and set aside.

Heat 1½ tablespoons of the oil in a soup pot and add the onion, ¼ teaspoon salt, and a pinch of pepper. Cook over medium heat until the onions begin to soften, 3 to 4 minutes. Stir in 1 tablespoon of the garlic, the carrots, celery, and porcini and cook another 3 to 4 minutes. Add ¼ cup sherry and the porcini soaking liquid and cook until the pan is nearly dry, 3 to 4 minutes. Add the farro, bay leaf, and 4 cups of stock and bring to a boil. Lower the heat, cover the pan, and simmer until the farro is tender, about 45 minutes.

While the farro is cooking, sear the mushrooms in 2 separate batches. Heat ½ tablespoon of the oil and ½ tablespoon of the butter in a large sauté pan and add half of the mushrooms, ¼ teaspoon salt, and a pinch of pepper. Sauté over medium-high heat until the mushrooms begin to release their juices, add half the remaining garlic and continue to cook until the juices evaporate. At this point the mushrooms will be golden and seared. Add half of the remaining sherry to deglaze. Add the mushrooms to the soup, making sure to include the flavorful pan juices. Return the pan to the heat and cook the remaining mushrooms in the same way, adding a little stock to loosen the juices from the pan, if needed.

Add 2 cups of stock and the herbs to the soup and cook for 5 to 10 minutes. Season to taste with salt and pepper and serve.

Giant Peruvian Lima Bean Soup

This simple bean soup is deeply satisfying. When it comes to Peruvian lima beans, the bigger and starchier, the better. They sweeten as they melt into the Vegetable Stock and give the broth just the right thickness.

MAKES ABOUT 2 QUARTS

Vegetable Stock (page 110), about 2 quarts

1½ cups giant lima beans, about 9 ounces, sorted and soaked overnight

2 fresh thyme sprigs

2 fresh marjoram or oregano sprigs

3 fresh sage leaves

6 flat-leaf parsley sprigs

1 bay leaf

1½ tablespoons extra-virgin olive oil, plus more for garnish

1 large yellow onion, chopped, about 2 cups

Salt and pepper

1 tablespoon minced garlic

1 medium carrot, peeled and diced, about 1 cup

1 medium red pepper, diced, about 1 cup

⅓ cup white wine

10 kale leaves, ribs removed, cut into thick ribbons, about 3 cups

Make the Vegetable Stock.

Drain the beans and rinse them well. Combine 6 cups of the stock, the beans, the herb sprigs and leaves, and the bay leaf in a soup pot and bring to a boil. Lower the heat and simmer, uncovered, until the beans are cooked all the way through and beginning to break apart, about 1½ hours.

While the beans are cooking, heat the oil in a large sauté pan and add the onions, ¼ teaspoon salt, and a pinch of pepper. Cook over medium heat until the onions begin to soften, about 3 minutes. Add the garlic and cook 1 minute more. Stir in the carrots, red peppers, ¼ teaspoon salt, and a pinch of pepper and cook about 10 minutes, adding a little stock as needed to keep the vegetables from sticking to the pan. Pour in the wine and cook until the pan is nearly dry, about 3 minutes.

Add the vegetables to the soup pot, along with the remaining stock, ¼ teaspoon salt, and a pinch of pepper and cook until the flavors begin to come together, about 20 minutes. Add the kale and cook until tender, about 10 minutes more. Season to taste with salt and pepper. Remove the bay leaf. Serve in warm bowls and drizzle a little olive oil over each serving.

VARIATION: You can garnish this soup in any number of ways. For options, see the variation for Borlotti Bean Soup with Roasted Garlic and Parmesan Croutons (page 94).

Favorite Big Beans

With the wild array of dried beans available, favorites are hard to choose, but we have a special affinity for the big ones that plump up to make fantastic soups, marinated salads, and rustic ragoûts. We love cannellini, white runner, emergo, corona, and giant Peruvian limas. At Greens we're especially fond of the gigandes grown by Phipps Ranch in Pescadero. Of course, borlotti and scarlet runner beans are also delicious—they just happen to be reddish brown. Here are three surefire tips for making a great pot of beans.

SOAKING

We always soak beans—both large and small—overnight in plenty of water, so there's time for them to plump slowly. (We find they cook more evenly and their skins tend to be softer when they've had a good, slow soaking.) We put them in the refrigerator, but if your kitchen is cool, leave them out overnight. Rinse the beans well before cooking to remove any toxins released during soaking.

SLOW-COOKING

Give the beans plenty of time to cook and you'll be rewarded in a couple of ways: They'll be tender and still hold their shape (unless you want them to fall apart) and be much easier to digest than rushed, undercooked beans. Cook them in plenty of water; the beans need room to circulate in the pot and will soak up a lot of the liquid. Toss in a bay leaf and a few fresh herb sprigs and leaves, such as oregano, thyme, and sage to flavor the beans and their broth. If the beans need more water while they're cooking, add more. But don't salt the water;

it constricts the skins and increases the cooking time. Times will vary according to their variety, size, and age; the older the beans, the longer they'll take to cook. Big beans tend to have tough skins that shrivel when cool, so be sure they're completely tender. It's better to overcook them a bit than undercook them.

SEASONING

We always season beans while they're warm—even when making a salad that will be served chilled—so they soak up the flavor. Don't be shy with the seasonings—olive oil, vinegar, garlic, salt and pepper, and fresh herbs. Just be sure to toss the beans gently so they hold their shape. Hold on to that flavorful bean broth and add it to soups or ragoûts for great flavor and a little body.

107

Curry-Laced Lentil Soup

This curried soup— our version of Julie Sahni's recipe— is surprisingly light but rich tasting, and full of the enticing, aromatic flavors of India. We add a splash of lemon juice and chopped cilantro to finish, but you can also cool down the soup with a spoonful of tangy yogurt.

MAKES 2 QUARTS

¾ cup lentils, about ¼ pound, sorted and rinsed

6 cups cold water

1 bay leaf

1 tablespoon olive oil or vegetable oil

1 large yellow onion, diced, about 2 cups

Salt

1 tablespoon grated fresh ginger

1 tablespoon minced garlic

1 teaspoon yellow mustard seeds, toasted (page 214)

½ tablespoon cumin seeds, toasted (page 214) and ground

1 teaspoon coriander seeds, toasted (page 214) and ground

1 celery rib, diced, about ⅓ cup

1 small carrot, peeled and diced, about ½ cup

1 medium zucchini, diced, about 1 cup

One 14½-ounce can tomatoes, chopped, including the juice

Cayenne pepper

½ tablespoon fresh lemon juice

2 to 3 tablespoons chopped cilantro

Place the lentils in a large saucepan with the water and the bay leaf and bring to a boil. Lower the heat and simmer, uncovered, until tender, about 20 minutes.

While the lentils are cooking, heat the oil in a soup pot and add the onions and ¼ teaspoon salt and sauté over medium heat until soft, about 5 minutes. Add the ginger and garlic and cook for 1 minute. Stir in the spices and cook for 1 or 2 minutes, adding a little water if needed. Add the celery, carrots, zucchini, and ½ teaspoon salt and cook over low heat until tender, about 5 minutes. Add the tomatoes and simmer for 15 to 20 minutes.

Remove the bay leaf from the lentils. Add the lentils and their broth, ½ teaspoon salt, and 2 pinches of cayenne to the vegetable mixture and simmer for 20 minutes. Add the lemon juice and the cilantro just before serving and season to taste with salt and cayenne.

A Stock Pep Talk

Vegetable stock lays the foundation for so many of our dishes—soups, stews, ragoûts, and curries. It's essential to our cooking—there's no way around it. Besides, it's easy to make and just as easy to freeze.

Good stock is all about flavor and freshness. You can vary the ingredients, depending on the dish you're making, but don't use too much of one ingredient or too many ingredients overall. If leeks aren't in season, use a yellow onion or scallions instead. (We use yellow onions because they're less expensive than red ones and they make a lighter colored stock. We also stay away from onion skins because they darken the stock and can make it bitter.) If you're making a stock for a winter squash soup, don't throw out the seeds and the skin of the squash; use them to add flavor to the stock. You can always add another carrot or potato, but be careful with mushrooms, because they darken the stock and can take over. But if you're making a mushroom sauce or soup, use as many as you like. If you're crazy about garlic, go ahead and add a few extra cloves. Fresh herbs are delicious, but oregano, thyme, and sage can be overpowering, so use them sparingly. Don't even think of including rosemary, unless it's a tiny sprig for a hearty bean soup. And be sure to include salt, as it draws out all the flavors.

Don't be tempted to use old vegetables or members of the brassica family—the strong taste of broccoli, cauliflower, and cabbage takes over. Toss your old vegetables in your compost bin or better yet, feed them to your hardworking worms (page 371). They'll get down to business on those weary vegetables and turn them into a dark, rich worm compost, which is simply out of this world for everything growing in your garden.

Vegetable Stock

This versatile stock is surprisingly rich, adding tremendous depth of flavor to many of our favorite dishes. It is just right for risotto and all kinds of soups and stews, both delicate and hearty. It's great for thinning leftover soups, ragoûts, and pasta dishes, so double the recipe and freeze half of it for later. It keeps nearly indefinitely in the freezer, but only a day or two in the refrigerator.

MAKES ABOUT 2 QUARTS

1 large yellow onion, sliced

2 to 3 leek tops, chopped and washed

3 celery ribs, sliced

2 large carrots, sliced

½ pound white mushrooms, sliced

1 large potato, sliced

6 garlic cloves, smashed with the flat side of a knife, skins left on

1 teaspoon salt

½ teaspoon peppercorns

6 parsley sprigs

3 to 4 fresh thyme sprigs

2 fresh oregano or marjoram sprigs

5 fresh sage leaves

1 bay leaf

10 cups cold water

Combine all the ingredients in a stockpot and bring to a boil. Lower the heat and simmer, uncovered, for about 45 minutes, stirring as needed. Pour the stock through a strainer, pressing as much liquid from the vegetables as possible, then discard them.

Corn Stock

We make this easy stock for corn soups. After cutting the kernels from the cobs, we pile the shaved cobs in a stockpot with a few vegetables and sprigs of parsley. This stock is much lighter in color than Vegetable Stock, so it keeps the soups from discoloring and the flavor is sweet and fresh. It can stay nearly indefinitely in the freezer, but only a day or two in the refrigerator.

MAKES ABOUT 2 QUARTS

6 to 8 corncobs, shaved, broken in half

1 large yellow onion, sliced

2 celery ribs, sliced

1 large potato, sliced

5 garlic cloves, smashed with the flat side of a knife, skins left on

1 teaspoon salt

½ teaspoon peppercorns

5 parsley sprigs

2 fresh thyme sprigs

10 cups cold water

Combine all the ingredients in a stockpot and bring to a boil. Lower the heat and simmer, uncovered, for about 45 minutes, stirring occasionally. Pour the stock through a strainer, pressing as much liquid from the vegetables as possible, then discard them.

Mushroom Stock

This deep, full-bodied stock is the secret ingredient that gives our mushroom soups and sauces their intensity and richness. We use dried shiitake mushrooms, but you can use dried porcini instead. Either way, the dried mushrooms give the stock its essential mushroom flavor, so be sure to include them. This is a great place for those cast-off portobello mushroom stems, which are too tough to roast or sauté. The stock keeps nearly indefinitely in the freezer, but only a day or two in the refrigerator.

MAKES ABOUT 2 QUARTS

1 large yellow onion, sliced

1 leek top, chopped and washed

2 medium carrots, chopped

½ pound white mushrooms, sliced

1 ounce dried shiitake mushrooms

4 garlic cloves, smashed with the flat side of a knife, skins left on

6 parsley sprigs

3 fresh thyme sprigs

2 fresh oregano or marjoram sprigs

1 bay leaf

1 teaspoon salt

½ teaspoon black peppercorns

10 cups cold water

Place all the ingredients in a large soup pot and bring to a boil. Lower the heat and simmer for about 45 minutes. Strain the stock, pressing as much liquid from the vegetables as possible, and then discard them.

TIP: You can reduce the stock to intensify the mushroom flavor. Simmer over medium-high heat until the stock concentrates in flavor; just a little will enhance a wild mushroom pasta or risotto.

Sandwiches

Sourdough Baguette with Goat Cheese, Watercress, and Tomatoes

Make the most of your juicy, ripe tomatoes with this simple sandwich. Use the best sourdough baguette and the tastiest goat cheese you can find. We use Laura Chenel's chef's chèvre— which is largely distributed— but any creamy, fresh goat cheese will do. Go lightly on the watercress or its strong flavor takes over.

SERVES 4; MAKES 4 SANDWICHES

1 sourdough baguette
4 to 6 ounces creamy, fresh goat cheese
1 large ripe tomato, about ½ pound, sliced
Salt and pepper
A handful of watercress

Slice the baguette in half lengthwise and spread the goat cheese lightly on both sides. Layer the tomatoes on the bottom, sprinkle with salt and pepper, and place the watercress on top. Place the top of the baguette on the sandwich and slice diagonally into 4 sandwiches.

TIP: If the goat cheese is hard to spread, add a little milk or heavy cream to thin it.

VARIATION: This sandwich is delicious with grilled or roasted peppers instead of tomatoes. Piquillo peppers—spicy jarred or canned roasted peppers from Spain—are also good. (Piquillo means "with a little bite.") You can also substitute arugula for the watercress.

Avocado and Tomato Sandwich with Chipotle Aïoli

Rich avocado, juicy, ripe tomatoes, sharp cheddar cheese, crisp romaine leaves, and spicy Chipotle Aïoli make a winning sandwich. Be sure to use a hearty, fresh whole wheat bread. Take it on a picnic or a bike ride, or enjoy it after an exhilarating dip in the Bay.

SERVES 4

Chipotle Aïoli (recipe follows)

8 slices of whole wheat bread

6 to 8 ounces New York or Vermont cheddar cheese, thinly sliced

2 firm, ripe avocados, peeled and sliced

Salt and pepper

2 large, ripe tomatoes, about 1 pound, sliced

8 to 12 romaine leaves, trimmed

Make the Chipotle Aïoli.

Spread each slice of bread with a little of the aïoli and place the cheese on 4 of the slices. Make an avocado layer and sprinkle with salt and pepper. Add the tomatoes and sprinkle with salt and pepper. Follow with the romaine and place the bread on top. Slice in half on the diagonal.

TIP: You can slice the avocados ahead of time. Just brush with a little fresh lemon or lime juice to keep them from discoloring.

Chipotle Aïoli:
You can use either lime or lemon juice here, but lime juice goes particularly well with the smoky flavor of the chipotle chilies.

MAKES ABOUT 1 CUP

1 large egg yolk

½ tablespoon fresh lime or lemon juice

1 cup olive oil

Chipotle Puree (page 163), 1 teaspoon or to taste

¼ teaspoon minced garlic

¼ teaspoon salt

115

Whisk the egg yolk with a few drops of the citrus juice and whisk in the oil, very slowly at first, until the aïoli begins to emulsify. After all the oil has been added, season with the remaining juice, chipotle puree, the garlic, and salt.

Baguette with Tapenade, Grilled Peppers, and Fontina

This sandwich features creamy Fontina, salty black olive spread, smoky grilled peppers, and pungent arugula, all layered onto a crusty baguette. We grill the peppers over coals, but you can use a stovetop grill or roast them in the oven instead. Red and yellow peppers make an especially beautiful sandwich. You don't need to peel the peppers, unless the skins are completely charred.

SERVES 4; MAKES 4 SANDWICHES

1 each red and yellow pepper, seeded and cut into thick strips

Garlic Oil (page 14)

Salt and pepper

Tapenade (recipe follows), about ½ cup

1 baguette

A large handful of arugula or mizuna

6 ounces Fontina cheese, thinly sliced

Prepare the grill.

Brush the peppers with garlic oil and sprinkle with salt and pepper. Grill until the skin is blistered and the flesh is soft, 2 to 3 minutes on each side.

Make the Tapenade.

Cut the baguette in half lengthwise. Spread the tapenade evenly over the top and bottom, using about ¼ cup per side. Layer the peppers on the bottom, follow with the greens, and the Fontina. Place the top of the baguette on the sandwich and slice diagonally into 4 sandwiches.

TIP: Fontina is difficult to slice, so we pop it in the freezer for about 5 minutes before we slice it. Don't forget it's in the freezer; if it stays in too long, the Fontina will lose its wonderful creamy texture.

Tapenade: We make this tasty olive spread in a food processor so it's smooth and easy to use. We love the flavors of plumped, dried currants and toasted ground fennel seeds with the saltiness of the olives.

MAKES ABOUT 1 CUP; ENOUGH FOR 2 BAGUETTES

1 ½ cups Kalamata or Gaeta olives, pitted, about ½ pound

1 ½ tablespoons dried currants, covered with hot water for about 15 minutes and drained

1 tablespoon capers, drained and rinsed

1 teaspoon fennel seeds, toasted (page 214) and ground

Pinch of pepper

Combine everything in a small food processor and puree until smooth.

Grilled Mexican Sandwich with Poblano Chilies and Cheddar

Chipotle and Fire-Roasted Poblano Chilies give this grilled cheese sandwich plenty of smoky heat. Good, sharp cheddar and sturdy whole wheat bread stand up to the big, bold flavors. We use a stovetop grill here, but you can grill the onions and chilies over coals. Serve with crisp romaine hearts, sliced avocado, and paper-thin radishes tossed with a sharp lime vinaigrette.

SERVES 4; MAKES 4 SANDWICHES

1 large red onion, peeled and sliced into ½-inch-thick rings
2 poblano chilies
Garlic Oil (page 14)
Salt and pepper
8 slices of whole wheat bread
1 to 2 tablespoons Chipotle Puree (page 163)
6 to 8 ounces sharp cheddar cheese, thinly sliced or grated
2 or 3 tablespoons chopped cilantro
Unsalted butter, softened

Brush the onions and chilies lightly with garlic oil and sprinkle with salt and pepper. Grill the onions until tender, allowing 3 to 4 minutes for each side. Season with salt and pepper and set aside. Grill the chilies until their skins are blistered and charred. Place them in a bowl and cover; set aside to steam. When cool, peel and seed them, and cut them into long, thin strips. Season with salt and pepper and set aside.

Place 4 slices of bread on a work surface and brush each slice lightly with Chipotle Puree. Layer the cheese, chilies, and onions on top and sprinkle with the cilantro. Place the other 4 slices of bread on top of the sandwiches and spread with butter. Place the sandwiches, buttered side down, in a heated skillet or on a griddle. Then spread the top side with butter. Cook over medium heat until golden, 4 to 5 minutes, then turn and cook the other side. Serve immediately.

VARIATION: Tomatoes, fresh or roasted, and cilantro pesto are always welcome additions.

Focaccia with Roasted Eggplant, Sun-Dried Tomatoes, and Asiago

Thick slices of eggplant are roasted until they're perfectly tender and then layered on moist focaccia with sun-dried tomatoes, creamy Asiago, and a big handful of arugula. We use an imported young Asiago, but Fontina or marinated mozzarella is also delicious. If focaccia isn't available use a crusty baguette or sturdy sandwich rolls. You can roast the eggplant a few hours ahead of time. Just be sure to brush it with the Reduced Balsamic Vinegar while it's warm. For an irresistible appetizer, cut the focaccia into little wedges and serve on a beautiful platter.

SERVES 6; MAKES 6 SANDWICHES

Reduced Balsamic Vinegar (page 126)

1 pound globe eggplant, ends trimmed, cut into ½-inch-thick rounds

Garlic Oil (page 14)

Salt and pepper

1 store-bought focaccia, about 1 pound

½ cup sliced oil-packed sun-dried tomato halves

A large handful of arugula

6 ounces fresh Asiago cheese, thinly sliced

Make the Reduced Balsamic Vinegar.

Preheat the oven to 375°F.

Lay the eggplant on a baking sheet; brush both sides generously with garlic oil and sprinkle with salt and pepper. Roast about 10 minutes, turn the slices over, and roast until completely tender, about 6 minutes. Brush the warm eggplant generously with the reduced vinegar and sprinkle with salt and pepper. Set aside to cool.

Cut the focaccia in half horizontally. Arrange the eggplant on the bottom half, all the way out to the edges. Sprinkle the sun-dried tomatoes over, followed by the arugula and the cheese.

Place the other half of the focaccia on top and slice into 6 sandwiches.

VARIATION: Spread the bread with Basil Aïoli (page 128) or sprinkle whole or chopped basil leaves over the eggplant. It's also delicious with roasted or juicy, ripe tomatoes and pesto. You can brush the focaccia with olive oil or the oil from the sun-dried tomatoes.

Fresh Mozzarella Sandwich with Grilled Onions and Wilted Chard

This meal-in-itself sandwich is loaded with big flavors and pleasing, contrasting textures. We wilt the chard with a splash of sherry vinegar and pile it on top of ripe tomatoes, grilled onions, and marinated mozzarella on round sandwich rolls— the savory juices soak into the layers below. It's best to marinate the cheese for at least 30 minutes, but you can let it sit as long as an hour. Serve with Yellow Finn Potato Salad with Green Beans and Tarragon.

SERVES 4; MAKES 4 SANDWICHES

½ pound fresh mozzarella cheese

6 tablespoons extra-virgin olive oil

1 tablespoon chopped fresh herbs: parsley, thyme, and oregano or marjoram

Red pepper flakes

Salt and pepper

1 large red or yellow onion, cut into ½-inch-thick rings

1 bunch of chard, stems removed, cut into thick ribbons, 6 to 8 cups packed leaves

½ tablespoon minced garlic

Sherry vinegar

4 round sandwich rolls

2 large ripe tomatoes, about 1 pound, cut into thick slices

Slice the mozzarella and layer in a flat-bottomed dish with ¼ cup of the oil, the herbs, a pinch of red pepper flakes, and ¼ teaspoon salt. Let the cheese marinate for 30 minutes to an hour, turning it once to distribute the flavors.

Brush the onions with a little of the oil and sprinkle with salt and pepper. Grill them on a stovetop grill until tender and cooked through, 3 to 4 minutes per side.

Heat the remaining oil in a large sauté pan and add the chard, garlic, a couple of pinches of salt, and a pinch of pepper. Cook over medium heat until wilted, about 3 minutes. Season with a splash or two of sherry vinegar and salt and pepper to taste. Keep the greens warm over low heat while you toast the rolls.

Toast the rolls on the stovetop grill. While still warm, brush with a little of the oil from the mozzarella. Layer the cheese on the bottom half of each roll, top with the tomatoes, and sprinkle with salt and pepper. Add the onions, heap on the greens, and replace the top of the sandwich. Serve right away.

TIP: We use a stovetop grill to grill the onions and the rolls. Of course, you can always roast the onions on a baking sheet at 400°F for 15 to 20 minutes and toast the rolls or grill them over coals.

VARIATION: Wilted kale is also delicious here, but you'll need to parboil it before you sauté it unless it's very young and tender; just drop it in salted boiling water for 2 to 3 minutes. You can also try succulent Roasted Tomatoes (page 261). Their rich flavor is perfect in this sandwich.

Santorini Sandwich on a Rosemary Roll

This Greek salad tucked in a roll with spinach leaves is really half salad/half sandwich. Cucumbers, peppers, red onions, and Kalamata olives are tossed in a Spicy Lemon Vinaigrette, with feta added at the last minute. For a spicier sandwich, add an extra pinch of cayenne to the vinaigrette.

SERVES 4; MAKES 4 SANDWICHES

½ medium red onion, thinly sliced, about ½ cup

Spicy Lemon Vinaigrette (recipe follows)

1 each red and yellow pepper, thinly sliced, about 2 cups

1 European cucumber, ends trimmed, cut in half lengthwise, seeded and thinly sliced

15 Kalamata or Gaeta olives, pitted and coarsely chopped, about ¼ cup

2 to 3 ounces feta cheese, crumbled, about ¾ cup

4 rosemary rolls or flavorful torpedo rolls

2 handfuls of spinach leaves, washed and dried

Place the onion in a small bowl, cover with cold water, and set aside for 30 minutes. Make the Spicy Lemon Vinaigrette.

Drain the onion and toss with the peppers, cucumbers, olives, and the vinaigrette. Set aside for a few minutes to allow the flavors to come together. Add the feta and quickly toss together.

Cut the rolls in half lengthwise and scoop out the centers. Place the spinach on the bottom of the rolls and spoon the filling on top, making sure to include all the juices. Press the tops over the filling and serve.

123

Spicy Lemon Vinaigrette

MAKES ABOUT ½ CUP

2 tablespoons fresh lemon juice

1 tablespoon Champagne vinegar

¼ teaspoon salt

Pinch each of cayenne and paprika

¼ cup extra-virgin olive oil

Whisk everything but the oil together in a small bowl; slowly pour in the oil, whisking, until emulsified.

TIP: We use European or "hothouse" cucumbers; their flesh is less watery and they have far fewer seeds than the domestic variety. Of course, you can use domestic cucumbers. Just be sure to peel them and scoop out their big pocket of seeds.

VARIATION: If you're using a plain roll, add a little chopped fresh mint to the filling. For an exceptional sandwich, toss marinated artichokes (page 53), grilled peppers, pickled red onions, ricotta salata cheese, and mint with the Spicy Lemon Vinaigrette. You can also spread the roll with a little Hummous (page 12).

Baguette with Grilled Summer Vegetables, Fromage Blanc, and Basil

Simplicity is often best and this delightful sandwich is no exception. We spread fromage blanc— a fresh cow's milk cheese— over a crusty baguette and layer it with grilled sweet peppers and zucchini and whole leaves of basil. A little reduced balsamic vinegar intensifies the flavors.

SERVES 4; MAKES 4 SANDWICHES

Reduced Balsamic Vinegar (page 126)

1 each red and yellow pepper, cut into thick strips

2 or 3 golden or green zucchini, about 1 pound, sliced ½ inch thick on the diagonal

Garlic Oil (page 14)

Salt and pepper

1 baguette

4 to 6 ounces fromage blanc or chèvre, about ½ cup

10 to 15 whole basil leaves

Make the Reduced Balsamic Vinegar.

Prepare the grill.

Brush the vegetables with garlic oil and sprinkle with salt and pepper. Grill until tender, 2 to 3 minutes on each side. Brush the warm zucchini with the reduced vinegar and set aside.

Cut the baguette in half lengthwise and spread the cheese on both sides. Place the peppers on the bottom half, layer the zucchini on top, and sprinkle with salt and pepper. Arrange the basil over the vegetables and cover with the top of the baguette. Slice diagonally into 4 sandwiches.

TIP: Brush the vinegar over the zucchini while it's still warm so it soaks up the intense balsamic flavor. Leave the pepper skins on unless completely charred.

VARIATION: If fromage blanc isn't available, use a creamy, fresh goat cheese or natural cream cheese instead. You can also roast the vegetables instead of grilling them. They will lose the smoky flavor, but are still delicious. This sandwich is great on torpedo rolls.

Reduced Balsamic Vinegar

This simple, inexpensive sauce couldn't be easier to make. It's the secret potion that gives our grilled and roasted vegetables, especially portobello mushrooms, eggplant, and peppers, a delicious, mouth-watering intensity. Save your fine, aged balsamic for another use; this is the place for the everyday supermarket variety. The reduced vinegar will hold indefinitely, so make as little or as much as you like. Add to leftover pasta or a make-ahead grilled vegetable salad or relish. A drop or two of this complex, sweet-tart syrup is all you need.

In a small saucepan over high heat, reduce the vinegar to half its original volume. For more intense flavor, you can reduce it further; just watch it closely to be sure the vinegar doesn't boil away. Cool and store in a sealed container or refrigerate.

Portobello Sandwich with Tomatoes, Roasted Onions, and Basil Aïoli

Smooth Basil Aïoli is spread on sturdy sandwich rolls and layered with roasted portobellos and onions, thick slices of tomatoes, and arugula. We brush the warm mushrooms with reduced balsamic vinegar to tease out their hidden flavors. For a bit of crunchy texture, try crisp romaine leaves instead of arugula.

SERVES 4; MAKES 4 SANDWICHES

Basil Aïoli (recipe follows)

Reduced Balsamic Vinegar (page 126)

1 pound portobello mushrooms, stems removed and gills lightly brushed if dirty

1 large red onion, cut into ½-inch-thick rings

Garlic Oil (page 14)

Salt and pepper

4 round sandwich rolls

2 large, ripe tomatoes, about 1 pound, sliced

A handful of arugula

Make the Basil Aïoli and the Reduced Balsamic Vinegar.

Preheat the oven to 400°F.

Brush the mushrooms and onions with garlic oil, sprinkle with salt and pepper, and place them on a baking sheet. Roast for 10 minutes, turn them over, and roast until completely tender, about 10 minutes more. Slice the warm mushrooms, toss with a little of the reduced vinegar, and season to taste with salt and pepper. Toss the onions with a little salt and pepper and set aside.

Slice and toast the rolls. Spread both sides of the rolls with aïoli. Place the mushrooms on the bottom of each roll, layer the tomatoes on top, and sprinkle lightly with salt and pepper. Spread the onion rings over, top with the arugula, and replace the top of the roll.

Basil Aïoli: Use this pale green aïoli as an accompaniment to grilled summer vegetables or to spread on toasted bread. We puree the basil with the olive oil, but you can chop it instead; you'll just need 2 or 3 tablespoons.

MAKES ABOUT 1 CUP

1 cup extra-virgin olive oil

1 cup basil leaves, packed

1 large egg yolk

½ tablespoon fresh lemon juice

¼ teaspoon minced garlic

¼ teaspoon salt

Place the oil and the basil in a blender and puree. Whisk the yolk with a few drops of the lemon juice and whisk in the basil oil a little at a time to start, then a little faster as it begins to emulsify. Season with the remaining lemon juice, the garlic, and salt.

VARIATIONS: Try grilled or roasted peppers and pickled onions. You can also grill the mushrooms and onions over coals instead of roasting them. Make Greens' Rancho Portobello Sandwich with Fire-Roasted Poblano Chilies (page 64), roasted onions, fresh or Roasted Tomatoes (page 261), sprigs of cilantro, and spicy Chipotle Aïoli (page 115).

Tai's Vietnamese Tofu Sandwich

This warm, braised tofu sandwich is reminiscent of sandwiches sold by street vendors in the cities of Vietnam. We simmer fried tofu in a spicy tomato sauce seasoned with shallots and fresh ginger. Then we spoon it into a hollowed French roll with crunchy Carrot-Daikon Radish Pickles and big sprigs of cilantro. The soft bread catches all the intriguing flavors of the juices.

SERVES 4; MAKES 4 SANDWICHES

Carrot-Daikon Radish Pickles (recipe follows)

1 package regular tofu, 14 to 16 ounces

Vegetable oil for frying

Salt and pepper

2 shallots, thinly sliced, about ½ cup

½ tablespoon minced garlic

½ tablespoon grated fresh ginger

2 cups flavorful canned tomatoes, chopped, with their juice

Tamari or soy sauce

Sugar

Pinch of cayenne pepper

4 soft French rolls

12 to 16 cilantro sprigs

Make the Carrot-Daikon Radish Pickles.

Cut the tofu into ½-inch-thick slices, cut each slice into quarters, and each quarter into two triangles. Pour enough oil into a large skillet to measure ¼ inch deep and heat until just below the point of smoking, when the first wisp of vapor appears. Fry the tofu until golden and crisp, about 3 minutes per side. Drain the tofu on paper towels, sprinkle with salt and pepper, and set aside.

Heat 1 tablespoon of the tofu frying oil in a skillet, add the shallots, ¼ teaspoon salt, and a pinch of pepper, and cook over medium heat for 2 minutes. Stir in the garlic and ginger, adding a little water if needed to keep everything from sticking to the pan. Add the tomatoes, the tamari, ½ teaspoon sugar, and the cayenne and cook until the tomatoes thicken, about 15 minutes. Add the tofu and simmer for about 5 minutes.

Cut the rolls in half lengthwise and scoop out the centers. Spoon the filling into the bottom halves of the rolls, making sure to include all of the sauce. Scatter ¼ cup of the pickles and a few sprigs of cilantro over the filling. Place the top on each sandwich, press it down to hold the filling in place, and slice in half on the diagonal.

Carrot-Daikon Radish Pickles: *These delicious little pickles are quick and easy to make and keep for several weeks in the refrigerator, so make them ahead of time. This is more than you'll need for the sandwich, so toss the leftovers with cold Asian noodles or serve them as a refreshing condiment.*

MAKES 1 QUART

2 large carrots, sliced into matchsticks, about 2 cups

¼ daikon radish, peeled and sliced into matchsticks, about 2 cups

½ medium yellow onion, thinly sliced, about ½ cup

1 jalapeño chili, seeded and thinly sliced

½ cup rice vinegar

¼ cup water

2 tablespoons sugar

¼ teaspoon salt

Place the carrots, daikon, onions, and chili in a bowl. Combine the remaining ingredients in a small saucepan, bring to a boil, and pour over the carrot mixture. Set aside for an hour to pickle, transfer to an airtight container, and refrigerate.

All Wrapped Up: Filo, Tarts, and Tortillas

A Filo Pep Talk

If you can't imagine yourself baking with filo pastry, here's some encouragement to get you started. Think of filo as a shortcut—the dough is already made; you just need to pull it from the freezer.

Filo is an essential ingredient in the Greens kitchen. For many years, we used beautiful, fresh filo made by hand by Mihran Sagatelyan at Shaharazad Bakery, but now that he's closed Shaharazad, we use commercially made filo, just like everyone else. We make all kinds of filo turnovers, layered filo dishes, and filo purses, which, believe it or not, are a good place to start; they're quick and easy to make. Most of the dishes can be made ahead of time, covered in plastic wrap, and refrigerated or frozen.

Filo is sold in 1-pound packages, which you'll find in the frozen food section of the grocery store. (It's often sold with 2 half-pound packages inside, so you can thaw and use it a half-pound at a time.) Unopened, it keeps indefinitely in the freezer. Once it's been thawed and opened, it will last for a few days in the refrigerator; just be sure to wrap the leftover sheets in plastic wrap to keep them from drying out. Do not refreeze.

We recommend thawing filo overnight in the refrigerator. That way, it's easy to use when you're ready to assemble a dish. Once you open the package, cover with a damp kitchen towel to keep the dough moist.

If you're using melted butter to brush over the filo, keep it warm on the stove or over hot water—you'll use far less of it that way. (A good-quality pastry brush really comes in handy here.) You can also use olive oil, but we prefer the rich flavor and golden color butter gives the filo.

Filo Purses with Artichokes, Mushrooms, and Asiago

We make these crisp, golden purses for special occasions and feature them on our dinner menu, filled with seasonal vegetable combinations and flavorful cheeses. Filo purses may sound complicated, but they're actually quite easy to make. Each purse is unique unto itself— they don't need to be perfect— and that's the beauty of this dish. Serve with Roasted Pepper Sauce, Braised French Lentils, and sautéed greens.

MAKES 4 PURSES

Roasted Pepper Sauce (page 290)

2 tablespoons olive oil

½ pound white mushrooms, quartered, about 2 cups

2 teaspoons minced garlic

Salt and pepper

½ cup white wine

2 medium leeks, white parts only, sliced in half lengthwise, thinly sliced and washed, about 1½ cups

1 pound small artichokes, trimmed (page 178) and quartered, about 2 cups

1 cup water

1 tablespoon chopped fresh herbs: oregano, parsley, thyme, and chives

2 ounces Asiago cheese, grated, about ½ cup

1 ounce Parmesan cheese, grated, about ⅓ cup

8 sheets frozen filo dough, thawed overnight in the refrigerator

4 tablespoons unsalted butter, melted and kept warm

Make the Roasted Pepper Sauce.

Preheat the oven to 375°F.

Heat 1 tablespoon of the oil in a large sauté pan and add the mushrooms, ½ teaspoon garlic, ¼ teaspoon salt, and a pinch of pepper. Cook over medium-high heat until the mushrooms are golden and tender, about 5 minutes. Add ¼ cup of the wine and cook until the pan is nearly dry. Transfer the mushrooms to a small bowl and set aside.

Heat the remaining oil in the pan and add the leeks, ¼ teaspoon salt, the remaining garlic, and a pinch of pepper. Cook over medium heat until the leeks are wilted, about 3 minutes, adding a little water if needed to keep them from sticking to the pan. Add the artichokes, the remaining wine, ¼ teaspoon salt and cook until the pan is nearly dry. Add the water and simmer until the artichokes are tender, about 10 minutes. Add the mushrooms and cook together for 5 minutes more. Drain the vegetables of any excess liquid and set aside to cool. Coarsely chop the vegetables and combine with the herbs and cheeses. Season to taste with salt and pepper.

Lay 8 sheets of filo on a clean work surface, cut in half widthwise, and place in a single stack. Lay two sheets in a horizontal direction, then place two sheets on top vertically, in a cross shape. Brush lightly with the butter and spoon ½ cup filling into the center. Gather the edges of the dough up around the filling and twist it just above the filling to seal the purse, allowing the top to fall naturally. Brush the outside lightly with butter, making sure to include the top edges, and place on a parchment-lined baking sheet. Make the rest of the purses in the same way.

Bake on the middle rack of the oven for 35 to 40 minutes until the filo is golden and crisp. Ladle ¼ cup of the Roasted Pepper Sauce on each plate and place a purse on top. Serve the remaining sauce at the table.

MAKE-AHEAD TIP: You can sauté the mushrooms and braise the artichokes and leeks ahead of time. (You can even slice the mushrooms and leeks and trim the artichokes the day before.) Just be sure to drain the vegetables before you toss them with the herbs and cheeses. Make the purses a couple of hours in advance and refrigerate until you're ready to bake them. Once baked, they keep well in a warm oven (250°F).

VARIATION: This is a great way to serve roasted root vegetables or butternut squash with leeks and Gruyère cheese. You can also try portobello or crimini mushrooms, peppers, fennel, and grilled or roasted onions. The mushrooms give off a lot of moisture—particularly the portobellos—so be sure to drain them to keep the filo from getting soggy.

The purses are also delicious made without cheese. Just brush them with olive oil instead of butter.

Tomato-Zinfandel Sauce (page 295) or Mushroom-Sherry Sauce (page 294) are also great accompaniments to this dish.

Filo Turnovers with Butternut Squash and Gruyère

Roasted butternut squash and Gruyère cheese are delicious together in these favorite fall and winter turnovers. The butternut squash is an inviting host for the flavors of all kinds of onions and distinctive cheeses— shallots, leeks, or caramelized onions are delicious here, as well as Fontina, Manchego, or Asiago cheese. This is a great place to use up leftover roasted root vegetables.

MAKES 16 LITTLE TURNOVERS

1 small butternut squash, cut into ½-inch cubes, about 2½ cups

1 tablespoon olive oil

Salt and pepper

½ small yellow onion, diced, about ½ cup

½ teaspoon minced garlic

¼ cup water

2 ounces Gruyère cheese, grated, about ½ cup

½ teaspoon chopped fresh thyme

½ teaspoon chopped fresh oregano or marjoram

½ tablespoon chopped flat-leaf parsley

8 sheets frozen filo dough, thawed overnight in the refrigerator

¼ cup unsalted butter, melted and kept warm

Preheat the oven to 400°F.

Toss the squash with ½ tablespoon of the oil, ¼ teaspoon salt, and a few pinches of pepper. Roast in a small baking dish until tender, about 20 minutes. Set aside. Lower the oven temperature to 375°F.

Heat the remaining oil in a medium-size sauté pan and add the onions, ¼ teaspoon salt, and a pinch of pepper. Sauté over medium heat for 3 to 4 minutes, add the garlic, and cook 1 minute more.

Lower the heat, add the squash, along with the water, and cook until the pan is nearly dry, about 3 minutes. Transfer to a bowl and set aside to cool. Toss in the cheese and herbs.

To assemble the turnovers, lay 8 sheets of filo on a clean work surface and cover with a damp cloth.

Lay a single sheet of filo out and place a second sheet on top. Brush lightly with butter and cut lengthwise into 4 strips. Place a heaping tablespoon of filling at the end of each strip, and then fold over at a 45-degree angle to form a triangle. As you roll the turnovers, think of folding a flag. Roll them loosely, so the filling will have room to expand during baking. Keep folding at an angle until you reach the end of the strip, trimming any excess filo. Make the rest of the turnovers in the same way, brush them with butter, and place on a parchment-lined baking sheet. The turnovers can be refrigerated or frozen at this point for later baking.

Bake until golden and crisp, about 15 minutes.

TIP: The roasted butternut squash filling is so flavorful that it stands on its own without the cheese. For a little added richness, sprinkle toasted, chopped walnuts between the two layers of filo before filling. If you'd like to skip dairy altogether, brush the filo with olive oil instead of butter.

Filo Turnovers Filled with Goat Cheese, Leeks, and Walnuts

These little turnovers are packed with big flavor. The creamy goat cheese melts into the leeks and bites of toasted walnuts up the ante. They freeze beautifully, so make them ahead of time for a quick, last-minute appetizer. Serve with Moroccan Beet Salad, caperberries, and marinated olives.

MAKES 16 LITTLE TURNOVERS

1 tablespoon olive oil

1 tablespoon unsalted butter

3 medium leeks, white parts only, cut in half lengthwise, thinly sliced, and washed, about
    3 cups

Salt and pepper

¼ cup white wine

¼ cup walnut pieces, toasted (page 46) and chopped

¼ pound mild goat cheese, crumbled, about ¾ cup

1 ounce Parmesan cheese, grated, about ⅓ cup

1 tablespoon chopped flat-leaf parsley

½ teaspoon chopped fresh thyme

8 sheets frozen filo dough, thawed overnight in the refrigerator

4 tablespoons unsalted butter, melted and kept warm

Preheat the oven to 375°F.

    Heat the oil and butter in a medium-size sauté pan and add the leeks, ½ teaspoon salt, and a pinch of pepper. Sauté over medium heat until the leeks begin to wilt, 3 to 4 minutes. Add the wine and simmer until the pan is almost dry, about 2 minutes more. Transfer to a bowl. When cool, add the walnuts, cheeses, herbs, and salt and pepper to taste.

    To assemble the turnovers, lay 8 sheets of filo on a clean work surface and cover with a damp cloth.

    Lay a single sheet of filo out and place a second sheet on top. Brush lightly with butter and cut lengthwise into 4 strips.

    Place a heaping tablespoon of filling at the end of each strip, and then fold over at a 45-degree angle to form a triangle. As you roll the turnovers, think of folding a flag. Roll them loosely, so the filling will have room to expand during baking. Keep folding at an angle until you reach the end of the strip, trimming any excess filo. Make the rest of the turnovers in the same way, brush with butter, and place on a parchment-lined baking sheet. The turnovers can be refrigerated or frozen at this point for later baking.

Bake until golden and crisp, about 15 minutes.

Artichoke and Spring Onion Tart

The rich flavors of artichokes and delicate spring onions make this a well-loved tart. You need only about a cup of artichokes; if there's too much of the dense artichoke filling, the custard won't set up and the tart will be difficult to cut and serve. We're lucky to have fresh spring onions— the young, green-topped onions on their way from being scallions to mature onions— but if they aren't available, you can use leeks, shallots, or regular onions instead.

SERVES 6 TO 8; MAKES ONE 9-INCH TART

Yeasted Tart Dough (page 150)

1 tablespoon olive oil

1 tablespoon unsalted butter

1 bunch spring onions, about ½ pound, tops removed, sliced, about 1½ cups
    (see headnote)

Salt and pepper

½ pound small artichokes, trimmed (page 178), cut in half, about 1 cup

1 tablespoon minced garlic

¼ cup white wine

1 cup water

3 large eggs

¾ cup milk

½ cup heavy cream

⅓ cup Crème Fraîche (page 98)

2 ounces white cheddar cheese, grated, about ¾ cup

1 to 2 tablespoons chopped chives

Make the Yeasted Tart Dough and follow the instructions for lining the tart pan.

Preheat the oven to 375°F.

Heat the olive oil and butter in a large sauté pan and add the onions, ¼ teaspoon salt, and a pinch of pepper. Sauté over medium heat until soft, about 3 minutes; add the artichokes, garlic, and ¼ teaspoon salt and cook 1 or 2 minutes. Add the wine and cook until the pan is nearly dry, about 3 minutes. Add the water, lower the heat, and simmer until the artichokes are tender and the pan is nearly dry, about 10 minutes. Set aside to cool. Coarsely chop the artichoke mixture. You should have about 1½ cups.

Beat the eggs in a bowl and whisk in the milk, cream, crème fraîche, ½ teaspoon salt, and a pinch of pepper.

Sprinkle the cheese and chives on the bottom of the dough, followed by the artichoke mixture. Pour the custard over and bake for 35 to 40 minutes, until the custard is golden and set.

VARIATION: The flavorful artichoke and spring onion filling goes beautifully with a number of cheeses. Good-quality white cheddar is outstanding here, but Gruyère, Fontina, Asiago, or Manchego work just as well.

Corn and Basil Tart

Sweet corn, fragrant basil, and good white cheddar cheese combine to make this an outstanding summer tart. We like to use locally made Saint George cheddar, but Vermont cheddar is also delicious. The tart goes together easily, particularly if you make the Yeasted Tart Dough the day before. Serve with roasted fingerling potatoes and tender lettuces tossed with fresh beans and red wine vinaigrette.

SERVES 6 TO 8; MAKES ONE 9-INCH TART

Yeasted Tart Dough (page 150)

½ tablespoon olive oil

½ tablespoon unsalted butter

2 large shallots, diced, about ½ cup

Salt and pepper

2 ears of corn, shaved, about 2 cups kernels

¼ cup water

3 large eggs

¾ cup milk

½ cup heavy cream

⅓ cup Crème Fraîche (page 98)

2 ounces Vermont or other flavorful white cheddar cheese, grated, about ½ cup

10 to 15 basil leaves, bundled together and thinly sliced, 2 to 3 tablespoons

Make the dough and follow the instructions for lining the tart pan.

Preheat the oven to 375°F.

Heat the olive oil and butter in a medium-size sauté pan and add the shallots, ¼ teaspoon salt, and a pinch of pepper. Sauté over medium heat until soft, about 2 minutes. Add the corn and the water, lower the heat, and cover the pan. Simmer until the corn is tender, about 5 minutes. Set aside to cool.

Beat the eggs in a bowl and whisk in the milk, cream, crème fraîche, ½ teaspoon salt, and a pinch of pepper.

Sprinkle the cheese and basil on the bottom of the dough, followed by the corn mixture. Pour the custard over and bake for 35 to 40 minutes, until the custard is golden and set.

TIP: Homemade crème fraîche adds a special richness to the custard, but if you don't have time to make it, use equal parts of milk and cream—¾ cup of each—instead. You can also use all half-and-half, but the custard will be lighter and less flavorful.

Provençal Tartlets

*All the full flavors of late summer— roasted
Japanese eggplant, sweet peppers, fennel, and zucchini— reveal their Provençal
soul when combined with fruity olive oil, black olives, and creamy Fontina cheese.
Roasted Tomatoes add intensity and keep the filling moist.*

*If fennel isn't available, use an extra pepper or zucchini instead. Serve with a salad
of crisp lettuces and bite-size cherry tomatoes tossed with Champagne Vinaigrette.*

MAKES 4 INDIVIDUAL TARTLETS

Tart Dough (page 148)

Roasted Tomatoes (page 261), 1 cup, coarsely chopped

2 small golden or green zucchini, diced, about 1½ cups

½ large yellow onion, diced, about 1 cup

1 medium red or yellow pepper, diced, about ¾ cup

2 medium Japanese eggplant, diced, about 2½ cups

1 fennel bulb, outer leaves and core removed, diced, about 1 cup

1½ tablespoons extra-virgin olive oil

½ tablespoon minced garlic

1 teaspoon each chopped fresh thyme and oregano

Salt and pepper

16 Gaeta olives, pitted and coarsely chopped, about ¼ cup

1 tablespoon chopped flat-leaf parsley

2 ounces Fontina cheese, grated, about ½ cup

½ ounce Parmesan cheese, grated, 2 to 3 tablespoons

Egg Wash (see box)

Make the Tart Dough and shape the tartlet rounds. Let them rest in the refrigerator while you prepare the filling.

Preheat the oven to 400°F.

Make the Roasted Tomatoes.

Toss the vegetables together in a large bowl with the oil, garlic, thyme, oregano, ¼ teaspoon salt, and a pinch of pepper. Spread the mixture in a single layer on two baking sheets and roast for 10 minutes. Rotate the pans from top to bottom and use a spatula to loosen and turn the vegetables so they cook evenly. Cook until just tender, about 10 minutes more. Transfer to a bowl and set aside to cool. Lower the oven temperature to 375°F.

Toss the tomatoes, olives, parsley, and cheeses into the vegetables and season to taste with salt and pepper. You should have 3 to 4 cups of filling. Place ¾ cup of the filling in the center of each dough. Pull up the sides and gently fold the dough to form 6 to 8 pleats as you move around the circle. A little of the filling will be visible in the center. Brush lightly with egg wash and place on a parchment lined baking sheet. Bake for 25 to 30 minutes, or until golden and bubbling.

VARIATION: The fresh taste of basil is classic here. Season the roasted vegetable filling with ⅓ cup chopped basil in place of the herbs and spoon a tablespoon of pesto into the center of the tartlets when you take them from the oven.

Egg Wash

We brush a simple egg wash over savory tartlets and turnovers just before baking to give them a shiny finish. We use water to thin the beaten egg, but you can use milk instead.

Whisk 1 large egg with 2 tablespoons water until smooth.

Chanterelle Tart
with Roasted Garlic Custard

Make this sleek, elegant tart in the fall when wild mushrooms are in season. The woodsy chanterelles and tender leeks blend perfectly into the rich roasted garlic custard. There's really no substitute for chanterelles, but if you can't find them, use crimini or white mushrooms instead. Just be sure to sear them with plenty of fresh garlic and deglaze the pan with white wine to capture all the juices. The chanterelles will be missed, but the earthy mushroom flavor will still be there.

SERVES 6 TO 8; MAKES ONE 9-INCH TART

Yeasted Tart Dough (page 150)

Roasted Garlic Puree (see box)

½ pound chanterelle mushrooms

3 large eggs

¾ cup milk

½ cup heavy cream

⅓ cup Crème Fraîche (page 98)

Salt and pepper

1 tablespoon unsalted butter

½ tablespoon olive oil

2 medium leeks, white parts only, cut in half lengthwise, thinly sliced, and washed, about 2 cups

¼ cup white wine

1 teaspoon chopped fresh thyme

2 ounces Gruyère cheese, grated, about ⅔ cup

Make the Yeasted Tart Dough and follow the instructions for lining the tart pan.

Preheat the oven to 375°F.

Make the Roasted Garlic Puree.

Using a brush or damp cloth, carefully clean the chanterelles. Remove the dirt and bits of organic matter, but don't wash them, or they'll soak up the water and lose their delicate flavor. Trim off the base of the stems if they're particularly dirty and discard. Cut the mushrooms into large pieces, or thickly slice them, being sure to include the stem. You should have about 2½ cups.

Beat the eggs in a bowl and whisk in the Roasted Garlic Puree followed by the milk, cream, crème fraîche, ½ teaspoon salt, and a pinch of pepper.

Heat the butter and oil in a large sauté pan and add the leeks, ¼ teaspoon salt, and a few pinches of pepper. Sauté over medium heat until the leeks begin to wilt, about 3 minutes. Add the wine and cook for 1 minute more. Add the chanterelles and a few pinches of salt and pepper and gently sauté until just tender and cooked through. (The cooking time will depend on the moisture in the mushrooms.) Stir in the thyme and set aside to cool.

Sprinkle the cheese on the bottom of the rolled dough and spread the mushroom mixture over it. Pour the custard over and bake for 35 to 40 minutes, until the custard is set and the top is golden.

Roasted Garlic Puree

Fresh garlic takes on a whole new range of flavors once it's roasted— its sharp, assertive taste becomes delicate, soft, and smooth. We spoon it into soups, sauces, and stews, spread it over pizza dough, and slather it on grilled or toasted bread. If you're a true garlic lover, roast a few extra heads while you're at it. It's the ultimate pick-me-up for leftover odds and ends, and keeps in a sealed container in the refrigerator for up to a week.

Preheat the oven to 375°F.

Place a head or two of garlic pointy end up in a small baking dish and drizzle with a little extra-virgin olive oil. Throw in a few fresh sage leaves or a sprig or two of fresh thyme if you like. Roast until tender all the way through, about 35 to 40 minutes, checking for doneness by inserting a paring knife or skewer. When cool enough to handle, cut off the top end and squeeze the cloves into a small bowl. (You can also do this later, but you'll get more garlic if you squeeze it warm.) Puree in a small food processor or mash with a fork until smooth. Two large heads of garlic make about ⅓ cup of puree.

Mexican Tartlets
with Roasted Winter Vegetables

Roasted portobello mushrooms, butternut squash, and Yellow Finn potatoes are taken south of the border by toasted cumin and the smoky heat of the chipotle and ancho chilies. For a spicier filling, you can always add more chilies. We serve these tartlets, also known as galettes, right out of the oven, but you can cut them into wedges and serve them at room temperature as appetizers.

SERVES 4

Masa Harina Dough (page 149)

Ancho Chili Puree (see box)

Chipotle Puree (page 163)

½ pound butternut squash, cut into ¾-inch cubes, about 1½ cups

½ pound Yellow Finn potatoes, cut into ¾-inch cubes, about 1½ cups

1 medium red onion, chopped, about 1½ cups

¼ pound white mushrooms, quartered, about 1 cup

1 pound portobello mushrooms, cut in large pieces, about 3 cups

1½ tablespoons olive oil

2 teaspoons minced garlic

1 teaspoon cumin seeds, toasted (page 214) and ground

Salt

Cayenne pepper

2 ounces white cheddar cheese, grated, about ½ cup

1 ounce smoked mozzarella cheese, grated, about ¼ cup

1 teaspoon chopped fresh sage

1 teaspoon chopped fresh oregano

Egg Wash (page 143)

Make the Masa Harina Dough and shape the tartlet rounds. Let them rest in the refrigerator while you prepare the filling. Make the Ancho Chili Puree and the Chipotle Puree.

Preheat the oven to 400°F.

Toss the vegetables together in a large bowl with the oil, garlic, cumin, ½ teaspoon salt, and a pinch of cayenne. Spread the mixture on two baking sheets and roast for 15 minutes. Use a spatula to loosen and turn the vegetables so they cook evenly. Cook until just tender,

10 to 15 minutes more. Transfer to a bowl and set aside to cool. Lower the oven temperature to 375°F.

Mix in 1 teaspoon Ancho Chili Puree, ½ teaspoon Chipotle Puree, the cheeses, and the herbs. You should have 3 to 4 cups of filling. Season to taste with salt, ancho, and chipotle purees. Make the Egg Wash.

Place ¾ cup of the filling in the center of each dough. Pull up the sides and gently fold the dough to form 6 to 8 pleats as you move around the circle. A little of the filling will be visible in the center. Brush lightly with egg wash and place on a parchment-lined baking sheet. Bake for 25 to 30 minutes, or until golden and bubbling.

SUMMER VARIATION: Make a filling with sweet corn, jalapeños, grilled onions, cilantro, and cheddar cheese. You can use Fire-Roasted Poblano Chilies (page 64) instead of the jalapeños. You'll need about a cup of filling per tartlet.

Ancho Chili Puree

This dark, spicy puree of dried poblano chilies adds depth and heat to all kinds of Mexican and Southwestern dishes; we use it every day. You never know how hot the chilies will be, so be sure to taste the puree before using.

MAKES ABOUT ½ CUP
2 dried ancho chilies
1 cup boiling water

Toast the chilies over an open flame, on a stovetop grill, or in a cast-iron skillet until they puff up—and they will. This can take as little as a minute or longer, depending on the source of heat; just don't let them burn. You can also roast the chilies in a 400°F oven for about 10 minutes. Pull out the stem, tear the chili open, and shake out the seeds. Place in a small bowl, cover with the water, and let soak for 15 to 20 minutes. Puree the chilies with 2 or 3 tablespoons of the soaking liquid in a blender or small food processor until smooth, adding more liquid if needed. The remaining soaking liquid can be strained and reserved as a seasoning. Store the puree in an airtight container and refrigerate; it will keep for a week or two.

Tart Dough

This buttery dough is the one we use for savory tartlets (also called galettes) and deep-dish pies. We make the dough in advance, roll it to size, wrap it, and freeze it until we're ready to use it. If you put it in the refrigerator, it will keep for up to a day. It's always best to freeze the dough (for up to 1 month) unless you're using it right away.

MAKES ENOUGH DOUGH FOR 4 INDIVIDUAL TARTLETS OR ONE 9-INCH TART

1½ cups all-purpose flour

¾ teaspoon salt

¼ pound cold unsalted butter, cut into small cubes

2 tablespoons solid vegetable shortening

3 to 4 tablespoons ice water

Flour for rolling out

Combine the flour and salt in the bowl of an electric mixer. Using the paddle attachment, mix together at low speed. Add the butter and mix until it resembles a coarse meal, then add the shortening and mix to distribute it evenly. Add 3 tablespoons ice water and work until the dough just holds together, adding the remaining tablespoon of water if needed. Shape the dough into a disk; cover with plastic wrap and let rest in the refrigerator for at least 30 minutes before rolling.

Cut the chilled dough into 4 equal pieces, about 3½ ounces, and flatten into disks. Roll each piece into a circle ⅛ inch thick and about 8 inches in diameter. The dough pieces can be rolled in advance and stored in the refrigerator or freezer, separated by parchment or wax paper, and wrapped tightly with plastic wrap.

TIP: At the restaurant, we use a small salad or dessert plate to trim the rolled dough to a consistent size. For a more rustic look, you can roll the dough to size and include the rough edges.

Masa Harina Dough: This rustic dough has the delectable flavor of corn tortillas. We use it for empanadas and Mexican Tartlets with Roasted Winter Vegetables (page 146). We're lucky to be able to buy fresh masa harina from La Palma Mexicatessen (if there's a sizable Mexican population in your area, no doubt there's a fresh masa harina source), but you can also use the dried masa harina that's commonly available.

Make the dough as directed, substituting ½ cup masa harina for ½ cup of the flour and using 4 tablespoons of ice water. Unlike the flour, masa harina doesn't produce gluten, so you'll need to work the dough a little more than you might expect to.

Making Tart and Pie Dough by Hand

If you've never made pie dough by hand, it may be time to learn, especially if you find yourself at a cottage on a lake or a cabin in the woods without a standing electric mixer. Just be sure to bring a pastry cutter with you. This efficient, old-fashioned tool makes a beautiful dough and works wonders in a rustic kitchen. If you don't have a pastry cutter, you can improvise with two table knives held side by side.

Mix the flour and salt (and sugar, when making sweet pastry dough) in a bowl. Using two knives or a pastry cutter, cut the butter and shortening into the flour mixture until it's evenly distributed and resembles coarse meal. Add the water, a little at a time, and work it into the dough, using a fork or your fingertips until it just comes together. Use a rubber spatula or plastic scraper to loosen any bits of dough from the side of the bowl and gently work the dough in. Shape the dough into a disk, wrap tightly in plastic wrap, and let rest in the refrigerator for at least 30 minutes before using.

149

Yeasted Tart Dough

We've used this lovely, supple dough since the early days of Greens. It has all the wonderful qualities of a dear old friend— it's forgiving, reliable, and always true. It's tender and moist just like brioche dough and it's easy to work by hand. Because the dough is yeasted, it doesn't need to be prebaked. Be sure the butter is soft, but not melted and the egg is warmed to room temperature before you mix it into the dough. You can make it a day ahead of time and keep it in the refrigerator. Just be sure to wrap it tightly in plastic wrap and allow it to return to room temperature before you roll it.

MAKES ONE 9-INCH TART SHELL

1 teaspoon active dry yeast

Pinch of sugar

¼ cup warm (110°F) water

1 cup all-purpose flour, plus extra for shaping

½ teaspoon salt

1 large egg, at room temperature

3 tablespoons unsalted butter, softened

Dissolve the yeast and sugar in the water and set in a warm place for 10 to 15 minutes, until foamy. Combine the flour and salt in a bowl and make a well. Whisk the egg and pour it into the middle of the well, along with the softened butter and yeast mixture. Mix with a wooden spoon to form a soft, smooth dough. Dust it lightly with flour and gather into a ball; place in a bowl and cover with plastic wrap or a kitchen towel. Let the dough rise in a warm place until it doubles in size, 45 minutes to 1 hour. If you're not ready to shape the dough, knead it and let it rise again.

Use a 9-inch tart pan with a removable bottom. Roll the dough into a 10-inch circle on a lightly floured board. Place the dough in the pan and press it evenly against the sides. It should be about ½ inch higher than the pan. Fold the edges over and press again, so the dough is just a little above the rim of the pan. Allow the dough to rest for a few minutes, then fill it, or refrigerate it until needed.

TIP: If you forget to take the egg out of the refrigerator, you can place it in a bowl of warm water for a few minutes to bring it to room temperature.

Corn Quesadillas

These summer quesadillas are simply the best— they're great for lunch, an afternoon snack, or a last-minute supper. We brush Chipotle Puree over the tortillas, but Fire-Roasted Poblano Chilies or jalapeños work beautifully. Serve with Guacamole, crème fraîche, salsa fresca, and big sprigs of cilantro.

Use your old cast-iron skillet here; it conducts heat like no other skillet can. Have all your ingredients ready before you warm the tortillas; they're best served straight from the pan.

MAKES 6 QUESADILLAS

Chipotle Puree (page 163)

½ tablespoon olive oil

2 ears of corn, shaved, about 2 cups kernels

Salt and pepper

1 or 2 scallions, both white and green parts, thinly sliced on the diagonal

¼ cup water

Oil for the pan

Six 9-inch flour tortillas

6 ounces white cheddar cheese, grated, about 1½ cups

⅓ cup coarsely chopped cilantro

Make the Chipotle Puree.

Heat the oil in a medium-size sauté pan and add the corn, ¼ teaspoon salt, and a pinch of pepper and cook over medium heat for 1 minute. Add the scallions and the water, cover the pan, and cook until the corn is tender, 3 to 4 minutes. Transfer to a bowl.

Heat a large cast-iron skillet or griddle over medium heat and add just enough oil to coat the pan. Place a tortilla in the pan and heat for about 30 seconds, until soft, then flip to heat the other side. Heat the remaining tortillas, adding oil to the pan as needed. Place the warm tortillas between clean kitchen towels to keep them supple.

Working as quickly as you can so the tortillas don't dry out, place the tortillas on a work surface and brush lightly with Chipotle Puree. Spread about ⅓ cup of the corn mixture on the lower half of each tortilla, follow with the cheese and cilantro, distributing them evenly over the corn, and fold the tortillas over the filling.

Heat the skillet, adding oil as needed, and place 1 or 2 quesadillas in the pan. Cook over medium-low heat, turning them when crisp and golden to cook the other side. Keep them warm in the oven while you make the rest. Serve whole or cut into wedges for appetizers.

Soft Tacos with Grilled Summer Vegetables

Make these seductive soft tacos when you're in the mood for grilling. We toss all kinds of summer vegetables and fresh chilies on the grill and then chop them up for a rustic filling. For exceptional color, try different varieties of summer squash and peppers. A little sautéed potato binds everything together, but you can use chayote squash instead. There's no substitute for aged cheddar, but queso fresco— fresh Mexican cheese— is also delicious. Serve with Corn and Tomatillo Salsa.

MAKES 12 TACOS

Chipotle Puree (page 163)

1 jalapeño or serrano chili

1 poblano chili

1 plum tomato, cored

1 red or yellow pepper, cut lengthwise into thick strips

1 small red onion, peeled and cut into ½-inch-thick rings

1 each golden and green zucchini, cut in half lengthwise and scored

Garlic Oil (page 14)

Salt and pepper

½ tablespoon olive oil

1 medium Yellow Finn or Yukon Gold potato, cut into ½-inch cubes, 1½ to 2 cups

¼ cup water

2 to 3 tablespoons coarsely chopped cilantro

Oil for the pan

2 dozen corn tortillas

6 ounces white cheddar cheese, grated, about 1½ cups

8 to 10 Romaine lettuce leaves, cut into ribbons

Crème Fraîche (page 98) or sour cream

Make the Chipotle Puree.

Prepare the grill.

Brush the chilies, tomato, peppers, onion, and zucchini with garlic oil and sprinkle with salt and pepper. Place the vegetables on the grill and cook, turning as needed, until completely tender. Remove from the grill and set aside.

Heat the olive oil in a medium-size skillet and add the potatoes, ¼ teaspoon salt, and a pinch of pepper. Lightly brown the potatoes over medium high heat, using a spatula to loosen them as needed. Add the water, cover the pan, lower the heat, and simmer until completely tender, 8 to 10 minutes. Transfer to a medium-size bowl.

Peel and seed the chilies, removing as much of the skin as you can. Finely chop and add them to the potatoes. Chop the grilled vegetables into ½-inch pieces and add to the potatoes and chilies, along with 1 teaspoon Chipotle Puree and the cilantro. Season to taste with salt and Chipotle Puree. You should have about 4 cups of filling.

Heat a little oil in a skillet and place two tortillas on top of each other. When the tortillas are soft and heated through, flip them over, and heat the other side. Sprinkle 2 to 3 table-spoons of the cheese over and spread ⅓ cup filling across the center. Fold the tortillas in half and keep them warm in the oven while you repeat with the rest of the tortillas. Garnish with lettuce and a dollop of crème fraîche or sour cream.

Soft Tacos with Butternut Squash, Plantain, and Poblano Chilies

In these winter soft tacos, there's a compelling combination of flavors— a squeeze of fresh lime juice, sweet roasted butternut squash, starchy plantain, and smoky chilies. Buy your plantain at least a few days ahead of time to give it time to ripen. If it's not available, just make the filling without it. Be sure to have all your ingredients ready before you heat the tortillas.

MAKES 12 TACOS

Chipotle Puree (page 163)

Fire-Roasted Poblano Chilies (page 64), diced, about ½ cup

½ large butternut squash, cut into small cubes, about 3 cups

1½ tablespoons olive oil

1 tablespoon minced garlic

1 teaspoon cumin seeds, toasted (page 214) and ground

Salt and pepper

A pinch of cayenne pepper

1 ripe plantain, about 10 ounces, peeled and chopped, about 1½ cups

1 large onion, diced, about 2 cups

2 large red peppers, diced, about 2 cups

1 tablespoon fresh lime juice

2 to 3 tablespoons coarsely chopped cilantro

2 dozen corn tortillas

6 ounces white cheddar cheese, grated, about 1½ cups

Oil for the pan

Romaine lettuce, cut into ribbons

Crème Fraîche (page 98)

Fire-Roasted Salsa (page 287)

Make the Chipotle Puree and the Fire-Roasted Poblano Chilies.

Preheat the oven to 400°F.

Toss the squash in a baking dish with ½ tablespoon of the olive oil, ½ tablespoon garlic, ½ teaspoon cumin, ¼ teaspoon salt, and a pinch each of black and cayenne pepper. Roast until tender, 15 to 20 minutes. Set aside.

Bring a small pot of water to a boil and drop in the plantains. Return to a boil, lower the heat, and simmer until tender, about 10 minutes. Drain and mash the plantains with a fork.

Heat the remaining olive oil in a large sauté pan and add the onions, ¼ teaspoon salt, and a pinch of pepper. Cook over medium heat until the onions begin to soften, about 3 minutes. Add the remaining garlic and cook 1 minute more. Stir in the peppers, the remaining cumin, ¼ teaspoon salt, and cayenne and cook until tender, about 4 minutes, adding water as needed to keep the vegetables from sticking to the pan. Stir in the plantains, the squash, 1 teaspoon chipotle puree, and the chilies and cook together for 1 minute. Add the lime juice and the cilantro and season to taste with salt and chipotle puree. Keep the filling warm over low heat. Have all your ingredients, including the toppings, ready before you make the tacos.

Heat a little oil in a skillet and place two tortillas on top of each other. When the tortillas are soft and heated through, flip them over and heat the other side. Sprinkle with 2 to 3 tablespoons of the cheese and spread ⅓ cup filling across the center. Fold the tortillas in half and keep them warm in the oven while you repeat with the rest of the tortillas. Garnish with lettuce, a dollop of crème fraîche, and a spoonful of salsa before serving.

Roasted Winter Vegetable Enchiladas

There's a great advantage to roasting the vegetables in this savory winter dish; it brings out their intensity and frees up the stove-top to cook the sauce and heat the tortillas. The deep, lusty flavor of Salsa Negra goes right into the corn tortillas and works its way into the roasted vegetable filling. Serve with Spicy Rattlesnake Beans and Basmati Rice with Pumpkin Seeds.

SERVES 6

Salsa Negra (page 288)

Chipotle Puree (page 163)

Ancho Chili Puree (page 147)

1 large yellow onion, diced, about 2 cups

2 large red peppers, diced, about 2 cups

½ pound white mushrooms, quartered, about 2 cups

1 chayote squash, peeled and diced, or 1 medium zucchini, diced, about 1½ cups

½ small butternut squash, cut into small cubes, about 2 cups

1½ tablespoons olive oil or vegetable oil

2 tablespoons minced garlic

½ tablespoon cumin seeds, toasted (page 214) and ground

Salt

1 tablespoon chopped fresh sage

1 tablespoon chopped fresh oregano

¼ pound smoked cheese, grated, about 1 cup

¼ pound dry jack cheese, grated, about 1¼ cups

Vegetable oil for frying

1 dozen corn tortillas

Make the Salsa Negra, Chipotle Puree, and Ancho Puree.

Preheat the oven to 400°F.

Toss the vegetables in a large bowl with the oil, garlic, cumin, and ½ teaspoon salt. Spread the vegetables on two baking sheets and roast for 15 minutes. Use a spatula to loosen and turn the vegetables and roast until tender, about 10 minutes more. Return the vegetables to the bowl and season with the chipotle and ancho purees (start with 1 teaspoon of chipotle and 1½ teaspoons of ancho), the herbs, and salt to taste.

Reduce the oven temperature to 375°F.

Combine the cheeses and reserve ½ cup for garnish.

Pour enough oil in a small skillet to measure ¼ inch deep and heat until just below the smoking point, when the first wisp of vapor appears. Using a pair of metal tongs, dip a tortilla into the oil just long enough to heat it through, 2 to 3 seconds. Place on a paper towel to drain the excess oil. Repeat with the rest of the tortillas, placing a paper towel between each of them.

Pour 3 cups of the Salsa Negra on the bottom of a 9- by 13-inch baking dish. Place ⅓ cup of the vegetables in the center of each tortilla and sprinkle with 2 tablespoons of cheese. Roll the tortillas, making sure the filling extends to the edges and place them in the dish, seam side down. Ladle enough sauce over the enchiladas to cover them completely. You should have about 1 cup left over.

Cover and bake until the enchiladas are hot and the sauce is bubbling, about 25 minutes. Sprinkle with the reserved cheese and serve.

MAKE-AHEAD TIP: You can make the Salsa Negra ahead of time, freeze it, and defrost when needed. (Be sure to adjust the seasoning with the chilies and salt to taste.) Roast the vegetables and make the filling ahead of time. You can also grate the cheese; just be sure to cover it. Last but not least: Assemble the enchiladas in the baking dish an hour or two ahead of time; they'll soak up the sauce on the bottom of the dish as they sit, but that's okay. Wait to pour the sauce over the top until just before you bake them.

Pizza

A Pizza Pep Talk

There's simply no comparison between the incredible flavor and texture of homemade and store-bought pizza-dough—and it's actually fun to make. There are just a few tricks. Be sure the water isn't too hot, so the yeast can grow comfortably. Feed it a little sugar to increase its appetite and set in a warm place to rise, so the dough is supple and light.

WINNING COMBINATIONS: If you like a mixture such as broccoli rabe, toasted almonds, and Manchego cheese with pasta, chances are it'll be great on pizza too. Accent flavors are essential here: Toasted pine nuts, capers, olives, sun-dried tomatoes, whole cloves of roasted garlic or Roasted Garlic Puree, and fresh herbs are always a hit.

COMBINING CHEESES: We like to combine two or three cheeses—one is often dry or crumbly (such as ricotta salata or feta) and the other is creamy (such as mozzarella or Fontina), plus a sprinkling of Parmesan. Substitute one cheese for another, use less cheese, or skip it altogether, as long as the topping ingredients are moist. (If there's no cheese on the pizza, brush the dough lightly with tomato sauce, Roasted Pepper or Tomatillo Sauce to keep it tasty and moist.)

USING UP LEFTOVERS: This is the place to use wilted greens, sautéed mushrooms, grilled or roasted tomatoes, onions, eggplant, summer squash, peppers, and potatoes. Be sure the ingredients are well seasoned and still taste fresh. Add a splash of balsamic or sherry vinegar to bring the flavors to life.

BAKING: We bake our pizzas on a stone, which makes all the difference in the crispness of the crust. So by all means, use a pizza stone and sprinkle the wooden peel (the big wooden paddle used to get pizza in and out of the oven) with fine cornmeal to keep the dough from sticking when you slide it onto the stone. We bake our pizzas at 500°F for 12 to 15 minutes, but the baking time will depend on the heat of your oven.

Tomato Pizza with Feta, Lemon, and Scallions

Save your best summer tomatoes for this pizza. We seed the tomatoes and cut them in big pieces, then season them with scallions and lemon zest. For a beautiful touch, use red and yellow tomatoes and sprinkle whole leaves of cilantro over the pizza instead of chopped. You can also use thinly sliced opal and green basil or flat-leaf parsley instead.

MAKES ONE 12-INCH PIZZA

Pizza Dough (page 172), ready to roll out

¾ pound ripe tomatoes, cored

1 teaspoon minced lemon zest

1 or 2 scallions, both white and green parts, thinly sliced on the diagonal

½ teaspoon salt

Pepper

Fine cornmeal for dusting

Garlic Oil (page 14)

¼ pound mozzarella cheese, grated, about 1 cup

2 ounces feta cheese, crumbled, about ½ cup

½ ounce Parmesan cheese, grated, 2 to 3 tablespoons

1½ to 2 tablespoons chopped cilantro (or whole leaves)

Make the Pizza Dough.

Preheat the oven to 500°F. If using a pizza stone, put it in the oven now.

Cut the tomatoes in half crosswise, gently squeeze to remove the juice and seeds, and cut in large pieces. Toss with the lemon zest, scallion, salt, and a pinch of pepper.

Roll out the dough and place it on a lightly oiled pizza pan (or a wooden peel if you're using a pizza stone) sprinkled with fine cornmeal; brush lightly with garlic oil. Spread one-third of the mozzarella over the dough, place the tomato mixture on top, and cover with the feta and the remaining mozzarella.

Bake the pizza in the pan or on the pizza stone, for 10 to 12 minutes, until the crust is golden and crisp. Remove it from the oven and sprinkle with the Parmesan and cilantro.

Mexican Pizza with Corn, Tomatillos, and Chipotle Chilies

Tender, sweet kernels of corn, tomatillos, and rings of roasted onion make this pizza a star of the summer menu. You can always grill the onions over coals or on the stovetop instead of roasting them. We opt for cilantro, but chopped sage leaves are also delicious.

MAKES ONE 12-INCH PIZZA

Pizza Dough (page 172), ready to roll out

1½ tablespoons Chipotle Puree (see box)

1 large red onion, peeled and cut into ½-inch-thick rings

Garlic Oil (page 14)

Salt and pepper

¼ pound tomatillos, husked and chopped into large pieces, about 1¾ cups

½ tablespoon olive oil

2 ears of corn, shaved, about 2 cups kernels

¼ cup water

Fine cornmeal for dusting

¼ pound white cheddar cheese, grated, about 1¼ cups

2 ounces dry jack or Monterey jack cheese, grated, about ¾ cup

2 tablespoons chopped cilantro

Make the Pizza Dough and the Chipotle Puree.

Preheat the oven to 400°F. If using a pizza stone, put it in the oven now.

Toss the onion rings with garlic oil, ¼ teaspoon salt, and a pinch of pepper. Lay the onions on a baking sheet and roast until they're tender, 15 to 20 minutes. Set aside to cool.

Raise the oven temperature to 500°F. Season the tomatillos with salt and pepper and set aside. Heat the oil in a medium-size skillet and add the corn, ¼ teaspoon salt, and a pinch of pepper; sauté over medium heat for 1 to 2 minutes. Add the water, lower the heat, cover the pan, and cook until tender, 3 to 4 minutes. Set aside to cool.

Roll out the dough and place it on a lightly oiled pizza pan (or a wooden peel if you're using a pizza stone) sprinkled with fine cornmeal. Brush the dough with garlic oil and follow with the Chipotle Puree. Toss the cheeses together and spread a thin layer over the dough, followed by the corn, onions, tomatillos, and the remaining cheese.

Bake the pizza in the pan or on a preheated pizza stone, until the crust is golden and crisp, 10 to 12 minutes. Remove it from the oven and sprinkle with the cilantro.

VARIATION WITH BLACK BEANS: This is a great place to use up leftover black beans, as long as they still hold their shape. Season ½ cup of drained, cooked black beans with salt and pepper and sprinkle over the dough, along with the other ingredients.

Chipotle Puree

This fiery puree of smoked jalapeño chilies is indispensable in our kitchen. We spread it over pizza dough, tortillas, and bread for Mexican grilled cheese sandwiches. It's the secret ingredient that gives many of our sauces, soups, and stews their smoky background flavor; a little goes a very long way. We use canned chipotle chilies packed in adobo, a spicy sauce of the chilies, tomatoes, and vinegar. We buy them at La Palma Mexicatessen in our Mission neighborhood, but they're also available at specialty markets. Puree a whole can at a time in a small food processor or blender and refrigerate in an airtight container. It keeps for weeks in the refrigerator.

Roasted Eggplant and Cherry Tomato Pizza with Basil

Here's what you do with those irresistible, slender eggplant and ripe, little multicolored cherry tomatoes. The thin flesh of Japanese eggplant really holds its shape when roasted or grilled over coals.

MAKES ONE 12-INCH PIZZA

Pizza Dough (page 172), ready to roll out

3 medium Japanese eggplant, about ¾ pound, sliced ½ inch thick on a diagonal

Garlic Oil (page 14)

Salt and pepper

½ pint ripe cherry tomatoes, preferably small ones

Fine cornmeal for dusting

¼ pound Fontina cheese, grated, about 1 cup

2 ounces provolone cheese, grated, about ½ cup

½ ounce Parmesan cheese, grated, 2 to 3 tablespoons

20 fresh basil leaves, bundled and thinly sliced, about ¼ cup

Make the Pizza Dough.

Preheat the oven to 375°F. If using a pizza stone, put it in the oven now.

Toss the eggplant with 1½ tablespoons garlic oil and sprinkle with salt and pepper. Roast on a baking sheet for 15 to 20 minutes, until soft in the center. Cool and slice into thick strips. If the cherry tomatoes are large, cut them in half and sprinkle with salt and pepper. Otherwise, leave them whole.

Raise the oven temperature to 500°F.

Roll out the pizza dough and place it on a lightly oiled pizza pan (or a wooden peel if you're using a pizza stone) sprinkled with fine cornmeal; brush it lightly with garlic oil.

Toss the Fontina and provolone cheeses together and spread one-third of it over the dough. Place the eggplant on top, sprinkle the cherry tomatoes over, and cover with the remaining cheeses.

Bake the pizza in the pan or on a preheated pizza stone for 10 to 12 minutes, until the crust is golden and crisp. Remove it from the oven and sprinkle with the Parmesan and basil.

Potato Pizza with Roasted Tomatoes, Olives, and Manchego

We roast vegetables— potatoes, tomatoes, and garlic— until they're tender and succulent and spread them over pizza dough. Manchego and Fontina cheeses are a great combination here— the salty Manchego cuts the "double starch" of the crisp crust and the roasted potatoes, while the creamy Fontina keeps everything moist. If Manchego isn't available, you can use Asiago or smoked mozzarella instead.

MAKES ONE 12-INCH PIZZA

Pizza Dough (page 172), ready to roll out

1 cup Roasted Tomatoes (page 261), coarsely chopped and drained

Roasted Garlic Puree (page 145), about ⅓ cup

Garlic Oil (page 14)

¾ pound Yellow Finn or Yukon Gold potatoes, sliced into ¼-inch-thick rounds

Salt and pepper

3 tablespoons chopped fresh basil

¼ pound Manchego cheese, grated, about 1 cup

2 ounces Fontina cheese, grated, about ½ cup

Fine cornmeal for dusting

20 Gaeta or 10 Kalamata olives, pitted and coarsely chopped, about ⅓ cup

Make the Pizza Dough.

Preheat the oven to 400°F. Make the Roasted Tomatoes and the Roasted Garlic Puree and set aside. If using a pizza stone, put it in the oven now.

Brush the potato slices on both sides with garlic oil, sprinkle with salt and pepper, and roast on a baking sheet for 10 minutes. Use a spatula to turn them over and roast until golden and tender, about 10 minutes more. When cool, cut them in half.

Raise the oven temperature to 500°F.

Toss the tomatoes in a small bowl with 1 tablespoon of the basil and set aside. Reserve half of the Manchego to sprinkle over the baked pizza; toss the remaining cheeses together.

Roll out the dough and place it on a lightly oiled pizza pan (or a wooden peel if you're using a pizza stone) sprinkled with fine cornmeal; brush with garlic oil. Spread the roasted garlic puree over the dough. Sprinkle a little of the cheese mixture over it, layer on the potatoes, followed by the tomatoes and olives; cover with the remaining cheese mixture.

Bake the pizza in the pan or on a preheated pizza stone for 10 to 12 minutes, until the crust is golden and crisp. Remove it from the oven and sprinkle with the reserved Manchego and chopped basil.

TIP: To maximize the oven time, you can roast the potatoes, tomatoes, and garlic all at the same time. You can even roast them a day in advance. Just be sure to adjust the seasoning with salt and pepper.

VARIATION: In the summer, we use chunks of fresh, ripe tomatoes instead of roasting them. You can also skip the tomatoes altogether and use grilled or roasted peppers in their place. Jarred or canned piquillo peppers from Spain, available in specialty stores, are delicious here.

Pizza with Wilted Greens, Goat Cheese, and Hot Pepper

We've chosen spinach and chard for this popular year-round pizza, but you can use all kinds of greens here, including broccoli rabe, kale, or beet greens, to name a few. We sauté the chard until it's tender and add the spinach at the last minute, just long enough to heat it through. The creamy goat cheese melts into the greens and salty Kalamata olives intensify the flavors.

MAKES ONE 12-INCH PIZZA

Pizza Dough (page 172), ready to roll out

1 tablespoon extra-virgin olive oil

1 medium red onion, diced, about 1½ cups

Salt and pepper

1 tablespoon minced garlic

1 bunch of chard, stems removed and leaves washed, 8 to 10 cups

1 bunch of spinach, stems removed and leaves washed, 6 to 8 cups

¼ teaspoon red pepper flakes, plus more to taste

Fine cornmeal for dusting

Garlic Oil (page 14)

5 ounces mozzarella cheese, grated, about 1½ cups

10 Kalamata olives, pitted and coarsely chopped, about ⅓ cup

2 to 3 ounces creamy goat cheese, crumbled, about ½ cup

½ ounce Parmesan cheese, grated, 2 to 3 tablespoons

Make the Pizza Dough.

Preheat the oven to 500°F. If using a pizza stone, put it in the oven now.

Heat the oil in a large sauté pan and add the onions, ¼ teaspoon salt, and a few pinches of pepper. Sauté over medium heat until it begins to soften, about 3 minutes; add the garlic and cook 1 minute more. Add the chard, ¼ teaspoon salt, and a pinch of pepper; sauté over medium heat until tender, about 3 minutes. Add the spinach and hot pepper flakes and cook 1 minute more, just long enough to wilt it. Cool in a strainer. Squeeze out the excess moisture with your hands and coarsely chop. You should have 1 heaping cup.

Roll out the dough and place on a lightly oiled pizza pan (or a wooden peel if you're using a pizza stone) sprinkled with fine cornmeal; brush lightly with garlic oil. Sprinkle 1 cup of the mozzarella over the dough. Spread the greens and onion mixture over, sprinkle with the olives, and the goat cheese. Cover with the remaining mozzarella.

Bake the pizza in the pan or on a preheated pizza stone for 10 to 12 minutes, until the crust is golden and crisp. Remove it from the oven and sprinkle with the Parmesan. For a spicier pizza, sprinkle with additional red pepper flakes.

TIP: If you're using broccoli rabe or kale, parboil the greens before you sauté them, unless they're very young and tender.

VARIATION: Try fromage blanc here instead of goat cheese. This tangy, fresh cow's milk cheese is similar to goat cheese, without the goaty flavor.

Artichoke and Roasted Shallot Pizza

Make this pizza in the spring and fall, when tasty, little artichokes are abundant. They're really quite quick to prepare, so it's worth a trip to a farmers' market or specialty produce store to find them. To speed things along, you can peel the artichokes the day before and roast the shallots ahead of time. Just be sure to store the artichokes in lemon water to keep their pale green color from turning.

MAKES ONE 12-INCH PIZZA

Pizza Dough, ready to roll out (page 172)

5 or 6 large shallots, about ½ pound, peeled

2 tablespoons extra-virgin olive oil

Salt and pepper

2 pounds small artichokes, trimmed (page 178) and halved, about 3 cups

1 tablespoon minced garlic

¼ cup white wine

1 cup water

Fine cornmeal for dusting

Garlic Oil (page 14)

6 ounces Asiago cheese, grated, about 2 cups

½ ounce Parmesan cheese, grated, 2 to 3 tablespoons

2 to 3 tablespoons chopped flat-leaf parsley

Make the Pizza Dough.

Preheat the oven to 400°F. If using a pizza stone, put it in the oven now.

Roast the shallots in a small baking dish, tossed with 1 tablespoon of the oil and sprinkled with salt and pepper, until caramelized and tender, 25 to 30 minutes. When cool, coarsely chop them and season with salt and pepper.

Increase the oven temperature to 500°F. Heat the remaining olive oil in a medium-size sauté pan and add the artichokes, garlic, ¼ teaspoon salt, and a pinch of pepper. Sauté over medium heat for 2 to 3 minutes, add the wine, and cook until the pan is nearly dry. Add the water and simmer, uncovered, until tender and the pan is nearly dry, about 10 minutes. When cool, coarsely chop and set aside.

Roll out the dough and place it on a lightly oiled pan (or a wooden peel if you're using a pizza stone) sprinkled with fine cornmeal; brush lightly with garlic oil. Spread a little of the Asiago over the dough, followed by the shallots, artichokes, and the remaining Asiago.

Bake the pizza in the pan or on a preheated pizza stone for 10 to 12 minutes, until the crust is golden and crisp. Remove it from the oven and sprinkle with the Parmesan and parsley.

Pizza with Portobello Mushrooms, Spring Onions, and Arugula

We go wild for spring onions, which look like pregnant scallions, when they first come into the market and feature them every way imaginable. In this pizza, their delicate onion flavor balances the intensity of the roasted portobello mushrooms and the arugula. If you don't have spring onions, use leeks or onions in their place.

MAKES ONE 12-INCH PIZZA

Pizza Dough (page 172), ready to roll out

Roasted Portobello Mushrooms (page 260), cut in half and thinly sliced

1 tablespoon extra-virgin olive oil

1 bunch of spring onions, about ½ pound, white or red parts only, sliced, about 3 cups

Salt and pepper

½ tablespoon minced garlic

¼ cup white wine

2 ounces Parmesan cheese, grated, about ½ cup

¼ pound Fontina cheese, grated, about 1 cup

Fine cornmeal for dusting

Garlic Oil (page 14)

A small handful of arugula leaves, about 1 cup

Make the Pizza Dough and the Roasted Portobello Mushrooms.

Preheat the oven to 500°F. If using a pizza stone, put it in the oven now.

Heat the olive oil in a large sauté pan and add the onions, ¼ teaspoon salt, and a pinch of pepper. Cook for 2 to 3 minutes over medium heat until softened. Add the garlic and cook for 1 minute; add the wine and cook until the pan is nearly dry, 3 to 4 minutes.

Reserve half of the Parmesan to sprinkle over the baked pizza and toss the remaining cheeses together. Roll out the dough and place it on a lightly oiled pizza pan (or a wooden peel if you're using a pizza stone) sprinkled with fine cornmeal; brush with garlic oil. Spread the onions evenly over the dough, follow with the mushrooms, and cover with the mixed cheeses.

Bake the pizza in the pan or on a preheated pizza stone for 10 to 12 minutes, until the crust is golden and crisp. Remove it from the oven, sprinkle with the remaining Parmesan, and scatter the arugula leaves over.

Pizza Dough

Our basic pizza dough has evolved over the years and this latest version is our best so far. We've pared down the ingredients and taken away the rye flour and the milk, so the distinctive taste and crunchy texture of the fine cornmeal come to the fore. At the restaurant we use bread flour, but you can use all-purpose flour instead; because it has less protein than bread flour, it makes a lighter, less toothy dough. Either way, this is an exceptional pizza crust.

MAKES ONE 12-INCH PIZZA

1½ teaspoons dry active yeast

½ teaspoon sugar

⅔ cup warm (110°F) water

1½ tablespoons extra-virgin olive oil, plus extra for the bowl

1½ tablespoons fine cornmeal

1½ cups bread flour or all-purpose flour, plus extra for rolling

½ teaspoon salt

In a large bowl, dissolve the yeast and sugar in the warm water; set aside in a warm place for 5 minutes, until foamy. Stir in the olive oil, cornmeal, flour, and salt, making a soft, workable dough.

Turn out onto a lightly floured work surface and knead for about 5 minutes, sprinkling in as little flour as possible to keep the dough from sticking to the surface.

Put the dough into an oiled bowl and turn it once so the surface is coated with oil. Cover the bowl with a kitchen towel or plastic wrap and let the dough rise in a warm place until it has doubled in size, about 45 minutes. Punch the dough down and form into a ball; let rise again for about 30 minutes.

TIP: This dough keeps well in the refrigerator overnight and freezes well. Just be sure to punch it down and cover tightly with plastic wrap before you refrigerate or freeze it. Allow the dough to return to room temperature before rolling it.

VARIATION: If you like the taste of rye flour and the complexity it adds to the dough, add 1 tablespoon of rye flour and decrease the fine cornmeal to 1 tablespoon.

Griddle Cakes and Crêpes

Corn and Scallion Griddle Cakes

These griddle cakes are tender and light and filled with the sweetness of corn. Aged cheddar works beautifully, but Fontina, Asiago, or smoked cheese are just as delicious. Add chopped basil or chives or diced fresh chilies for spice and heat.

SERVES 4 TO 6; MAKES 18 CAKES

½ tablespoon olive oil

½ medium yellow onion, diced, about ½ cup

2 scallions, sliced on the diagonal, white and green parts separated

½ teaspoon minced garlic

Salt and pepper

3 ears of corn, shaved, about 3 cups kernels

¼ cup water

2 large eggs, separated

½ pound whole milk ricotta cheese, about 1 cup

½ cup milk

2 ounces white cheddar cheese, grated, about ¾ cup

½ ounce Parmesan cheese, grated, 2 to 3 tablespoons

½ cup all-purpose flour

1 teaspoon baking powder

Vegetable oil for the pan

Heat the olive oil in a medium-size sauté pan and add the onions, white parts of the scallions, the garlic, ¼ teaspoon salt, and a pinch of pepper. Sauté over medium heat until the onions begin to soften, about 3 minutes. Add the corn and the water, lower the heat, and cover the pan. Simmer until the corn is tender, about 5 minutes. Transfer to a bowl, toss in the scallion greens, and set aside to cool.

Combine the egg yolks, ricotta, milk, and the cheeses in a mixing bowl. Stir in the corn mixture, flour, baking powder, ¼ teaspoon salt, and a pinch of pepper. Beat the egg whites with a pinch of salt until stiff and gently fold them into the batter.

Spoon the batter into a generously oiled skillet or griddle over medium-high heat, allowing about ¼ cup batter per cake. Cook for about 3 minutes on each side, until the cakes are golden. Add fresh oil to the pan between batches of cakes.

Spinach and Feta Griddle Cakes

These tender griddle cakes have classic Greek flavors— feta, lemon zest, rosemary, and spinach. Be sure to squeeze as much moisture as you can from the spinach. Otherwise, the ricotta batter will be too wet. You can make the batter ahead of time, but don't fold in the egg whites until you're ready to make the cakes. Put the first batch of cakes in a warm oven (250°F) while you make the rest and serve with Meyer Lemon Beurre Blanc and Niçoise olives.

SERVES 4 TO 6; MAKES 12 TO 15 CAKES

1 tablespoon extra-virgin olive oil

½ large yellow onion, chopped, about 1 cup

Salt and pepper

2 teaspoons minced garlic

1 bunch spinach, stems removed, leaves washed and dried, about 8 cups packed

1½ teaspoons minced lemon zest

½ tablespoon fresh lemon juice

3 large eggs, separated

½ pound whole milk ricotta cheese, about 1 cup

2 tablespoons milk

3 ounces feta cheese, crumbled, about ¾ cup

½ ounce Parmesan cheese, grated, 2 to 3 tablespoons

1 teaspoon chopped fresh rosemary

½ cup all-purpose flour

1 teaspoon baking powder

Vegetable oil for the pan

Heat the olive oil in a skillet and add the onions, ¼ teaspoon salt, and a pinch of pepper. Cook over medium heat until the onions begin to soften, about 3 minutes; add the garlic and cook 1 minute more. Toss in the spinach and cook until wilted, 3 to 4 minutes. Add the lemon zest and juice. Set aside to cool. Squeeze out the excess moisture in small handfuls and coarsely chop.

Combine the egg yolks, ricotta, milk, cheeses, and rosemary in a mixing bowl. Stir in the spinach mixture, flour, baking powder, ¼ teaspoon salt, and a pinch of pepper. Whisk the egg whites with a pinch of salt until stiff and gently fold them into the batter.

Generously coat a skillet with vegetable oil. Over medium-high heat, spoon the batter into the pan, allowing about ¼ cup per cake. Cook for about 3 minutes on each side, until the cakes are golden. Add fresh oil to the pan between batches of cakes.

VARIATIONS: We constantly vary the ingredients here, depending on the menu and the time of year. Scallions, spring onions, or leeks are always a welcome addition. Try chopped fresh dill or chives in place of the rosemary. You can also use chèvre or fromage blanc instead of the feta; they're equally delicious.

Artichoke Griddle Cakes with Gruyère

We braise artichokes and leeks in white wine until they're perfectly tender and then toss them into a light ricotta, Gruyère cheese, and lemon zest batter. Serve the cakes with Meyer Lemon Beurre Blanc or with golden and Chioggia beets tossed with mâche and crisp slices of fennel.

SERVES 4 TO 6; MAKES ABOUT 16 CAKES

½ tablespoons extra-virgin olive oil

2 medium leeks, white parts only, cut in half lengthwise, thinly sliced and washed, 1 heaping cup

Salt and pepper

1 teaspoon minced garlic

¼ cup white wine

2 pounds small artichokes, trimmed (page 178), 3½ to 4 cups

1 cup water

½ pound whole milk ricotta cheese, about 1 cup

3 large eggs, separated

2 to 3 ounces Gruyère cheese, grated, about ½ cup

½ ounce Parmesan cheese, grated, 2 to 3 tablespoons

⅓ cup milk

1 tablespoon chopped chives

1 tablespoon chopped flat-leaf parsley

½ teaspoon minced lemon zest

1 teaspoon fresh lemon juice

⅓ cup all-purpose flour

1 teaspoon baking powder

Vegetable oil for the pan

Heat the oil in a large sauté pan over medium heat and add the leeks, ½ teaspoon salt, and a pinch of pepper. Cook until they begin to soften, 2 to 3 minutes, add the garlic and cook 1 minute more. Pour in the wine and cook until the pan is nearly dry, about 3 minutes. Add the artichokes and water. Simmer until the artichokes are completely tender, about 10 minutes. Drain off any excess liquid and set aside to cool. Coarsely chop the artichoke mixture.

Combine the ricotta, egg yolks, cheeses, milk, herbs, lemon zest, and juice in a large bowl.

Stir in the artichoke mixture, flour, baking powder, ¼ teaspoon salt, and a pinch of pepper. Whisk the egg whites with a pinch of salt until they form stiff peaks and gently fold them into the batter.

Generously coat a skillet with vegetable oil. Over medium-high heat, spoon the batter into the pan, allowing about ¼ cup per cake. Cook for about 3 minutes on each side, until the cakes are lightly browned. Add fresh oil to the pan between batches of cakes.

RESTAURANT TIP: You can peel the artichokes a day ahead of time (see below). You can also slice the leeks and grate the cheese the day before. Just be sure to store them in sealed containers in the refrigerator.

VARIATION: Try using Manchego in place of the Gruyère. Its smooth, assertive flavor is great with the artichokes.

Prepping Little Artichokes

Little artichokes are easy to cook and once you realize how delicious they are, your resistance to trimming them will disappear. These beautiful little side shoots of the artichoke plant are too young to develop a choke inside, so all you need to trim are the top and bottom and peel away the tough outer leaves. There are two essentials here: a bowl of lemon water and a knife with a nonreactive blade, both to keep the artichokes from discoloring. At the restaurant, we trim the artichokes by the case and refrigerate them overnight in the lemon water. You can prepare them ahead of time too; just remember the lemon flavor develops as they sit.

For 1 pound of artichokes you'll need 1 quart of water and the juice of half a lemon. Combine the water and lemon juice in a large bowl; you can even throw in the rind. Trim the tops and base of the artichokes, peel away the dark outer leaves, down to the tender, pale green inner leaves, and trim the edges of the base. (A sharp paring knife makes the trimming easier.) Cut the artichokes in half or quarters, depending on their size (or the recipe instructions), and drop them into the lemon water. Place an inverted plate on top to ensure that the artichokes are submerged. When you're ready to cook them, just drain in a colander and discard the lemon rind; their lovely light green color will be vibrant.

Butternut Squash Risotto Griddle Cakes

This is the place to use that leftover Risotto with Roasted Butternut Squash and Kale, so be sure to set some aside the next time you make it. We toss the risotto with egg yolks, flour, and creamy Fontina cheese and fold in beaten egg whites to lighten it. You can serve these rustic cakes as an appetizer or a main course, depending on their size.

SERVES 4 TO 6; MAKES ABOUT 12 CAKES

2 cups Risotto with Roasted Butternut Squash and Kale (page 253)

2 large eggs, separated

3 tablespoons all-purpose flour

1 teaspoon chopped fresh thyme

2 ounces Fontina cheese, grated, about ½ cup

½ ounce Parmesan cheese, grated, 2 to 3 tablespoons

Salt and pepper

Vegetable oil for the pan

Place the risotto in a large bowl and combine with the egg yolks, flour, thyme, and cheeses. In a separate bowl, beat the egg whites with a pinch of salt until soft peaks are formed. Gently fold the whites into the mixture and taste for salt and pepper.

Heat a well-oiled skillet or griddle over medium-high heat, and spoon the batter on, allowing about ¼ cup per cake. Cook for 3 to 4 minutes on each side, until the cakes are golden and puffed. Add fresh oil to the pan between batches of cakes.

Yellow Finn Potato Cakes with Asiago

Starchy Yellow Finn potatoes are a delightful host for leeks, spring onions, or tender shoots of green garlic and a variety of cheeses. We've chosen Asiago here, but any creamy melting cheese will do; Manchego, Fontina, Gruyère, or chèvre are equally delicious. This is where we love to show off St. George cheddar, an exceptional cheese that's made locally by the Matos family in Petaluma and sold at the Cowgirl Creamery in Marin, which will mail order their cheeses.

The potato mixture keeps well in the refrigerator for a day or two, so you can make it ahead of time and cook up the cakes at the last minute. Serve with a generous spoonful of crème fraîche and warm Quince and Sour Cherry Compote.

SERVES 4 TO 6; MAKES 12 CAKES

2 pounds Yellow Finn potatoes

1 tablespoon olive oil

2 medium leeks, white part only, cut in half lengthwise, sliced and washed, about 1½ cups

Salt and pepper

2 teaspoons minced garlic

2 large eggs

2 tablespoons Crème Fraîche (page 98), plus extra for garnish

3 ounces Asiago cheese, grated, about ¾ cup

1 to 1½ tablespoons all-purpose flour

Oil for the pan

Place the potatoes in a pot of cold water and bring to a boil. Lower the heat and simmer, uncovered, until they're tender but not quite cooked through, about 25 minutes. Drain and set aside to cool. Peel the potatoes and grate on the largest hole of a hand grater or in a food processor.

Heat the olive oil in a medium-size skillet and add the leeks, ¼ teaspoon salt, and a few pinches of pepper. Cook over medium heat until the leeks begin to soften, about 3 minutes. Add the garlic and cook 1 minute more, adding a little water if needed to keep the leeks from sticking to the pan.

Combine the leeks, potatoes, ½ teaspoon salt, and a pinch of pepper in a mixing bowl. Beat the eggs and the crème fraîche together and mix into the potatoes along with the cheese and flour.

Form into little cakes about 3 to 4 inches in diameter and ½ inch thick. Cook in a well-oiled skillet or on a griddle over medium heat, until the cakes crisp and turn golden, about 5 minutes per side.

Two Potato Griddle Cakes

Garnet yams lend their deep, rich flavor and warm, inviting color to these griddle cakes. The Gruyère draws out their natural sweetness without overpowering them. Once roasted, yams are incredibly moist, so don't be surprised if the batter is a little wet; not to worry. We serve the cakes with a spoonful of crème fraîche and a fall salad of bitter greens tossed with crisp apples, pomegranate seeds, and Cider Vinaigrette.

SERVES 4 TO 6; MAKES 12 CAKES

1 small yam or sweet potato, about ½ pound

1½ pounds Yellow Finn potatoes

1 tablespoon olive oil

4 to 6 large shallots, about ½ pound, thinly sliced, 1½ cups

Salt and pepper

1 teaspoon minced garlic

¼ cup white wine

2 large eggs

2 tablespoons Crème Fraîche (page 98)

3 ounces Gruyère cheese, grated, about ½ cup

1 ounce Parmesan cheese, grated, about ⅓ cup

3 tablespoons all-purpose flour

Oil for the pan

Preheat the oven to 375°F.

Prick the yam with a fork and roast in a small baking dish until just tender, about 30 minutes. When cool enough to handle, peel and mash the yam.

Place the potatoes in a pot of cold water and bring to a boil. Lower the heat and simmer, uncovered, until they're tender but not quite cooked through, about 25 minutes. Test for doneness with a paring knife or skewer. Drain the potatoes and set aside to cool. Peel them and grate on the largest hole of a hand grater or in a food processor.

Heat the olive oil in a medium-size skillet and add the shallots, ¼ teaspoon salt, and a few pinches of pepper. Cook until they begin to soften, 2 to 3 minutes. Add the garlic and cook 1 minute more, adding a little water if needed to keep the shallots from sticking to the pan. Add the wine and cook until the pan is nearly dry, about 3 minutes.

Combine the yams, potatoes, and shallots with ½ teaspoon salt and a pinch of pepper in a mixing bowl. Beat the eggs and crème fraîche together and stir into the potato mixture along with the cheeses and flour.

Form into little cakes about 3 to 4 inches in diameter and ½ inch thick. Cook in a well-oiled skillet or on a griddle top over medium heat, allowing the cakes to crisp and turn golden, about 4 to 5 minutes per side.

Potato Gordas

Masa harina— the toasted corn flour used in tortillas— gives these rustic cakes their exceptional flavor. Be sure to use fresh, moist masa harina if you can find it. If not, you can use the dried masa harina available in most grocery stores. Serve with New Mexican Border Stew or with Fire-Roasted Salsa, big sprigs of cilantro, and a spoonful of crème fraîche.

MAKES 18 2-INCH CAKES

1 pound Yellow Finn or Yukon Gold potatoes

½ cup masa harina, about 2 ounces

1 or 2 jalapeño chilies, seeded and diced, 2 to 3 tablespoons

1 ounce white cheddar cheese, grated, about ¼ cup

1 ounce dry jack cheese, grated, about ⅓ cup

1 teaspoon baking powder

¾ teaspoon salt

Pinch of cayenne pepper

Oil for the pan

Place the potatoes in a large saucepan, cover generously with cold water, and bring to a boil. Lower the heat and simmer until tender but still firm in the center, about 25 minutes. Drain the potatoes and reserve 1 cup of the cooking liquid. When cool enough to handle, peel the potatoes and grate on the largest hole of a hand grater or in a food processor. Toss in a large bowl with the remaining ingredients. Add the cooking liquid and use a rubber spatula to combine, being careful not to overwork the mixture. Shape into small patties about 2 inches in size.

Heat a thin coating of oil in a large sauté pan or on a griddle and cook the patties over medium-high heat until they're golden and crisp, about 3 minutes per side. Keep in a warm oven (250°F) while you cook the rest.

VARIATION: Substitute ⅓ cup Manchego or smoked cheese for the dry jack.

Masa Harina Crêpes with Summer Vegetables, Poblano Chilies, and Cheddar

The tastes of summer— corn, sweet peppers, and zucchini— are tucked into crêpes stuffed with poblano chili, cilantro, and cheddar cheese, and topped with tangy Tomatillo Sauce and a spoonful of crème fraîche.

If you do some preparation in advance, this delightful dish can be made with a minimum of fuss (see Make-ahead tip).

MAKES 10 TO 12 CRÊPES

Masa Harina Crêpes (page 192)

Tomatillo Sauce (page 289)

1 tablespoon olive oil

½ medium yellow onion, chopped, about ¾ cup

1 teaspoon minced garlic

Salt

Cayenne pepper

2 ears of corn, shaved, about 2 cups kernels

¼ cup water

1 large zucchini, diced, 1 heaping cup

½ medium red pepper, diced, about ⅔ cup

1 poblano chili, roasted, peeled, seeded, and diced (page 64), about 3 tablespoons

3 to 4 tablespoons chopped cilantro

¼ pound good quality, white cheddar cheese, grated, about 1 cup

Milk or heavy cream

Crème Fraîche (page 98) to garnish

Make the crêpes and set them aside. Make the Tomatillo Sauce and set aside.

Heat the oil in a medium-size sauté pan and add the onions, garlic, ¼ teaspoon salt, and a pinch of cayenne. Cook over medium heat until the onions begin to soften, about 2 minutes. Add the corn and the water, cover the pan, and simmer for 5 minutes.

Add the zucchini, peppers, and ¼ teaspoon salt and cook until tender, about 5 minutes. Drain thoroughly and transfer to a bowl. Stir in the chili, the cilantro, and season to taste with salt and cayenne.

Preheat the oven to 375°F.

Place the crêpes on a flat work surface. Spread ⅓ cup filling over the bottom half of each crêpe and sprinkle with 1 heaping tablespoon of the cheese. Fold the top over the filling, then fold in half again, to form a quarter circle. Place the filled crêpes on a parchment-lined baking sheet, brush with a little milk or cream, and bake until hot, about 15 minutes.

To serve, place two crêpes, slightly overlapping, on each plate and ladle ⅓ cup of the Tomatillo Sauce over them and spoon crème fraîche on top.

MAKE-AHEAD TIP: You can make the crêpe batter the day before. Make the crêpes, the filling, and the sauce a few hours ahead of time, but don't make the sauce too early or it will lose its freshness. You can even fill the crêpes in advance. Just cover with plastic wrap to keep them moist until you're ready to bake.

Rosemary Crêpes with Goat Cheese and Wilted Greens

Spinach, chard, and leeks blend beautifully with creamy goat cheese and a hint of fresh rosemary in these savory crêpes. They don't need much filling, just about ¼ cup per crêpe. You can make the filling a few hours ahead of time, but not much earlier, or the greens begin to lose their freshness. Serve them with Herb Cream.

MAKES 10 TO 12 CRÊPES

Rosemary Crêpes (page 192)

Herb Cream (page 297)

1 bunch of chard, about 1½ pounds with stems

2 tablespoons extra-virgin olive oil

1 medium leek, white part only, cut in half lengthwise, sliced, and washed, about 1 cup

Salt and pepper

½ teaspoon minced garlic

1 to 2 bunches of spinach; stems removed, washed and dried, 12 cups packed leaves

2 ounces creamy goat cheese, crumbled, about ⅓ cup

1 ounce Parmesan cheese, grated, about ⅓ cup

Milk or heavy cream

Make the crêpes and the Herb Cream and set aside.

Tear the chard leaves away from the stems, wash, and drain in a colander. Trim the stems, remove the strings, and slice on the diagonal, about ¼ inch thick. You should have 6 to 8 cups of leaves and 1 heaping cup of stems.

Heat 1 tablespoon of the oil in a large sauté pan and add the leeks, chard stems, ¼ teaspoon salt, and a pinch of pepper. Cook over medium heat until tender, about 5 minutes, adding a little water if needed. Transfer to a bowl.

Heat the remaining oil in the pan and add the chard leaves, garlic, ¼ teaspoon salt, and a pinch of pepper. Cook over medium heat until tender, about 3 minutes. Add the spinach and cook just long enough to wilt, about 1 minute more. Transfer to a colander. When cool enough to handle, use your hands to squeeze as much moisture as you can from the greens. Coarsely chop and add to the leek mixture. Add the cheeses and season with salt and pepper to taste.

Preheat the oven to 375°F.

187

Place the crêpes on a flat work surface. Spread ¼ cup filling over the bottom half of each crêpe and fold the top over the filling. Fold in half again, to form a quarter circle. Place the filled crêpes on a parchment-lined baking sheet, brush each on top with a little milk or cream and bake until hot, about 15 minutes.

To serve, place two crêpes, slightly overlapping, on each plate and ladle about ¼ cup of the Herb Cream over them.

TIP: Be sure to squeeze the excess moisture from the greens before you combine them with the leeks and cheeses for the filling. Otherwise, the filling will be too wet and the crêpes will be soggy.

VARIATION: Add 1 teaspoon minced lemon zest to the filling. You can use fromage blanc or a good quality feta cheese instead of the goat cheese. Kale is also delicious here. Since it takes much longer to cook than chard or spinach, be sure to parboil it for 3 to 4 minutes, or until it's tender, before sautéing it with the other greens.

Buckwheat Crêpes with Winter Vegetables and Caramelized Onions

Earthy Buckwheat Crêpes perfectly embrace these hearty ingredients: roasted butternut squash, parsnips, and Yellow Finn potatoes, caramelized onions, and nutty Fontina cheese. We love these flavors together, but celery root, rutabagas, and other varieties of winter squash are also delicious. Their cooking times will vary, so just be sure the vegetables are roasted evenly. Herb Cream is a perfect finish to this homey winter dish.

MAKES 10 TO 12 CRÊPES

Buckwheat Crêpes (page 192)

1 large Yellow Finn potato, cut into ¾-inch pieces, about 2 cups

¾ pound butternut squash, cut into ¾-inch pieces, about 2 cups

1 medium parsnip, peeled and cut into ¾-inch pieces, about 1 cup

2 tablespoons olive oil

1 teaspoon minced garlic

Salt and pepper

Herb Cream (page 297)

2 large yellow onions, sliced in thin half moons, about 4 cups

¼ cup white wine

1½ tablespoons chopped fresh sage

1 tablespoon chopped flat-leaf parsley

1 cup Vegetable Stock (page 110) or water

¼ pound Fontina cheese, grated, about 1 cup

2 ounces Parmesan cheese, grated, about ⅔ cup

Milk or heavy cream

Make the crêpes and set aside.

Preheat the oven to 400°F.

In a large bowl toss the potatoes, squash, and parsnips with 1 tablespoon of the oil, the garlic, ¼ teaspoon salt, and a pinch of pepper. Spread the mixture on a baking sheet and roast for 15 minutes. Use a spatula to loosen and turn the vegetables so they cook evenly. Cook until tender, 10 to 15 minutes more. Transfer to a bowl and set aside to cool.

While the vegetables are roasting, make the Herb Cream.

Reduce the oven temperature to 375°F.

Heat the remaining oil in a large sauté pan and add the onions, ½ teaspoon salt, and a pinch of pepper. Cook the onions over medium heat until they're soft and a deep golden color, about 20 minutes, using a wooden spoon to loosen them from the pan as they caramelize. Add the wine and cook until the pan is nearly dry, about 3 minutes. Add the roasted vegetables, the herbs, the stock or water, and simmer until the vegetables absorb the liquid, about 3 minutes. Adjust the seasoning. Set aside to cool.

Mix the cheeses into the filling. Place the crêpes on a flat work surface. Spread ⅓ cup filling over the bottom half of each crêpe and fold the top over the filling, then fold in half again, to form a quarter circle. Place the filled crêpes on a parchment-lined baking sheet, brush with a little milk or cream and bake until hot, about 15 minutes.

To serve, place two crêpes, slightly overlapping, on each plate and ladle about ¼ cup of the Herb Cream over them.

MAKE-AHEAD TIP: Make the crêpes early in the day or even the day before. You can caramelize the onions ahead of time and roast the vegetables in advance; just be sure to adjust the seasonings before you fill the crêpes.

Crêpe Batter

This recipe makes perfect crêpes every time. You can vary it in a number of ways, depending on the flavors of the filling. Be sure to let the batter rest for at least two hours after you make it. You can also make the batter a day ahead of time and refrigerate it overnight. The batter will thicken as it sits, so just add a little milk to thin it before cooking. The thinner the batter, the lighter the crêpes.

MAKES 10 TO 12 CRÊPES

¾ cup milk, plus additional milk to thin the batter

¾ cup water

2 large eggs

½ teaspoon salt

1⅓ cups all-purpose flour

3 tablespoons unsalted butter, melted with 1 tablespoon vegetable oil

Butter and vegetable oil for the pan

Puree ¾ cup milk, the water, eggs, and salt in a blender for 30 seconds. Add the flour and blend until smooth, about 1 minute. Scrape down the sides of the blender with a rubber spatula and pour in the melted butter. Blend another 30 seconds and pour through a fine-mesh strainer to remove any lumps. Refrigerate in a covered container for at least two hours or overnight.

Check the consistency of the batter before making the crêpes. It should be the consistency of heavy cream. If thicker, thin it with a little milk.

Heat a 9-inch sauté pan or crêpe pan over medium-high heat and coat with a thin layer of butter, plus a little oil. Ladle about ¼ cup of batter in the center of the pan, tilting and swirling to spread it evenly over the surface.

Cook the crêpe over medium heat until golden and easily loosened from the pan, 1 to 2 minutes. Flip it over, and cook for another 30 to 40 seconds. Layer the crêpes like shingles on a parchment-lined baking sheet to keep them from sticking together.

Once cool, the crêpes can be stacked, wrapped in a plastic wrap, and refrigerated or frozen until ready to use.

Rosemary Crêpes: Make the batter as directed, adding 1 teaspoon finely chopped fresh rosemary after you strain it. Fill with sautéed greens— spinach, chard, and different varieties of kale are always a good bet— with goat cheese, ricotta, or feta.

Buckwheat Crêpes: Make the crêpe batter as directed, substituting 1/3 cup buckwheat flour for 1/3 cup of the flour. Fill with wild mushrooms and leeks, roasted root vegetables, or caramelized onions with goat cheese and sage. For a luscious dessert, fill the crêpes with apples sautéed in butter and Calvados and dab fromage blanc over the filling.

Masa Harina Crêpes: Make the batter as directed, substituting 1/3 cup masa harina for 1/3 cup of the flour. Fill with roasted butternut squash, poblano chilies, and sage. In the summer, try a filling of sweet white corn and fresh chilies.

Herb Crêpes: Make the batter as directed, adding 2 to 3 teaspoons finely chopped herbs such as cilantro, basil, chives, marjoram, oregano, parsley, chervil, or sage after you strain the batter.

Scallion Crêpes: Make the batter as directed, adding 1 minced scallion (both white and green parts) after you strain it. Fill with fresh corn, little cherry tomatoes, and basil.

Curries, Ragoûts, and Stews

Indian Curry with Tamarind and Chilies

The warm, enticing flavors of south India— coconut milk, tamarind, ginger, and fresh chilies— permeate this simple curry. There's really no substitute for tamarind; its tart flavor is a perfect balance to the richness of coconut milk and the heat of the chilies. We use tamarind pulp; you'll find it in Indian and Asian markets.

For a spicier curry, add another chili or a pinch or two of cayenne. Serve over Basmati Rice with Mustard Seeds.

SERVES 4 TO 6

1 ounce tamarind pulp, about 2 tablespoons

¾ pound English peas, shelled, or frozen peas, about 1 cup

1½ tablespoons vegetable oil

1 large onion, chopped, about 2 cups

Salt and pepper

1 pound Yellow Finn potatoes, peeled and cut into ¾-inch cubes, about
     3 cups

2 medium carrots, cut in half lengthwise, cut diagonally into ½-inch thick slices,
     about 2½ cups

1 tablespoon minced garlic

1½ tablespoons grated fresh ginger

1 or 2 jalapeño chilies, seeded and diced

½ medium head of cauliflower, cut into large florets, about 3 cups

2 large red or yellow peppers, cut into thick strips and then triangles, about 3 cups

1 teaspoon coriander seeds, toasted (page 214) and ground

½ teaspoon paprika

Cayenne pepper

One 14-ounce can unsweetened coconut milk

⅓ cup chopped cilantro

Bring a small pot of water to a boil and salt lightly. Place the tamarind in a small bowl, pour ¾ cup of the water over it, and set aside to soak. Drop the peas, fresh or frozen, into the boiling water and cook until tender, about 2 minutes. Drain, rinse under cold water, and set aside.

When the tamarind is cool enough to handle, use your fingers to work the seeds out of the pulp and discard the seeds. Puree the tamarind with the soaking liquid in a small food processor or blender and set aside.

Heat the oil in a deep sauté pan or Dutch oven over medium heat and add the onions, ½ teaspoon salt, and a pinch of pepper. Sauté until they begin to soften, about 3 minutes; stir in the potatoes, carrots, garlic, 1 tablespoon of the ginger, the chilies, and a few spoonfuls of water. Lower the heat, cover the pan, and simmer for 6 to 7 minutes. Add the cauliflower, peppers, the remaining ginger, the tamarind, coriander, paprika, ½ teaspoon salt, and a pinch each of cayenne and black pepper. Cover the pan and cook for 5 minutes more. Stir in the coconut milk and simmer, uncovered, until the cauliflower is tender, about 15 minutes.

Add the peas and cook for 1 to 2 minutes, just long enough to heat them through. Stir in the cilantro and season to taste with salt and cayenne.

Red Curry with Summer Vegetables and Thai Spices

In this luscious curry, the exotic flavors of galangal, ginger, lime leaves, and Thai basil (all available at most Asian markets) blend into the rich sauce of coconut milk, Lemongrass Stock, and Red Curry Spices. Wedges of patty pan and sunburst squash are especially beautiful here, but if they're not available, use golden and green zucchini instead. Serve over jasmine rice.

SERVES 4 TO 6

THE SAUCE

1¼ cups Lemongrass Stock (page 199)

2½ teaspoons Red Curry Spices (recipe follows)

½ large yellow onion, chopped, about 1 cup

2 medium red peppers, coarsely chopped, about 2 cups

1 teaspoon minced garlic

½ teaspoon salt

2 kaffir lime leaves

1 tablespoon grated fresh ginger

1 tablespoon minced galangal

One 14-ounce can unsweetened coconut milk

Make the Lemongrass Stock and prepare the Red Curry Spices.

Combine 1 cup of the stock, 1 teaspoon of the spices, and everything but the coconut milk in a saucepan and bring to a boil. (Reserve ¼ cup of the stock and 1½ teaspoons of the spices to add to the curry later.) Lower the heat, cover the pan, and simmer for 5 minutes. Remove the lime leaves and set them aside. Puree the sauce in a blender until smooth, add the coconut milk and the lime leaves, and set aside.

THE STEW

1 tablespoon vegetable oil

½ large yellow onion, chopped, about 1 cup

Salt and pepper

1 pound Yellow Finn potatoes, peeled and cut into ¾-inch cubes, about 3 cups

1 carrot, cut in half lengthwise, sliced ½ inch thick on the diagonal, about 1 cup

1 teaspoon minced garlic

1 tablespoon grated fresh ginger

1 stalk lemongrass, tops and outer leaves removed, finely chopped, about 1 tablespoon

1 pound pattypan and sunburst squash, cut into thick wedges, about 4 cups, or ½-inch
  chunks of zucchini, cut on the diagonal

2 medium red peppers, cut into thick strips and then triangles, about 2 cups

1 cup bamboo shoots, drained and rinsed

¼ pound green beans, ends trimmed, cut in half on the diagonal, about 1 cup

⅓ cup chopped Thai basil

Whole Thai basil leaves for garnish

Heat the oil in a deep sauté pan and add the onions, ¼ teaspoon salt, and a pinch of pepper. Cook over medium heat until the onions begin to soften, about 3 minutes. Stir in the potatoes, carrots, garlic, ginger, and lemongrass and cook for 2 to 3 minutes. Add the reserved Lemongrass Stock; lower the heat, cover the pan, and simmer for 2 to 3 minutes. Add the squash, peppers, reserved spices, and ½ teaspoon salt; cover the pan and cook for 5 minutes. Stir in the sauce and bamboo shoots, and cook, uncovered, for 15 to 20 minutes. The sauce will be thick at first but as the vegetables cook they'll release their juices and thin it.

Bring a small pot of water to a boil and salt lightly. Drop in the green beans and cook until tender, 3 to 4 minutes. Drain and rinse under cold water. Add the green beans to the curry and cook just long enough to heat them through, 1 to 2 minutes. Remove the lime leaves, add the basil, and season with salt and pepper to taste. Garnish with whole Thai basil leaves.

Red Curry Spices: These spices are fiery and sweet— toasted fennel and coriander seeds, black pepper, red chili flakes, and paprika to give the curry its deep, rich color. Be sure to store the leftover spices in an airtight container, they'll keep for up to a month in your cupboard.

MAKES 5 TEASPOONS; ENOUGH FOR TWO CURRIES

1½ teaspoons fennel seeds

1½ teaspoons coriander seeds

¾ teaspoon paprika

¾ teaspoon red pepper flakes

½ teaspoon black pepper

Toast the fennel and coriander seeds together in a small skillet over medium-low heat until fragrant, 1 to 2 minutes. Combine everything in a spice mill or coffee grinder and grind to a fine powder.

MAKE-AHEAD TIP: Make the Lemongrass Stock in advance, freeze it and defrost when needed. The spice mixture can be made weeks ahead and stored in a sealed container. You can also prepare the vegetables the day before and the sauce a few hours ahead of time.

VARIATIONS: Galangal adds its earthy, pungent flavor, but if you can't find it, make the curry without it and add a little extra ginger. If Thai basil isn't available, use regular basil or cilantro instead. For a delectable fall or winter curry, substitute butternut squash and roasted root vegetables for the summer vegetables.

Lemongrass Stock

The fresh, clean taste of lemongrass is essential to our Southeast Asian dishes, balancing the richness of coconut milk in our favorite curries, stir-fries, and soups. This simple stock is quick and easy to make. Just be sure to give the lemongrass a good whack with the side of a knife, to release all the flavor. Our curry recipes use only about 1¼ cups stock, so make a full recipe and freeze the rest in small containers.

MAKES ABOUT 1 QUART

4 lemongrass stalks

1 yellow onion, sliced

6 thick coins of fresh ginger

10 cilantro sprigs

1 teaspoon coriander seeds

½ teaspoon salt

6 cups cold water

Trim off the tough tops of the lemongrass stalks and discard them. Smash the base of the stalks with the side of a knife and chop into large pieces. Combine the ingredients in a medium-size saucepan and bring to a boil. Reduce the heat and simmer, uncovered, for about 40 minutes, stirring occasionally. Strain the stock and discard the vegetables. The stock will keep in the freezer for several months.

Vietnamese Yellow Curry

This traditional Vietnamese curry is mild instead of fiery, with lime leaves, fresh ginger, and Lemongrass Stock mingling with coconut milk and sweet curry spices. Frozen petite peas are a good, reliable substitute if peas are out of season or you're short on time. Be sure to use sweet yellow peppers here— without their luxurious yellow color, the sauce isn't the same. Garnish with cilantro and serve with Jasmine Rice with Cashews.

SERVES 4 TO 6

THE SAUCE

1¼ cups Lemongrass Stock (page 199)

2½ teaspoons Yellow Curry Spices (recipe follows)

½ large yellow onion, coarsely chopped, about 1 cup

2 medium yellow peppers, coarsely chopped, about 2 cups

1 teaspoon minced garlic

½ teaspoon salt

2 kaffir lime leaves

1 tablespoon grated fresh ginger

1 stalk lemongrass, tops and outer leaves removed, finely chopped, about 1 tablespoon

One 14-ounce can unsweetened coconut milk

Make the Lemongrass Stock and prepare the Yellow Curry Spices.

Place 1 cup of the stock, 1 teaspoon of the spices, and everything but the coconut milk in a saucepan and bring to a boil. (Reserve ¼ cup of the stock and 1½ teaspoons of the spices to add to the curry later.) Lower the heat, cover the pan, and simmer for 5 minutes. Remove the lime leaves and set them aside. Puree the sauce in a blender until smooth, add the coconut milk and the lime leaves; set aside.

THE STEW

1 tablespoon vegetable oil

½ large yellow onion, chopped, about 1 cup

Salt and pepper

½ pound Yellow Finn potatoes, peeled and cut into ¾-inch cubes, 1½ to 2 cups

1 carrot, peeled, cut in half lengthwise, sliced ½ inch thick on a diagonal, about 1 cup

1 teaspoon minced garlic

1 tablespoon grated fresh ginger

1 stalk lemongrass, tough tops and outer leaves removed, finely chopped, about 1 tablespoon

1½ pounds Garnet yams or sweet potatoes, peeled and cut into ¾-inch cubes, about 4 cups

2 medium red peppers, cut into thick strips and then triangles, about 2 cups

½ pound English peas, shelled, or frozen peas, about ¾ cup

½ medium head cauliflower, cut into florets, about 2 cups

⅓ cup chopped cilantro

Cayenne pepper (optional)

Heat the oil in a deep sauté pan over medium heat and add the onions, ¼ teaspoon salt, and a pinch of pepper. Cook until softened, about 3 minutes. Stir in the potatoes, carrots, garlic, ginger, and lemongrass and cook for 2 to 3 minutes. Add the reserved Lemongrass Stock, lower the heat, cover the pan, and simmer for 2 to 3 minutes. Add the yams, peppers, the reserved spices, ½ teaspoon salt, and a pinch of pepper; cover the pan and cook for 5 minutes.

Meanwhile, bring a small pot of water to a boil and salt lightly. Drop in the peas and cook until tender, about 2 minutes. Rinse under cold water and set aside. Add the cauliflower to the vegetables. Add the sauce and simmer, uncovered, over low heat for 15 to 20 minutes.

Remove the lime leaves, stir in the peas, and cook just long enough to heat them through, 1 to 2 minutes. Add the cilantro and season with salt and pepper to taste. Add a pinch or two of cayenne for a spicier curry.

Yellow Curry Spices: *Be sure to measure the whole cloves carefully or they'll overpower the other spices. Store this sweet spice mixture in an airtight container and it will keep for weeks.*

MAKES ABOUT 5 TEASPOONS; ENOUGH FOR TWO CURRIES

1¼ teaspoons coriander seeds

1¼ teaspoons cumin seeds

¾ teaspoon allspice berries

¾ teaspoon anise seeds

½ teaspoon whole cloves

1½ teaspoons turmeric

Toast everything but the turmeric in a small skillet over medium-low heat until fragrant, 1 to 2 minutes. Add the turmeric and grind the spices to a fine powder in a spice mill or coffee grinder.

VARIATIONS: We vary the vegetables for this curry, depending on the time of year. Just about any combination of vegetables will do, as long they're cut to a similar size. Be careful to cook them evenly.

MAKE-AHEAD TIP: There are a number of steps you can do in advance to simplify the preparation. See Red Curry with Summer Vegetables and Thai Spices (page 196).

RESTAURANT TIPS: We often include pearl onions in the curry, in addition to the yellow onion. A 10-ounce bag or basket of pearl onions—yellow, red, or white—are just the right amount here. You can prepare them a day in advance.

Bring a small pot of water to a boil and drop in the onions for about 2 minutes. Drain and rinse under cold water. Trim away the onion tops and hairs at the stem end, leaving the base of the stem end intact, then peel. Add the onions to the curry, along with the yams and peppers.

You can also use little creamer potatoes instead of the large ones and roast them ahead of time, so they're already cooked and ready to add to the curry. Once they're cool, cut them in halves or quarters (depending on their size) and add them to the curry 5 to 10 minutes before serving.

Fall Vegetable Ragoût with White Beans

Starchy white beans and their flavorful broth are the soul of this fine ragoût. Cubes of butternut squash melt into the Roasted Tomatoes with ribbons of chard, salty black olives, and a surprising hint of toasted fennel seeds. Serve with thick slices of grilled rustic bread to sop up all the delicious juices. This dish can be made ahead; in fact, it's even better the second day.

SERVES 4 TO 6

½ cup cannellini beans, sorted and soaked overnight

6 cups cold water

1 bay leaf

2 fresh oregano sprigs

2 fresh thyme sprigs

3 tablespoons extra-virgin olive oil

Salt and pepper

Roasted Tomatoes (page 261), cut into large pieces, about 2 cups

1 small butternut squash, about 1½ pounds, cut into ¾-inch cubes, about 3 cups

1½ tablespoons minced garlic

1 large yellow onion, chopped, about 2 cups

1 medium fennel bulb, halved, cored, and cut into 1-inch pieces, about 1 cup

2 medium red or yellow peppers, cut into thick strips, then triangles, about 3 cups

1 teaspoon fennel seeds, toasted (page 214) and ground

¼ cup white wine

8 chard leaves, stems removed, washed and cut into thick ribbons, about 2 cups

1 tablespoon chopped fresh oregano

2 teaspoons chopped fresh thyme

10 Kalamata olives, pitted and coarsely chopped

Preheat the oven to 400°F.

Drain the beans and rinse them well. Place them in a large saucepan with the water, bay leaf, and herb sprigs and bring to a boil. Lower the heat and simmer, uncovered, about 1½ hours, until the beans are tender but still hold their shape. Remove the bay leaf and herb sprigs and season with 1 tablespoon of the oil, ½ teaspoon salt, and a pinch of pepper. Leave the beans in their broth and set aside.

While the beans are cooking, make the Roasted Tomatoes and roast the butternut squash. In a large baking dish, toss the squash with 1 tablespoon of the oil, ½ tablespoon of the garlic, ½ teaspoon salt, and a pinch of pepper. Roast until just tender, about 20 minutes. Set aside.

Heat the remaining oil in a large skillet and add the onions, ½ teaspoon salt, and a pinch of pepper. Sauté over medium heat until the onions begin to soften, 3 to 4 minutes. Add the remaining garlic and cook 1 minute more. Stir in the fennel, peppers, and ground fennel seeds and cook for about 5 minutes. Add the wine and cook until the pan is nearly dry, about 3 minutes. Add the beans and their broth; simmer over medium-low heat until they begin to break down and the sauce thickens, about 15 minutes. Add the squash, the Roasted Tomatoes, and chard and cook until the chard is tender, about 10 minutes. There should be plenty of broth in the pan. If not, add a little water to make the ragoût saucy. Stir in the fresh herbs and olives just before serving and season to taste with salt and pepper.

MAKE-AHEAD TIP: Cook the beans a day in advance and season them while they're still warm—that's when they soak up all the flavors. They keep beautifully in their broth. Prepare the vegetables up to a day ahead of time. Roast the butternut squash and the tomatoes. You can even pit the olives and toast the fennel seeds.

VARIATIONS: Try dinosaur kale in place of the chard, but it's best to parboil it for 2 to 3 minutes before adding it to the ragoût. If you're short on time, use high-quality canned fire-roasted tomatoes with their juice instead of Roasted Tomatoes. The intense tomato flavor will be missed, but the ragoût will still be delicious.

Winter Vegetable Ragoût with Portobello Mushrooms

Earthy mushroom stock is the essence of this rich, inviting ragoût. The Mushroom-Sherry Sauce will appear thin at first, but will thicken a bit as the roasted winter roots slowly simmer together and begin to break down. We add the portobellos at the last minute to keep them from discoloring the stew. Serve over grilled or creamy, soft polenta with a spoonful of crème fraîche.

SERVES 4 TO 6

Mushroom-Sherry Sauce (page 294), 1½ quarts

2 to 3 portobello mushrooms, about ¾ pound, stems removed

Garlic Oil (page 14)

Salt and pepper

1 large yellow onion, cut into 1-inch cubes, about 2 cups

2 large fennel bulbs, outer leaves and cores removed, cut into 1-inch cubes,
    about 2½ cups

1 small butternut squash, 1½ pounds, cut into 1-inch cubes, about 3 cups

1 to 2 rutabagas, about ¾ pound, peeled and cut into 1-inch cubes, about 2 cups

1 pound Yellow Finn potatoes, peeled and cut into 1-inch cubes, about 3 cups

8 chard leaves, stems removed, washed and cut into thick ribbons, about 2 cups

1 tablespoon chopped fresh herbs: flat-leaf parsley, thyme, oregano or marjoram,
    and sage

Crème Fraîche (page 98) for garnish (optional)

Make the Mushroom-Sherry Sauce and keep it warm over low heat.

Preheat the oven to 400°F.

Brush the portobellos generously with garlic oil and sprinkle with salt and pepper. Place them gill side up on a baking sheet and roast for 10 minutes. Use tongs to turn them over and roast another 10 minutes, until tender. When cool, cut the mushrooms in half, and then cut in thick slices. Set aside.

Toss the cubed vegetables in a large bowl with 2 tablespoons garlic oil, ¾ teaspoon salt, and a few pinches of pepper. Roast them on a baking sheet for 15 minutes. Use a spatula to turn and loosen them and roast until tender, about 15 minutes more.

Combine the roasted vegetables (do not add the mushrooms at this time) and the Mushroom-Sherry sauce in a deep sauté pan or Dutch oven and cook over medium-low heat for about 10 minutes. Add the chard and cook until tender, about 10 minutes more. Add the mushrooms and cook just long enough to heat them through. Just before serving, add the herbs and season to taste with salt and pepper. Add the crème fraîche if using.

TIP: The ragoût will thicken as it sits — thin with a little stock as needed.

MAKE-AHEAD TIP: Make the Mushroom Stock (page 112) in advance, freeze it and defrost when needed. You can also make the sauce a day ahead of time and roast the vegetables in advance.

VARIATION: Try roasting other root vegetables here, but don't overlook the butternut squash. Its superior flavor, texture, and warm, tawny color really make the ragoût.

Spring Vegetable Tagine

Saffron, ginger, and Ras el Hanout— a mixture of exotic Moroccan spices— blend magically into this North African vegetable and chick-pea stew. Little artichokes, fennel, and peas are especially tasty here, but you can vary the vegetables with the seasons. Serve on Almond-Cherry Couscous.

SERVES 4 TO 6

THE CHICK-PEAS

½ cup dried chick-peas, about ¼ pound, sorted and soaked overnight

6 cups cold water

1 bay leaf

3 coins of fresh ginger

One 3-inch cinnamon stick

Drain and rinse the chick-peas and place them in a large saucepan with the water, bay leaf, ginger, and cinnamon stick. Bring to a boil, lower the heat and simmer, uncovered, until completely tender, about 1½ hours. Set the beans aside to cool in their broth.

THE SAUCE

1 tablespoon Ras el Hanout (recipe follows)

Roasted Tomatoes (page 261), chopped, about 2 cups

1½ tablespoons extra-virgin olive oil

½ large yellow onion, coarsely chopped, about 1 cup

½ teaspoon salt

Pinch of cayenne pepper

1 medium red pepper, coarsely chopped, about 1 cup

1 tablespoon minced garlic

1 tablespoon grated fresh ginger

1 generous pinch of saffron threads, soaked in ¼ cup hot water

⅓ cup golden raisins

Make the Ras el Hanout. Make the Roasted Tomatoes.

Heat the oil in a large saucepan and add the onions, salt, and cayenne; cook over medium heat until the onions begin to soften, 2 to 3 minutes. Add the peppers, garlic, and ginger and cook until the peppers release their juices, about 4 minutes. Stir in the Ras el Hanout and cook

1 minute more. Add the saffron threads and their soaking liquid, along with the raisins and the Roasted Tomatoes. Simmer, uncovered, for 15 to 20 minutes. Puree in a blender and set aside.

THE STEW

6 ounces English peas, shelled, or frozen peas, about ½ cup

1½ tablespoons extra-virgin olive oil

½ large yellow onion, coarsely chopped, about 1 cup

Salt and cayenne pepper

¾ pound small artichokes, trimmed (page 178), cut in halves or quarters, about 1 cup

1 medium red pepper, cut into thick strips, then triangles, about 1 cup

1 medium fennel bulb, halved, cored, and cut into ½-inch-thick slices, about 1 cup

1 tablespoon minced garlic

1 tablespoon grated fresh ginger

¼ cup white wine

1 medium Yellow Finn potato, peeled and cut into ¾-inch cubes, about 1½ cups

1 carrot, peeled, cut in half and cut into ½-inch-thick slices on the diagonal, about 1 cup

¼ cup chopped cilantro

Bring a small pot of water to a boil and salt lightly. Drop in the peas and cook until just tender, 2 to 3 minutes. Drain, rinse under cold water, and set aside.

Heat the oil in a Dutch oven and add the onions, ½ teaspoon salt, and a pinch of cayenne. Cook over medium heat until soft, 3 to 4 minutes. Add the artichokes, peppers, fennel, garlic, ginger, and a pinch of salt and cayenne. Cook for 1 minute, add the wine, and cook until the pan is nearly dry, 3 to 4 minutes.

Remove the spices and bay leaf from the chick-peas. Add the chick-peas and their broth, the potatoes, and the carrots to the vegetables. Simmer, uncovered, for 10 minutes. Add the sauce and cook until the vegetables are tender, about 30 minutes.

Add the peas and cook until heated through. Stir in the cilantro and season to taste with salt and cayenne.

Ras el Hanout: *According to Paula Wolfert, in her* World of Food, *Ras el Hanout means "top of the shop." For "top of the shop" quality, be sure to use whole spices here and store the spice mixture in an airtight container. This makes enough spice mixture for two recipes of tagine.*

MAKES ABOUT 2 TABLESPOONS
1 teaspoon cumin seeds
1 teaspoon coriander seeds
1 teaspoon whole black peppercorns
5 whole cloves
15 allspice berries
1½ teaspoons ground cinnamon

Toast the cumin and coriander seeds in a dry skillet over medium-low heat until fragrant, 1 to 2 minutes. Combine everything but the cinnamon and grind the spices to a fine powder in a spice mill or coffee grinder. Add the cinnamon.

MAKE-AHEAD TIP: You can cook the chick-peas the day before. Just be sure to remove the spices and bay leaf from the broth before you refrigerate the chick-peas. Make the Ras el Hanout and Roasted Tomatoes a day or two ahead of time. You can always use high-quality fire-roasted canned tomatoes (we use Muir Glen organic) instead of roasting them, but their intense tomato flavor will be missed. Prepare the artichokes the day before, cover them with lemon water, and refrigerate.

Spring Stir-Fry with Peanut Sauce and Thai Basil

This quick and easy Asian stir-fry always sells out at Greens. The flavors of the peanut sauce are perfectly balanced with lots of ginger. Have all your ingredients ready so the vegetables stay vibrant and crisp. If Thai basil isn't available, use cilantro instead. Fresh pea shoots are a tasty addition; you can find them in Asian markets. Serve over Coconut Jasmine Rice.

SERVES 4 TO 6

Peanut Sauce (recipe follows), about 2 cups

Vegetable oil for frying

½ pound firm tofu, sliced ½ inch thick, brushed with 2 tablespoons of tamari or soy sauce

Salt and pepper

1½ tablespoons toasted sesame oil

3 scallions, white parts minced and green tops cut into 2-inch lengths on the diagonal

1 tablespoon grated fresh ginger

1 tablespoon minced garlic

2 medium carrots, cut in half lengthwise, thinly sliced on the diagonal, about 1 cup

1 large red pepper, cut into 1-inch thick strips, then into triangles, about 1 cup

½ pound asparagus, tough stalks removed, cut into 2-inch pieces on the diagonal, 1½ cups

¼ pound snow peas, trimmed and cut in half on the diagonal, about 1½ cups

20 Thai basil leaves, bundled and thinly sliced, or 3 tablespoons chopped cilantro

1 ounce fresh pea shoots, about 3 cups (optional)

Make the Peanut Sauce and set aside.

Pour a thin layer of oil in a skillet and heat it just below the point of smoking, until the first wisp of vapor appears. Fry the tofu until golden and crisp, 3 to 4 minutes per side. Drain the tofu on paper towels and sprinkle lightly with salt and pepper. When cool, cut into thin strips and toss with ¼ cup of the Peanut Sauce. Set aside.

Heat the sesame oil in a wok or large sauté pan over high heat and stir in the minced scallions, ginger, garlic, and ¼ teaspoon salt. Cook for 1 minute, stirring constantly. Lower the heat to medium-high and add the carrots, peppers, the scallion tops, and ¼ teaspoon salt. Cook for 2 minutes, add the asparagus, a couple of pinches of salt, and a little water. Cook until the asparagus is a vibrant green and just tender. Add the snow peas and cook 1 or 2 minutes more. The vegetables should be tender but firm. Add the remaining Peanut Sauce, the basil, and tofu and cook just long enough to heat the sauce. If using the pea shoots, toss them in at the last minute or arrange them on a platter and spoon the vegetables over.

Peanut Sauce: *This rich, silky sauce gets lighter and thinner when it's tossed into the hot pan with the vegetables and their juices. Be sure to use high-quality, nonhydrogenated peanut butter; it makes all the difference here.*

MAKES ABOUT 1 CUP

¼ cup smooth, natural peanut butter

¼ cup peanut oil

¼ cup light brown sugar, packed

2 tablespoons tamari or soy sauce

2 tablespoons water

½ tablespoon grated fresh ginger

½ teaspoon salt

Puree the ingredients in a blender until smooth.

211

New Mexican Border Stew

Make this homey stew in the early fall, when butternut squash comes into season and peppers are still at their peak. The vegetables simmer in a spicy sauce of tomatoes, plantain, ancho and chipotle chilies. Serve with Potato Gordas or over creamy, soft Polenta.

SERVES 6; MAKES ABOUT 2 QUARTS

PLANTAIN-CHILI SAUCE

1 tablespoon Ancho Chili Puree (page 147)

1 teaspoon Chipotle Puree (page 163)

1 cup water

½ ripe plantain, about ½ pound, diced, 1 cup

One 28-ounce can tomatoes, coarsely chopped, including the juice

1 teaspoon cumin seeds, toasted (page 214) and ground

½ teaspoon dried oregano, toasted (page 214)

Pinch of salt

Make the Ancho Chili Puree and the Chipotle Puree.

Bring the water to a boil in a large saucepan. Add the plantain, lower the heat, and simmer for 5 minutes. Add the remaining ingredients and cook over medium-low heat for about 20 minutes. Set aside.

THE STEW

1 medium butternut squash, 2½ to 3 pounds, cut into ¾-inch cubes, about 4 cups

2½ tablespoons olive oil

1 tablespoon minced garlic

Salt and pepper

1 large onion, chopped, about 2 cups

1 teaspoon cumin seeds, toasted (page 214) and ground

½ teaspoon dried oregano, toasted (page 214)

1 medium yellow or red pepper, cut into thick strips, then in triangles, about 1 cup

½ cup canned hominy, rinsed

2 medium zucchini, cut in half lengthwise and sliced ½ inch thick on the diagonal, 2 cups

1 cup water

Fresh lime juice

3 tablespoons chopped cilantro
Chipotle Puree (page 163)

Preheat the oven to 400°F.

Toss the squash in a large bowl with 1 tablespoon of the oil, ½ tablespoon of the garlic, ¼ teaspoon salt, and a pinch of pepper. Roast on a baking sheet for 10 minutes. Use a spatula to loosen and turn the squash and cook until tender, about 10 minutes more. Set aside.

Meanwhile, heat the remaining oil in a Dutch oven and add the onions, ¼ teaspoon salt, and a pinch of pepper. Cook until the onions begin to soften, about 3 minutes. Add the remaining garlic, the cumin, and oregano and cook for a minute or two. Add the peppers and cook for 3 to 4 minutes, adding a little water to keep the vegetables from sticking to the pan. Add the hominy, the sauce, the roasted butternut squash, the zucchini, water, ¼ teaspoon salt, and a pinch of pepper; lower the heat and cover the pan. Simmer until the flavors come together, about 20 minutes.

Add a squeeze of lime juice and the cilantro just before serving. Season to taste with salt, Chipotle Puree, and more lime juice, if needed.

TIPS: Be sure the plantain is ripe; otherwise, it won't be sweet. The one you want may not be the one you'd ordinarily choose. If it's really ripe, it will be soft, dark-skinned, and ugly.

We use water to thin the stew, but if you have leftover vegetable stock, by all means use it here.

Toasting and Grinding Herbs and Spices

Toasting herbs and whole spices brings their complex flavors and fragrance to life and takes only a few minutes; if you've never tried it before, you'll be amazed at the difference it makes. A small, heavy-bottomed skillet and an electric coffee grinder (page 370) are the tools you need. Whether you're toasting whole cumin seeds, mustard seeds, dried oregano, or fenugreek, there are a few key things to keep in mind: Always use a dry skillet and toast most herbs and spices separately, unless they're of similar size. Stay at the stove and don't let your attention stray; toasted herbs and spices hold on to their heat and can incinerate in the blink of an eye. You can toast and grind herbs and spices ahead of time; just allow them to cool completely, then store in an airtight container.

Heat the herb or spice in a dry skillet over very low heat, shaking the pan as needed, until their fragrance intensifies and the color begins to turn—a minute or two, sometimes three, depending on the herb or spice. When it smells toasty, remove from the heat, and allow to cool in the skillet. Grind to a powder and transfer to an airtight container. If it's toasted a little too long and has begun to turn dark, all is not lost if you move quickly—transfer it to a cool surface.

Baked in
a Casserole

Asparagus Bread Pudding *We feature this delightful dish—*
inspired by Georgeanne Brennan's recipe— in late spring, when the local asparagus season is under way. Of course, you can use all kinds of vegetables and cheeses, depending on the time of year. Remember, the flavor and texture of the bread makes all the difference— we use day-old ciabatta or sourdough Italian.

SERVES 6 TO 8

1 pound rustic bread, crust removed, cut into ½-inch-thick slices

1½ cups milk

1 cup heavy cream

6 large eggs

¾ teaspoon salt

Pinch of pepper

1 pound asparagus, tough stem ends removed, cut into 2-inch pieces

¼ pound Fontina cheese, grated, about 1 cup

3 ounces Parmesan cheese, grated, about 1 cup

¼ cup chopped mixed herbs: thyme, oregano or marjoram, chives, and flat-leaf parsley

Place the bread in a large shallow dish and pour the milk over. Set aside to soak until the milk is mostly absorbed, about 35 minutes.

Preheat the oven to 350°F.

Bring a medium-size pot of water to a boil and lightly salt it.

Butter a 2-quart soufflé or square baking dish and set aside. Combine the cream, eggs, salt, and pepper in a medium-size bowl and whisk together. Set the custard aside.

Drop the asparagus in the boiling water and cook until just tender, 1 to 2 minutes. Drain and rinse under cold water. Set aside to drain.

Combine the cheeses in a small bowl. Place one-third of the soaked bread in the bottom of the soufflé or baking dish. Place half of the asparagus over, sprinkle with one-third of the cheese mixture, and half of the herbs. Layer half of the remaining bread over, cover with the rest of the asparagus, half of the remaining cheese, and the rest of the herbs. Cover with the last of the bread and the cheese. Pour the custard over the top. Bake until golden, about 1 hour. Check for doneness with a skewer or paring knife; the custard should be set and the tester should come out clean.

Corn Pudding

Make this simple, satisfying pudding when corn is tender and sweet. We use locally made St. George cheddar, but any aged white cheddar will do. Fresh basil is especially tasty with the corn and creamy cheddar, but parsley, chives, and cilantro are also good. You can even include diced fresh jalapeños or Fire-Roasted Poblano Chilies if you like heat.

We wait for the pudding to cool down a bit before cutting it, then serve each piece on a bed of peppery greens— watercress, curly cress, ancho cress, or arugula— with a sprinkling of little cherry tomato halves tossed with a sharp red wine vinaigrette.

SERVES 6 TO 8

Garlic Bread Crumbs (page 219), about ½ cup

6 ears of corn, shaved, about 6 cups

1 cup milk

1 cup heavy cream

6 large eggs

¼ pound good-quality, white cheddar cheese, grated, about 1 cup

1 tablespoon chopped basil

½ teaspoon salt

Pinch of pepper

Make the Garlic Bread Crumbs.

Preheat the oven to 350°F.

Butter a 2-quart, square baking dish and sprinkle with the Garlic Bread Crumbs.

Reserve 1 cup of corn kernels and set aside. Puree the remaining corn and milk in a blender until smooth. Transfer to a large bowl and whisk in the cream, eggs, cheese, reserved corn, basil, salt, and pepper. Pour into the prepared baking dish. Place it in a large baking pan and add enough hot water to come halfway up the sides of the dish. Bake until puffed and golden, about 1 hour. Let cool a bit before slicing.

Macaroni and Cheese

This knockout version of the great American classic is full of rich flavors and definitely qualifies as comfort food. We steep the milk and cream with garlic and fresh herbs and thicken it ever so slightly so it coats the pasta nicely. Good, aged white cheddar is the essential ingredient here, so be sure to use it. Crunchy garlic bread crumbs add just the right texture. Serve with a refreshing salad of watercress, crisp apples, slivers of fennel, and Cider Vinaigrette.

SERVES 6 TO 8

Garlic Bread Crumbs (see box), about 1 cup

1 quart milk

½ cup heavy cream

½ large yellow onion, chopped, about 1 cup

2 garlic cloves, smashed with the flat side of a knife, skin left on

3 parsley sprigs

2 fresh oregano or marjoram sprigs

2 fresh thyme sprigs

2 to 3 fresh sage leaves

2 tablespoons unsalted butter

2 tablespoons all-purpose flour

1 tablespoon Dijon mustard

Salt and pepper

½ pound penne

½ pound aged white cheddar cheese, grated, about 2 cups

2 ounces Parmesan cheese, grated, about ⅔ cup

¼ cup chopped chives

Make the Garlic Bread Crumbs and set aside.

Combine the milk, cream, onions, garlic, and herb sprigs and leaves in a large, heavy-bottomed saucepan and bring to a simmer. Cook over medium-low heat for 15 minutes. Set aside to steep for 15 minutes. Pour through a strainer and return to the pan.

Melt the butter in a heavy-bottomed saucepan, whisk in the flour to make the roux, and cook over medium-low heat for 2 to 3 minutes. Slowly whisk 1 cup of the seasoned milk into the roux to make a paste. Add the remaining milk, 1 cup at a time, until all the milk has been incorporated. Continue to cook—still whisking—over medium-low heat for about 5 minutes. The sauce will be just slightly thickened. Season with the Dijon, ¼ teaspoon salt, and a pinch of pepper.

Preheat the oven to 375°F. Butter a 2-quart baking dish.

Bring a large pot of water to a boil and salt lightly. Drop in the penne and cook until al dente, about 8 minutes. (It should be slightly undercooked to allow for baking time.) Drain the penne and place in a large bowl. Pour the sauce over and toss in the cheeses and all but 1 tablespoon of the chives. Season to taste with salt and pepper.

Pour the pasta mixture into the baking dish, making sure to include all of the sauce. Sprinkle with the garlic bread crumbs and bake until golden and bubbling, about 40 minutes. Sprinkle with the remaining chives and serve.

MAKE-AHEAD TIP: Cook the pasta a day ahead of time and toss it with a little oil to keep it from sticking together. Steep the milk and make the sauce. Make the Garlic Bread Crumbs and grate the cheese. When you're ready to bake, just assemble the ingredients in the baking dish and pop it in the oven.

Garlic Bread Crumbs

These tasty morsels of toasted bread add crunch and delicious garlic flavor to bubbling gratins and pastas. Tossed with Fontina, toasted pine nuts, and lemon zest, they make a sumptuous stuffed artichoke filling. We like the coarse crumb of crusty breads—levain, ciabatta, and sourdough Italian—but just about any leftover bread will do. Trim off the crusts or not; it's up to you.

Preheat the oven to 325°F. Cut the bread into thin slices and place on a baking sheet; brush with garlic oil, generously or lightly, as you like. Bake until golden and very crisp, about 15 minutes. Allow to cool. Break up the bread with your hands and pulse in a food processor, leaving the texture a little coarse. Serve right away or store for a few days in a sealed container in the refrigerator. Bread crumbs keep indefinitely in the freezer, but you'll need to crisp them for a few minutes in a 325°F oven before using.

Potato and Green Garlic Gratin

This simple gratin is one of the joys of early spring. We take full advantage of tender garlic shoots by steeping their tops in the cream and sautéing the white parts. Starchy Yellow Finns soak up the garlic-infused cream.

The taste of green garlic varies with the age and the size of the shoots and we never know how intense it will be. A little goes a long way, but if you're a true garlic lover, you can always use more. If green garlic isn't available, use the Roasted Garlic Variation.

SERVES 6 TO 8

2 to 3 shoots green garlic, about ¼ pound (or see Roasted Garlic Variation)

1 cup milk

1 cup heavy cream

½ teaspoon black peppercorns

4 flat-leaf parsley sprigs

2 fresh thyme sprigs

1 fresh oregano or marjoram sprig

1 bay leaf

1½ tablespoons olive oil

Salt and pepper

2 pounds large Yellow Finn or Yukon Gold potatoes

¼ pound Gruyère cheese, grated, about 1⅓ cups

2 tablespoons chopped chives

1 ounce Parmesan cheese, grated, about ⅓ cup

Trim off the base of the garlic shoots and discard. Thinly slice the white parts until you have ½ cup; set aside. (If there's extra garlic, save it for another dish.) Roughly chop the tops until you have ½ cup. In a small heavy-bottomed saucepan, combine the milk and cream with the garlic tops, peppercorns, herb sprigs, and bay leaf. Bring to a simmer and cook over medium-low heat for 5 minutes. Remove the pan from the heat and set aside to steep for 30 minutes.

Preheat the oven to 375°F.

Heat the oil in a small skillet and add the sliced garlic, ¼ teaspoon salt, and a pinch of pepper. Cook over medium heat until soft, about 3 minutes, adding a little water if needed to keep the garlic from sticking to the pan.

Butter a 2-quart, square baking dish. With a mandoline or sharp knife, thinly slice the potatoes. Lay one-quarter of them in the bottom of the dish, overlapping the slices and rows as you go. Sprinkle with salt and pepper, half the Gruyère, and 1 tablespoon of the chives. Continue with another layer of potatoes, sprinkle with salt and pepper, and spread the garlic on top. Make another layer of potatoes, sprinkle with salt and pepper, the remaining Gruyère, and the chives. Make the final layer of potatoes and sprinkle with salt and pepper. Strain the cream and pour it over the top. Cover the dish and bake for 45 to 50 minutes. Uncover, and use a spoon to push the potatoes under the cream. (The gratin will cook more quickly and evenly if you do this a couple of times during the baking.) Sprinkle the Parmesan over and bake, uncovered, until golden brown and bubbling, about 20 minutes. Allow the gratin to set for a few minutes before you cut it.

ROASTED GARLIC VARIATION: If green garlic isn't available, use a combination of roasted garlic and sautéed onions or leeks in its place. Roast a head of garlic (page 145) until it's very soft, squeeze it out of the skin, and add it to the cream and steep, as directed. When you strain the cream, use a spoon to push the garlic through the strainer, so you don't miss a bit of its flavor. Thinly slice an onion or a couple of leeks and sauté in olive oil with a few cloves of chopped garlic, salt, and pepper. Divide the onions in half and spread them over two of the potato layers. Layer the rest of the ingredients as directed and bake.

Butternut Squash Gratin

This rustic gratin is the perfect beginning to a simple autumn supper. It's also a great choice for a holiday meal because you can make it ahead and bake it at the last minute.

SERVES 4 TO 6

Parmesan Bread Crumbs (recipe follows), about ½ cup

1 large butternut squash, about 2½ pounds, cut into ¾-inch cubes, 5 to 6 cups

2 teaspoons minced garlic

2 tablespoons unsalted butter, melted

1 tablespoon all-purpose flour

½ teaspoon salt

Freshly ground pepper

½ cup half-and-half

Preheat the oven to 375°F.

Make the Parmesan Bread Crumbs and set aside.

Place the squash in a large bowl and toss with the garlic, butter, flour, salt, and a couple of pinches of pepper. Butter a small baking dish and spoon the mixture into it. Pour the half-and-half over, cover, and bake for 30 minutes. Sprinkle the Parmesan bread crumbs over the top and continue to bake, uncovered, until golden brown and crisp, about 15 minutes. Test for doneness with a paring knife or skewer; the squash should be completely tender. Let the gratin sit for a few minutes before serving.

TIP: Butternut squash loses its moisture toward the end of its season, so if you're making the gratin in late winter, increase the half-and-half to ¾ cup.

Parmesan Bread Crumbs

MAKES ABOUT ½ CUP

1½ tablespoons unsalted butter

½ cup bread crumbs

1 ounce Parmesan cheese, grated, about ⅓ cup

Melt the butter in a small skillet; add the bread crumbs and toast over medium heat until golden, 3 to 4 minutes. Cool and toss in a small bowl with the cheese.

Polenta Gratin with Fire-Roasted Poblano Chilies and Roasted Garlic

Don't be scared off by this recipe; it's much easier to make than it first appears. With the exception of the Polenta and the Fire-Roasted Poblano Chilies, this is an oven-roasted dish and you can do all the roasting at the same time. Once that's done, you have the ingredients for the gratin as well as the smooth, spicy sauce.

SERVES 6 TO 8

Polenta (page 280)
Roasted Tomatoes (page 261), about 2 cups
1 each red and yellow pepper, roasted and peeled (page 291)
24 whole garlic cloves, peeled, 2 to 3 heads
3 tablespoons olive oil
Salt and pepper
Fire-Roasted Poblano Chilies (page 64)
1 or 2 tablespoons Ancho Chili Puree (page 147)
⅓ cup chopped cilantro
2 ounces aged white cheddar cheese, grated, about ½ cup
1 ounce dry jack cheese, grated, about ⅓ cup

223

Preheat the oven to 400°F.

Make the Polenta and cut into triangles as directed.

Make the Roasted Tomatoes. Roast the peppers.

Toss the garlic with the oil in a small baking dish and sprinkle lightly with salt and pepper. Cover and roast until tender, 20 to 25 minutes. When cool, pour off the oil and reserve it for the sauce. Place the garlic in a medium-size bowl and set aside.

While the vegetables are roasting, make the Fire-Roasted Poblano Chilies and the Ancho Chili Puree.

To make the sauce, puree half of the tomatoes in a blender with the reserved garlic oil, half a roasted red pepper, 3 of the garlic cloves, 1 tablespoon of the ancho chili puree, and ½ teaspoon salt until smooth. Season to taste with ancho chili puree.

Coarsely chop the remaining tomatoes and add to the garlic. Slice the chilies and remaining peppers in thin strips and toss into the tomatoes, along with 3 tablespoons of the cilantro and a pinch or two of salt and pepper.

Lower the oven temperature to 375°F.

Pour the sauce into the bottom of a 9- by 13-inch baking dish. Arrange the polenta triangles upright in rows across the width of the dish, overlapping them slightly. Spoon the vegetable mixture between the triangles. Combine the cheeses and sprinkle over the top, tucking it into the vegetables as you go. Cover and bake for 25 minutes. Remove the cover and bake 10 to 15 minutes more, until bubbling. Sprinkle with the remaining cilantro and serve.

MAKE-AHEAD TIP: Make the polenta a day in advance and cut into triangles. Roast the Fire-Roasted Poblano Chilies and the vegetables ahead of time. You can even make the sauce and grate the cheese.

VARIATION: If dry jack cheese isn't available, use smoked cheese instead or skip it altogether and increase the cheddar to 3 ounces.

Winter Root Vegetable Gratin

Winter root vegetables star in this hearty, satisfying gratin. We layer celery root and rutabagas with leeks and Yellow Finn potatoes and bake them in an herbaceous cream. You can use all kinds of root vegetables here— turnips, parsnips, and sunchokes are equally delicious. Give the gratin plenty of time to bake, and you'll be rewarded when you pull it, tender and bubbling, from the oven.

SERVES 6 TO 8

2 large leeks, roots trimmed

1 cup milk

1 cup heavy cream

2 garlic cloves, smashed with the flat side of a knife, skin left on

1 teaspoon coriander seeds, toasted (page 214)

½ teaspoon black peppercorns

6 flat-leaf parsley sprigs

3 to 4 fresh thyme sprigs

2 fresh oregano or marjoram sprigs

5 fresh sage leaves

1 bay leaf

1 tablespoon unsalted butter

1 tablespoon olive oil

Salt and pepper

1 tablespoon minced garlic

¼ cup white wine

1½ tablespoons chopped fresh herbs: flat-leaf parsley, sage, and thyme

1 large rutabaga, about ¾ pound

1 large celery root, about 1 pound

2 ounces Parmesan cheese, grated, about ⅔ cup

3 ounces Fontina cheese, grated, about ¾ cup

1¼ pounds Yellow Finn or Yukon Gold potatoes

1 heaping tablespoon all-purpose flour

Preheat the oven to 375°F.

Trim the green tops from the leeks. Coarsely chop 1 cup of the tops, wash them well, and drain. Cut the white part of the leeks in half lengthwise and thinly slice them. You should have about 2 cups. Wash well and drain.

In a small, heavy-bottomed saucepan, combine the milk and cream with the leek tops, whole garlic, coriander, peppercorns, herb sprigs and leaves, and bay leaf. Bring to a simmer and cook over medium-low heat for 5 minutes. Set aside to steep for 30 minutes. Strain the cream.

Heat the butter and oil in a small skillet and add the leeks, ¼ teaspoon salt, and a pinch of pepper. Cook over medium heat until soft, about 3 minutes; add the garlic and cook for 1 minute. Add the wine and cook until the pan is nearly dry, about 3 minutes. Transfer to a bowl and mix in the herbs.

Bring a medium-size pot of water to a boil and salt lightly. Peel and quarter the rutabaga and celery root. Use a vegetable slicer or sharp knife to thinly slice them, keeping them in separate piles. Drop the rutabaga into the pot and cook until just tender, 2 to 3 minutes. Using a strainer, scoop out the rutabaga, rinse under cold water, and drain. Repeat with the celery root.

Combine the cheeses and set aside.

Butter a 2-quart baking dish. Thinly slice the potatoes and lay one-third of them in the bottom of the dish, overlapping the slices and rows as you go. Sprinkle with salt and pepper, half of the flour, and spread half of the leeks on top. Layer on the rutabaga and sprinkle with one-third of the cheese. Follow with half of the remaining potatoes, sprinkle with salt and pepper, and the rest of the flour. Spread the remaining leeks over, layer on the celery root, and follow with one-third of the cheese. Layer on the last of the potatoes, sprinkle with salt and pepper, and pour the cream over.

Cover the dish and bake for 45 minutes. Uncover, press the potatoes down with a spoon, and continue to bake, uncovered, until completely tender, 15 to 20 minutes more. Test for doneness with a paring knife or skewer. Sprinkle the rest of the cheese on top and return to the oven until golden on top, about 5 minutes more. Let the gratin sit for a few minutes before serving. It will soak up any excess cream as it begins to cool.

TIP: Parboiling the rutabagas and celery root ahead of time ensures that they'll cook evenly with the starchy potatoes. It also removes some of their acidity, which helps keep the cream from separating as the gratin bakes. Sprinkling a little flour over the layers of vegetables also stabilizes the cream.

Artichoke and Portobello Mushroom Lasagne

Braised artichokes, delicate leeks, and meaty roasted portobello mushrooms are layered between sheets of fresh pasta in this excellent lasagne. Tomato-Zinfandel Sauce, creamy Asiago, and a smooth layer of fresh ricotta finish the dish.

SERVES 8

Tomato-Zinfandel Sauce (page 295)

Roasted Portobello Mushrooms (page 260), cut in half and thinly sliced, about 1½ cups

2 tablespoons extra-virgin olive oil

2 large leeks, white parts only, cut in half lengthwise, thinly sliced and washed, about 3 cups

Salt and pepper

½ tablespoon minced garlic

2 pounds small artichokes, trimmed (page 178) and cut in half, about 3 cups

¼ cup white wine

1 cup water

1 tablespoon chopped fresh herbs: flat-leaf parsley, oregano or marjoram, and thyme

1 pound whole-milk ricotta cheese, about 2 cups

2 large eggs

5 ounces Parmesan cheese, grated, about 1¼ cups

2 or 3 pinches of freshly grated nutmeg

¼ pound Asiago cheese, grated, about 1 cup

1 pound fresh pasta sheets

Make the Tomato-Zinfandel Sauce and the Roasted Portobello Mushrooms.

Heat the oil in a large sauté pan and add the leeks, ½ teaspoon salt, and a pinch of pepper. Sauté over medium heat until wilted, about 3 minutes. Add the garlic and the artichokes and cook for about 4 minutes. Add the wine and cook until the pan is nearly dry, about 3 minutes. Add the water and simmer, uncovered, until the artichokes are tender and the pan is nearly dry, about 10 minutes. Add the portobellos and the herbs, and set aside.

Preheat the oven to 350°F.

Combine the ricotta, eggs, ¼ cup of the Parmesan, the nutmeg, ¼ teaspoon salt, and a pinch of pepper in a bowl and whisk together. Combine the remaining Parmesan with the Asiago, reserving ¼ cup to sprinkle on top during baking.

Spread 1½ cups of the sauce in the bottom of a 9- by 13-inch baking dish and cover with a layer of pasta. Pour another cup of sauce over the pasta, followed by half the artichoke mixture. Sprinkle with half the mixed cheeses and another layer of pasta. Spread the ricotta mixture evenly over the pasta and cover with another layer of pasta. Spread 1 cup of the sauce over, followed by the remaining artichoke mixture and cheeses, and the final layer of pasta. Top with 1½ cups of sauce, cover, and bake for 35 minutes. Sprinkle with the reserved cheeses and bake, uncovered, until set, 10 to 15 minutes.

VARIATION: If Asiago isn't available, you can use Fontina or Gruyère.

MAKE-AHEAD TIP: Prepare and braise the artichokes a day or two in advance. You can roast the mushrooms and sauté the leeks ahead of time; just be sure to adjust the seasonings before you assemble the lasagne. By all means, make the Tomato-Zinfandel Sauce well in advance and take it from the freezer.

Roasted Winter Vegetable Lasagne

This rustic, well-loved lasagne boasts parsnips, butternut squash, and celery root. If you roast the vegetables and make the Tomato-Zinfandel Sauce ahead of time, you'll be amazed by how quick this is to assemble. We toss the vegetables with roasted garlic puree, but you can also use whole cloves of roasted garlic instead.

SERVES 8

Tomato-Zinfandel Sauce (page 295)

2 to 3 tablespoons Roasted Garlic Puree (page 145)

1 large yellow onion, diced, about 2 cups

½ pound parsnips, peeled and cut into ½-inch cubes, about 1½ cups

1 pound butternut squash, cut into ½-inch cubes, about 2 cups

1 pound celery root, peeled and cut into ½-inch cubes, about 2 cups

2 tablespoons extra-virgin olive oil

½ tablespoon minced garlic

Salt and pepper

1 tablespoon chopped fresh herbs: flat-leaf parsley, oregano or marjoram, and thyme

1 pound whole-milk ricotta cheese, about 2 cups

2 large eggs, beaten

5 ounces Parmesan cheese, grated, about 1½ cups

2 or 3 pinches of freshly grated nutmeg

¼ pound Gruyère cheese, grated, about 1 cup

1 pound fresh pasta sheets

Make the Tomato-Zinfandel Sauce and set aside.

Make the Roasted Garlic Puree. Preheat the oven to 400°F.

Toss the vegetables in a large bowl with the olive oil, minced garlic, ½ teaspoon salt, and a pinch of pepper. Spread the vegetables on two baking sheets and roast for 10 minutes. Use a spatula to loosen and turn them and cook until golden and tender, about 10 minutes more. Set aside to cool.

Lower the heat to 350°F.

Transfer the vegetables to a bowl and toss with the garlic puree and the herbs.

Whisk the ricotta, eggs, ¼ cup of the Parmesan, the nutmeg, ¼ teaspoon salt, and a pinch of pepper together in a medium-size bowl. Combine the remaining Parmesan with the Gruyère, reserving ¼ cup to sprinkle on top during baking.

Spread 1½ cups of the sauce in the bottom of a 9- by 13-inch baking dish and cover with a layer of pasta. Pour another cup of sauce over the pasta, followed by half the vegetable mixture. Sprinkle with half the mixed cheeses and another layer of pasta. Spread the ricotta mixture over the pasta and cover with another pasta sheet. Spread 1 cup of the sauce over, followed by the remaining vegetables and cheeses, and the final layer of pasta. Top with 1½ cups of sauce, cover, and bake for 35 minutes.

Sprinkle with the reserved cheeses and bake, uncovered, until set, 10 to 15 minutes more.

VARIATION: This is a great place to try different combinations of root vegetables and use up leftover odds and ends—turnips, rutabagas, and Yellow Finn potatoes are just a few of the possibilities.

Pasta and Risotto

Fusilli Col Bucco with Grilled Tomatoes, Gorgonzola, and Pine Nuts

This long spiral pasta looks just like a telephone cord and wraps itself around the grilled tomatoes and catches every bit of the creamy Gorgonzola, basil, and sweet tomato juices. You'll find fusilli col bucco at specialty markets. If it isn't available, try spaghettini, fusilli, or penne instead. Be sure to use your good, fruity olive oil here; its flavor won't be lost on these ingredients.

SERVES 4 TO 6

Grilled Tomatoes (see box), about 3 cups

½ pound fusilli col bucco or penne

¼ cup extra-virgin olive oil

1 tablespoon minced garlic

Salt and pepper

2 to 3 ounces Gorgonzola cheese, about ⅓ cup

¼ cup pine nuts, toasted (page 46)

20 fresh basil leaves, bundled and thinly sliced, about ¼ cup

Grated Parmesan cheese

Prepare the Grilled Tomatoes and set aside.

Bring a large pot of water to a boil and salt lightly. Drop in the pasta and cook until tender, 12 to 14 minutes.

While the pasta is cooking, heat the oil in a large sauté pan and add the garlic, tomatoes, ½ teaspoon salt, and a pinch of pepper. Cook over medium-low heat for 3 to 4 minutes. Drain the pasta and add it to the pan. Add half of the Gorgonzola and cook about 1 minute, tossing gently to coat the pasta.

Just before serving, toss in the pine nuts, the basil, and the remaining Gorgonzola. Sprinkle with Parmesan at the table.

MAKE-AHEAD TIP: To speed up the preparation, grill the tomatoes and cook the pasta in advance. Toss the pasta with a little oil to keep it from sticking together.

VARIATIONS: For a delicious addition, toss a handful of little cherry tomatoes into the pan and cook about 1 minute, just long enough to heat through. If you don't have time to make grilled tomatoes, use 2 pounds of fresh, ripe tomatoes and remove their seeds before you cut them into large pieces. Try combining golden and red tomatoes in this dish.

Grilled Tomatoes

This is a great way to use juicy summer tomatoes that are simply too ripe for a salad. We grill them until their skins blister and char, then we chop them—skins and all—and use them for a fiery salsa, rustic pasta sauce, or crostini spread. If your tomatoes are flavorful, don't add much seasoning—a little olive oil, fresh herbs, or chilies are all you'll need.

MAKES ABOUT 3 CUPS

2 pounds flavorful ripe tomatoes
Extra-virgin olive oil
Salt and pepper

Prepare the grill.

Core the tomatoes, coat them lightly with oil, and sprinkle with salt and pepper. Place them on a medium-hot grill and cook, using metal tongs to turn them, until the skin is charred. The flesh will be soft and juicy, but still firm in the center. Chop when cool, making sure to include the juice. You should have about 3 cups altogether.

TIP: The tomatoes will keep in the freezer in plastic freezer bags for at least a month.

Linguine with Summer Beans, Gremolata, and Olives

The fresh taste of gremolata— minced flat-leaf parsley, lemon zest, and garlic— adds zip to this summer pasta, and green beans and yellow wax beans are especially beautiful. The cooking time varies with each variety, so be sure to cook them separately. You can use Kalamata or little Niçoise olives instead of Gaeta as long as you don't use too many— ⅓ cup pitted and coarsely chopped is all you'll need. Toss in the olives just before serving to keep the colors bright.

SERVES 4 TO 6

Gremolata (recipe follows)

¾ pound summer beans, preferably Blue Lake, and yellow wax beans, stem ends trimmed, cut in half on the diagonal

¾ pound fresh linguine

¼ cup extra-virgin olive oil

½ teaspoon minced garlic

Salt and pepper

1 tablespoon fresh lemon juice

20 Gaeta olives, pitted and coarsely chopped, about ⅓ cup (see headnote)

1 ounce Parmesan cheese, grated, about ⅓ cup, plus more to serve at the table

Make the Gremolata and set aside.

Bring a large pot of water to a boil and salt lightly. Drop in the beans, one variety at a time, and cook until tender, 2 to 3 minutes depending on their size. Scoop out the beans, rinse under cold water, and set aside to drain.

Drop the pasta into the water and cook until just tender, 2 to 3 minutes.

While the pasta is cooking, heat 1 tablespoon of the oil in a large sauté pan and add the beans, the garlic, ¼ teaspoon salt, and a pinch of pepper. Sauté over medium heat for 1 minute. Add 1 cup of the pasta cooking water to the pan, along with the lemon juice, the gremolata, the remaining oil, ¼ teaspoon salt, and a pinch of pepper. Drain the pasta, add it to the pan, and cook for 1 minute, tossing it gently to coat with the gremolata and the sauce. Toss in the olives and the cheese at the last minute. Serve with freshly grated Parmesan.

Gremolata: This intense, fresh condiment adds a bright touch to our pastas and vegetable dishes. You can make it an hour or two in advance, but not much more or it will lose its freshness.

¼ cup finely chopped flat-leaf parsley
1½ tablespoons minced lemon zest
3 garlic cloves, minced

Mix everything together in a small bowl.

TIP: Have everything ready before you cook the pasta. You can use dried pasta instead and cook it ahead of time, if you like. Be sure to rinse it under cold water and toss it with a little olive oil to keep it from sticking together.

Pappardelle with Spring Vegetables and Lemon Cream

This lovely spring pasta celebrates green: asparagus, English peas, and fava beans are tossed with wide noodles and a rich lemon-infused cream. We steep the cream with lemon rind to intensify the flavor. If Meyer lemons are available, by all means use them here. You can substitute spring onions or leeks for the shallots. If you're short on time, skip the peas and fava beans and simply go with the asparagus. A sprinkling of chive blossoms adds a beautiful touch.

SERVES 4 TO 6

2 lemons

1 cup heavy cream

Salt and pepper

½ pound fava beans, shelled, about ¾ cup

½ pound asparagus, tough stem ends removed, cut into 2-inch pieces on the diagonal, about 1 cup

½ pound English peas, shelled, about ½ cup

1½ tablespoons olive oil

3 large shallots, sliced, about ½ cup

2 teaspoons minced garlic

¼ cup white wine

¾ pound fresh pappardelle

1 ounce Parmesan cheese, grated, about ⅓ cup, plus more to serve at the table

Chive blossoms (optional)

Use a sharp knife or vegetable peeler to remove three wide strips of rind from one of the lemons. Combine in a small saucepan with the cream and a pinch each of salt and pepper. Bring the cream to a simmer over medium heat, remove from the heat, and steep for 30 minutes. Strain the cream.

Bring a large pot of water to a boil and salt lightly.

Use a zester to remove threads from the remaining lemon, keeping the threads as long as possible. You should have about ¼ cup; place them in a small bowl. Squeeze the juice of ½ lemon; you should have about 1½ tablespoons. Scoop enough hot water from the pot to cover the lemon threads and allow them to soak for 30 seconds. Drain and set aside.

Drop the fava beans into the pot and cook for 1 to 2 minutes. Scoop them out and rinse under cold water, then slip them out of their skins. Drop in the asparagus and the peas separately, cooking them until just tender and still bright green: allow 2 to 3 minutes for the asparagus and 1½ to 2 minutes for the peas. Rinse them under cold water and drain.

Heat the oil in a large sauté pan and add the shallots, ¼ teaspoon salt, and a pinch of pepper. Cook over medium heat until the shallots begin to soften, 2 to 3 minutes; add the garlic, and cook 1 minute more. Add the wine and 1 tablespoon of the lemon juice and cook until the pan is nearly dry, about 3 minutes.

Meanwhile, drop the pasta into the boiling water and cook until just tender, about 3 minutes. Just before you drain the pasta, scoop out ½ cup of the pasta cooking liquid, and add it to the sauté pan. Drain the pasta. Add the cream to the sauté pan and cook for 1 to 2 minutes. Add the pasta, the vegetables, the lemon threads, the remaining lemon juice, ¼ teaspoon salt, and a pinch of pepper. Gently toss everything together to coat with the sauce and cook for a minute or two to heat the vegetables through. Remove from the heat, toss in the Parmesan, and season to taste with salt and pepper. Sprinkle with the chive blossoms, if using, and serve with freshly grated Parmesan.

TIP: If you don't have a zester, peel wide strips of rind with a vegetable peeler and cut them into skinny strips.

MAKE-AHEAD TIP: Shell the English peas and fava beans and steep the cream. You can even blanch the fava beans and slip them out of their skins a few hours in advance.

Spinach Tagliarini with Corn, Cherry Tomatoes, and Basil

Tender kernels of corn and tasty little cherry tomatoes are an inspired combination in this simple summer pasta. Cut the cherry tomatoes in half; their acidic juices balance the richness of the creamy sauce. The fresh spinach noodles really absorb all the flavors. To take this dish over the top, try aged white cheddar instead of the Parmesan.

SERVES 4 TO 6

1 tablespoon olive oil

2 tablespoons unsalted butter

2 large shallots, diced, about ⅓ cup

1 teaspoon minced garlic

Salt and pepper

2 ears of corn, shaved, about 2 cups kernels

¼ cup water

½ pound fresh spinach tagliarini

¾ cup heavy cream

1½ cups ripe, little cherry tomatoes, cut in half

1 ounce Parmesan cheese, grated, about ⅓ cup, plus more to serve at the table

⅓ cup chopped fresh basil, about 30 leaves

Bring a large pot of water to a boil and salt lightly.

Heat the oil and butter in a large sauté pan and add the shallots, garlic, ¼ teaspoon salt, and a pinch of pepper. Cook over medium heat until the shallots begin to soften, about 3 minutes. Stir in the corn and water, lower the heat, and simmer until the corn is tender, about 5 minutes.

Drop the pasta into the boiling water and cook until just tender, 2 to 3 minutes. Meanwhile, add 1 cup of the pasta cooking water to the corn mixture along with the cream, ½ teaspoon salt, and a pinch of pepper. Turn the heat to medium high and cook for 1 minute to reduce the cream. Drain the pasta, add it to the pan, and lower the heat. Toss in the cherry tomatoes, the cheese, and half the basil and cook until the cherry tomatoes are heated through. Serve the pasta and garnish with Parmesan and the remaining basil.

Pasta and White Beans with Roasted Garlic, Rainbow Chard, and Olives

The succulent flavor of whole cloves of roasted garlic and their roasting oil make this a memorable fall and winter pasta. To speed up the preparation, roast the tomatoes, onions, and garlic at the same time; you can even roast them in advance. If rainbow chard isn't available, use red or green chard instead. Be sure to include the chard stems for their good taste and crunchy texture.

SERVES 6 GENEROUSLY

½ cup white emergo or cannellini beans, sorted and soaked overnight

8 cups cold water

1 bay leaf

2 fresh thyme sprigs

2 fresh oregano sprigs

3 fresh sage leaves

Roasted Tomatoes (page 261), about 2 cups, chopped into large pieces

1 large yellow onion, sliced into ½-inch-thick rings

Extra-virgin olive oil

Salt and pepper

24 whole garlic cloves, peeled, about 2 heads

¼ pound penne

1 bunch of rainbow chard, about 1½ pounds with stems

20 Gaeta olives, pitted and coarsely chopped, about ⅓ cup

½ tablespoon chopped fresh herbs: oregano or marjoram, sage, and thyme

Grated Parmesan cheese

239

Preheat the oven to 400°F.

Rinse and drain the beans. Combine the beans, water, bay leaf, and the herb sprigs and leaves in a saucepan and bring to a boil. Lower the heat and simmer, uncovered, until the beans are tender but still hold their shape, about 1½ hours.

While the beans are cooking, make the Roasted Tomatoes.

Arrange the onions on a baking sheet, brush with a little of the oil, and sprinkle with salt and pepper. Roast for 10 minutes, turn them over, and roast until tender, about 15 minutes more. When cool, chop in large pieces.

Meanwhile, toss the garlic with ½ cup of the oil in a small baking dish and sprinkle lightly with salt and pepper. Cover and bake until tender, about 25 minutes. Pour off the roasted garlic oil and set aside. You should have about ½ cup.

Bring a large pot of water to a boil and salt lightly. Drop in the penne and cook until just tender, about 8 minutes. Drain and rinse under cold water.

Remove the bay leaf and herb sprigs and leaves from the beans and season them with 1 tablespoon of the roasted garlic oil, ½ teaspoon salt, and a pinch of pepper.

Tear the chard leaves away from the stems, wash, and drain. Bundle the leaves and cut into thick ribbons. Trim the stems, remove the strings, and slice on the diagonal about ¼ inch thick. You should have 6 to 8 cups of leaves and 1 heaping cup of stems.

Heat 1 tablespoon of the roasted garlic oil in a Dutch oven. Add the chard stems, a pinch each of salt and pepper, and cook over medium-heat until tender, about 3 minutes. Stir in the onions, the chard leaves, and a pinch each of salt and pepper. Lower the heat and add the beans and their broth, tomatoes, garlic, penne, and the remaining roasted garlic oil. Cook over medium-low heat until the broth is slightly thickened, 8 to 10 minutes.

Toss in the olives and the herbs, and season to taste with salt and pepper. Serve in warm bowls and pass the Parmesan at the table.

Orecchiette with Broccoli Rabe, Almonds, and Manchego

Toasted almonds and the rich, distinctive taste of Manchego are flavors you'll remember in this classic pasta. The orecchiette is a little tricky; be sure these "little pigs' ears" are cooked all the way through. When the cooked orecchiette hits the sauce, it gives off starch, slightly thickening the liquid, and catches the flecks of hot pepper. We like spring onions here, but you can use leeks or thinly sliced onions instead. Try pecorino pepato or dry jack cheese as a substitute for the Manchego.

SERVES 4 TO 6

1 large bunch of broccoli rabe, about ¾ pound

½ pound orecchiette

¼ cup extra-virgin olive oil

½ pound spring onions, sliced, about 2 cups

Salt and pepper

½ tablespoon minced garlic

Red pepper flakes

¼ cup unskinned almonds, toasted (page 46) and chopped

¼ pound Manchego cheese, grated, about 1 cup

Bring 2 large pots of water to a boil and salt lightly.

Trim the tough lower stems from the broccoli rabe and discard them. Chop the tops into 2-inch pieces; you should have about 8 cups of florets and stems. Drop the broccoli rabe into one of the pots and cook until tender, 2 to 3 minutes. Drain in a colander, rinse under cold water, and set aside.

Drop the orecchiette into the boiling water and cook until tender, 12 to 15 minutes. While the pasta is cooking, heat 2 tablespoons of the oil in a large sauté pan and add the onions, ½ teaspoon salt, and a pinch of pepper. Cook over medium heat until wilted, 2 to 3 minutes, add the garlic, and cook 1 minute more. Add 1½ cups of the pasta cooking water to the onions, along with the broccoli rabe, the remaining oil, ¼ teaspoon red pepper flakes, ¼ teaspoon salt, and a pinch of pepper.

Drain the pasta, add the pasta to the sauté pan, and cook for 1 to 2 minutes, tossing it gently to coat with the sauce. There will be a lot of liquid at first, but the pasta will absorb it. Toss in a pinch of red pepper flakes, the almonds, and half of the cheese and season to taste with salt and additional red pepper flakes.

Divide the pasta into warm bowls and sprinkle with the remaining Manchego.

Italian Sprouting Broccoli

Also known as *broccoli di ciccio,* this delightful Bay Area newcomer produces little side shoots of broccoli, which are incredibly tender and sweet; there are no tough stems to discard. Organically grown and available at farmers' markets, *broccoli di ciccio* turns up on the menus of those Bay Area restaurants lucky enough to find it. Sauté the shoots for just a minute or two in olive oil with garlic and red pepper flakes or toasted almonds and it's ready to serve. Toss it into a stir-fry or include in pasta with Garlic Bread Crumbs, fruity olive oil, and Parmesan cheese.

Linguine with Arugula, Sun-Dried Tomatoes, and Ricotta Salata

This pasta is fiendishly simple, particularly if you cook the linguine ahead of time. Just be sure to toss in the arugula at the very last minute; it wilts in the blink of an eye. Little bites of the crumbled salty ricotta salata cheese (which is just salted ricotta, drained and formed into cheese) coat the pasta and mingle with toasted pine nuts and sun-dried tomatoes.

SERVES 4 TO 6

½ pound dried linguine

¼ cup extra-virgin olive oil

6 large shallots, sliced, about 1 cup

½ tablespoon minced garlic

12 oil-packed sun-dried tomato halves, thinly sliced, about ½ cup

¼ cup white wine

3 large handfuls of arugula, 4 to 6 cups leaves

¼ pound ricotta salata cheese, crumbled, about 1 cup

1 tablespoon chopped fresh herbs: flat-leaf parsley, oregano or marjoram, and thyme

⅓ cup pine nuts, toasted (page 46)

Grated Parmesan cheese

Bring a large pot of water to a boil and salt lightly. Drop in the pasta and cook until just tender, about 10 minutes.

While the pasta is cooking, heat 3 tablespoons of the oil in a large sauté pan and add the shallots, ½ teaspoon salt, and a pinch of pepper. Cook over medium heat until softened, 3 to 4 minutes; add the garlic and the sun-dried tomatoes and cook for 1 minute more. Add the wine and cook until the pan is nearly dry, about 3 minutes.

Just before you drain the pasta, scoop 1½ cups of the pasta cooking water from the pot and add it to the sauté pan. Drain the pasta and add it to the pan along with the remaining oil, ¼ teaspoon salt, and a pinch of pepper. Cook for 1 minute to reduce the liquid. Toss in the arugula, half of the ricotta salata, the herbs, and the pine nuts and cook just long enough to wilt the arugula, about 30 seconds. Season with salt and pepper to taste.

Serve the pasta in warm bowls and garnish with the remaining ricotta salata cheese. Pass the Parmesan at the table.

Penne with Roasted Butternut Squash, Brown Butter, and Sage

Nutty brown butter coats tender cubes of butternut squash, toasted walnuts, and pungent sage in this hearty fall and winter pasta. We use the pasta's cooking water to make the sauce, but you can use vegetable stock instead. Roast the squash and cook the pasta ahead of time and this earthy, satisfying dish comes together in a snap. If you can find penne made with farro, it will be delicious in this dish. Look for it in Italian specialty stores.

SERVES 4 TO 6

Brown Butter (recipe follows)

1 pound butternut squash, cut into ½-inch cubes, about 2½ cups

2 tablespoons olive oil

2 teaspoons minced garlic

1½ tablespoons chopped fresh sage

Salt and pepper

½ pound penne

6 large shallots, thinly sliced, about 1 cup

¼ cup white wine

⅓ cup walnut pieces, toasted (page 46) and chopped

Grated Parmesan cheese

Make the Brown Butter.

Preheat the oven to 400°F.

Toss the squash in a baking dish with 1 tablespoon of the oil, the garlic, ½ tablespoon of the sage, ½ teaspoon salt, and a pinch of pepper. Roast until tender, about 20 minutes, and set aside.

Bring a large pot of water to a boil and salt lightly. Drop in the penne and cook until tender, about 10 minutes. While the pasta is cooking, heat the remaining oil in a large sauté pan and add the shallots, ¼ teaspoon salt, and a pinch of pepper. Cook over medium heat until the shallots begin to soften, about 3 minutes. Add the wine and cook until the pan is nearly dry, about 3 minutes.

Just before you drain the pasta, add 1 cup of the pasta cooking water to the shallots, along with the squash, the brown butter, ¼ teaspoon salt, and a pinch of pepper. Drain the pasta and add it to the pan. Cook over medium heat for 1 or 2 minutes. Toss in the walnuts and the remaining sage and season to taste with salt and pepper. Serve with freshly grated Parmesan.

Brown Butter: A little of this versatile butter goes a long way. It's great to have on hand to enrich a quick leftover pasta or to toss with roasted winter roots or wilted greens. Be sure to use unsalted butter here, or its sweetness will be lost to salt. Keep an eye on it in the last minute or two of cooking, so it doesn't turn too dark. The butter should be a rich amber color when you remove it from the heat.

MAKES ABOUT ⅓ CUP

¼ pound unsalted butter

Heat the butter in a small heavy-bottomed saucepan over medium-low heat. As the butter simmers, the milk solids will settle to the bottom of the pan, coloring the butter as it cooks. When it turns a deep golden color, after 8 to 10 minutes, strain through a cheesecloth lined sieve or a coffee filter. The butter can be used immediately or cooled and refrigerated in an airtight container.

VARIATION: A handful of spinach leaves or ribbons of rainbow chard or dinosaur kale are delicious additions. The spinach can be tossed in at the last minute, but chard or kale will take longer to cook. If using chard, add it to the pan after the wine has reduced and cook for 3 to 4 minutes before you toss in the pasta. If you're using kale, it's best to boil it until completely tender, about 5 minutes, and add it to the pan along with the pasta.

Udon with Miso, Shiitake Mushrooms, and Bok Choy

For this saucy Asian noodle dish, we make a Quick Asian Stock and whisk in just enough miso to give it depth and richness. Assertive red miso is our favorite here, but you can also use mild, sweet yellow miso or a combination of the two. The udon noodles release their starches and add body to the steamy miso broth. Use fresh or dried udon or big, fat Shanghai noodles if they're available— buckwheat soba is also delicious.

SERVES 4

Quick Asian Stock (recipe follows), about 3 cups

½ pound firm tofu, sliced ½ inch thick

Tamari or soy sauce

Vegetable oil for frying

Salt and pepper

2 heads baby bok choy or 1 large head bok choy

¼ pound shiitake mushrooms, stemmed and cut into wedges, about 2 cups

1 medium carrot, peeled and cut into matchsticks, about 1½ cups

1 tablespoon grated fresh ginger

½ tablespoon minced garlic

½ pound fresh or dried udon

1 tablespoon toasted sesame oil

2 to 3 scallions, both white and green parts, sliced on the diagonal, about ½ cup

Red pepper flakes

1½ tablespoons red miso

2 to 3 tablespoons chopped cilantro

1 teaspoon sesame seeds, toasted (page 46), for garnish

Make the Asian Quick Stock and keep it warm over low heat.

Brush the tofu with tamari. Pour a thin layer of vegetable oil in a skillet and heat it just below the point of smoking, until the first wisp of vapor appears. Fry the tofu until golden and crisp, 3 to 4 minutes per side. Drain the tofu on paper towels and sprinkle lightly with salt and pepper. When cool enough to handle, cut into thin strips.

Trim the stem end off the bok choy and remove the bruised outer leaves. Cut the head in quarters and trim away the inner core to separate the leaves. Cut the larger leaves lengthwise through the stem, leaving the small, inner leaves whole; you should have 4 to 6 cups. Set aside.

Bring a large pot of water to a boil and salt lightly.

Heat 2 tablespoons of vegetable oil in a wok or large sauté pan over medium-high heat and add the shiitakes and ¼ teaspoon salt. Cook for 2 minutes, stirring constantly, adding a little stock as needed to keep them from sticking to the pan. Add the carrots, ginger, garlic, a pinch of salt, and up to ½ cup of the stock. Lower the heat to medium and cook until the vegetables are just tender, about 5 minutes.

Meanwhile cook the udon noodles as directed on the package until tender. Drain and toss with the sesame oil.

Add the bok choy to the vegetables and cook until just wilted, 2 to 3 minutes. Toss in the noodles, the scallions, the tofu, and a pinch of red pepper flakes.

Place the miso in a small bowl and whisk in ½ cup of the stock until smooth. Then whisk the miso into the stock and pour over the noodles. Toss in the cilantro and cook everything together for 1 to 2 minutes, until heated through. Serve in warm bowls sprinkled lightly with sesame seeds.

Quick Asian Stock: *Fresh ginger, kombu (dried seaweed), and dried shiitake mushrooms give this stock its robust flavor. Like all vegetable stocks, this freezes well.*

MAKES ABOUT 3 CUPS

4 to 6 scallions, both white and green parts, or ½ large yellow onion, chopped, about 1 cup

1 large carrot, peeled and chopped, about 1½ cups

1 large potato, chopped, about 1½ cups

6 coins of fresh ginger

2 to 3 garlic cloves, smashed with the flat side of a knife, skin left on

Two 2-inch pieces of kombu

½ ounce dried shiitake mushrooms

A handful of cilantro stems

½ teaspoon salt

1 tablespoon tamari or soy sauce

6 cups cold water

Combine all of the ingredients in a large saucepan and bring to a boil. Lower the heat and simmer, uncovered, for 30 minutes. Pour the stock through a strainer and discard the vegetables. Return the stock to the pot, bring it to a boil, and reduce it to 3 cups.

MAKE-AHEAD TIP: Make the Quick Asian Stock in advance, freeze it, and defrost when needed. Cook the noodles a few hours ahead of time. Just be sure to rinse them under cold water and toss them with the toasted sesame oil to keep them from sticking together. You can also prepare the vegetables, fry the tofu, and toast the sesame seeds in advance.

VARIATION: The crisp stems of bok choy have a fresh taste and crunchy texture, but you can use pak choi or other Asian greens instead.

Risotto with Asparagus, Morels, and Parmigiano-Reggiano

There's a magical time in the late spring when the local asparagus and morels first appear in the markets— that's when we make this elegant risotto. These woodsy wild mushrooms may be pricey, but a quarter pound is all you need; their intense, haunting flavor is perfect with the asparagus and the saucy rice. This is the place for a fine Parmigiano-Reggiano.

SERVES 4 TO 6

Vegetable Stock (page 110), about 6 cups

½ pound asparagus, tough stem ends removed, sliced on the diagonal into 1-inch pieces, about 2 cups

1 tablespoon olive oil

4 tablespoons (½ stick) unsalted butter

1½ tablespoons minced garlic

¼ pound fresh morel mushrooms, cut in half if large, about 2 cups (see Variation)

Salt and pepper

½ cup white wine

2 medium leeks, white parts only, cut in half lengthwise, sliced and washed, about 2 cups

½ pound Carnaroli or Arborio rice, about 1 cup

2 tablespoons chopped fresh herbs: flat-leaf parsley, thyme, oregano or marjoram, and chives

3 ounces Parmigiano-Reggiano cheese, grated, about 1 cup, plus more to serve at the table

Make the Vegetable Stock and keep it warm over low heat.

Bring a medium-size pot of water to a boil and salt lightly. Drop in the asparagus and cook until just tender, about 2 minutes. Rinse under cold water and drain.

Heat the oil and 1 tablespoon of the butter in a deep sauté pan and add ½ tablespoon of the garlic, the morels, ¼ teaspoon salt, and a pinch of pepper. Cook over medium heat until the mushrooms are tender, about 5 minutes. Add half the wine and cook until the pan is nearly dry, about 3 minutes. Transfer the mushrooms to a bowl.

Heat 2 tablespoons of the butter in the pan and add the leeks, ½ teaspoon salt, the remaining garlic, and a pinch of pepper; cook until the leeks are soft, about 3 minutes. Add the rice and cook for 1 to 2 minutes, stirring constantly. Add the stock 1 cup at a time, stirring gently, allowing the rice to absorb each cup before adding more. After the rice has absorbed 2 cups of stock, add the remaining wine, lower the heat to medium-low and cook, continuing to add the stock 1 cup at a time, until the rice is tender. The grains of rice should be a little toothy and the risotto quite saucy.

Add the remaining butter, the morels, the asparagus, and half the herbs, and cook until the vegetables are heated through, 1 to 2 minutes. Stir in half the cheese and season to taste with salt and pepper. Serve in warm bowls and sprinkle with the remaining cheese and herbs.

VARIATION: If morels aren't available, you can use grilled or roasted portobello mushrooms instead. Thinly slice the caps and stir them into the risotto at the last minute to keep them from discoloring the rice. For a beautiful presentation, loosely arrange the mushrooms on top of each serving, then sprinkle with the herbs and cheese.

TIP: If the morels are dirty, use a pastry brush to clean them.

Risotto the Restaurant Way

The best risotto is made with flavorful stock and cooked slowly and gently, allowing the grains to plump gradually. After 40 to 45 minutes of attentive stirring, and adding the stock a cup at a time, the rice is tender and saucy and ready to serve. Since it's too much to ask our customers to wait 45 minutes for risotto, we've found another delicious way to make it. Here's how we do it:

We take it to the final stage of cooking, just to the point of adding the vegetables, the butter and cheese, and the last of the stock. Then, we remove the pan from the heat, spread the risotto on a baking sheet, and allow it to cool in the refrigerator. When the time comes, we finish each serving of risotto in a small sauté pan, adding a little stock at first to moisten and warm it. We then add the final ingredients, the last of the stock (or as needed), and cook over medium heat, stirring constantly, until it's perfectly cooked.

This is a wonderful technique for the busy home cook who loves risotto, but can't imagine serving it at a dinner party or special gathering. You can even keep the rice in the refrigerator overnight, as long as it's tightly covered. The texture of the rice will suffer a little, but it will still be very tasty. Try it the next time you're having a party.

Summer Risotto with Tomatoes, Mascarpone, and Basil

Make this risotto when summer's tomatoes are juicy, sweet, and ripe. This dish is about simple flavors, so use the best ingredients you can find. We toss the tomatoes with fruity olive oil and basil and add them at the last minute, so they hold their shape and keep their skins.

SERVES 4 TO 6

Vegetable Stock (page 110), about 6 cups

¾ pint ripe, little cherry tomatoes, about 1½ cups, cut in half

½ pound flavorful ripe tomatoes, cored, seeded, and cut into large pieces, about 1 cup

3 tablespoons extra-virgin olive oil

30 to 40 basil leaves, bundled together and cut into thin ribbons, about ½ cup

Salt and pepper

2 tablespoons unsalted butter

2 medium leeks, white parts only, cut in half lengthwise, sliced, and washed, about 2 cups

1 tablespoon minced garlic

½ pound Carnaroli or Arborio rice, about 1 cup

⅓ cup white wine

¼ cup mascarpone cheese

½ ounce Parmigiano-Reggiano cheese, grated, 2 to 3 tablespoons, plus more to garnish

Make the Vegetable Stock and keep it warm over low heat.

Toss all the tomatoes together in a mixing bowl with 2 tablespoons of the oil and 2 tablespoons of the basil. Season with ¼ teaspoon salt, a pinch of pepper, and set aside.

Heat the butter and the remaining oil in a large sauté pan and stir in the leeks, the garlic, ½ teaspoon salt, and a pinch of pepper. Cook over medium heat until the leeks are soft, about 3 minutes. Add the rice and cook for 1 to 2 minutes, stirring constantly. Add the stock 1 cup at a time, stirring gently, allowing the rice to absorb each cup before adding more. After the rice has absorbed 2 cups of stock, add the wine, lower the heat to medium low, and cook, continuing to add the stock 1 cup at a time, until the rice is tender. The grains of rice should be a little toothy and the risotto quite saucy.

Add the cheeses, the tomatoes, and ¼ cup of the basil and cook until the tomatoes are just heated through. Adjust the seasoning with salt and pepper. Garnish each serving with a little Parmigiano-Reggiano and the remaining basil.

VARIATION: You can make this risotto without the mascarpone; just increase the butter to 3 or 4 tablespoons and add a little extra Parmesan.

Risotto with Roasted Butternut Squash and Kale

This comforting fall risotto has tender cubes of roasted butternut squash, Fontina cheese, and hearty kale. A sprinkling of freshly grated nutmeg makes all the difference in the flavor, so be sure to include it. You can use any variety of kale, but dark green dinosaur kale is especially good.

SERVES 6 GENEROUSLY

Vegetable Stock (page 110), 7 to 8 cups

1 small butternut squash, cut into ½-inch cubes, about 2 cups

2 tablespoons olive oil

2 teaspoons minced garlic

Salt and pepper

½ bunch of kale, stems removed, about 2 cups packed leaves

2 tablespoons unsalted butter

3 medium leeks, white parts only, cut in half lengthwise, sliced, and washed, about 3 cups

1½ cups Carnaroli or Arborio rice

½ cup white wine

A pinch or two of freshly grated nutmeg

2 ounces Fontina cheese, grated, about ½ cup

½ ounce Parmesan cheese, grated, 2 to 3 tablespoons, plus more to garnish

Make the Vegetable Stock and keep it warm over low heat. Preheat the oven to 400°F.

Toss the squash in a baking dish with 1 tablespoon of the oil, half of the garlic, ¼ teaspoon salt, and a pinch of pepper. Roast until tender, about 20 minutes.

Bring a pot of water to a boil and salt lightly. Drop in the kale and cook until tender, 3 to 4 minutes. Drain and when cool, squeeze out any excess moisture. Coarsely chop the kale and set aside.

Heat the butter and the remaining oil in a large sauté pan and add the leeks, ¼ teaspoon salt, and a pinch of pepper. Cook over medium heat until the leeks begin to soften, about 2 minutes; add the remaining garlic and cook 1 minute more. Add the rice and cook for 1 to 2 minutes, stirring constantly. Add the stock, 1 cup at a time, stirring gently, allowing the rice to absorb each cup before adding more.

After the rice has absorbed 4 cups of stock, stir in the wine, the squash, and the kale. Lower the heat to medium low and cook, continuing to add the stock 1 cup at a time, until the rice is tender and the squash is beginning to break down. The grains of rice should be a little toothy and the risotto quite saucy. Add a pinch of nutmeg, and stir in the cheeses. Adjust the seasoning with salt, pepper, and nutmeg to taste. Serve in warm bowls and sprinkle with the Parmesan.

TIP: There's a delicious recipe for Butternut Squash Risotto Griddle Cakes (page 179) to use any leftovers.

Roasted and Stuffed Vegetables

Roasted Butternut Squash Rounds with Sage Leaves

This simple fall dish is a delightful alternative to roasted potatoes. The deep orange rounds of squash caramelize as they roast in the oven, releasing their natural sweetness. The squash rounds look beautiful arranged on a rustic platter or smothered with Rainbow Chard with Pumpkin Seeds.
It's a perfect savory holiday side dish, quick and easy to prepare.

SERVES 4 TO 6

Two butternut squash with long necks
1 tablespoon Garlic Oil (page 14)
10 to 15 sage leaves, chopped, about 2 tablespoons
Salt and pepper

Preheat the oven to 400°F.

Cut the squash at the base of the neck, reserving the bulbous part with the seeds for another dish. Remove the stem and skin of the neck and cut into ¾-inch-thick rounds. You should have about 12 slices.

Lay the squash slices on a baking sheet. Brush both sides of the slices with garlic oil and sprinkle with the sage and a little salt and pepper. Roast for 15 minutes, then use a spatula to loosen the rounds. Cook another 5 minutes, until the squash is tender and the color vibrant. Serve warm.

TIP: Be sure to select butternut squash with slender, long necks—you'll be using just the necks—and save the bulbs and seeds for a soup or ragoût.

Glazed Cipollini Onions

These Italian disk-shaped onions are great for roasting. They slowly caramelize in their juices and their sweet-and-sour flavor— with a surprising hint of cinnamon— is addictive. They keep well, so make them a day or two ahead. Serve warm or at room temperature.

Cipollini onions are available at farmers' markets and specialty produce stores. If you can't find them, use regular red or yellow onions. Just cut into quarters and keep the stem ends intact so they hold together as they roast.

SERVES 4 TO 6

1 pound cipollini onions, peeled

1 tablespoon olive oil

½ teaspoon salt

1 tablespoon light brown sugar

One 3-inch cinnamon stick

½ cup water

2 tablespoons balsamic vinegar

1 tablespoon Champagne vinegar

Preheat the oven to 400°F.

Toss everything together in a small baking dish. Cover and roast for 20 minutes, and give the onions a stir. Roast, uncovered, until they're tender and caramelized, about 20 minutes more. Stir to coat the onions with the caramelized juices. Spoon a little of the juice over each serving.

Crisp Sliced Potatoes with Garlic and Fresh Thyme

These satisfying, oven-roasted gems have the allure of fried potatoes without the excess oil. Choose large, firm Yellow Finns or Yukon Golds and don't cut them too thin or they'll dry out in the oven. Sprigs of fresh thyme leave their imprint on each slice, giving this humble dish a lovely, warm presentation. They're best served right away.

SERVES 4 TO 6

2 pounds large Yellow Finn or Yukon Gold potatoes
2 tablespoons Garlic Oil (page 14)
Salt and pepper
Fresh thyme sprigs

Preheat the oven to 400°F.

Cut the potatoes into slices about ¾ inch thick and discard the rounded end pieces. Place the slices in a single layer on an oiled baking sheet, brush with garlic oil, and sprinkle generously with salt and pepper. Lay 2 or 3 small thyme sprigs on each slice. Roast for 15 minutes, flip them over, and roast until puffy and golden, about 15 minutes more. Arrange on a platter with the thyme sprigs facing up. Serve immediately.

VARIATION: Include some purple Peruvian potatoes for a striking contrast of colors. You can also try whole sage leaves or small sprigs of rosemary instead of the thyme.

Gingered Yams

This festive make-ahead dish adds a lively element to the holiday table. We feature it each year at Thanksgiving. All the traditional seasonings are here, with fresh ginger to heighten the flavors. The yams keep well, covered, in a warm oven (250°F); they also reheat beautifully.

SERVES 4 TO 6

2 pounds Garnet yams or sweet potatoes

1 teaspoon grated fresh ginger

2 tablespoons maple syrup

1 tablespoon light brown sugar

3 tablespoons unsalted butter

Salt and pepper

Preheat the oven to 375°F.

Prick the yams in several places with a fork, place in a baking dish, and roast until they're completely tender when pierced with a skewer or paring knife, about 30 minutes.

When cool enough to handle, peel the yams and place them in a large bowl. Use a potato masher to mash the yams with the ginger, maple syrup, sugar, and butter. Season with salt and pepper to taste and serve.

Roasted Portobello Mushrooms

This humble supermarket mushroom has all the quality of its fancy cousins foraged in the wild. We brush the caps with garlic oil and roast them until their big gills open and juices bubble. Once cool, they're ready to stuff, slice, or chop.

Here are a few of the ways we use them: tossed into wilted greens or mixed into risotto or a hearty ragoût. We also like to layer them with roasted peppers, pickled red onions, and arugula on a toasted roll slathered with Basil Aïoli.

½ pound portobello mushrooms, 2 or 3 caps
Garlic Oil (page 14)
Salt and pepper

Preheat the oven to 400°F.

Remove the mushroom stems. Brush both sides of the mushroom caps generously with garlic oil and sprinkle with salt and pepper. Roast the mushrooms, gill side up, on a baking sheet for 10 minutes. Use metal tongs to turn them over and roast until tender, about 10 minutes more.

Roasted Tomatoes

Roasted tomatoes have a rich, lusty flavor that adds depth and complexity to many of our soups, stews, and vegetable fillings. These tomatoes are versatile and can be made ahead; they take just about an hour from beginning to end. The tomatoes keep well for up to a week, so double the recipe and save extra to spoon over grilled bread, leftover pasta, or risotto.

MAKES 2 CUPS

2 pounds plum tomatoes
Extra-virgin olive oil
Salt and pepper
Fresh herbs: 4 sage leaves and 4 to 5 thyme sprigs

Preheat the oven to 400°F.

Core the tomatoes, cut them in half crosswise, and place them cut side down on a parchment-lined baking sheet. Brush lightly with olive oil and sprinkle with salt, pepper, and the herbs. Roast until their skin is blistered and the flesh is very soft, about 45 minutes. When cool enough to handle, remove their skins, if they slip off easily. Otherwise, leave them on. Use immediately or store in a sealed container in the refrigerator for up to a week—be sure to include the sweet roasting juices.

TIP: Use parchment paper here. Line your baking sheet with it to save time—and your baking sheet—when cleaning up.

Mashed Yellow Finn Potatoes

When we mash potatoes, we use the very best. Our mashing favorites are: Yellow Finns for their creamy texture and unbeatable richness, and German Butterballs for their remarkable, deep golden color. If you can't find either one, good old Yukon Golds will do fine.

Ours is a classic recipe and on the simple side. Of course, you can add fresh herbs and Parmesan cheese, or substitute buttermilk for a tangy taste and lower fat. Or go in the other direction and add a little luxurious mascarpone.

SERVES 4 TO 6

2 pounds Yellow Finn potatoes
½ cup heavy cream
2 tablespoons unsalted butter
Salt and pepper

Peel the potatoes, place in a large pot, and cover with cold water. (If they're large, cut into halves or quarters to speed up the cooking time.) Bring to a boil, lower the heat, and simmer until completely tender, 25 to 30 minutes. Drain and use a potato masher to work in the cream, butter, and ½ teaspoon salt. Season to taste with salt and pepper and serve hot.

GARLIC VARIATIONS

Roasted Garlic: Add 2 to 3 tablespoons Roasted Garlic Puree (page 145) to the potatoes along with the cream, butter, and salt and pepper.

Green Garlic: Trim off the top and base of 1 or 2 shoots of green garlic and thinly slice the white part. Sauté in a little butter or olive oil with a pinch of salt and pepper until tender. Puree with a little of the potato cooking liquid and add to the potatoes, along with the cream, butter, and salt and pepper.

TIP: Save the potato cooking water for a quick and easy soup stock.

Roasted Portobello Mushrooms Filled with Winter Vegetables and Fontina

This deeply flavored dish appears on our menu throughout the year, and we vary the vegetables with the seasons. The portobello caps are roasted and heaped with a savory filling of mushrooms, fennel, peppers, leeks, and a little sun-dried tomatoes. The creamy Fontina and crunchy Garlic Bread Crumbs add the right flavor and texture. For a hearty, satisfying meal, serve with Mushroom-Sherry Sauce and Mashed Yellow Finn Potatoes.

SERVES 4

½ cup Garlic Bread Crumbs (page 219)

4 large portobello mushrooms, about 1 pound, stems removed

Garlic Oil (page 14)

Salt and pepper

2 tablespoons extra-virgin olive oil

½ pound white mushrooms, quartered, about 2 cups

1 tablespoon minced garlic

¼ cup white wine

2 medium leeks, white part only, cut in half lengthwise, sliced and washed, about 2 cups

1 fennel bulb, halved, cored, and outer leaves removed, cut into large dice, about 1 cup

1 large red pepper, cut into large dice, about 1½ cups

6 oil-packed sun-dried tomatoes, diced, about ¼ cup

2 tablespoons chopped fresh herbs: flat-leaf parsley, chives, thyme, and oregano

2 ounces Fontina cheese, grated, about ½ cup

½ ounce Parmesan cheese, grated, 2 to 3 tablespoons

Make the Garlic Bread Crumbs.

Preheat the oven to 400°F.

Brush the mushrooms with garlic oil, sprinkle lightly with salt and pepper, and place them gill side up on a baking sheet. Roast for about 10 minutes, turn them over, and roast until tender, about 10 minutes more.

Lower the heat to 375°F.

Heat 1 tablespoon of the oil in a large sauté pan and add the quartered white mushrooms, half of the garlic, ¼ teaspoon salt, and a pinch of pepper. Sauté over high heat until the mushrooms are tender and golden, about 5 minutes, adding a little water if needed to keep them from sticking to the pan. Add the wine to deglaze and cook until the pan is nearly dry. Transfer to a bowl.

Return the pan to the heat with the remaining oil and add the leeks, the remaining garlic, ¼ teaspoon salt, and a pinch of pepper. Sauté over medium heat until the leeks are wilted, about 3 minutes. Stir in the fennel and red pepper and cook until tender, 3 to 4 minutes more. Add the mushrooms and the sun-dried tomatoes and cook everything together for 5 minutes. Transfer to a bowl and set aside to cool. Add the herbs, the Fontina, and the Parmesan to the vegetables.

Heap the filling in the mushroom caps, firmly cupping the top to make a dome. Place them in a lightly oiled baking dish. Sprinkle the garlic bread crumbs over the mushrooms. Bake until the filling is heated through and the top is crisp and golden, 15 to 20 minutes.

SUMMER VARIATION: In summer, use grilled or roasted onions and summer squash instead of the leeks and fennel. You can also use Roasted Tomatoes in place of sun-dried tomatoes. Almost any flavorful cheese works; Asiago or Manchego are particularly delicious.

Anaheim Chilies Filled with Corn, Cheddar, and Cilantro

The mild heat and long, tapered shape of Anaheim chilies make them ideal for stuffing. At the restaurant, we grill them directly over an open flame until their skins blister and char, then let them steam in their own heat so they're easy to peel.

We season the corn filling with jalapeños, but you can use a serrano or other chilies instead. Just be sure their fiery heat doesn't overpower the sweet, fresh taste of the corn. Serve with Fire-Roasted Salsa.

SERVES 4

4 Anaheim chilies, about 1 pound
½ tablespoon olive or vegetable oil
½ medium yellow onion, diced, about ½ cup
Salt and pepper
2 ears of corn, shaved, about 2 cups kernels
1 or 2 jalapeño chilies, seeded and diced
¼ cup water
1 tablespoon coarsely chopped cilantro
2 ounces white cheddar cheese, grated, about ½ cup

Grill the Anaheim chilies directly over the flame, using metal tongs to turn them until the skin is blistered and charred. Transfer to a bowl, and cover; the chilies will steam as they cool.

Preheat the oven to 375°F. Lightly oil the baking dish.

Heat the olive oil in a sauté pan and add the onions, ¼ teaspoon salt, and a pinch of pepper. Sauté over medium heat until the onions begin to soften, about 3 minutes. Add the corn, jalapeño, and water. Cover and cook over low heat until the corn is tender, about 5 minutes. Set aside to cool.

Peel the Anaheim chilies, carefully removing the skin around the stems as you go. Make a lengthwise slit in each chili and remove the seeds. Sprinkle lightly with salt.

Toss the corn mixture with the cilantro, cheese, ¼ teaspoon salt, and a pinch of pepper. Stuff each chili with ⅓ to ½ cup filling, depending on their size, being careful to keep the stems in place. The stuffed chilies should be firm, but not overly full. Place them seam side down in the dish and bake, uncovered, until the filling is heated through and the chilies are puffed, 15 to 20 minutes. Serve immediately.

TIP: El Asador, an inexpensive stovetop grill, is a great tool for grilling vegetables in the home kitchen.

Gypsy Peppers Filled with Fromage Blanc and Fines Herbes

These beautiful peppers appear in the farmers' markets in late summer and early fall. With their sweet, thick flesh, they're easy to peel and great for stuffing. If they're not available, use any sweet pepper that's up to 4 or 5 inches long; pimiento is a good choice.

We roast the peppers and stuff them with fromage blanc, but you can use chèvre or ricotta instead. Fines herbes— the classic combination of fresh parsley, chervil, tarragon, and chives— contribute their distinctive flavor, but basil, marjoram, and scallions are also a delicious mix.

SERVES 4

4 medium gypsy peppers, about 1 pound

Olive oil

Salt and pepper

1½ cups fresh cheese: fromage blanc, ricotta, or chèvre

1 large egg

1 tablespoon each: chopped flat-leaf parsley, chervil, tarragon, and chives

Preheat the oven to 400°F.

Rub the peppers lightly with olive oil and place on a baking sheet. Roast until the skin is blistered and the flesh is soft, 15 to 20 minutes. When cool enough to handle, peel the peppers, carefully removing the skin around the stems. Make a lengthwise slit in each pepper, removing the seeds and leaving the stem in place. Sprinkle lightly with salt and pepper.

Lower the heat to 375°F. Lightly oil a small baking dish.

Whisk together the cheese, egg, herbs, ½ teaspoon salt, and a pinch of pepper in a small bowl. Gently fill the peppers and place them seam side down in the baking dish. Bake until the peppers are puffed and the filling is set, 25 to 30 minutes.

MAKE-AHEAD TIP: You can roast and peel the peppers the day before. You can also make the filling and stuff the peppers a few hours ahead of time so they're ready just to pop in the oven.

Using Fresh Herbs

Chopping fresh herbs by hand is a daily ritual in our kitchen. Every morning, we pile big bunches of aromatic sprigs and leaves on a wooden countertop to prepare them—it's an extravagant array of fragrant greens. We use fresh herbs two ways: alone, for bold accent flavors; and combined, to add complexity and enhance key ingredients. We use a mixture of herbs to season all kinds of savory dishes—crisp roasted potatoes, tartlets, lasagne, and filo fillings, hearty soups, and rustic ragoûts.

HERB BUTTER: You can mix herbs into softened butter and slather it over grilled vegetables or add a generous spoonful to pasta at the last minute to coat the noodles and bind the sauce. (Herb butter is a great way to use up leftover herbs if you've chopped too many, and, refrigerated in a sealed container, it will keep for weeks.)

Our favorite combination is equal parts fresh parsley, thyme, oregano or marjoram, and chives, a variation on what is traditionally known as *bouquet garni*. It has a distinctive, well-balanced flavor that blends beautifully into a number of dishes. You can vary the herbs and the quantities, according to the dish you're preparing. If you include fresh sage or rosemary, go lightly—they can be overpowering. Remember, the more parsley you use, the milder the flavor will be.

Artichokes Stuffed with Garlic Bread Crumbs, Lemon, and Pine Nuts

We marinate big, sturdy artichokes in a lemon vinaigrette and fill them until brimming with Garlic Bread Crumbs, pine nuts, and creamy Fontina cheese. Lemon zest— and lots of it— is the ingredient that makes this filling so delectable. We bake the artichokes until the flavors melt together and serve them warm, drizzled with more vinaigrette.

The artichokes are beautiful served on individual plates with sprigs of watercress all around and a sprinkling of Niçoise olives. If Meyer lemons are available, use them here. Their exotic taste and fragrance shine in this dish.

SERVES 4

1 cup Garlic Bread Crumbs (page 219)

Lemon Vinaigrette (recipe follows)

Zest and juice of 1 lemon

4 large artichokes, about 2 pounds

Artichoke Marinade (page 53)

⅓ cup pine nuts, toasted (page 46)

2 ounces Fontina cheese, grated, about ½ cup

½ ounce grated Parmesan cheese, 2 to 3 tablespoons

2 to 3 tablespoons coarsely chopped flat-leaf parsley

1 teaspoon minced garlic

Preheat the oven to 375°F.

Make the Garlic Bread Crumbs and the Lemon Vinaigrette.

Mince the lemon zest and set aside to add to the filling. Fill a large bowl with water and add the lemon juice. Trim off the artichoke tops, the stem ends, and peel away the thorny outer leaves. Use your thumb to loosen the inner leaves, and, using a small spoon, scoop out the choke. Place the artichokes in the lemon water and set aside.

Make the Artichoke Marinade and cook as directed. Drain the artichokes, reserving ½ cup of the cooking liquid to bake with them later.

In a small bowl, combine the garlic bread crumbs with the remaining ingredients, and season to taste with salt and pepper. Spoon the filling into the artichokes, filling the cavities, and stuffing it between the leaves. Pour the reserved cooking liquid in a small baking dish and place the artichokes in upright. Bake, uncovered, until the filling is golden and crisp on top,

25 to 30 minutes. Place the artichokes on individual plates or on a serving platter and spoon 1 tablespoon of the vinaigrette over each. Serve the remaining vinaigrette at the table.

Lemon Vinaigrette

MAKES ½ CUP

1 teaspoon minced lemon zest

2 tablespoons fresh lemon juice

1 tablespoon Champagne vinegar

¼ teaspoon salt

⅓ cup extra-virgin olive oil

Whisk everything but the oil together in a small bowl; slowly pour in the oil, whisking until emulsified.

MAKE-AHEAD TIP: There are a number of steps you can do ahead. Trim and marinate the artichokes the day before. (You can even trim the artichokes the day before you marinate them, as long as they're covered with lemon water.) Toast and grind the bread crumbs and grate the cheese. (This can also be done the day before; store in an airtight container.) Make the vinaigrette and toast the pine nuts.

VARIATION: You can use the delicious filling to stuff summer squash, mushrooms, or tomatoes.

Warm Beans and Grains

Spicy Rattlesnake Beans

Not many restaurants have the word "rattlesnake" on the menu, but Greens always does. These light brown heirloom beans with dark speckles are featured on our Sunday brunch each week next to eggs-over-easy on warm tortillas smothered with Fire-Roasted Salsa. These saucy beans are also delicious served alongside Soft Tacos with Butternut Squash, Plantain, and Poblano Chilies.

Rattlesnake beans are medium size, but they take a full 90 minutes to cook. If you can't find them at a specialty food store, try borlotti, pinto, or black beans instead.

SERVES 6

10 ounces rattlesnake beans, 1½ cups sorted and soaked overnight

8 cups cold water

1 large yellow onion, diced, about 2 cups

1 tablespoon minced garlic

½ tablespoon cumin seeds, toasted (page 214) and ground

10 fresh sage leaves, chopped, about 1 tablespoon

1 bay leaf

Chipotle Puree (page 163)

Salt

3 tablespoons fresh orange juice

½ teaspoon rice vinegar

Drain and rinse the beans and place them in a large saucepan with the water, onions, garlic, cumin, sage, and bay leaf. Bring to a boil, lower the heat, and simmer until the beans are tender, about 1½ hours.

Make the Chipotle Puree.

Discard the bay leaf. Season with 1 teaspoon salt, 1 teaspoon chipotle puree, the orange juice, and vinegar. Use a potato masher to lightly mash the beans, leaving most of them whole. If the broth is still thin, cook them a little longer. Add salt and chipotle puree to taste.

Warm White Beans

Big, starchy white beans have huge status in the Greens kitchen. We simmer them with fruity olive oil and sprigs of fresh herbs; the beans soak up these flavors and make their own delectable sauce as they slowly release their starches. We splash a little vinegar over the dish to finish and serve them with savory Filo Purses. If you have leftovers, spread on crusty grilled levain bread and top with wilted greens.

Cannellini beans are our first choice, but we often use giant Peruvian limas, white runners, or white emergo beans instead. Their cooking times vary, according to size and age (if you've had them in your cupboard for a long time, they may take longer to cook), but there's one thing they all have in common: they need plenty of time, so don't be in a hurry when you make them.

SERVES 4 TO 6

1 cup cannellini beans, about 6 ounces, sorted and soaked overnight

7 cups cold water

1 bay leaf

2 or 3 sprigs fresh marjoram or oregano

5 sprigs parsley

3 or 4 fresh sage leaves

2 tablespoons extra-virgin olive oil

½ large yellow onion, diced, about 1 cup

Salt and pepper

½ tablespoon minced garlic

1 celery rib, diced, about ½ cup

1 small carrot, peeled and diced, about ½ cup

½ cup white wine

1 teaspoon sherry vinegar

Drain and rinse the beans. Place them in a large saucepan with the water, bay leaf, and herbs. Bring to a boil, lower the heat and simmer, uncovered, until they're tender but still hold their shape, at least 1 hour.

While the beans are cooking, heat 1 tablespoon of the oil in a small skillet. Add the onions, ¼ teaspoon salt, and a pinch of pepper and cook over medium heat until the onions begin to soften, about 3 minutes. Add the garlic, celery, and carrots and cook until tender, about 4 minutes. Add the wine and cook until the pan is nearly dry, about 3 minutes.

Remove the bay leaf and herbs and add the vegetables, the remaining olive oil, ½ teaspoon salt, and a pinch of pepper. Cook over medium-low heat until the beans begin to break apart and the broth is slightly thickened, about 30 minutes. Add the vinegar and season to taste with salt and pepper just before serving.

Braised French Lentils

Little lentils are unique unto themselves— they have their own distinctive flavor and when cooked hold their shape instead of turning to mush, as ordinary brown lentils do. We use a couple of varieties here: French du Puy lentils and American-grown beluga, named after the black caviar they resemble. We braise them with red wine until they're saucy and serve them alongside Provençal Tartlets and filo purses filled with roasted winter roots. The lentils get better as they sit, so make them a few hours ahead of time or even the day before. You can always thin your leftovers with Vegetable Stock for an elegant, rich-tasting lentil soup.

SERVES 6 TO 8

2 tablespoons extra-virgin olive oil

½ large yellow onion, diced, about 1 cup

Salt and pepper

1 tablespoon minced garlic

1 medium carrot, peeled and diced, about ¾ cup

2 celery ribs or ½ fennel bulb, diced, about ¾ cup

1 medium red or yellow pepper, diced, about ¾ cup

½ cup red wine

1 cup French lentils

4 cups cold water

1 bay leaf

2 sprigs fresh thyme

3 fresh sage leaves

Heat the oil in a Dutch oven. Add the onions, ¼ teaspoon salt, and a pinch of pepper and cook over medium heat until they begin to soften, 3 to 4 minutes. Add the garlic, the vegetables, ¼ teaspoon salt, a pinch of pepper and cook until tender, about 5 minutes. Pour in the wine and cook until the pan is nearly dry, 3 to 4 minutes. Add the lentils, water, bay leaf, and herbs and simmer until the beans are completely tender, but still hold their shape, 30 to 35 minutes. The lentils should be saucy, but not soupy. If the broth is thin, cook the lentils longer to reduce it. Remove the bay leaf and herbs and season to taste with salt and pepper.

Basmati Rice with Pumpkin Seeds

This distinctively flavored, long-grain rice is delicious on its own or tossed with a little butter and fresh herbs or toasted nuts or seeds. Here is our surefire method for free-boiling basmati rice. It works like a charm as long as you cook it in plenty of water and give the grains time to open up completely.

SERVES 4 TO 6

1½ cups basmati rice

1 tablespoon unsalted butter

Salt and pepper

¼ cup pumpkin seeds, toasted (page 46)

Bring a large pot of water to a boil and salt lightly. Add the rice, give it a stir, and cook at a rolling boil for 10 to 12 minutes. Remove from the heat, cover, and set aside to steam for 2 minutes. Drain the rice and transfer to a bowl. Toss with the butter, ¼ teaspoon salt, a pinch or two of pepper, and the pumpkin seeds. Adjust the seasoning with salt and pepper and serve right away. You can also cover it and keep it in a warm oven (250°F).

VARIATION: Make the rice as directed, substituting 1 teaspoon toasted black mustard seeds (page 214) or ¼ cup cashews for the pumpkin seeds, a perfect choice if you're serving the rice with Indian curries. To complement a spicy Mexican stew, substitute almonds or pine nuts for the pumpkin seeds.

Jasmine Rice with Cashews

This starchy, short-grained rice has a unique flavor and slightly sticky texture and is the perfect accompaniment to Red Curry with Thai Spices and Vietnamese Yellow Curry. Toasted cashews are our favorite addition, but you can always use toasted peanuts instead.

The rice cooks up beautifully every time. Just be sure to use a pot with a tight-fitting lid and don't lift it when you set the rice aside to steam.

SERVES 4 TO 6

2 cups water

Salt and pepper

1½ cups jasmine rice

¼ cup cashews, toasted and chopped (page 46)

1 tablespoon unsalted butter (optional)

Bring the water to a boil in a small, heavy-bottomed saucepan. Stir in ¼ teaspoon salt and the rice. Cook at a rolling boil for 1 minute. Lower the heat, give it a stir, cover, and cook over low heat for 10 minutes. Turn off the heat and leave the rice to steam for 3 to 4 minutes, resisting the temptation to lift the lid.

Just before serving, use a fork to fluff the rice and stir in the nuts and butter, if using. Season to taste with salt and pepper. Serve immediately or cover and keep in a warm oven (250°F) until you're ready to serve it.

Coconut Jasmine Rice

Pair this coconut-infused rice with spicy curries and grilled vegetable brochettes with Peanut-Ginger Sauce. The starchy, plump grains of rice absorb every bit of the coconut flavor. For a special touch, sprinkle toasted coconut over the rice.

MAKES ABOUT 4 CUPS

1½ cups water

1 cup unsweetened canned coconut milk

Salt and pepper

1½ cups jasmine rice

Heat the water and coconut milk in a small, heavy-bottomed saucepan and bring to a boil. Stir in ¼ teaspoon salt and the rice. Cook at a rolling boil for 1 minute. Lower the heat, give it a stir, cover, and cook over medium-low heat for 10 minutes. Turn off the heat and leave the rice to steam for 2 to 3 minutes, resisting the temptation to lift the lid.

Just before serving, use a fork to fluff the rice and season to taste with salt and pepper.

Almond-Cherry Couscous

Instant couscous has its virtues: It's quick and easy to prepare. Toasted almonds and dried tart cherries spice this simple, versatile dish. Vegetable Stock adds tremendous flavor, but if you're short on time, you can use water instead. Just be sure to toast the couscous grains in butter to bring out their nuttiness. We serve it with Spring Vegetable Tagine and alongside our classic grilled vegetable brochettes with Charmoula.

SERVES 4 TO 6

2 tablespoons unsalted butter

1½ cups instant couscous

Salt and pepper

2 cups Vegetable Stock (page 110) or water

2 to 3 tablespoons dried tart cherries

1 tablespoon dried currants

¼ cup almonds, in their skins, toasted (page 46) and chopped

Melt the butter in a medium-size sauté pan. Add the couscous, ¼ teaspoon salt, and a pinch of pepper and stir over medium heat for 4 to 5 minutes to toast the grains. Remove from the heat.

Combine the stock or water, cherries, and currants in a small saucepan and bring to a boil. Pour over the couscous and give it a quick stir. Cover the pan with a tight-fitting lid and set aside for 15 to 20 minutes. Use a fork to fluff the couscous, add the almonds, and season with salt and pepper to taste. Serve immediately or cover and keep in a warm oven (250°F) until you're ready to serve it.

Polenta

We've adapted this basic recipe endlessly over the years and keep finding new ways to serve it. We've chosen Parmesan here, but you can use any flavorful cheese— cheddar, Asiago, smoked mozzarella, and dry jack— depending on the dish you're preparing. You can also make it without butter or cheese. For creamy, soft polenta, serve right away and garnish with your favorite toppings— ours are grilled portobello mushrooms, Fire-Roasted Poblano Chilies, or caramelized onions with toasted walnuts and Gorgonzola.

SERVES 6 TO 8; MAKES 24 POLENTA TRIANGLES

4 cups water

¾ teaspoon salt

1 cup coarse cornmeal

2 tablespoons unsalted butter

1½ ounces Parmesan cheese, grated, about ½ cup

Pepper

Bring the water to a boil in a large saucepan. Add the salt and whisk in the cornmeal. Lower the heat and cook at a low boil for about 25 minutes, stirring frequently, until the grains have opened up and the polenta is smooth.

Remove the pan from the heat, stir in the butter, cheese, and a pinch of pepper. Serve immediately, or— if using in another recipe— pour into a lightly oiled 9- by 13-inch baking dish, using a rubber spatula to scrape the pan and smooth the top of the polenta. Set aside to cool. Cut into 12 squares, then cut each square into two triangles.

Crisp Polenta Triangles with Gorgonzola Cream, Walnuts, and Basil

At the restaurant this delicious polenta is served as an appetizer, but it's so satisfying it can be a main course. We pour a reduced Gorgonzola cream over crisp polenta triangles and sprinkle toasted walnuts and basil on top. A bed of arugula leaves wilts underneath and adds a fresh touch. This is a great last-minute dish if you prepare the polenta a day ahead of time and make the cream in advance. Use a high-quality Gorgonzola— it makes a big difference in the flavor of the sauce.

SERVES 6 TO 8

Polenta (page 280)

2 cups heavy cream

½ medium yellow onion, thinly sliced, about ½ cup

2 garlic cloves, smashed with the flat side of a knife, skin left on

1 bay leaf

1 or 2 fresh thyme sprigs

1 or 2 fresh oregano or marjoram sprigs

3 fresh sage leaves

5 to 6 ounces Gorgonzola cheese, crumbled, about 1 cup

Salt and pepper

Oil for the griddle

A large handful of arugula

2 ounces Fontina cheese, grated, about ½ cup

½ cup walnut pieces, toasted (page 46), and chopped

10 basil leaves, stacked and thinly sliced, about ⅓ cup

Make the polenta, cut it into triangles as directed, and set aside.

Combine the cream, onions, garlic, bay leaf, and herb sprigs and leaves in a heavy-bottomed saucepan. Bring to a boil, being careful not to let it boil over; lower the heat, and simmer until reduced by one-quarter, 12 to 15 minutes. Pour the cream through a strainer. You should have about 1½ cups. Whisk in half of the Gorgonzola and season with a couple of pinches of salt and a pinch of pepper. Keep warm over low heat.

Heat a little oil on a griddle or in a large sauté pan. Grill the polenta triangles over medium heat until crisp and golden, 3 to 4 minutes on each side. Keep in a warm oven (250° F) until you're ready to serve.

Place a small handful of arugula on each plate and shingle 3 or 4 polenta triangles on top. Sprinkle the Fontina and remaining Gorgonzola over each serving. Ladle ½ cup of the cream over and garnish with the walnuts and basil. Serve immediately.

Salsas
and Sauces

Cucumber Raita

This extremely refreshing condiment goes with curries (and Middle Eastern dishes, for that matter), but it's very good all by itself too. Sprinkle a little minced mint on top and serve it with grilled pita bread.

MAKES ABOUT 3 CUPS

1 European cucumber
1 cup plain yogurt
¼ cup chopped fresh mint
Salt and cayenne pepper

Slice the cucumber in half lengthwise and use a spoon to scoop out the seeds. Dice finely and toss with the yogurt, mint, ½ teaspoon salt, and a pinch of cayenne. Cover and refrigerate for an hour or two. Adjust salt and cayenne to taste before serving.

TIP: You can make this with a regular cucumber as well but it will need to be peeled first, and the raita will have a slightly watery texture.

Avocado-Mango Salsa

In this beloved salsa, the fresh taste of lime, creamy avocado, and succulent mango are like a spicy dessert. Be sure the avocado and mango are perfectly ripe, yet still firm. Spoon over warm flour tortillas with Spicy Rattlesnake Beans or serve alongside quesadillas.

MAKES ABOUT 3 CUPS

½ medium red onion, diced, about ½ cup

Champagne or rice vinegar

1 ripe, firm avocado, cut into ½-inch cubes, about 1½ cups

1 large mango, peeled, seeded, and cut into ½-inch cubes, about 1½ cups

1 red or green jalapeño chili, seeded and diced

1 tablespoon fresh lime juice

¼ teaspoon salt

1 to 2 tablespoons chopped cilantro

Cayenne

Bring a small pot of water to a boil and drop in the onions for 15 seconds. Drain and toss with a splash of vinegar. Toss with the remaining ingredients except the cilantro and cayenne. Set aside for 20 to 30 minutes to allow the flavors to come together. Just before serving, toss in the cilantro and season to taste with cayenne.

Mango-Tomatillo Salsa:

Tart tomatillos and juicy, sweet mangoes work well together. The sharp flavor of the tomatillos softens as this salsa sits, so give it 30 minutes to an hour before serving.

MAKES ABOUT 2½ CUPS

Substitute ¼ pound diced tomatillos for the avocado. You should have about 1 cup. Prepare as directed and add up to ½ tablespoon of sugar to balance the tartness of the tomatillos.

Corn and Tomatillo Salsa

The simple fresh flavors of this summer salsa sing— tart tomatillos, refreshing lime, and sweet corn. The heat of the chilies will vary, so taste them first— you can always add more. Serve with scrambled eggs, queso fresco, and warm corn tortillas or Soft Tacos with Grilled Summer Vegetables.

MAKES ABOUT 3 CUPS

½ medium red onion, diced, about ½ cup

Champagne or rice vinegar

¼ cup water

2 ears of corn, shaved, about 2 cups kernels

Salt

¼ pound tomatillos, husked and diced, about 1 cup

1 jalapeño or serrano chili, seeded and diced

1½ tablespoons fresh lime juice

Sugar (optional)

Cayenne pepper

2 tablespoons chopped cilantro

Toss the onions with a splash of vinegar.

Combine the water, the corn and ¼ teaspoon salt in a small saucepan and cook over medium-low heat until the corn is tender, about 5 minutes. Transfer to a bowl and toss with the tomatillos, the chili, and the onions. Season with ¼ teaspoon salt, the lime juice, and a pinch of sugar, if needed. For a hotter salsa, add a pinch or two of cayenne. Adjust the seasoning with salt and a splash of vinegar. Toss in the cilantro just before serving.

Fire-Roasted Salsa

This rustic salsa has a taste that's smoky and rich. The plum tomatoes are grilled over coals— their firm, dense flesh keeps the salsa from being watery— and cilantro and lime juice keep the flavors bright. We serve it with soft tacos or Corn Quesadillas.

MAKES ABOUT 2 CUPS

1 pound plum tomatoes, cored

½ medium onion

1 or 2 jalapeño or serrano chilies

Garlic Oil (page 14)

Salt and pepper

1½ to 2 tablespoons fresh lime juice

2 tablespoons coarsely chopped cilantro

Prepare the grill.

Brush the tomatoes, onions, and chilies with garlic oil and sprinkle with salt and pepper. When the coals are ready, grill until the tomatoes and chilies are soft and their skins are blistered and the onion is grilled on all sides. Set aside to cool.

Coarsely chop the onion and tomatoes and toss in a bowl. Slice the chili in half lengthwise and remove the stem and seeds. Chop the chili and toss with the tomato mixture, along with 1½ tablespoons lime juice, ¼ teaspoon salt, and a pinch of pepper. Season to taste with salt and lime juice, if needed. Toss in the cilantro just before serving.

TIP: Keep this salsa in mind the next time you're grilling. Take advantage of the dying coals to grill the vegetables and make the salsa the next day.

287

Salsa Negra

Ancho chilies, bittersweet chocolate, and plantain are magical here, adding depth and complexity to this smooth, spicy sauce. The starchy plantain thickens the sauce, so to thin it we add water and the ancho chili soaking liquid. If plantains aren't available, you can still make the sauce— just don't add the water. We spoon it over Masa Harina Crêpes or bake it as the sauce for polenta or Roasted Winter Vegetable Enchiladas.

MAKES ABOUT 1½ QUARTS

2 cups water

2 ancho chilies, toasted (page 64) and seeded

1 tablespoon olive oil or vegetable oil

½ large yellow onion, diced, about 1 cup

Salt

1 tablespoon minced garlic

½ ripe plantain, about ½ pound, diced, 1 cup

One 28-ounce can whole tomatoes with their juice, pureed

½ ounce bittersweet chocolate, chopped

Bring 1 cup of the water to a boil. Place the chilies in a small bowl and cover with the boiling water. Set aside to soak for 20 minutes. Puree the chilies and ¼ cup of their soaking liquid in a blender or the bowl of a small food processor until smooth. (Reserve the rest of the soaking liquid to add to the sauce later.)

Heat the oil in a large saucepan and add the onions and ¼ teaspoon salt. Cook over medium heat until the onions begin to soften, about 3 minutes. Add the garlic and cook 1 minute more. Stir in the plantain, the reserved ancho soaking liquid, the remaining 1 cup water, and ¼ teaspoon salt. Cover and cook until the plantain softens, about 8 minutes. Add the tomatoes and the chocolate, lower the heat, and simmer for 20 to 25 minutes. Puree in a blender until smooth.

TIP: The sweetness and quality of the chocolate affect the flavor of the sauce. There are many types and grades to choose from, including the Mexican chocolates; we use Guittard's bittersweet.

Tomatillo Sauce

This smooth, tangy sauce is great with tortillas, polenta, and just about any dish made with corn. The tart taste of the tomatillos mellows as they simmer with onions, green pepper, and chili. For a hotter sauce, add another jalapeño or serrano chili, or try a smoky, dark green poblano. You can make the sauce a few hours ahead of time, but no earlier or it will lose its fresh, clean flavor. We serve it with enchiladas and Masa Harina Crêpes with Summer Vegetables, Chilies, and Cheddar or Roasted Winter Vegetable Enchiladas.

MAKES ABOUT 2½ CUPS

½ tablespoon olive oil or vegetable oil

½ medium yellow onion, chopped, about ¾ cup

Salt

Cayenne pepper

½ medium green pepper, coarsely chopped, about ½ cup

1 or 2 jalapeño or serrano chilies, seeded and chopped

1 pound tomatillos, husked and chopped

Sugar (optional)

Heat the oil in a saucepan and add the onions, ½ teaspoon salt, and a pinch of cayenne. Cook over medium heat until the onions begin to soften, about 3 minutes. Add the peppers and chili and cook for 1 minute. Add the tomatillos, cover the pan, and cook over medium-low heat until the tomatillos break down, 15 to 20 minutes. Puree in a blender until smooth. Adjust the seasoning with salt, cayenne, and a pinch or two of sugar, if needed, to round out the flavor.

TIP: Soak the tomatillos in a bowl of warm water before you husk them. The warm water will soften the husks and loosen them from the sticky skin of the tomatillos. Peel them a day ahead if you like.

The ripeness of the tomatillos makes all the difference in the flavor of the sauce. Sometimes you can find really ripe ones in the market; they take on a yellowish color and there's a wonderful lingering taste that's just like bananas. If the sauce is sharp, add a spoonful of crème fraîche (page 98) to smooth the flavors.

Roasted Pepper Sauce

Make this smooth, versatile sauce in late summer when peppers are sweet, cheap, and abundant. Spice it up with a pinch of cayenne, fresh chilies, or a spoonful of Chipotle or Ancho Chili Puree, or add a splash of lemon juice or balsamic vinegar to brighten the flavors. It's delicious with Filo Purses, spooned over grilled bread, or spread over pizza dough with Asiago cheese and black olives.

MAKES ABOUT 1 QUART

3 or 4 large red peppers, about 1½ pounds, cut in half lengthwise, stem and seeds removed

1 large plum tomato, cored, cut in half

Extra-virgin olive oil

Salt and pepper

4 fresh sage leaves

4 to 5 fresh thyme sprigs

Preheat the oven to 400°F.

Rub the peppers and tomato with oil, sprinkle with salt and pepper, and place on a parchment-lined baking sheet. Sprinkle the herbs on top and roast until the pepper skins are blistered and the flesh is soft, about 15 to 20 minutes. The tomatoes will take a little longer, about 30 minutes.

When cool enough to handle, peel the peppers and slip the skin off the tomatoes. Puree in a blender until smooth. Season with salt and pepper to taste.

TIP: If there are any pan juices, be sure to include them in the sauce.

MAKE-AHEAD TIP: This sauce keeps for 2 to 3 days in the refrigerator.

Roasting Peppers

Late summer is prime pepper season, and that's when they're at their very sweetest. Every color, shape, and variety fill the bins of our local farmers' markets. We roast red and yellow bell peppers most of the year, but gypsy, lipstick, and thick-fleshed pimientos are a peak of the season treat. They're great tossed into pasta, tucked into a gratin, or heaped on grilled or toasted bread, or lavish them with fruity olive oil, thin ribbons of basil, and a splash of good balsamic vinegar. Roasting peppers may sound like a lot of work, but it really isn't, so don't miss out on this delicious opportunity.

Preheat the oven to 400°F. Slice the peppers in half lengthwise, remove the stems, seeds, and as much as you can of the white membrane. Don't fuss over the membrane—it will disappear once the peppers are roasted. Lay the pepper halves cut side down on a parchment-lined baking sheet, brush them lightly with olive oil or garlic oil and sprinkle with salt and pepper. Roast until the skins blister and pull away from the flesh, 15 to 20 minutes. (You can also roast whole peppers on a stovetop grill or over hot coals until their skins are blistered and charred.) Transfer to a bowl or a container with a lid and cover right away; the peppers will steam as they cool. Once cool, peel off the skins. The peppers don't have to be perfect; the little bits of skin left behind are a tasty sign that they're truly roasted. Leave the slabs whole or slice, dice, or puree. They'll keep for a few days in the refrigerator and for weeks in the freezer in plastic bags.

Grilled Tomato, Garlic, and Basil Sauce

This rustic Mediterranean sauce— traditionally known as aillade— isn't pretty, but its flavor is transcendent. Just be sure your tomatoes are juicy and ripe. It's delicious with grilled eggplant, peppers, sunburst squash, and rings of sweet red onions, or as a pasta sauce tossed with spaghettini, garlic bread crumbs, and pecorino.

MAKES 1½ CUPS

1 large tomato, about ½ pound, cored

1 teaspoon minced garlic

½ cup extra-virgin olive oil

½ teaspoon salt

⅛ teaspoon pepper

1 cup basil leaves, packed

Red wine vinegar

Prepare the grill.

Grill the tomato, using metal tongs to turn it until the skin is blistered; coarsely chop. Combine everything but the basil and the vinegar in a blender and blend until smooth. Add the basil and pulse until chopped. The sauce will be slightly thickened with flecks of green. Add a splash of vinegar to brighten the flavor.

TIP: If your tomatoes are acidic, add a pinch of sugar to balance the flavors of the sauce.

MAKE-AHEAD TIP: This sauce keeps well in the refrigerator for a day or two, so throw an extra tomato on the grill and double the recipe.

Charmoula

The big tastes of the eastern Mediterranean are here— fruity olive oil, cumin, paprika, cilantro, lemon, and the heat of cayenne. Freshly toasted cumin brings out all the enticing flavors, so be sure to take that extra little step. We serve this spicy Moroccan sauce over simply grilled vegetables— fingerling potatoes, peppers, and summer squash of all colors and shapes— and Almond-Cherry Couscous.

MAKES ABOUT ¾ CUP

6 tablespoons extra-virgin olive oil

3 tablespoons fresh lemon juice

2 tablespoons water

2 or 3 garlic cloves, peeled

1 teaspoon paprika

1 teaspoon cumin seeds, toasted (page 214) and ground

½ teaspoon salt

A pinch or two of cayenne pepper

⅓ cup flat-leaf parsley leaves, packed

⅓ cup cilantro sprigs, packed

Combine everything but the parsley and cilantro in a blender and puree until emulsified, about 1 minute. Add the herbs and pulse just long enough to chop them, about 30 seconds. The sauce should be a warm, tawny brown with flecks of bright green.

MAKE-AHEAD TIP: This sauce is best served right away, but will keep in the refrigerator for a day or two.

Mushroom-Sherry Sauce

Dried porcini, sherry, and roasted garlic give this smooth, silky sauce depth and intensity. It's slightly thickened with a roux— just enough to bind it together. Try a spoonful of crème fraîche or cream for added richness. Serve with Roasted Portobello Mushrooms Filled with Winter Vegetables and Fontina or Filo Purses with Artichokes, Mushrooms, and Asiago.

MAKES 1½ QUARTS

5 cups Mushroom Stock (page 112)

⅓ cup Roasted Garlic Puree (page 145)

½ ounce dried porcini, soaked in ½ cup hot water for 10 minutes

¼ cup sherry

4 tablespoons (½ stick) unsalted butter

5 tablespoons all-purpose flour

1 tablespoon mushroom soy sauce or tamari

Salt and pepper

1 to 2 tablespoons heavy cream or Crème Fraîche (page 98), (optional)

Make the Mushroom Stock and the Roasted Garlic Puree.

Pour the porcini through a fine sieve and save the liquid. Finely chop the porcini and set aside. Combine the Mushroom Stock, porcini soaking liquid, and the sherry in a medium-size saucepan; whisk in the Roasted Garlic Puree and bring to a boil. Lower the heat and simmer for 5 minutes.

Melt the butter in a large, heavy-bottomed saucepan, whisk in the flour to make a roux, and cook over medium-low heat— still whisking— for 2 to 3 minutes. Slowly whisk 1 cup of the seasoned stock into the roux to make a paste. Add the remaining stock, 1 cup at a time, until all the stock has been incorporated. Add the porcini, the mushroom soy, and a pinch of pepper; simmer over low heat until the sauce is slightly thickened, 10 to 15 minutes. Season to taste with salt and pepper and add the cream or crème fraîche, if using.

MAKE-AHEAD TIP: Make the Mushroom Stock in advance, freeze it and defrost when needed. Roast the garlic and soak the porcini the day before; you can even make the roux a day ahead. Assemble the sauce ahead of time; just add the crème fraîche or cream, if using, right before serving.

VARIATION: Use red wine or port instead of the sherry. You can also make the sauce without the roasted garlic.

Tomato-Zinfandel Sauce

This basic tomato sauce with dried porcini is rich, complex, and satisfying on all levels. It's what makes our lasagne, filo purses, and baked polenta dishes so outstanding. The flavor of the tomatoes is essential here, so be sure to use the best— we like Muir Glen organic. If you don't have zinfandel, any good red wine will do.

If you're making this sauce for Artichoke and Portobello Mushroom Lasagne or Roasted Winter Vegetable Lasagne, you'll have a cup or so leftover. Freeze and use in another dish.

MAKES ABOUT 1½ QUARTS

½ ounce dried porcini, soaked in ½ cup hot water for 10 minutes

1½ tablespoons olive oil

1 large yellow onion, finely chopped, about 2 cups

Salt and pepper

1 tablespoon minced garlic

⅓ cup Zinfandel or dry red wine

Two 28-ounce cans whole tomatoes with juice, pureed

1 bay leaf

1 tablespoon chopped fresh herbs: flat-leaf parsley, thyme, and oregano or marjoram

Sugar (optional)

Drain the porcini through a fine sieve and save the soaking liquid. Finely chop the porcini and set aside.

Heat the oil in a large saucepan over medium heat and add the onions, ¼ teaspoon salt, and a pinch of pepper. Cook until the onions begin to soften, about 3 minutes. Add the garlic and cook 1 minute more. Pour in the wine and simmer until the pan is nearly dry, about 3 minutes.

Add the tomatoes, the porcini and their soaking liquid, the bay leaf, ½ teaspoon salt, and a pinch of pepper. Simmer over medium-low heat for about 30 minutes. Remove the bay leaf, add the herbs, and season with salt and pepper to taste. If the sauce is acidic, add a pinch of sugar.

VARIATION: Instead of the wine, try aged sherry, or skip the porcini and add roasted garlic instead.

Meyer Lemon Beurre Blanc

This rich sauce is one of our all-time favorites. We serve it with Spinach and Feta Griddle Cakes and Artichoke Griddle Cakes with a generous spoonful of crème fraîche and little Niçoise olives— the flavors are sensational.

Meyer lemons are truly one of our Bay Area backyard treasures. If you're lucky enough to have a source for these fragrant, soft-skinned lemons (they've started appearing in East Coast markets), one or two are all you'll need. If they're not available, use equal parts of fresh lemon and orange or tangerine juice.

MAKES ABOUT 1 CUP

½ tablespoon minced Meyer lemon zest or minced lemon and orange or tangerine zest

¼ cup Meyer lemon juice or 2 tablespoons each fresh lemon and orange or tangerine juice

1 tablespoon Champagne vinegar

¼ cup dry white wine

2 shallots, finely diced, about ¼ cup

2 sticks cold unsalted butter, cut in small pieces

Salt and pepper

Set the citrus zest aside.

Place the citrus juice, vinegar, wine, and shallots in a small saucepan. Reduce over medium-high heat until the liquid is almost evaporated; there should be a tablespoon or two of liquid in the pan. Turn the heat to medium-low and whisk in the butter, a little at a time, making sure each addition is incorporated before adding the next. Whisk constantly until all the butter is added, remove from the heat, and stir in the zest, ¼ teaspoon salt, and a pinch of pepper. Serve immediately or keep warm over hot water until ready to serve.

Herb Cream

This simple, elegant sauce is steeped with fresh herbs and seasoned with a little Dijon mustard to temper the richness of the cream. Serve with Buckwheat Crêpes with Winter Vegetables and Caramelized Onions. Toss with leftover noodles, freshly grated Parmesan, and a sprinkling of herbs for a last-minute supper.

MAKES ABOUT 1½ CUPS

2 cups heavy cream

½ medium yellow onion, sliced

2 to 3 fresh thyme sprigs

2 to 3 fresh oregano sprigs

1 bay leaf

½ tablespoon Dijon mustard

½ teaspoon chopped fresh thyme

½ teaspoon chopped fresh oregano

½ tablespoon chopped flat-leaf parsley

Salt and pepper

Combine the cream, onions, herb sprigs, and bay leaf in a small, heavy-bottomed saucepan and bring to a boil. Lower the heat to medium-low and cook until the cream is thick enough to coat a spoon, about 15 minutes. Don't let the cream boil over as it reduces. Pour the cream through a strainer. You should have about 1½ cups. If there's more, return the cream to the pan and reduce it further.

Whisk in the Dijon and the chopped herbs and season with a pinch or two of salt and a pinch of pepper. Keep the sauce warm over low heat until you're ready to serve it.

MAKE-AHEAD TIP: You can make this sauce ahead of time; it keeps in the refrigerator for a day or two.

297

A Few of Our Favorite Greens

Broccoli Rabe with Hot Pepper

Broccoli rabe, also known as rapini, isn't broccoli at all. It's actually a flowering turnip green with a wonderfully pungent, spicy flavor. It's a delicious accompaniment to Filo Purses Filled with Mushrooms, Artichokes, and Asiago; served alongside Warm White Beans; or scattered over Pizza with Wilted Greens, Goat Cheese, and Hot Pepper. Save leftovers and mix them with white beans or fresh cheese for a quick pasta sauce or crostini spread.

SERVES 4 TO 6

2 bunches broccoli rabe, about 1½ pounds

2 tablespoons extra-virgin olive oil

1 teaspoon minced garlic

Salt and pepper

Red pepper flakes

Bring a large pot of water to a boil and salt lightly. Trim the tough lower stems from the broccoli rabe and discard. Chop the tops and remaining stems into 2-inch pieces; you should have about 4 quarts of florets, leaves, and stems. Drop the broccoli rabe into the boiling water and cook until tender, 2 to 3 minutes; drain.

Heat the oil in a large sauté pan and add the broccoli rabe, garlic, ¼ teaspoon of salt, and a pinch each of pepper and red pepper flakes. Cook for 2 to 3 minutes over medium heat, using metal tongs to toss the greens. Adjust the seasoning with salt and red pepper flakes.

TIP: We always parboil the broccoli rabe before we sauté it, unless it's very young and tender. It may seem like an extra step, but it actually speeds cooking times. You can do this ahead of time (just leave it in the colander), so it's ready to sauté at the last minute.

Dinosaur Kale with Toasted Almonds

This funny-looking kale goes by many names— Tuscan kale, cavolo nero, lacinato, or, simply, dino kale. We call it dinosaur kale, with its thick center rib that runs straight like a spine down pebbly, dark green leaves. With a color and texture unlike any other, dinosaur kale is incomparable in hearty fall and winter soups and ragoûts. It's also delicious spooned over Warm White Beans or served alongside Roasted Winter Vegetable Lasagne.

Parboil the greens before you sauté them, so they're tender when you add them to the pan. This step softens their strong flavor and shortens the cooking time all around.

SERVES 4

1 or 2 bunches dinosaur kale, about ½ pound, stems and ribs discarded, leaves cut into
    thick strips, about 10 cups
2 tablespoons extra-virgin olive oil
2 teaspoons minced garlic
Salt and pepper
1 or 2 tablespoons unskinned almonds, toasted (page 46) and chopped

Bring a large pot of water to a boil and salt lightly. Drop in the kale, cook until tender, about 5 minutes, and drain.

Heat the oil in a large sauté pan and add the kale, garlic, ¼ teaspoon salt, and a pinch of pepper. Sauté over medium heat for 3 to 4 minutes, adding a little water if needed to keep the kale from sticking to the pan. Toss in the almonds just before serving and season to taste with salt and pepper.

Rainbow Chard with Pumpkin Seeds

This simple sauté is as much about the wildly colorful chard stems as it is about delicious sautéed greens. The bright ribs of pale pink, deep magenta, and gold reach up like fingers into the crinkly, dark green leaves. We slice the stems and sauté them with plenty of olive oil and garlic until just tender, then add the greens, making sure to cook them all the way through. If rainbow chard isn't available, you can still make this dish, using red or green chard instead.

To turn this into a satisfying supper, skip the pumpkin seeds and pile the greens and stems on top of creamy polenta with grilled portobello mushrooms and a sprinkling of Parmesan cheese.

SERVES 4

1 bunch of chard, about ¾ pound

1½ tablespoons extra-virgin olive oil

1 teaspoon minced garlic

Salt and pepper

1 teaspoon fresh lemon juice

1 to 2 tablespoons pumpkin seeds, toasted (page 46)

Wash the chard and drain. Tear the chard leaves away from the stems, keeping the stems and leaves separate. Bundle the leaves and cut them into wide strips. Trim the stems, remove the strings, and slice on the diagonal about ¼ inch thick. You should have about 8 cups of leaves and 1 heaping cup of stems.

Heat the oil in a large sauté pan; add the stems, garlic, and a pinch of salt and pepper. Cook over medium heat for 2 to 3 minutes, until the stems begin to soften, adding a little water to keep them from sticking to the pan. Turn the heat to medium-high, add the chard leaves, 2 pinches of salt, and a pinch of pepper. Cook until tender, 3 to 4 minutes, using a pair of metal tongs to toss the greens. Just before serving, add the lemon juice, toss in the pumpkin seeds, and season to taste with salt and pepper.

TIP: Big chard stems take longer to cook than the tender little ones. Slice the stems thinly and—if the greens are tough—give them more time in the pan, adding a little water if needed to keep them moist, or cover the pan to steam them before adding the greens.

VARIATION: We like the crunch of toasted pumpkin seeds, but you can use pine nuts, almonds, walnuts, or a pinch of red pepper flakes instead. A splash of sherry vinegar is another great way to finish the greens. Add just before serving to keep the greens from discoloring.

Rainbow Chard

Rarely does a week go by that we don't feature rainbow chard. You can find it in big, beautiful bunches at farmers' markets and specialty food stores, or you can grow your own from organic seed. These showy plants with their brilliantly colored leaves brighten the fallow Green Gulch fields on gray winter days and bring good cheer to the Greens kitchen.

Be sure to save the stems when you strip them from the greens. Slice and add them to the dish; they add texture and—unlike the gorgeous leaves—actually hold their color beautifully when sautéed. Stunning colors aside, the leaves and stems of this vibrant plant taste just like other varieties of chard.

Sautéed Winter Greens

Chard and kale are great partners in this hearty winter sauté. We always include the chard stems for added crunch and flavor. Don't hold back on the seasonings here— fruity olive oil, lots of garlic, and a splash of lemon juice. You can add toasted pine nuts for sweetness and complexity.

SERVES 4 TO 6

1 bunch of chard, about ¾ pound

1 bunch of kale, about ½ pound, stems removed, leaves cut into wide strips, about 10 cups

2 tablespoons extra-virgin olive oil

½ tablespoon minced garlic

Salt and pepper

1 tablespoon fresh lemon juice

Bring a large pot of water to a boil and salt lightly.

Wash the chard and kale separately and set them aside to drain. Tear the chard leaves from the stems, bundle the leaves, and cut into wide strips. Trim the chard stems, remove the strings, and slice on the diagonal about ¼ inch thick. You should have about 8 cups of leaves and 1 heaping cup of stems. Cut the kale in wide strips to make about 10 cups.

Drop the kale into the boiling water and cook until tender, 3 to 4 minutes. Drain and set aside. Heat the oil in a large sauté pan and add the chard stems, garlic, ¼ teaspoon salt, and a pinch of pepper. Cook over medium heat for 2 to 3 minutes, until the stems are translucent. Turn the heat to medium high, add the chard leaves and cook until wilted, 3 to 4 minutes. Add the kale and cook until the greens are completely tender, 1 to 2 minutes more. Add the lemon juice just before serving and season to taste with salt and pepper.

TIP: The key to this dish is to parboil the kale for a few minutes before you sauté it with the chard stems and leaves. It's an extra step, but it works every time; when you combine the chard with the kale, they cook together evenly. It's a good step to do ahead, so you can then finish the dish in just a few minutes.

Spicy Asian Greens

Bok choy is our Asian green of choice for this quick, spicy sauté. With its fresh, clean taste and crisp, sturdy leaves it's a perfect match for the bold flavors of fresh ginger, garlic, and fermented black beans. For even spicier greens, you can increase the ginger and fermented black beans, but be careful— the salt in the beans can sneak up on you.

SERVES 4 TO 6

4 small heads of bok choy or pak choi, about 2 pounds
1½ tablespoons vegetable oil
½ tablespoon grated fresh ginger
½ tablespoon minced garlic
½ teaspoon fermented black beans (page 363), mashed to a paste
¼ teaspoon salt
1 teaspoon toasted sesame oil
½ teaspoon tamari or soy sauce

Trim the stem end off the bok choy and remove the bruised outer leaves. Cut the head in quarters and trim away the inner core to separate the leaves. Cut the larger leaves lengthwise through the stem, leaving the small, inner leaves whole; you should have about 10 cups.

Heat the vegetable oil in a large sauté pan or wok over medium-high heat and add the ginger, garlic, and fermented black beans. Cook for about 30 seconds; add the bok choy, the salt, and cook for 3 to 4 minutes, using a pair of metal tongs to toss the greens. The leaves should be tender and the stems translucent and crisp. Stir in the sesame oil and tamari just before serving.

Desserts and Pastries

Ginger Cookies

These spicy cookies are inspired by a recipe from one of our favorite pastry chefs, Emily Luchetti. They're a snap to make— though they're not gingersnaps— and guaranteed to please.

MAKES 2½ DOZEN 2½-INCH COOKIES

2½ cups all-purpose flour

2 teaspoons baking soda

2 teaspoons ground ginger

1 teaspoon cinnamon

½ teaspoon allspice

½ teaspoon salt

2 sticks unsalted butter

1 cup sugar

½ cup light brown sugar, packed

1 large egg

⅓ cup molasses

In a large bowl, sift together the flour, baking soda, spices, and salt. Set aside.

Beat the butter in the bowl of an electric mixer or by hand; add ½ cup of the sugar, the brown sugar, and beat until fluffy, about 4 minutes. Add the egg, followed by the molasses, and beat until smooth, about 2 minutes. Scrape down the bowl. On low speed add the dry ingredients and mix until just incorporated. Cover with plastic wrap and refrigerate for 30 minutes.

Preheat the oven to 350°F and set the oven rack to the middle position.

Roll the dough into ¾-inch balls and roll them in the remaining sugar. Place them on a parchment-lined baking sheet, 2 to 3 inches apart. Bake until golden, about 12 minutes. Let cool for 5 minutes, then remove the cookies from the pan.

Almond Macaroons

These pop-in-your-mouth macaroon bites are simple to make— just four ingredients— and excellent with sorbet or a bowl of fresh berries. Like all macaroons, they're great keepers.

MAKES 2 DOZEN MACAROONS

6 ounces almond paste, about ¾ cup
½ cup sugar, plus more for rolling
1 large egg white
Pinch of salt

Preheat the oven to 350°F.

Mix the almond paste and the sugar together in the bowl of an electric mixer. Add the egg white and the salt and mix until it comes together, 4 to 5 minutes. Cover with plastic wrap and refrigerate for 20 minutes.

Use a teaspoon to scoop the dough into balls, about ½ inch in diameter. Roll them in sugar and place on a parchment-lined baking sheet, about 2 inches apart. Bake until puffed and golden, about 10 minutes.

VARIATION: Just before baking make a small impression in each macaroon with your thumb. Fill with a dab of your favorite jam and bake as directed.

Candied Ginger Shortbread

The supple dough of this spicy shortbread is exceptionally forgiving; you can roll it flat and cut it into all kinds of shapes with your favorite cookie cutters or just roll it into a cylinder and slice it into simple rounds. They're a perfect finish to a spicy Asian meal, served alongside Blackberry Sorbet.

One thing we love about this easy recipe is that you can embellish the flavors endlessly. We've included some of our favorite variations. You can fearlessly double a batch without complications, and, once baked, the cookies keep well in an airtight container.

MAKES 2½ TO 3 DOZEN 2-INCH COOKIES

½ cup sugar

2 sticks unsalted butter, chilled and cubed

1 teaspoon pure vanilla extract

2 cups all-purpose flour

¼ teaspoon salt

¼ pound candied ginger, finely chopped, about ½ cup

Place the sugar in the bowl of an electric mixer or food processor and work the butter in for 1 minute. (You can also do this by hand.) Add the remaining ingredients and mix until the dough just begins to come together. Wrap the dough in plastic wrap and refrigerate for at least 30 minutes before rolling out. (The dough freezes beautifully at this point, just be sure to wrap it well and defrost before proceeding.)

Preheat the oven to 350°F.

Lightly flour the work surface and rolling pin. Roll the dough to about ¼ inch thick and cut into different shapes with cookie cutters. (You can use the remaining scraps of dough to make more cookies, just make sure to handle it lightly.) You can also form the dough into a cylinder about 1½ inches in diameter and 10 inches long. Roll it tightly in plastic wrap and chill until firm, about 30 minutes. Slice into ¼-inch-thick rounds. Place the cut shortbread on a parchment-lined baking sheet and bake until the edges are just beginning to color, about 10 minutes.

Chocolate Espresso Bean Shortbread:

Make the dough as directed, substituting ½ cup chopped chocolate covered espresso beans for the candied ginger and adding 1 teaspoon of vanilla extract.

Pistachio Shortbread: Make the dough as directed. Substitute ½ cup toasted (page 46), chopped pistachios for the candied ginger.

Vanilla Bean Shortbread: Slice 1 vanilla bean in half lengthwise and scrape the seeds into the sugar. Make the dough as directed, omitting the candied ginger and adding 1 teaspoon of vanilla extract.

Citrus Shortbread: Make the dough as directed, adding 1 tablespoon minced citrus zest along with the sugar. Good candidates include lemon, especially Meyer lemon, tangerine, and orange.

Debbie's Pecan Brownies

At Greens, these over-the-top brownies sell out every day. Our pastry chef, Debbie, belongs to the fudgy, dense school of brownies. Unsweetened chocolate is essential here— we use Guittard. We've also made them at home with ordinary supermarket baking chocolate and they were excellent.

SERVES 8

1 stick unsalted butter

3 ounces unsweetened chocolate, chopped

1 cup sugar

2 large eggs

1 teaspoon pure vanilla extract

¼ teaspoon salt

¾ cup all-purpose flour

1 cup pecan pieces, toasted (page 46) and chopped

Preheat the oven to 350°F.

Butter and flour an 8- x 8-inch baking dish. Melt the butter and chocolate in a double boiler and set aside. Whisk the sugar, eggs, vanilla, and salt together in a medium-size bowl and whisk in the chocolate mixture. Sift the flour and add until incorporated. Fold in the pecans. Pour the batter into the pan and smooth the top. Bake for about 45 minutes. Test for doneness with a skewer or paring knife; it should come out clean. Allow to cool slightly before cutting.

Raspberry-Plum Cobbler

Raspberries and plums are an amazing combination, but you can also use blueberries or blackberries with stone fruits such as nectarines or peaches in this simple dessert. The shortcake topping is made with pecans, but you can substitute hazelnuts or almonds. The season for this homiest of homey classics stretches from midsummer right into fall, when prune plums arrive and raspberries are still on the market.

SERVES 6 TO 8

Shortcake (page 314)

1 pint raspberries

1½ pounds firm, ripe plums, cut in eighths

¼ cup sugar

3 tablespoons tapioca starch

Pinch of salt

Turbinado or raw sugar

Lightly sweetened whipped cream or vanilla ice cream for serving

Make the shortcake dough. Cover the bowl and refrigerate.

Preheat the oven to 350°F. Butter an 8-inch-square baking dish.

Toss the fruit with the sugar, tapioca starch, and salt and spoon it into the baking dish. Cover the fruit with tablespoon-size pieces of the Shortcake dough, using about three-quarters of it. Sprinkle with turbinado sugar and bake until the top is golden and cooked through and the fruit is bubbling, about 40 minutes. Allow to cool for a few minutes before serving with whipped cream or ice cream.

TIP: Use the leftover shortcake dough to make a few biscuits. Bake them right along with the cobbler until golden on top; they'll be done before the cobbler is done. You can reheat them up to 2 days later.

Shortcake

It's hard to imagine a simpler dessert than one based on shortcake. This one is simple, but a bit rich: It's made with both cream and butter, and includes toasted pecans. You can use almonds or peeled hazelnuts instead of pecans.

MAKES 8 INDIVIDUAL SHORTCAKES

2 cups all-purpose flour

¼ cup sugar, plus more for sprinkling

1 tablespoon baking powder

½ teaspoon salt

½ cup pecan pieces, toasted (page 46) and finely chopped

6 tablespoons (¾ stick) unsalted butter, chilled and cubed

1 cup heavy cream, chilled

Pastry Egg Wash (page 327)

Preheat the oven to 375°F and set the oven rack to the middle position.

Combine the flour, sugar, baking powder, salt, and pecans in the bowl of an electric mixer. Using the paddle attachment, work in the butter until the pieces are pea-size. (You can also do this by hand with a pastry blender.) Transfer to a bowl and use a rubber spatula to fold in the cream. Gently mix together, being careful not to overwork the dough. It should just hold together without any pockets of dry ingredients. Wrap the dough in plastic wrap and use the palm of your hand to flatten it and form a disk. Refrigerate for 15 to 20 minutes.

Dust a work surface and rolling pin lightly with flour, and roll the dough into a 10- by 6-inch rectangle, about ¾ inch thick.

Use a small cookie cutter or glass to cut the dough into rounds, 2½ inches in diameter. Press the remaining dough into a rectangle large enough to cut out 2 more rounds. Place on a parchment-lined baking sheet and chill for 10 to 15 minutes.

Make the egg wash, brush the top of each round, and sprinkle with sugar. Bake for 30 minutes. Move to the top rack and bake until golden, 5 to 10 minutes more.

Nectarine-Blackberry Shortcake

When nectarines and blackberries are at their peak, at the height of summer, we make this shortcake and show off the fruits' pure flavors and gorgeous colors. A pinch of salt in the sauce brings out the full flavor of the berries. You can, of course, include other berries— blueberries or raspberries— or replace the nectarines with peaches, which need to be peeled first.

MAKES 8 INDIVIDUAL SHORTCAKES

Shortcake (page 314)
1 pound firm, ripe nectarines, cut into thin wedges
½ pint blackberries
2 to 3 tablespoons sugar
Blackberry Sauce (recipe follows)
Whipped cream for garnish

Bake the shortcakes. When cool, slice them in half and set aside.

Gently toss the nectarines and the berries with the sugar.

Make the Blackberry Sauce.

Place the bottom half of each shortcake on a dessert plate and spoon the fruit on top. Pour a little sauce over each serving and top with the other half of the shortcake. Serve with a generous dollop of whipped cream.

Blackberry Sauce: *To adjust to your liking, you can increase the sugar or add a splash of juice.*

MAKES 1¼ CUPS

1 pint blackberries
⅓ cup sugar
Pinch of salt

Combine all of the ingredients in a blender and puree until smooth, about 3 minutes. Pour through a fine mesh strainer.

Ginger Crunch Cake with Poached Pears

I'll go out on a limb here: If you make no other dessert from this book, choose this one. It's intense, with all the separate elements contributing to the distinct big ginger flavor, a knockout finale for a dinner party. We use three kinds of ginger— crystallized, dried, and fresh— and in the kitchen it's known as the triple-ginger threat. All this joy comes at a price: The separate elements are recipes in themselves, so you can't just throw it together at the last minute.

Fortunately, there's a shortcut or two: The pears can be poached in advance and the ginger cookies for the streusel can be made ahead of time. You can also use store-bought gingersnaps. In summer, you can substitute plums for the pears and they don't need poaching.

SERVES 12

Ginger-Pecan Streusel (recipe follows)

3 Poached Pears (page 322), cut in half

1½ cups all-purpose flour

1 teaspoon baking soda

½ teaspoon salt

1 teaspoon ground ginger

1 stick unsalted butter, at room temperature

½ cup light brown sugar, packed

1 large egg

¼ cup light molasses

¼ cup dark corn syrup

1 tablespoon chopped crystallized ginger

1 tablespoon grated fresh ginger

½ cup buttermilk

Make the Ginger-Pecan Streusel and the Poached Pears.

Brush a 9-inch springform pan with melted butter, line with a round of parchment paper, and brush with a little more butter. Press the Ginger-Pecan Streusel firmly and evenly in the bottom of the pan. Cut the pears crosswise in ¼-inch-thick slices, leaving the pear shape intact. Using a spatula, lay the pears on a paper towel to drain while you make the cake batter.

Preheat the oven to 325°F and set the oven rack to the top position.

Sift the flour, baking soda, salt, and ground ginger together in a large bowl and set aside. In the bowl of an electric mixer or by hand, beat the butter until fluffy, about 4 minutes. Add the sugar and beat for 3 minutes. Scrape down the sides of the bowl, add the egg, and beat for 2 minutes. Add the molasses, corn syrup, the crystallized and fresh ginger, and beat until smooth, about 2 minutes more. Alternately, add the dry ingredients and the buttermilk, beginning and ending with the dry ingredients.

Pour the batter into the pan and smooth it. Using a spatula, arrange the pears on top with the narrow stem ends in the center, leaving a ¼-inch border of batter around the edge. Don't press the pears into the batter; they'll sink in as the cake bakes.

Place the pan on a parchment-lined baking sheet and bake until the cake has a deep golden color and a knife or skewer inserted into the center comes out clean, about 1½ hours.

Let cool for 10 minutes, invert onto a plate, and carefully remove the pan and the parchment paper.

Ginger-Pecan Streusel

Ginger Cookies (page 308), finely ground, about ½ cup
½ cup light brown sugar, packed
½ cup pecan pieces, toasted (page 46) and chopped
2 tablespoons unsalted butter, melted

Combine everything in a small bowl and set aside.

Almond Brown Butter Cake with Plums

The traditional French little cakes called financiers *are baked in small rectangular pans and resemble gold bricks. Our version is baked as a single-layer, round cake and includes plums, several sources of almond flavor, and the nutty taste of brown butter. The result is a buttery cake that's crunchy on the outside, moist and tender inside.*

This cake is particularly good served with raspberries and whipped cream.

SERVES 8

12 tablespoons (1½ sticks) unsalted butter, plus melted butter for the pan

½ cup all-purpose flour

1⅓ cups powdered sugar

½ cup unskinned almonds, toasted (page 46) and ground

4 large egg whites, at room temperature

¼ teaspoon salt

¼ teaspoon pure almond extract

½ pound firm, ripe plums, sliced in eighths

¼ cup sliced almonds, lightly toasted (page 46)

Powdered sugar for garnish

Preheat the oven to 350°F and set the oven to the middle position.

Brush an 8-inch cake pan with melted butter, line with a round of parchment paper, and brush with a little more butter. Cook the butter over medium heat until the solids settle to the bottom and the butter turns a deep tawny brown and smells nutty, 8 to 10 minutes. Pour through a fine mesh strainer lined with cheesecloth or a coffee filter.

Sift the flour and sugar together and add the ground almonds.

Beat the egg whites and salt in the bowl of an electric mixer until they form stiff peaks. Add the flour mixture in a steady stream and mix until smooth. Add the brown butter and the almond extract and mix until just combined. Pour the batter into the pan, arrange the plums in a circular pattern on top, and sprinkle with the sliced almonds. Bake until the top is golden brown and the sides of the cake have pulled away slightly from the pan, about 45 minutes.

Cool the cake in the pan. Sift a little powdered sugar over the top before serving.

VARIATION: Substitute ½ pound pitted, whole fresh cherries in place of the plums.

To make 12 individual cakes: Brush a muffin tin with melted butter and distribute the batter, fruit, and almonds evenly. Bake until golden brown and cooked through, about 25 minutes.

Nectarine-Almond Upside-Down Cake

Upside-down cake is a classic American dessert and for good reason— caramel topping over the fresh fruit and luscious cake is addictive. This version outshines tradition: It also has almond paste in the cake and brandy in the caramel. The fruit doesn't have to be nectarines; peaches, apricots, plums, and pitted fresh cherries are just as delicious.

SERVES 8

2 sticks unsalted butter, softened

½ cup light brown sugar, packed

¼ cup brandy or dark rum

¾ cup almond paste

¾ cup sugar

4 large eggs

1 cup all-purpose flour

½ teaspoon baking powder

¼ teaspoon salt

2 large, ripe nectarines, about ¾ pound, sliced in eighths

Preheat the oven to 350°F and set the oven rack to the middle position.

Melt ½ stick of the butter in a 9-inch ovenproof sauté pan over medium-low heat. Whisk in the brown sugar and cook until bubbling. Slowly add the brandy, a little at a time, and cook until the brown sugar dissolves, about 2 minutes. (If the heat is too high or the brandy is added too quickly the brandy will flame up.) Set the pan aside to cool.

Beat the remaining butter and almond paste together in the bowl of an electric mixer or by hand. Add the sugar and continue to mix until fluffy and light. Beat in the eggs, one at a time, mixing thoroughly after each addition. Sift the dry ingredients together. Using a rubber spatula, fold the dry ingredients into the batter.

Arrange the nectarines over the caramel in the bottom of the pan in a circular pattern. Pour the batter over and smooth the top. Bake until a skewer comes out clean and the cake bounces back to the touch, about 1 hour. Let cool in the pan for 10 to 15 minutes. Invert onto a serving platter while still warm.

TIPS: Use a mini food processor fitted with a metal blade to cut the almond paste into the sugar before creaming with the butter. This makes incorporating it easier, particularly if the almond paste is dry, and can be done ahead of time.

If you don't have an ovenproof sauté pan, just make the caramel and pour immediately into a 9-inch cake pan, spreading it evenly over the bottom. Assemble and bake the cake according to the directions.

Poached Pears

These fragrant pears are essential to our Ginger Crunch Cake, but you can enjoy them on their own. Be sure to select fruit that is firm to the touch— we like to use Bosc, Comice, or Anjou pears. They keep beautifully in their poaching liquid, so you can make them a few days ahead of time. Just remove the cinnamon stick once they're cool, so it doesn't eclipse their delicate flavor. Serve with Candied Ginger Shortbread for a more elaborate dessert.

SERVES 4 TO 8; MAKES 8 HALVES

2 cups water

Three ½-inch strips orange zest

1 cup fresh orange juice

¼ cup fresh lemon juice

1 cup sugar

4 coins of fresh ginger

One 3-inch cinnamon stick

1 vanilla bean, sliced in half lengthwise, seeds scraped with a knife blade

4 Bosc, Anjou, Comice, or other firm pears, peeled, cored, and cut in half

Combine everything but the pears in a deep sauté pan and bring to a boil. Lower the heat and place the pears, cut side down, in the liquid. Gently simmer for about 10 minutes. Turn them over and cook until just tender, 5 to 10 minutes more, testing for doneness with a paring knife or skewer. Set aside to cool in their liquid. If serving the pears on their own, transfer them to a bowl and reduce the poaching liquid to 1 cup. Strain the syrup and spoon over the pears.

Poached Sour Cherries

Tart cherries are packed with flavor, especially the ones from Michigan. They're further enhanced with apple and orange juice, and spiced with cinnamon and fresh ginger. A vanilla bean adds a subtle final touch.

You can serve the cherries at room temperature or warm. They keep a very long time, several weeks at least in the refrigerator, and you'll think of lots of interesting ways to use them, from a fruit compote to an ice cream topping.

MAKES ABOUT 2 CUPS

¼ pound dried, pitted cherries, about 1 cup

1 cup unfiltered apple juice

½ cup fresh orange juice

½ cup water

2 tablespoons sugar

One 3-inch cinnamon stick

3 coins of fresh ginger

1 vanilla bean, sliced in half lengthwise, seeds scraped with a knife blade

Place everything in a small saucepan and bring to a boil. Lower the heat and simmer until the cherries are plump, 10 to 12 minutes. Set aside to steep until cool. Remove the cinnamon stick, ginger, and vanilla bean.

323

Rhubarb Tartlets with Almond Streusel

If you're a rhubarb fan, these little, crunchy-topped tartlets, also known as galettes, will be a revelation. This is rhubarb taken to new heights, with the fruit cooked in concentrated rhubarb juices. Real vanilla bean seeds and a touch of orange zest make the flavor soar. Serve warm from the oven with vanilla ice cream.

MAKES 8 INDIVIDUAL TARTLETS

Cream Cheese Dough (page 331)

Almond Streusel (recipe follows)

3 pounds rhubarb, 9 to 10 large stalks, cut into ½-inch cubes, about 9 cups

1 vanilla bean, sliced in half lengthwise, seeds scraped with a knife blade

2 cups sugar, plus additional to sprinkle over the tartlets

Pastry Egg Wash (page 327)

1 tablespoon minced orange zest

6 tablespoons tapioca starch

Make the Cream Cheese Dough.

Lightly flour a rolling pin and work surface. Roll the dough into six 8-inch rounds, about ⅛ inch thick. Stack the dough rounds on a plate with a layer of parchment paper between each, cover with plastic wrap, and refrigerate.

Make the Almond Streusel and set aside.

Preheat the oven to 375°F and set the rack to the top position.

Combine 3 cups of the rhubarb, the vanilla bean and seeds, and 1 cup of the sugar in a medium-size saucepan. Cook over medium-low heat until the rhubarb releases its juices and they thicken to a syrup, about 20 minutes. Set aside to cool. It will continue to thicken as it cools.

Line a baking sheet with parchment paper and place another baking sheet underneath.

Make the Pastry Egg Wash and remove the dough rounds from the refrigerator.

Toss the remaining rhubarb and sugar in a large bowl with the orange zest, tapioca starch, and the cooked rhubarb. Scoop ½ cup of filling in the center of each round and brush the edge with the egg wash. Pull up the sides and gently fold the dough to form 6 to 8 pleats as you move around the circle. A little of the filling will be visible in the center. Brush lightly with the egg wash, sprinkle generously with sugar, and place on the baking sheet.

Bake for 20 minutes. Remove from the oven and sprinkle about ¼ cup of the streusel in the center of each tartlet. Bake until golden brown and the streusel is crisp, about 15 minutes more. The filling will be bubbling and juicy, so transfer the tartlets with a spatula to a cooling rack immediately to keep them from sticking.

Almond Streusel

MAKES ABOUT 2 CUPS

¼ cup light brown sugar, packed
¼ cup sugar
¾ cup all-purpose flour
¼ cup unskinned almonds, toasted (page 46) and chopped
Pinch of salt
6 tablespoons (¾ stick) unsalted butter, chilled and cubed

Combine the sugars, flour, almonds, and salt in the bowl of an electric mixer. Using the paddle attachment, mix in the butter until the streusel is crumbly and begins to hold together.

TIP: Press along each pleat of the tartlets with the tines of a fork before baking. This helps to seal the tartlets and is an attractive, rustic touch. Be careful not to poke through the dough, or the juices will leak.

Apricot Lattice Tart

This is the ultimate dessert for apricot lovers, eager to celebrate the arrival of these first stone fruits in the summer market. That's not to say that peaches, nectarines, and plums (or even apples and quinces) won't also be delicious in this simple, crunchy-crusted tart. A few pitted cherries are a fine addition to the apricots. Serve with Toasted Almond Ice Cream.

SERVES 8

Sweet Tart Dough (recipe follows)

1 pound ripe, firm apricots, cut into eighths

½ cup sugar

2½ tablespoons tapioca starch

Pastry Egg Wash (see box)

1 to 1½ tablespoons sugar or turbinado sugar for sprinkling over the lattice

Make the Sweet Tart Dough.

Preheat the oven to 375°F.

Divide the dough in half. Lightly flour a work surface and roll one piece into a 10- by 12-inch rectangle, about ⅛ inch thick. Use a sharp knife or crimped pastry cutter to cut ten 1-inch strips. Set aside. Roll the remaining dough into a 10-inch circle. Place it in a 9-inch tart pan with a removable bottom and trim the edges so they're even with the rim of the pan.

Toss the apricots, the ½ cup sugar, and tapioca starch together and spoon into the tart shell. Make the Pastry Egg Wash. Brush the lattice strips with the egg wash. Lay five strips down, evenly spaced, over the filling. Weave the remaining five strips into the first strips on the diagonal. (Or, you can just lay the remaining strips diagonally right over the first strips.) Press around the edges of the tart, removing any excess pieces of dough, making sure the edges of the strips are well attached to the edges of the tart. Sprinkle with the sugar and bake until the fruit is bubbling and the crust is golden, 35 to 40 minutes.

Sweet Tart Dough: *A little bit of cornmeal gives this supple dough crunch, color, and flavor. It's a perfect partner for stone fruit.*

2 cups all-purpose flour

¼ cup fine cornmeal

3 tablespoons sugar

½ teaspoon salt

6 tablespoons (¾ stick) unsalted butter, cubed and chilled

6 tablespoons vegetable shortening, chilled

¼ cup ice water

Combine the flour, cornmeal, sugar, and salt in the bowl of a food processor and cut in the butter until the pieces are pea-size. (You can also do this by hand with a pastry blender.) Add the shortening and pulse it into the flour mixture until it resembles coarse meal. Transfer to a bowl. Add the water and gently toss with a fork or your fingertips, being careful not to over-work the dough. Wrap in plastic wrap and use the palm of your hand to flatten it and form a disk. Refrigerate for 30 minutes. Roll as directed.

MAKE-AHEAD TIP: The dough can be refrigerated for a few days or frozen for up to 1 month. Defrost before using.

Pastry Egg Wash

This glossy egg wash gives our pastries a lustrous finish. We brush it over tarts, pies, and turnovers just before baking.

Whisk 1 egg yolk and 2 tablespoons milk or heavy cream together until smooth. This makes enough to cover the tops of 8 turnovers, a lattice tart, or a pie.

Apple-Quince Turnovers

Quince and apples come onto the market in the fall and seem made for each other. Spiced with a little cinnamon, the fruit is irresistibly fragrant, especially when these turnovers are just out of the oven. They're great for breakfast, reheated and served with lots of coffee.

MAKES 8 TURNOVERS

Cream Cheese Dough (page 331)

1 tablespoon unsalted butter

¼ cup plus 2 tablespoons sugar

Pinch of salt

½ teaspoon fresh lemon juice

2 large Granny Smith or other tart, green apples, about ¾ pound, peeled and cut into
¾-inch cubes, about 3 cups

1 cup unfiltered apple juice

½ cup water

One 2-inch cinnamon stick

2 large quince, about ¾ pound, peeled, cored, and cut into ¾-inch cubes, about 3 cups

2½ tablespoons tapioca starch

Pastry Egg Wash (page 327)

Cinnamon Sugar (recipe follows)

Make the Cream Cheese Dough.

Lightly flour a rolling pin and work surface. Roll the dough into six 8-inch rounds, about ¼ inch thick. Stack the dough rounds on a plate with a layer of parchment paper between each, cover with plastic wrap, and refrigerate.

Melt the butter in a medium-size sauté pan, add 2 tablespoons sugar, the salt, and lemon juice; cook over medium heat until the sugar is dissolved and bubbling, 2 to 3 minutes. Add the apples and cook until just tender, about 5 minutes. Transfer to a medium-size bowl and set aside to cool.

Combine the apple juice, water, cinnamon stick, and ¼ cup sugar in a medium-size saucepan and bring to a boil. Lower the heat, add the quince, and simmer until tender, 5 to 6 minutes. Set aside to cool. Drain the quince (saving the liquid if you like—see tip), add to the apples, and toss the fruit with the tapioca starch and the remaining sugar.

Preheat the oven to 375°F and set the oven rack to the middle position. Remove the dough rounds from the refrigerator.

Make the Pastry Egg Wash and the Cinnamon Sugar.

Place ⅓ cup of the fruit in the center of each round and brush the edge with the egg wash. Fold the dough over the filling to form a half-moon. Seal and crimp the edges with the back of a fork. Brush the turnovers with egg wash and sprinkle lightly with cinnamon sugar. Place on a parchment-lined baking sheet and bake until golden, about 25 minutes.

Cinnamon Sugar: This spicy sugar is good to have on hand to sprinkle over pastries, cookies, and toast.

1 tablespoon ground cinnamon
1 cup sugar

Combine and store in an airtight container.

MAKE-AHEAD TIP: The dough rounds can be rolled in advance and stored in the refrigerator for up to 2 days, or in the freezer, layered with parchment or wax paper; just be sure to wrap them tightly with plastic wrap. Thaw before using. (You can also thaw them in the refrigerator overnight.)

You can poach the quince several days ahead and leave it in the poaching liquid; just be sure to remove the cinnamon stick before refrigerating it. The flavor will actually intensify if you make it ahead.

TIP: Use leftover quince poaching liquid to poach dried fruit, such as sour cherries.

VARIATION: For an early summer treat, use the apricot filling from the Apricot Lattice Tart to make the turnovers. Increase the apricots to 1½ pounds, the tapioca starch to 3 tablespoons, and add sugar to taste. Apricots are juicier than apples and quince, so a scant ⅓ cup of filling is all you'll need. Don't fill the turnovers too full, or they'll explode when you bake them.

Quince

This unique old-world fruit—with a flavor that's somewhere between an apple and a pear—is high on our list of fall favorites. We buy them by the case and poach them with fruit juice and spices for warm compotes—both savory and sweet—and exquisite baked turnovers, lattice tarts, and pies. Leave a couple of quince on your kitchen windowsill to ripen on a warm sunny day, and their incredible fragrance will fill the room. There's a catch here: You simply can't eat them raw. When poached, though, their firm, astringent flesh becomes soft and sweet. Keep an eye out for that magical moment when their color turns rosy; that's when you know they're done. With their high pectin content, they thicken their poaching liquid, making a kind of homey preserve.

In San Francisco, we know Chinese New Year is near when slender branches of ornamental flowering quince appear all over Chinatown. Red quince—not the pale, delicate white ones—is the color to look for here. It's the ultimate symbol of life and good luck in the New Year.

Cream Cheese Dough

This supple dough is easy to make and incredibly forgiving. It includes cornmeal and natural cream cheese for a pleasant, smooth texture punctuated with crunchiness. If you're making pastry with a juicy fruit filling, be sure to use this dough.

MAKES 8 TURNOVERS

2 cups all-purpose flour

⅓ cup fine cornmeal

3 tablespoons sugar

½ teaspoon salt

2 sticks unsalted butter, chilled and cubed

½ pound natural cream cheese

Sift the dry ingredients together in the bowl of an electric mixer. Use the paddle attachment to cut in the butter until the pieces are pea-size. (You can also do this by hand with a pastry blender.) Add the cream cheese and work until just combined, being careful not to overmix. There will still be white streaks of cream cheese striating the dough. Wrap in plastic wrap and chill for 30 minutes. Roll as directed in the recipe.

MAKE-AHEAD TIP: The dough can be refrigerated for a few days or frozen for up to 1 month. Defrost before using.

Fromage Blanc Cheesecake with Pistachio Crust

This distinctive cheesecake has a wonderfully tangy flavor. The secret ingredient that makes it different from all other cheesecakes is fromage blanc, a simple, fresh, creamy cheese available at specialty stores and some supermarkets. If it's not, don't substitute ricotta.

The other unusual element is the shortbread crust with chopped nuts. We make it with pistachios but you can substitute chopped candied ginger for the nuts.

SERVES 10 TO 12

Pistachio Shortbread (page 311), ½ recipe of dough

Melted butter for brushing the pan

1½ pounds fromage blanc

1 pound natural cream cheese

1 cup sugar

1 teaspoon minced orange, tangerine, or Meyer lemon zest

Pinch of salt

2 large eggs

Make the Pistachio Shortbread dough and chill.

Preheat the oven to 325°F.

Brush a 9-inch springform pan with melted butter, line with a round of parchment paper, and brush with a little more butter. Roll the pistachio shortbread dough to fit the pan and press it gently and evenly into the bottom. Bake until golden, 12 to 15 minutes.

Combine the fromage blanc, cream cheese, sugar, citrus zest, and salt in the bowl of an electric mixer; using the paddle attachment, mix until smooth. (You can also do this by hand.) Mix in the eggs, one at a time, scraping down the sides of the bowl and combine until smooth after each addition. Pour the batter over the crust. Place a pan of hot water on the bottom rack of the oven to prevent a crust from forming on the top of the cheesecake. Bake on the top rack of the oven until just set, 45 to 50 minutes. It will continue to cook as it cools, so the center should be a little soft when you remove it from the oven.

Triple Chocolate Angel Food Cake

This ethereal cake is food for those angels who can never get enough chocolate. Chunks of bittersweet chocolate melt into the airy cocoa-flavored batter, creating delectable little bites of chocolate throughout. We finish the cake with a glossy Chocolate Glaze.

SERVES 8 TO 10

1 cup cake flour

⅓ cup unsweetened cocoa powder

Pinch of salt

10 egg whites, about 1¾ cups, at room temperature

1 teaspoon cream of tartar

1¾ cups sugar

1½ teaspoons pure vanilla extract

1 teaspoon fresh lemon juice

3½ ounces bittersweet chocolate, finely chopped, about ¾ cup

Chocolate Glaze (recipe follows)

Preheat the oven to 350°F.

Sift the flour, cocoa, and salt together. Beat the egg whites and cream of tartar in the bowl of an electric mixer until foamy. Slowly pour in the sugar and beat until the whites are glossy and firm, but not dry.

Sift one-third of the dry ingredients into the whites and fold in gently with a rubber spatula. Add the vanilla and lemon juice, sift in another one-third of the flour mixture, and fold in gently. Sift the remaining dry ingredients and fold in, along with the chocolate.

Pour the batter into an ungreased tube pan with a removable bottom. Pass a skewer or long, thin knife blade through the batter to remove any air pockets. Bake until golden brown and cooked through, 35 to 40 minutes. Check for doneness with a skewer or paring knife; it should come out clean. Invert the pan on a rack (see Tip) and let the cake cool completely before removing from the pan, about 1 hour.

Make the Chocolate Glaze. Pour the glaze over the top of the cake.

Chocolate Glaze: This silky glaze can be made ahead of time and refrigerated. Just spoon it over the top of the cake and let gravity do the rest.

MAKES ABOUT ¾ CUP

¼ pound bittersweet chocolate, finely chopped, scant 1 cup

7 tablespoons heavy cream

1 tablespoon unsalted butter

1 teaspoon light corn syrup

Combine everything in a small heavy-bottomed saucepan and cook over medium-low heat, whisking until smooth. Allow the glaze to cool and thicken slightly, then drizzle over the cake. To reheat, transfer to a small bowl and heat over a pan of barely simmering water or in a double boiler. If the glaze is thick, add a little cream or milk to thin it.

TIPS: To ensure a light, airy cake that rises all the way to the top of the pan, use a scrupulously clean pan—the same goes for the bowl of the electric mixer—so the whites beat to their fullest volume.

Angel food cakes are cooled upside down. A real angel food cake pan has little feet to accomplish this, but you can get the same effect by hanging the cake upside down over the neck of a large bottle.

Chocolate Mousse with Filo Crisps

With its smooth velvety texture, you'd never guess this decadent mousse is made without eggs or cream— vanilla soy milk is the secret ingredient here. The Poached Sour Cherries are a nice twist on the classic chocolate-cherry affinity, and the Filo Crisps provide a good crunch.

All the elements can be made ahead of time: The mousse keeps for up to a week in the refrigerator, the crisps keep well in a sealed container, and the cherries will still be tasty a week or two after you make them.

SERVES 4 TO 6

Filo Crisps (recipe follows)
1½ cups vanilla soy milk
¾ pound bittersweet chocolate, chopped, about 2½ cups
Poached Sour Cherries (page 323)

Make the Filo Crisps.

Bring the soy milk to a boil in a small, heavy-bottomed saucepan. Add the chocolate and whisk until smooth. Remove the pan from the heat and whisk until slightly thickened, 2 to 3 minutes. Transfer to a bowl and set aside to cool. Place a layer of plastic wrap directly over the surface of the mousse and refrigerate for 2 to 3 hours. It will thicken as it cools.

Make the Poached Sour Cherries.

To serve, place a filo crisp on each plate and scoop 2 to 3 spoonfuls of mousse on top of each. Spoon ¼ cup cherries and their poaching liquid over and place a filo crisp on top. Serve right away to keep the crisps from getting soggy.

RESTAURANT TIP: We use a small ice cream scooper or large melon ball scoop to serve the mousse.

Filo Crisps: *These light treats are sprinkled with crunchy sugar. They can also be sprinkled with cinnamon sugar and rolled like little cigars.*

MAKES 12 TO 16 CRISPS

6 frozen filo pastry sheets, thawed overnight in the refrigerator

Canola oil or melted unsalted butter

2 to 3 tablespoons turbinado or raw sugar

Preheat the oven to 350°F.

Lay one sheet of filo on a work surface, brush it lightly with oil, and sprinkle lightly with the sugar. Top with another sheet of filo; brush with oil and sprinkle with sugar. Continue with the remaining sheets of filo. Cut the stack into 3- to 4-inch squares, depending on the size of the filo. Place on a parchment-lined baking sheet. Place another baking sheet underneath and bake on the top shelf of the oven until golden and crisp, 5 to 7 minutes.

Allow to cool. Serve or transfer to an airtight container and layer parchment paper between the crisps to keep them from breaking.

TIP: We use two sheet pans together—one laid on top of the other—to help the filo crisps bake evenly and keep them from getting too dark.

Chocolate-Rum Steamed Pudding

This old-fashioned dessert is delicious on its own. Dress it up for a special occasion with a gorgeous Chocolate Glaze, or simply dust it lightly with powdered sugar just before serving. Poached Sour Cherries and whipped cream are fine accompaniments.

Don't be scared off by the very idea of making a steamed pudding; it's just a cake baked in a Bundt pan in a water bath. There's no fuss about it.

SERVES 10 TO 12

1½ sticks unsalted butter, at room temperature

1 cup light brown sugar, packed

½ cup sugar

4 large eggs, at room temperature

1¼ cups all-purpose flour

½ cup unsweetened cocoa powder

1½ teaspoons baking powder

¾ teaspoon baking soda

Pinch of salt

⅔ cup buttermilk

¼ cup dark rum

3½ ounces bittersweet chocolate, finely chopped, about 1 cup

½ cup pecan pieces, toasted (page 46) and chopped

Preheat the oven to 350°F and set the oven rack to the middle position. Butter and flour a Bundt pan.

In the bowl of an electric mixer, beat the butter and sugars together until fluffy. (You can also do this by hand.) Scrape down the sides of the bowl and add the eggs, one at a time, mixing thoroughly after each addition. Sift the flour, cocoa, baking powder, baking soda, and salt together in a large bowl. Alternate adding the dry ingredients, the buttermilk, and the rum to the butter mixture, beginning and ending with the dry ingredients. Fold the chocolate and pecans into the batter and pour it into the pan.

Place the pan in a baking dish large enough to hold it. Add enough hot water to make a water bath that comes halfway up the sides of the Bundt pan. Cover the pans completely with foil and seal the edges tightly around the baking dish. Bake for about 2 hours, or until a testing skewer comes out clean.

Remove the pan from the water bath and cool for 10 to 15 minutes. Use a thin spatula to loosen the cake from the pan and invert onto a serving platter.

Chocolate-Chestnut Mousse Cakes

Make this elegant dessert for a special occasion in the fall or winter. The distinctive taste of chestnut provides balance to the two kinds of chocolate here, bittersweet and milk. You have two choices when serving: hot from the oven, when the cakes are light, fluffy, almost souffléd; or cooled, as we serve them, when they become more like creamy mousse.

MAKES 6 INDIVIDUAL CAKES

Melted butter for the ramekins

Sugar for the ramekins

3 large eggs

¼ cup sugar

4 tablespoons (½ stick) unsalted butter

¼ pound bittersweet chocolate, chopped

¼ pound milk chocolate, chopped

¼ pound sweetened chestnut puree, crumbled, about ½ cup

½ cup heavy cream

Brush six ½-cup ramekins with melted butter, sprinkle generously with sugar, tapping out the excess, and set aside. Preheat the oven to 350°F and set the oven rack to the middle position.

Beat the eggs in the bowl of an electric mixer until foamy. Add the sugar and beat until the eggs are pale and fluffy, about 5 minutes.

Melt the butter and chocolates together in a double boiler and stir in the chestnut puree. There will be a little texture from the chestnut puree. Remove from the heat and set aside to cool.

Whip the cream until it forms soft peaks. Fold the eggs into the chocolate mixture, then fold in the whipped cream. Spoon the batter into the ramekins, filling them three-quarters full. Place the ramekins in a large baking pan. Add enough hot water to make a water bath that comes halfway up the sides of the ramekins.

Bake on the middle rack of the oven until set and puffed like soufflés, 45 to 50 minutes. The center will be a little wet but they will continue to cook as they cool.

VARIATION: Substitute almond butter for the chestnut puree.

Basmati Rice Pudding with Mascarpone

This is rice pudding with an exotic twist. The heady fragrance of the spices combine with the nutty taste of basmati rice, enriched here with a luxurious touch of mascarpone. The pudding is best served with fruit alongside, especially tropical fruit such as mango tossed with lime juice. Strawberries are also delicious.

SERVES 6 TO 8

3 cups half-and-half

⅓ cup plus 2 tablespoons sugar

½ vanilla bean, sliced in half lengthwise, seeds scraped with a knife blade

One 3-inch cinnamon stick

4 cardamom pods, smashed with the side of a knife

3 coins of fresh ginger

Salt

6 cups water

1 cup basmati rice, rinsed

½ cup mascarpone cheese

3 large egg yolks

339

Combine 1 cup of the half-and-half, ⅓ cup of the sugar, the vanilla bean and seeds, the spices, and a pinch of salt in a small, heavy-bottomed saucepan and cook over medium-low heat until the sugar is dissolved, about 10 minutes. Remove from the heat and steep for 30 minutes. Pour through a strainer and reserve the spices and the vanilla pod. Return the seasoned half-and-half to the pan and set aside.

Meanwhile, bring the water to a boil in a medium-size saucepan, add ¼ teaspoon salt, and the rice, and cook at a rolling boil for 10 minutes. Remove from the heat, cover, and let sit for 10 minutes. Drain and add the rice to the seasoned half-and-half. Cook over medium-low heat until the liquid is absorbed, about 5 minutes. Remove from the heat, stir in the mascarpone, and set aside.

Whisk the egg yolks in a small bowl. In a small, heavy-bottomed saucepan, heat the remaining half-and-half with the reserved spices and the vanilla pod, the rest of the sugar, and a pinch of salt over medium-low heat. Gradually whisk ½ cup of the warm half-and-half into the yolks and add them to the rest of the half-and-half. Cook over medium-low heat, stirring constantly, until the mixture thickens enough to coat the back of a spoon, 10 to 12 minutes. Pour through a fine mesh strainer and discard the spices and the vanilla pod. Gently stir the custard into the rice mixture until incorporated. Set aside to cool for 15 to 20 minutes. It will thicken as it cools. Serve warm or at room temperature.

VARIATION WITH COCONUT MILK: Substitute 1 cup of unsweetened canned coconut milk for 1 cup of the half-and-half and combine with ⅓ cup of the sugar, the vanilla bean pod and seeds, the spices, and a pinch of salt. Follow the recipe as directed.

Cranberry Compote with Tangerines

This brilliantly colored compote is intensely flavored, so a little goes a long way. It's a perfect partner for Fromage Blanc Cheesecake with Pistachio Crust. If you're not using one of the tangerine varieties listed below, choose carefully; you want bright flavor and no seeds. The compote keeps in the refrigerator for weeks, but its glory fades after a couple of days.

MAKES ABOUT 3 CUPS, SERVES 8

8 seedless tangerines, such as Satsuma, Mineolas, and Pixie

12 ounces whole fresh cranberries, about 3½ cups

1 cup sugar

½ cup water

Pinch of salt

Squeeze the juice from 2 or 3 of the tangerines; you should have ½ cup. With a sharp knife, trim and discard the peel and white pith from the remaining tangerines. Remove each section by slicing between the center membranes; place in a small bowl, and set aside. You should have 1½ to 2 cups of sections.

Combine everything but the tangerine sections in a nonreactive saucepan and bring to a boil. Lower the heat, and simmer until the cranberries begin to pop and the sugar is dissolved, about 8 minutes. Remove from the heat, add the tangerine sections, and set aside to cool.

Bittersweet Chocolate Sauce

This luscious sauce couldn't be easier to make. Be sure to use a high-quality chocolate with a flavor you prefer; we use Guittard. Spoon over Toasted Almond Ice Cream or just keep on hand for a late-night chocolate craving.

MAKES 1½ CUPS

1 cup heavy cream

6 ounces bittersweet chocolate, chopped, about 1¼ cups

1 teaspoon pure vanilla extract

Pinch of salt

Place the cream in a small, heavy-bottomed saucepan and bring to a boil. Lower the heat, whisk in the remaining ingredients and cook, whisking constantly, until the chocolate is melted and the sauce is smooth, 2 to 3 minutes. Remove from the heat and set aside to cool. The sauce keeps very well, for several weeks, sealed in an airtight container and refrigerated.

TIPS: To reheat the sauce, transfer it to a small bowl and heat over a pan of barely simmering water. You can also use a double boiler here.

Look for chocolate with a high percentage of cocoa solids and the presence of cocoa butter; they're a sure indication of fine chocolate. Scharffen Berger, Valhrona, Callebaut, and El Rey are excellent choices.

Rose Geranium Ice Cream

If you don't have rose geraniums growing in your garden or in a pot, this ice cream isn't for you. But if you do, you'll be amazed at the heady quality of this rich ice cream. This is one of those desserts that drives people crazy with delight.

Serve it with berries and shortbread, garnished with a rose geranium leaf or flower.

MAKES 1 QUART

3 cups heavy cream

1 cup milk

⅔ cup sugar

10 rose geranium leaves

Pinch of salt

8 large egg yolks

Combine the cream, milk, sugar, rose geranium leaves, and salt in a medium-size heavy-bottomed saucepan. Heat the mixture to just below boiling, remove from the heat, and set aside to steep for 20 minutes. Taste the cream mixture. If the rose geranium flavor is strong enough, remove the leaves, if not, continue to steep 10 to 15 minutes more. Pour through a fine mesh strainer and discard the leaves. Return the cream mixture to the pan.

Whisk the egg yolks in a bowl and slowly pour in a little of the hot cream mixture, whisking constantly. Pour the warmed yolks back into the pan and cook over medium-low heat, stirring constantly, until the mixture coats the spoon, 10 to 12 minutes. Pour through a fine mesh strainer and cool. Freeze according to the manufacturer's directions for your ice cream maker.

Toasted Almond Ice Cream

Steeping toasted almonds in cream brings out every bit of their extraordinary flavor, which is then boosted with both pure almond and vanilla extracts. Purity of flavor counts here, so use the best almonds you can find— natural foods stores and farmers' markets are good sources. This ice cream is a natural partner for chocolate (especially Bittersweet Chocolate Sauce), nectarines, and peaches.

MAKES 1 QUART

1½ cups unskinned almonds

2 cups heavy cream

2 cups milk

½ cup sugar

Pinch of salt

8 large egg yolks

1 teaspoon pure vanilla extract

1 teaspoon pure almond extract

Preheat the oven to 350°F.

Toast the almonds on a baking sheet until golden and fragrant, 8 to 10 minutes. Coarsely chop when cool.

Combine the cream, milk, sugar, and salt in a medium-size heavy-bottomed saucepan and heat to just below boiling. Whisk the egg yolks in a small bowl and pour in a little of the hot cream mixture, whisking constantly. Pour the warmed yolks into the pan and cook over medium-low heat, stirring constantly, until the mixture coats the spoon, 10 to 12 minutes. Pour through a fine mesh strainer, stir in the vanilla and almond extracts, and cool.

Freeze according to the manufacturer's directions for your ice cream maker. Transfer to a container, fold in the almonds, and freeze until ready to serve.

Plum Sorbet

We usually make this sorbet with Santa Rosa plums, which are widely available, but other varieties, such as Golden or the wonderful big Elephant Heart plums with their deep red centers, are also excellent. You can use just one variety or mix them, or, for a gorgeous presentation, make two sorbets using different plum varieties with different colors. Serve the sorbet with Candied Ginger Shortbread.

MAKES 1 QUART

2 pounds flavorful, ripe plums, cut in quarters

¾ cup sugar

Pinch of salt

1 to 2 tablespoons fresh orange juice (optional)

Combine the plums, sugar, and salt in a medium-size, heavy-bottomed saucepan. Cover and cook over medium heat until the plums break down and the sugar dissolves, about 30 minutes. When cool, transfer to a blender and puree until smooth, about 3 minutes. Pour through a fine-mesh strainer and chill. Stir in the orange juice, if using, and freeze according to the manufacturer's directions for your ice cream maker. The sorbet will be fluffy and lighter in color when it's ready.

Blackberry Sorbet

Simplicity itself, this sorbet is made in just a few minutes. The flavor of the berries can vary a lot. If they're very sweet or too tart, you may need to use more lemon juice or more sugar. A pinch of salt brings out the flavor.

MAKES 1 QUART

Three 1-pint baskets of blackberries, about 6 cups
¾ cup sugar
1 teaspoon fresh lemon juice
Pinch of salt

Puree the berries and sugar in a blender until completely smooth, about 3 minutes. Pour through a fine-mesh strainer to remove the seeds; you should have about 3½ cups of puree. Add the lemon juice and the salt. Freeze the sorbet according to the manufacturer's directions for your ice cream maker.

Blackberry Sherbet: *Stir 1 cup half-and-half into the puree before freezing.*

Blueberry-Orange Bread

This quick bread is truly quick, and is always on the menu for Greens' summer Sunday brunches. Blueberries are great, but any summer berry— or frozen berries— will be fine too. For a winter version, see the variation with dried fruit.

The bread is delicious toasted, and, unlike most quick breads, it keeps well for several days.

MAKES 1 LOAF

1¾ cups all-purpose flour

1 teaspoon baking powder

¼ teaspoon salt

1 stick unsalted butter, softened

¾ cup sugar

2 large eggs

1 tablespoon minced orange zest

¼ cup fresh orange juice

½ cup Crème Fraîche (page 98) or sour cream

1 pint blueberries

Preheat the oven to 350°F.

Butter and flour a 9- by 5-inch loaf pan. Sift the dry ingredients together in a large bowl and set aside. Whip the butter and sugar in the bowl of an electric mixer until fluffy. Add the eggs, one at a time, scraping down the bowl after each addition. Combine the zest, juice, and the crème fraîche. Add the dry ingredients and the crème fraîche mixture alternately to the batter, beginning and ending with the dry ingredients. Gently fold in the blueberries.

Spread the batter into the loaf pan and bake until golden brown and cooked through, about 1½ hours. Check for doneness with a skewer or paring knife, which should come out clean.

VARIATION WITH DRIED SOUR CHERRIES OR CRANBERRIES: Plump 1 cup dried sour cherries or cranberries in hot water to cover for about 15 minutes. Drain and gently fold into the batter. Add ½ cup toasted, chopped pecans, walnuts, or skinned hazelnuts to the batter.

Currant-Pecan Scones

Fresh scones are popular for Sunday brunch and every day at our take-out counter, Greens to Go. These have extra richness and the fresh touch of orange juice and zest. You can freeze them or keep them for a couple of days before toasting them for breakfast or a midmorning snack.

MAKES 8 SCONES

1 tablespoon minced orange zest

⅓ cup dried currants

¼ cup fresh orange juice

3 cups all-purpose flour

1 tablespoon baking powder

6 tablespoons sugar

¼ teaspoon salt

1 stick unsalted butter, chilled and cubed

½ cup pecan pieces, toasted (page 46) and chopped

1 cup heavy cream

½ cup buttermilk

Pastry Egg Wash (page 327)

Preheat the oven to 375°F and set the oven rack to the middle position. Set the zest aside and plump the currants in the orange juice.

Sift the flour, baking powder, sugar, and salt into the bowl of an electric mixer. Use the paddle attachment to cut the butter into the flour mixture and work it until it resembles coarse meal. (You can also do this by hand with a pastry blender.) Transfer to a large bowl and stir in the nuts.

Combine the zest, currants, cream, and buttermilk. Add to the dry ingredients and gently mix together until it just holds together, being careful not to overwork the dough.

Sprinkle the work surface lightly with flour and shape the dough into an 8-inch round, about 1 inch high. Cut the round into 8 wedges and place 1 inch apart on a parchment-lined baking sheet, stacked on top of another baking sheet. (The double pan helps keep the bottoms from browning too quickly.) Make the egg wash and brush it over the scones.

Bake for 30 minutes. Rotate the pan and bake until golden and cooked through, 10 to 15 minutes more.

Maple-Pecan Spice Muffins

Light, warmly spiced, and crunchy on top, these simple muffins are so easy to make you can toss them together for breakfast. There are a couple of key ingredients you'll need to have on hand: maple sugar and vanilla soy milk, both available at natural food stores.

MAKES 10 MUFFINS

Canola oil for the muffin tins

Maple-Pecan Streusel (recipe follows)

1 cup all-purpose flour

1 cup cake flour

3 tablespoons maple sugar

1 teaspoon baking powder

½ teaspoon ground allspice

¼ teaspoon ground ginger

¼ teaspoon ground cardamom

¼ teaspoon salt

¾ cup vanilla soy milk

¾ cup maple syrup, plus 2 tablespoons

¼ cup canola oil

2 tablespoons pure vanilla extract

1 tablespoon unfiltered apple cider vinegar

Preheat the oven to 350°F and set the oven racks to the middle and top positions. Lightly brush the muffin tins with canola oil.

Make the Maple-Pecan Streusel and set aside.

Sift the dry ingredients together in a large bowl. Whisk the remaining ingredients together and gently fold into the dry ingredients until just mixed, being careful not to overwork the batter. Divide the batter into the muffin tins, filling them two-thirds full. Sprinkle 1 tablespoon of the streusel over each muffin. Bake on the middle rack for 15 minutes. Rotate the pan, move to the top rack, and bake until the muffins are golden and the center springs back to the touch, about 10 minutes more. Allow the muffins to cool in the pan for about 10 minutes, then transfer to a cooling rack.

TIP: If you don't have cake flour, just use another cup of all-purpose flour. The muffins won't be as light, but they'll still be delicious.

Maple-Pecan Streusel

MAKES ABOUT ¾ CUP

½ cup pecan pieces, toasted (page 46) and finely chopped
¼ cup maple sugar
1½ tablespoons canola oil

Combine the ingredients in a small bowl and use your fingertips to mix them together.

Blueberry-Maple-Pecan Spice Muffins: *Gently fold 1 pint blueberries into the batter.*

Maple-Pecan Streusel Cake: *Double the streusel recipe. Lightly brush a 9-inch springform pan with canola oil and spoon half of the batter into it. Sprinkle 1 cup of the streusel over and spread the remaining batter on top, smoothing it to the edges of the pan. Top with the rest of the streusel and bake on the middle rack for 30 minutes. Rotate the pan, move to the top rack, and bake 10 to 15 minutes more. Check for doneness by inserting a skewer or paring knife in the center; it should come out clean.*

The Kitchen Cupboard

WINES WITH GREENS

In the very beginning—in 1979—there was no plan to serve wines at Greens. But we started to discuss wines for this new style of food, and talk turned into organized tastings, which is the way to find out what works and what doesn't. Twenty-four years later, Greens has an excellent wine list that includes hundreds of wines, sixteen by the glass. There are no house wines, but tasting is still very much encouraged. There are also beers, ciders, and Navarro's elegant but nonalcoholic grape juices from Pinot Noir and Gewürztraminer grapes.

There are still no real rules to serving wine with our food, just a few guidelines to keep in mind. The point of matching foods to wines, after all, is to enhance both elements—the food tastes better because of the wine; the wine tastes better because of the food.

Almost invariably, the best wines for this food are young, fresh wines with a taste of fruit and not wood (which comes from fermentation or aging in small barrels). Fruit refers to the fruity qualities of the wine grape, not sweetness. In fact, a fruity wine is often dry. A Riesling has flavors that hint at apricot or peach or raspberry; Chardonnay may remind us of apple. Of course, these flavor memories are all highly subjective, and your own taste may identify different qualities in the wine, but you will always taste the fruit element.

With these younger wines, their bright flavors make a good match with the similarly bright-tasting fresh vegetables. Many of these wines are made to be drunk young and they're usually modestly priced. Current vintages work well with our lighter food, while the long-cellared, treasured reds such as special vintage Barolos and Cabernets aren't so easy to match, except with full-flavored dishes such as lasagne.

The right wine is an appropriate wine; appropriate to the occasion, the weather, the company, and the food. Food and wine that spring from the same region go together naturally and almost magically. With a classic Ligurian pasta with pesto, you might serve a fresh Vermentino from Liguria or another similarly brisk white wine. With almonds and olives in Spanish tapas, consider a crisp, young, very dry sherry.

Asian food can match with either wine (a young white wine with good fruit and sometimes just a little sweetness) or with a good beer. Mediterranean dishes are often best with bright red smooth wines with some richness, such as a rich Rhône Syrah or an Italian Barbera. Middle Eastern and North African food often need fully flavored, bold rosés. Look for rosés from California and Provence.

Indian food is good with full-flavored white and rosé wines, such as Riesling or a California Sauvignon Blanc. If it's spicy, a full red such as Syrah will be in order. But beer or ale is always a good choice with Indian food. The same choices work with Mexican food.

Light beers are especially good matches because they can handle many flavors. At Greens there are excellent beers to choose from, including the organic Wolaver's, a favorite of many customers and staff.

A few special cases: With egg dishes, a white such as Riesling is delicious. When the food is delicate, champagne immediately comes to mind. Or consider Prosecco, the Italian sparkling wine that goes well with lighter foods and makes a good apéritif that can continue into the first course.

A simple risotto is a dish unto itself that's based on the rice, the wine, and the stock it's cooked with. It's easy to match: Just choose the wine you want to drink and use the same wine in the risotto.

Herbs are another special case. Although parsley is wine-friendly, other fresh herbs such as rosemary can be hard on wine; because they're spirited, pungent, and sometimes forceful, these herbs can dim the flavor of wine.

Artichokes are infamously difficult with wine. Try a rosé from the south of France, or a Viognier or even a dry vermouth on the rocks.

Each wine, each dish, each occasion is different, and no guidelines can cover it all. The most important element of matching food and wine is your own pleasure. If you think both the food and the wine are delicious, and they're delicious together, then you've done a brilliant job.

OILS IN THE GREENS KITCHEN

We use oils for both cooking and flavoring our dishes. Because they're the major carrier of flavor, it's important to have high-quality oils. Here's what's in our pantry.

EXTRA-VIRGIN OLIVE OIL

In these heady days of specialty ingredients, extra-virgin olive oil from all over the map has flooded the marketplace. Finding a fine extra-virgin is no longer the problem, it's deciding on which fantastic variety to buy. Of course, price is important, but your own taste is what's really essential. We keep it pretty simple at Greens, featuring two delicious California olive oils— Marsala and Sevillano— made by Nick Sciabica and Sons nearby in Modesto. Marsala is smooth and buttery, while Sevillano is fruity and assertive. Both work beautifully for pasta, wilted salads, sautéing, and intensely flavored vinaigrettes. For some special dishes, we use a peppery, dark green extra-virgin from Tuscany. These fine oils are available at Ferry Plaza farmers' market in San Francisco.

PURE OLIVE OIL

This mild, refined olive oil is unremarkable in itself, so it's a good vehicle for picking up other flavors. It provides a subtle background for sparkling citrus vinaigrettes and balances the assertive flavor of nut oils, such as walnut and hazelnut, without taking away their richness. It's also great for mayonnaise when we want to play down the big taste of olive. We use an Italian import in a big pink can with a tiger on the front. We call it Tiger, but its real name is Tiger Brand, made by Fortuna Fontana. There are many brands of pure olive oil to choose from; just look for a mild, inexpensive oil with a clean, light taste.

CANOLA OIL

This light-tasting, rapeseed oil is fine for spicy Asian curries and Mexican soups and stews, where spices and chilies have a field day. There's no point in using olive oil for these dishes, when this inexpensive all-purpose oil will do. Like pure olive oil, it's a good vehicle for dishes with big, bold flavors.

PEANUT OIL

Peanut oil is very tolerant of high temperatures, so it's the perfect oil for frying. It's also a natural complement to the flavors in many of our Asian dishes. Be aware that some people are highly allergic to peanuts; we're always careful to tell our customers we've used peanut oil in a dish.

TOASTED SESAME OIL

This toasted oil with the big sesame flavor is a natural seasoning for noodle dishes, stir-fries, and Asian-inspired vegetable fillings. Its dark, assertive flavor can be overpowering, so use it sparingly and taste the dish before you add that extra spoonful. It's highly perishable, so buy it in small bottles and keep it in the refrigerator.

NUT OILS

Walnut and hazelnut oils make fine vinaigrettes and are a delicious accent for pastas tossed with toasted walnuts and hazelnuts. Nut oils are fragile and turn rancid quickly, so find a good-quality brand and keep it in the refrigerator. They're also expensive, but very much worth the splurge.

INFUSED OILS

These intensely flavored specialty oils are a delicious enhancement to salads, pasta, and risotto. They're expensive, so here's how you justify the investment: They're to be used only as a flavoring—a little goes a very long way.

LEMON OIL

This fragrant extra-virgin olive oil, made by the Sciabica family, is fresh, light, and clean. Eureka lemons are actually pressed with the olives, so a lemony essence infuses the oil. We toss it with roasted beets and peppery arugula or into a salad of fresh summer beans. It's also great spooned over penne with artichokes and salty black olives.

PORCINI AND WHITE TRUFFLE OILS

These distinctive oils with their incredible wild essence come to us from Connie Green, our wild mushroom forager from Wine Forest Wild Mushrooms in Napa Valley. A light drizzle of these extraordinary oils takes pasta and risotto into the stratosphere. They'll dress up simple pappardelle with grilled portobello mushrooms or intensify the subtle fall flavors of risotto with leeks and woodsy chanterelles. If a truffle oil price seems too good to be true, it probably is — cheap truffle oils are made from chemicals, not truffles.

SOME OUTSTANDING LOCALLY MADE CHEESES

The beautiful, rolling hills of Sonoma and West Marin counties are home to a fresh generation of creameries and artisan cheese makers who share an unwavering commitment to their herds of sheep, goats, and cows and the cheeses they make with the milk. We have the extraordinary good fortune of featuring these exceptional cheeses on our menu. They're available at cheese shops and specialty food stores, at farmers' markets, by mail order, and over the internet. You can taste a sampling of many of these cheeses here in San Francisco at the Ferry Plaza Farmers' Market.

From Bellwether Farms in Petaluma, Sonoma County organic sheep and cow's milk cheeses (bellwethercheese.com; 888-527-8606):

CRESCENZA

This buttery, soft-ripened cow's milk cheese is slightly tart and yeasty. We spread it over grilled or toasted bread and feature it in a trio of crostini along with warm chanterelles and Picholine Olive Tapenade.

FROMAGE BLANC

This fresh, smooth cow's milk cheese is wonderfully tangy like chèvre, but without the goaty flavor. We spread it on croutons and spoon it over a peperonata or Greek pizza and spread it on grilled bread with a sprinkling of chives.

PECORINO PEPATO

Made in the pecorino style with raw sheep's milk, this lovely soft cheese is studded with whole peppercorns and aged for two to three months. It's a delightful table cheese served with warm almonds and good, crusty bread. We shave it over a smoky salad of grilled portobello mushrooms and endive.

RICOTTA

We feature two different ricottas here—one from sheep's milk and the other from Jersey cow milk, prized for its rich flavor and golden color. Both are light and sweet, but the cow's milk ricotta is unforgettably buttery and creamy. Both come to us in the shape of the artisan baskets in which they're formed. Savor this exquisite fresh cheese with succulent figs and sliced melon.

From Cowgirl Creamery in Point Reyes Station, in West Marin County (cowgirlcreamery.com; 415-663-9335):

FROMAGE BLANC

Like all the Cowgirl cheeses, this tangy, fresh cheese is made with Straus organic milk. Made in the French style, it's light, yet full of rich flavor. It makes an incredibly delicious cheesecake and a fantastic open-face sandwich with juicy heirloom tomatoes and whole leaves of opal basil.

MT TAM

Named for beautiful, rugged Mount Tamalpais—which we can see from our dining room windows just across the Bay—this mold-ripened, triple cream cheese is aged for two to three weeks. This versatile cheese can be paired with all kinds of flavors—try lemony Artichoke Relish and olives or sliced Fuyu persimmons and Warm Spiced Almonds.

ST PATS

This mellow, soft whole milk cheese is wrapped in stinging nettle leaves (which have been frozen to take away the "sting"), giving it a little kick and a hint of artichoke flavor. Like Mt Tam, it's a wonderfully versatile cheese.

RED HAWK

This triple cream cheese is made in the same manner as Mt Tam, using the same mold, and washed with a brine solution as it ages. Its rind has a pale hint of orange color. If left to ripen, it becomes slightly runny and all the more delicious.

From Laura Chenel's Chèvre in Sebastopol, Sonoma County (707-996-4477):

CHEF'S CHÈVRE

This fresh, tangy chèvre is easy to spread, so it's great for sandwiches and crostini. We feature it every day on a sourdough baguette with watercress and sliced tomatoes.

CHÈVRE

This exceptional cheese is the one that first got us hooked on baked goat cheese, but it's also great crumbled over pasta or into a wilted spinach salad with tart apples, toasted pumpkin seeds, and rings of sweet roasted onions.

CABECOU

These little rounds of nutty, aged chèvre are packed in extra-virgin olive oil, produced by the Sciabica family here in Modesto. Be sure to spoon the delicious oil over the cheese when you serve it. We serve it with warm almonds, olives, and thick slices of spicy piquillo peppers.

TOME

This firm, aged goat cheese shaves beautifully over crisp romaine hearts and grilled vegetable salads.

From Redwood Hill Farm in Sebastopol, Sonoma County (redwoodhill.com; 707-823-8250):

CALIFORNIA CROTTIN

These little rounds of goat cheese with the soft rind are intensely flavored. Similar to the French crottin, they're soft and creamy when they're young and grow firmer as they age. As Brigitte, one of our longtime servers who recently returned to her French home in Toulouse, likes to say, "Crottin means little turd."

BUCHARET

A little larger than crottin, this dense, buttery, rind-ripened cheese is inspired by the French Bucheron.

CAMELLIA

This small Camembert-style goat cheese with a bloomy rind is named for a favorite, all white doe, Camellia, a champion milk producer. Aged six to eight weeks, it grows softer and riper as it matures.

From the all-organic Straus Family Creamery in Marshall on the shores of Tomales Bay, West Marin County (strausmilk.com; or order through Tomales Bay Foods 415-663-9335):

UNSALTED BUTTER

Freshly churned in small batches at the creamery, this unsalted butter is rich, sweet, and creamy. Most of the year the cows are pastured, so the butter reflects the nuances of the seasonal grasses.

NONFAT YOGURT

This tangy yogurt is made with milk and live cultures; it looks and tastes like homemade. A spoonful is all that's needed to cool down a spicy Curry-Laced Lentil Soup. It makes a refreshing Cucumber Raita with garden mint.

From the Vella Cheese Company in Sonoma (vellacheese.com; 800-848-0505):

VELLA DRY JACK

This exceptional cow's milk cheese is made just like Monterey jack, then coated with oil, cocoa, and black pepper, and aged for almost three years. The result is a hard, pale yellow cheese with a sweet, nutty flavor, a delicious substitute for grated or shaved Parmesan. This cheese keeps almost forever.

357

MEZZO SECCO

A creamy, young version of Dry jack, Mezzo Secco means half dry; it is aged for six months. This distinctive cheese is great for slicing. Be sure to include the smooth peppery rind—it's delicious.

From the Giacomini family just outside Point Reyes Station in West Marin (pointreyescheese.com; 800-591-6878):

ORIGINAL BLUE

This tangy, creamy blue cheese is full flavored, with clear blue veins throughout.
It's perfect crumbled over bitter greens with juicy, ripe pears and toasted pecans. It makes an addictive creamy blue cheese dressing, spooned over an heirloom tomato and garden cucumber salad.

From the Matos family in Santa Rosa (707-584-5283; or through cowgirlcreamery.com):

SAINT GEORGE CHEDDAR

This luscious aged cheddar is named after an island in the Azores and made to the original recipe of the island cheese. It's similar to a sharp New York cheddar—balanced and full of rich flavor. We feature it in all kinds of savory dishes, including our classic Macaroni and Cheese.

From Mytime Ranch in Eureka (capriciouscheese.com; 707-442-3209):

CAPRICIOUS

This sensational cheddar-like goat cheese is great for shaving over a salad of grilled figs and endive or crumbled into baked pasta or a rich tomato bisque. Handmade at a beautiful goat farmstead on the northern California coast and aged for ten months in a cave by the sea, it's available at the Ferry Plaza Farmers' Market in San Francisco every Saturday.

THE ASIAN PANTRY

Here in San Francisco—in this rich melting pot of Asian culture and cuisine—most supermarkets have extensive Asian food sections, stocked with all kinds of noodles, condiments, miso, dried mushrooms, and a wide array of seasonings. In both Chinatowns—the old and new ones—as well as in little Vietnam in the Tenderloin, here are some of the fresh ingredients you'll find at extraordinarily low prices:

DAIKON RADISH

These long, white radishes are pungent and spicy, adding kick to noodle salads, stir-fries, and spring roll fillings. They're mildest in fall and winter when the days are cool. They develop a bit of heat in the warm summer months. It's not easy to find a small daikon in San Francisco—where gigantic radishes fill the Asian market bins—so use part of it fresh and make pickles with the rest.

GALANGAL

Also known as Laos root, this rhizome is a favorite Thai ingredient, adding earthy, pungent flavor to fiery red curries and fragrant, steaming lemongrass broth. It's prepared in a number of ways—pounded with a mortar and pestle, minced, or sliced and tossed with lemongrass stalks and whole kaffir lime leaves into curries and soups. You'll find galangal in most Asian markets.

GINGER

This vibrant, fresh rhizome adds spicy heat to our Asian curries, Moroccan soups and stews, and all kinds of desserts—from simple Poached Sour Cherries and Ginger Cookies to addictive Ginger Crunch Cake with Poached Pears. To peel or not to peel: We leave the skin on when slicing ginger for stocks and poaching fruit. When it comes to mincing and grating ginger, we always peel it first. Look for firm hands of ginger, a sure sign of freshness, and leave the old, shriveled ginger behind in the bin. It keeps best when stored in a paper bag in the refrigerator.

GREEN PAPAYA

These large, unripe papayas are not to be confused with the ripened fruit. They should be firm to the touch, with dark green skin and pale flesh inside. There's really no substitute for this crunchy fruit, the essential ingredient in Green Papaya Salad. Texture is the point with green papayas; they have very little flavor.

KAFFIR LIME LEAVES

The fragrant leaves of the kaffir lime tree are indispensable in the Thai kitchen. Combined with lemongrass, galangal or ginger, and fresh lime juice, these whole citrus leaves brighten our stir-fries, curries, and soups. Slice into thin slivers for a garnish or to distribute their flavor evenly throughout the dish. But watch out—they're a little chewy. You'll find them in most Asian markets, both fresh and frozen. They're best eaten fresh, but they keep well in a Ziploc bag in the freezer.

LEMONGRASS

This long, fragrant grass with the delicate lemon flavor—essential to Southeast Asian cooking—is so delicious it's become a mainstream ingredient in our kitchen, along with ginger, cilantro, Thai basil, and fresh chilies. You can use every bit of the lemongrass stalk; the fibrous upper stalk goes right into the stockpot, while the tender inner core can be minced or pounded with a mortar and pestle. Give it a good, solid whack with the side of a chef's knife or cleaver so it releases its flavor while cooking. Look for lemongrass with a vibrant, pale yellow color—you'll know it's fresh. It's available in most Asian markets and keeps well in the vegetable bin of the fridge.

LOTUS ROOT

This relative of the water lily is cultivated throughout Asia for its beautiful flowers. Its long, slender root with the pale, smooth skin is linked just like big, funny-looking sausages. Peel away the skin and you'll find a beautiful, open-laced pattern inside. The starchy white flesh oxidizes quickly, so have a bowl of lemon water ready when you slice it to keep lotus root from discoloring. It adds lovely texture to Asian soups and makes a good, crunchy pickle.

PEA SHOOTS

These tendrils of young pea plants are available in the spring when the plants grow like crazy. You could mistake them for cultivated pea sprouts, which are sometimes sold in their place. But it doesn't really matter—both are delicious, fresh, and crunchy. We toss them into Asian-inspired salads and stir-fries, and wilt them in toasted sesame oil. Just add them at the last minute; their fresh sweet flavor and bright green color are fragile.

SHALLOTS

This delicate member of the onion family is an essential ingredient in Southeast Asian kitchens. Shallots are often sliced and fried until golden and crisp and used for a garnish or pounded or minced and sautéed with lemongrass, chilies, and galangal or ginger.

THAI BASIL

The purplish leaves of this aromatic basil are much smaller than the larger Mediterranean varieties. With its spicy anise flavor, Thai basil is a delicious addition to Green Papaya Salad, soups, and red curries. Chop the leaves or stack and slice them in thin ribbons; you can also leave them whole. If you're lucky, you'll find Thai basil at Asian and farmers' markets. You can also grow your own from organic seed. In a pinch, use one of the Mediterranean varieties in its place.

TOFU OR BEAN CURD

Tofu is the cheese made from soymilk. The firmness of the curd depends on how much whey is pressed out when it's made. We use organic tofu made by Wildwood; the firm and regular varieties are great for grilling and frying. Silken tofu is creamy and light and makes a wonderfully smooth dressing, dip, or sauce.

CONDIMENTS AND SEASONINGS

COCONUT MILK

This essential ingredient gives our Asian curries, soups, sauces, and desserts their full, rich flavor and lustrous, silky texture. Look for unsweetened coconut milk from Thailand in 14-ounce cans. Get the real thing: Light or low-fat coconut milk will give disappointing results. If you don't use the entire can, transfer the coconut milk to a sealed container and refrigerate; it will keep for several days.

HOISIN SAUCE

This dark, intensely flavored sauce has a perfect balance of sweet and salt; that's what makes it so deliciously addictive. Think of it as Chinese catsup or Asian barbecue sauce. To brighten the flavor, we toss in crisp fried shallots, thin it with Vegetable Stock or water, and add a splash of rice vinegar, if needed. Brush it over grilled vegetables or dab it on fresh Vietnamese Spring Rolls.

MISO

This aged, fermented soybean paste has a wide range of flavor, salt, and intensity, depending on the ingredients and how long it's aged. White miso is mild and sweet, yellow miso is stronger but still mellow, while red miso is salty and intensely flavored. Some misos are smooth, while others are chunky with whole fermented grain, usually rice or barley. Combine two different varieties to soften or bring up flavors. It's good to have on hand to season a last-minute bowl of buckwheat soba or for a quick, restorative broth. Miso keeps virtually forever in the refrigerator. You'll find it in the Asian section of most grocery stores.

MUSHROOM SOY SAUCE

This flavored soy sauce lacks the purity and clarity of aged tamari; there's just enough molasses to give it a little sweetness and viscosity. It's great for deglazing a pan of seared mushrooms, seasoning noodles, stir-fries, and mushroom soups and sauces. A splash is often all you need for flavor and to intensify the color of the soup or sauce. You'll find it in Asian markets.

RICE VINEGAR

The light, clean taste of this versatile vinegar is perfect for Asian vinaigrettes and sauces; we even use it to season our classic black bean chili. You can turn it into a delicious quick dipping sauce by adding sugar, a splash of tamari, and a sprinkling of hot pepper flakes. Be sure to select unseasoned vinegar; the seasoned vinegar has added salt and sugar. Rice vinegar is widely available in most grocery stores.

SAMBAL

This incendiary condiment is made from chilies that are ground, salted, and fermented. It's pretty spicy—and gaining in popularity. Look for it in the Asian section of grocery stores.

TAMARI

True Japanese tamari is a dark, rich soy sauce brewed without wheat. Most tamari available in today's marketplace is brewed with wheat. Whether it's made with or without wheat, it's generally superior to many of the Chinese and Japanese soy sauces.

TAMARIND

Also known as tamarindo in Latin American markets, this condiment adds a tangy, sour background flavor to curries, soups, and sauces. This multinational ingredient is widely used in Latin American, Asian, and Indian kitchens. Soak the pods or paste in hot water for 15 minutes, and then push the pulp through a fine mesh strainer with a rubber spatula, leaving the large seed and fibers behind.

TOASTED SESAME OIL

This dark oil made from toasted sesame seeds breaks down quickly under heat, so we generally use it as a seasoning. It's great for vinaigrettes and finishing sauces, stir-fries, and noodle dishes. It's prone to rancidity, so buy a small bottle and keep it in a cool place or refrigerate it.

NOODLES AND WRAPPERS

RICE NOODLES

Rice noodles—also known as cellophane noodles or bean thread noodles—are most often packaged in eight 2-ounce packages. Soak them in hot water, but don't boil them. A quick soak for 20 to 30 seconds is just about right.

UDON

These starchy, white Japanese noodles come both round and flat. They're great for brothy dishes and Asian pasta salads. You'll find fresh Udon in most Japanese markets and dried Udon in the Asian section of most supermarkets.

RICE WRAPPERS

These paper-thin sheets—used for fresh Vietnamese spring rolls—are brittle when dry and should be handled carefully. Moisten with a spray bottle of cool water, layer between paper towels or damp kitchen towels, and let sit until workable. Rice wrappers are difficult to handle if you're working with them for the first time, but once you get past the uncertainty, filling and rolling them goes smoothly. They're available in two sizes in most Asian markets. Check the clear plastic container to see that they're not cracked.

DRIED, CANNED, AND PRESERVED VEGETABLES

BAMBOO SHOOTS

Now that I have my own tangled bamboo grove, I finally understand how bamboo grows and what bamboo shoots really are. As a dear gardening friend once described it to me, "First they sleep, then they creep, then they leap!" Keep your bamboo happy—prune away the little shoots—and they'll produce edible tender, fresh shoots.

Canned bamboo shoots are available in the Asian food section of most supermarkets. The best shoots are white rather than yellow and the liquid should smell fresh when you open the can. Rinse bamboo shoots under cold water before using.

BLACK FUNGUS

Also known as Tree Fungus, Tree Ear Mushroom, and Wood Ear, this dark fungus has a mild, nondescript flavor, but adds a wonderful chewy texture to noodle and vegetable dishes and spring roll fillings. A small piece has tremendous expanding power. Pour boiling water over it and soak until tender, about 10 minutes, then rinse before slicing and cooking. Black fungus is available in Asian markets.

DRIED SHIITAKE MUSHROOMS

These dried black mushrooms—widely used in Korean, Japanese, and Chinese cooking—are available in the Asian section of most grocery stores. With their strong meaty flavor, they're a natural seasoning for soups, stocks, stir-fries, and Asian noodle dishes. Their short, flavorful stems are too tough for cooking, so save them to add to Mushroom Stock.

FERMENTED BLACK BEANS

These salty black beans are extremely potent; a small spoonful adds depth and intensity to noodle dishes, stir-fries, and wilted Asian greens. They're available in most supermarkets packed in jars in a thin spicy sauce. We prefer the dried fermented black beans, available in most Asian markets.

THE DESSERT PANTRY

Our longtime pastry chef, Debbie Hughes, assembled this collection of key ingredients—the ones we use again and again. We've also included a handful of important tips and tools.

BITTERSWEET CHOCOLATE

We use this flavorful but not too sweet chocolate for most of our desserts. As with all chocolates, it's most important to find a brand you like—we prefer locally made Guittard. Look for a deep chocolate flavor; high quality bittersweet chocolates have 65 to 70 percent cocoa solids.

SEMISWEET CHOCOLATE

Quality semisweet chocolate has between 35 to 54 percent cocoa solids and is a bit sweeter than bittersweet.

UNSWEETENED CHOCOLATE

This chocolate, also known as baking chocolate, is a combination of cocoa liqueur and cocoa butter, with no added sugar. There are all grades of unsweetened chocolate, but Bakers' is the brand that's best known. You'll find it in the baking section of most supermarkets.

COCOA POWDER

Look for a dark, unsweetened cocoa powder. Avoid "dutched" cocoa powder; Dutch process cocoa powder is treated with alkaline, so it won't activate baking soda in leavened recipes and you won't get a good rise. (However, "dutched" cocoa powder is acceptable in nonleavened recipes.) Our recipes call for natural cocoa powder.

CAKE FLOUR

Cake flour is milled from soft wheat, which produces a low protein flour that's low in gluten, so it makes light, tender baked goods. It may seem excessive to keep this airy flour on hand, but it makes a significant difference in angel food and unleavened chocolate cakes. Use non-self-rising cake flour and look for unbleached organic flour.

VANILLA BEANS

These fragrant beans are essential to our desserts, creating layers of flavor, both subtle and intense. Vanilla beans come from all over the world: Indonesia, Tahiti, Mexico, and Bourbon-Madagascar, each with its own distinctive character. We prefer the Tahitian beans, with their sweet-floral flavor. Always look for moist, plump beans. Split the bean lengthwise down the center and use a paring knife to scrape out the seeds. There's no question that vanilla beans are expensive, but they're worth every penny. Maximize your investment by storing the used pods in a jar of sugar to scent it and create vanilla sugar or add them to poaching liquid for fruit.

VANILLA EXTRACT

Pure vanilla extract, the real thing, is at the top of our list of essential ingredients. Its flavor is far superior to imitation vanilla, which should be avoided.

ALMOND EXTRACT

This intensely flavored extract is a delicious enhancement to just about any dessert or pastry made with stone fruit or pears. Use it sparingly, by the drop; it can easily overpower other flavors. Look for pure almond extract. Artificial almond extract has a harsh, unpleasant flavor and should be avoided.

NATURAL CREAM CHEESE

Natural cream cheese has tangy flavor and a creamy texture that's good for spreading and for making cheesecake and pastry dough. Its flavor and texture are far better suited to our desserts than commercially made cream cheese, which is full of additives. You'll find natural cream cheese in natural food stores and specialty markets.

TAPIOCA STARCH (TAPIOCA FLOUR)

We think this excellent starch, which is extracted from the root of the cassava plant, is the best thickening agent for fruit pies, turnovers, tarts, cobblers, and crisps. Here are some of its fine qualities: Unlike cornstarch, it thickens without boiling. Unlike flour, which becomes cloudy and gummy, it thickens fruit juices into a clear, glossy syrup. Because it's flavorless, it doesn't mask the full flavor of the fruit. You'll find tapioca starch in natural food stores and Asian markets. Stock up on it and store in an airtight container; it's good to have a supply on hand.

TURBINADO SUGAR

This crunchy, caramel-flavored sugar is a raw sugar that has had the molasses steamed away and is then dried into crystals. It's a nice finishing touch sprinkled over cookies, pies, and tartlets.

SOY MILK

Soy milks are flavored and sweetened differently according to the brand, so choose one based on the flavor you like. For desserts and pastries, we prefer vanilla soy milk to plain soy milk; with its smooth vanilla flavor, it's especially good with chocolate.

ALMOND PASTE

This versatile ingredient is just plain almonds ground with sugar. Look for a natural variety with no artificial flavors. You'll find it in natural food stores and specialty markets. Marzipan is another thing altogether, with lots more sugar. It's used for molding into cute little shapes of fruit, nuts, and so on.

DRIED CHERRIES

Dried cherries come in two varieties: sour Michigan and sweet Bing cherries. Sour cherries provide a distinctive contrast to ingredients such as bittersweet chocolate, oranges and tangerines, pears, apples, and dried apricots. Bings are just plain sweet and lack the complexity of sour cherries.

NUTS

Select fresh nuts whenever possible. They're in open bins at supermarkets, natural food stores, and farmers' markets. With their high oil content, nuts go rancid easily, so be sure to freeze them.

FLAVORED SUGARS

VANILLA SUGAR

This flavorful sugar is a classic for cookies, sweet pastry dough, and whipped cream. If you're feeling extravagant, use a whole vanilla bean, including the seeds. Split the pod lengthwise with a paring knife and scrape out the seeds. Mix the seeds into a cup or two of sugar and bury the bean inside. Ours is a more frugal version, simply made with the leftover pod. Store in an airtight container; the sugar will keep indefinitely.

ROSE GERANIUM SUGAR

This heady rose-scented sugar is a delicious seasoning for fresh berries, fruit compotes, sauces, sorbets, and jams. Rinse a few rose geranium leaves, pat them dry, and bury in sugar. Like vanilla sugar, it will keep indefinitely in an airtight container.

LAVENDER SUGAR

Use this lovely, fragrant sugar for special shortbread cookies, pound cake, ice cream, and crème anglaise. The subtle flavor will depend on the variety of lavender you're using. Lightly rub a few heads of lavender with your fingertips to release their fragrance and bury in a cup or two of sugar. Store in an airtight container.

FRESH HERBS AND THEIR USES

ROSE GERANIUM

We use the scented leaves to make ice cream, compotes, jam, crème caramel, crème brûlée, crème anglaise, and to season rhubarb, fresh berries, and stone fruit. If you don't have this wonderful plant in your garden, a pot of it will produce lots of leaves.

LEMON VERBENA

These long slender leaves with their intense herbal lemon flavor are great for ice cream, compotes, sugar syrup for poaching fruit, tossed into macerating stone fruit and berries, crème anglaise, crème caramel, and sorbet. For a refreshing lift, rub a leaf or two with your fingertips and add to a glass of sparkling water. It also makes delicious hot or iced tea.

LAVENDER FLOWERS

We steep these gorgeous, fragrant flowers in citrus juice and brush it over tea cakes and pound cakes, in custards for ice cream and crème caramel, and in honey to drizzle over fromage blanc, fresh figs, and raspberries.

ENGLISH BLACK PEPPERMINT

This elegant mint with its small, dark leaves adds intense flavor to chocolate sauce, ganache, and chocolate glazes. We steep the leaves in custard for crème anglaise, pots de crème, and outrageous mint chocolate chip ice cream. Bundle the leaves, slice in thin ribbons, and sprinkle over a citrus compote or melon. It makes a delicious, restorative fresh mint tea.

ANISE HYSSOP

This beautiful herb has spiky pale purple flowers and dark, pointed heart-shaped leaves. Its subtle licorice flavor is surprisingly sweet, a delicious flavoring for ice creams, crème anglaise, berries, and stone fruit.

A FEW IMPORTANT TIPS AND TOOLS

PLUMPING DRIED FRUIT

Soaking dried fruit helps to reconstitute its sweetness, softens the texture, and helps to keep it from drying or burning. Soak dried fruit in hot water, fruit juice, or alcohol.

DOUBLE PANNING

We often use two baking sheets, one on top of another, to insulate delicate baked goods and prevent them from browning too quickly. If something you're baking on a single sheet begins darkening too quickly and still requires more baking time, place another baking sheet underneath it to help slow down the browning.

COOLING DOWN CUSTARDS

It's always a good idea to set up a bath of ice water before making custard just in case it cooks a little too long at too high a heat and threatens to scramble. (It's also a great way to simply cool it down.) If you notice little curds beginning to develop, quickly remove the pan from the heat and, stirring constantly, set it in the ice water. Continue to stir the custard until it's completely cool. Refrigerate in an airtight container.

OVEN RACK SETTINGS

If you're baking a single item, place the rack in the middle of the oven. When baking cookies, place the racks in the middle and lowest position, rotating the pans halfway through for even baking. For angel food cake, place the rack on the bottom level.

PARCHMENT PAPER

This ovenproof paper (page 371) provides a clean, nonstick surface when baking. If you make a lot of cakes, cake rounds and pre-cut parchment rounds can be purchased at cake supply stores and through mail order. Rolls of parchment paper tend to curl up, so the pre-cut rounds are easier to work with.

PASTRY BRUSH

Keep a separate pastry brush on hand that's used only for desserts and pastries. Use it for brushing excess flour from rolled doughs (to avoid toughening), washing sugar from the sides of pan when caramelizing sugar, and brushing egg wash over rolled dough. To clean, dip the brush in warm soapy water and swish it around. Rinse very well and let it drip dry.

STANDING MIXER

A 4½- to 5-quart KitchenAid or other heavy-duty standing mixer makes baking a pleasure. And for anyone who enjoys baked goods, the savings at the bakery will quickly offset the cost of the machine. This wonderfully efficient tool will pay for itself again and again, so invest in a good one—you'll have it for years.

FOOD PROCESSOR

See page 370.

A FEW GOOD PANS

Bakers need a 9-inch springform pan, a couple of 9-inch cake pans, a 9-inch tart pan with a removable bottom, and a Bundt pan. If you're crazy for angel food cakes, then splurge on an angel food cake pan; this specialty pan has little feet to help the cake cool evenly. Two sturdy baking sheets and a few baking dishes (page 371) are an excellent investment. For individually baked desserts, ½-cup ramekins are a must.

See below for information on zesters, citrus juicers, and all kinds of tools. If you don't have a standing mixer, an old-fashioned pastry blender is a wonderfully efficient way to make dough.

KITCHEN TOOL BOX

You can make delicious meals in any kitchen, as long as you have the tools you need — the more fun they are, the more fun it will be to cook. Our cooking doesn't require a lot of fancy, specialized equipment, but there are a few key items that make a tremendous difference and they're included below.

KNIVES

Three good knives — and I don't mean expensive ones — are really all you need: An 8-inch French chef's knife or a Japanese knife with a non-corrosive blade, is perfect for cutting and slicing vegetables. A paring knife is essential for all kinds of jobs, such as peeling fresh ginger and scraping vanilla beans or seeds from fresh chilies. The elegant imported paring knives are very attractive, but the little inexpensive ones always get the job done. A serrated knife is indispensable for slicing tomatoes and bread.

Keep your knives sharp and they'll perform beautifully for years. If you're nervous about using a sharpening stone or steel, find a reliable cutlery service (in many hardware and kitchen supply stores) to keep them sharp.

A word on shopping for knives: Give yourself plenty of time so you make the right choice. The knife you choose should feel good in your hand — well balanced and not too heavy — almost like an extension of your hand. If it doesn't, try another until you find the one that's right for you.

VEGETABLE PEELER

A high-quality swivel vegetable peeler makes quick work of peeling apples, carrots, potatoes, winter roots, just about anything that needs its skin removed. For shaving fine, aged cheeses over grilled vegetables and salads, this is your tool.

VEGETABLE SLICER

A Japanese vegetable slicer or mandoline is fantastic for paper-thin slices of potatoes for gratins or a julienne of crisp vegetables for Asian salads and pickles. It isn't a substitute for a good, sharp knife, but it's great for specific uses. We have three kinds at Greens including a top-of-the-line, classic French one and a cheap Japanese slicer.

CITRUS JUICER

A small hand-held wooden reamer is the perfect tool for squeezing lemons and limes. It gets the job done quickly; you just need to strain out the seeds. An old-fashioned glass citrus juicer is also good for quick juicing. For orange juice, the sleek hand-pressed juicers are a pleasure to use. At home, I avoid the electric juicer, with all its parts that need washing.

CITRUS ZESTER

This invaluable tool is at the top of my list. Once an obscure item for professional chefs, zesters—of all shapes and sizes—are now all the rage for home cooks. They've learned that minced colored rind performs miracles in vinaigrettes, savory vegetable fillings, salads, and desserts. Whether you prefer a hand-held zester or a Microplane (which is really a fine wood-working tool), it's up to you; the Microplane avoids the extra step of mincing and just delivers grated rind. You can also use a vegetable peeler or the finest holes of a cheese grater; just be sure to avoid the bitter white citrus pith. My favorite zester is the wooden-handled six-hole zester made by Victorinox—it's a perfect fit.

SPRING-LOADED TONGS

These metal tongs are essential for the big jobs—turning vegetables on the grill, sautéing greens, and tossing pasta and salads. They come in several lengths; short and medium are the most useful for the home kitchen. Check to see that they spring nicely; a good pair will last a very long time.

SPICE GRINDER

An electric coffee grinder grinds dried herbs, spices, and seeds beautifully. Be sure to wash the top and wipe the blades with a damp cloth after every use so it's clean and ready for the next time. If you're a serious coffee drinker and grind your own beans, buy a second grinder that's used only for coffee.

FOOD PROCESSOR

This state-of-the-art tool is a timesaver for grinding bread crumbs, pureeing vegetables for spreads and fillings, chopping vegetables, and grating cheese. A mini food processor is handy for chopping garlic, ginger, galangal, and making chipotle or ancho puree—the important little jobs that are too small for the food processor or blender.

BLENDER

Compared to a food processor, a blender may seem out of date, but it isn't. If you're looking for a silky, smooth sauce or soup, or emulsifying a citrus vinaigrette, a blender is the right machine for the job.

PARCHMENT PAPER

This ovenproof paper is a big timesaver when it comes to cleaning baking sheets and roasting pans. It's available by the roll in many grocery stores and hardware stores. Don't think twice about buying it; it's worth every penny.

POTS AND PANS

Invest in a few good pans and they'll last for a lifetime. The Master Chef line from All-Clad is our choice—in the restaurant, at home, and the test kitchen—for most of our needs. Here are the basics: a medium-size and large or deep sauté pan, a small and medium-size heavy-bottomed saucepan, a Dutch oven, a stockpot, a small cast-iron or heavy enamel skillet for toasting nuts and spices, and a large cast-iron skillet for warming tortillas and grilling sandwiches.

BOWLS AND BAKING DISHES

A set of stainless-steel bowls and two or three standard-size baking dishes are necessary.

FOOD MILL

For making smooth pureed soups, this ingenious tool is indispensable.

ODDS AND ENDS

You'll need two good whisks—small and medium-size—for vinaigrettes and sauces, two stainless-steel colanders, and a couple of fine mesh strainers. (We like the large teardrop-shaped strainers—without the hooks on the sides—which are great for dipping vegetables and pasta right out of the pot.) You can use a few rubber spatulas and sturdy wooden spoons, a metal dough knife, and a couple of hand-held plastic scrapers for dough. For those who love chilies, a stovetop grill (El Asador) for roasting is essential.

WORM COMPOSTING

For those of us cooks who love to garden, worm compost is a treasure trove of nutrients, great riches if you measure your wealth in healthy garden soil. Why throw your food scraps in the garbage, when you could be feeding an industrious colony of worms, which, in turn, will feed your garden with their castings, the secret black gold of compost? It all comes down to the waste stream and the never-ending benefits of recycling your food scraps. If you're still not convinced, just think of it as an earth science project with delicious results. As with all science projects, there's a big payoff for careful observation.

I'll always be a novice in the garden and I'll never be a composting superstar; I'm simply too lazy and disorganized to take it that far. I learned my worm-composting tricks from my

dear friend, Susan, in Seattle—the green capital of the west—where the city gives away countless compost and worm bins every year to their wildly enthusiastic population of gardeners and
cooks. I was reluctant and squeamish at first, but I'll be the first to admit that worms eat my
garbage and I'm proud of it. Besides, it's fun and easy to do and once you get a bin going, it's
self-regulating, including population control. Here's what you'll need to get started.

THE BIN
You can start your first bin with very little or no money; all you need is an old wooden cupboard that's placed on its back or a box with a loose-fitting lid. Once you're hooked, you can
take the next step and invest in a *can of worms*, an ingenious three-tiered worm condo (made
from recycled materials), which is designed to give worms a top-of-the-line livework environment. It has all the modern conveniences, including a spigot to drain off *worm tea*, another
beneficial by-product of hardworking worms. Your plants will love this natural liquid fertil-
izer. It's highly concentrated, so dilute it with water by at least 50 percent before using it. I add
water intuitively; if it looks too dark, I simply add more until the color lightens.

THE WORMS
You'll need to invest in a small container of little red composting worms—not the big garden
variety—but a friend can also help you get started with a handful of wriggly worms from
their bin. Composting worms are available at nurseries and garden centers.

BEDDING
Unlike earthworms that live out in the cold, composting worms like a cozy environment and
good bedding so they can get right down to work. A couple of options for bedding: Shredded
paper is a good first step and a great way to use up those shredded documents from your
office. Newspaper is okay, but it isn't my first choice because it tends to clump. Sawdust and
fine wood shavings make a luxurious, fluffy bed—they're the best of all. I've made fantastic
forays all over the city in my search for the perfect bed. My favorite spot was a fine wood-
working shop in an old rubble-walled building built just after the 1906 earthquake. The
owner gladly left garbage bags full of wood shavings on his loading dock, far more than I
could ever use, so I'd spread the wealth to my worm composting friends. I'm still working off
a big haul from nearly a year ago. Find a local carpentry shop for a steady source of wood
shavings. Carpenters are happy to part with them.

RECIPE FOR LAYERING
Starting the bin is simple—think of layering a sandwich or assembling lasagne. Here's the
recipe: Spread a layer of bedding on the bottom of the bin, spread a layer of food scraps on

top, add the worms, and top with a layer of bedding, just enough to cover the scraps. Sprinkle with enough water to keep everything moist, just like a moist kitchen sponge. It will take a little time for the worms to adjust to their new environment, but I guarantee their hunger will quickly take over. Once they start eating, their work of converting food scraps to worm castings has begun. Cover the bin and leave them to enjoy their meal until it's time for their next feeding. Worms prefer their privacy, so keep your curiosity in check and leave them to their feast. Keep the bin moist, particularly out at the edges, where it tends to dry out.

FOOD SCRAPS: THE HEART OF THE MATTER

Since I don't cook meat, fish, or fowl, just about everything in my kitchen compost bucket goes to the worms. I'm not fussy when it comes to food scraps. If it's in the compost bin (including dairy products), I feed it to the worms. There are a few exceptions: big batches of acidic orange rinds, partial loaves of bread, or too many beans or grains. Worms like a light diet of fruit and vegetable trimmings, coffee grounds, and even paper towels.

A BALANCED ENVIRONMENT

You'll know there's too much acidity in the bin if flies begin to appear. This is almost unavoidable, since most food is highly acidic. There are a couple of things I do to correct the bin balance: First I aerate the bin with a garden trowel, a sturdy stick, or any good tool for digging. This moves the scraps around and gets the air circulating. Then I sprinkle on a little ash from the Greens mesquite grill to neutralize the acidity. Go lightly with the ash; I found this one out the hard way. (You can avoid this if you think of the ash as garnish.) Fortunately, I didn't decimate the population, it just took a while for their numbers to come back, and they did. If you don't have ash, then skip it. The flies will go away on their own. If the bin takes on an unpleasant odor, poke around with a trowel or stick to open up the pockets that need oxygen to breathe. The worms will go on eating and reproducing, as always.

HARVESTING

Here's the payoff: Those hardworking worms have converted your food scraps to a bed of moist, rich worm castings, nutritious natural food for your plants. This can take a number of weeks, even a month or two, depending on the food source, the bin, and the number of worms. If you have a *can of worms,* harvesting is pretty simple. Since the worms migrate naturally to the top layer, harvest the bottom layer. It's hard to avoid every single worm, but that's okay. If they don't survive the rigors of life in the garden, they're good for the soil in their afterlife. It's a little trickier if you're harvesting from a box or bin. Dig out the castings and heap them on a tarp in a warm, sunny spot. The worms will migrate to the bottom to avoid the light and heat, so harvest the top. Repeat this several times until the castings are reduced to a big pile of worms. That's the time to dig the castings into your garden, return the worms to the bin, and start all over again.

My worms have been feasting on a voluminous diet of food scraps from the recipes we've tested again and again for this book. I've let many things drop away during this intense time of work and writing, but for some crazy reason, my dedication to those worms has been unwavering. It's just about time to harvest those brimming bins, spread it around, and enjoy the labors of those industrious, insatiable worms.

If this worm exposé piques your interest and you'd like to know more, read Mary Appelhof's book *Worms Eat My Garbage,* the ultimate bible of worm composting.

Acknowledgments

Everyday Greens is the work of a handful of generous, hard-working people who focused their energies on this new collection of Greens recipes. I'm the fortunate one here, for without their dedication and love of Greens, *Everyday Greens* would never have made it to publication.

I'm deeply grateful to my dear friend Chris Leishman, who worked diligently and wholeheartedly in the test kitchen each day. As a professional chef and working mom who cooks delicious meals for her family every day, she had the confidence and the know-how to simplify the recipes without sacrificing an ounce of flavor. Her knack for turning leftovers into creative new dishes was a revelation and an inspiration for many of the tips and boxes throughout the book. In addition to her kitchen work, Chris literally put the book together—writing, revising, and editing the recipes; her computer savvy is dazzling.

Debbie Hughes, our pastry chef, is the star of the Desserts and Pastries chapter. With her quirky sensibility and love of good food—and not just pastries—her stellar contributions to Greens are broad and far-reaching. There's a big demand from our dining room and Greens to Go customers for the addictive desserts and pastries she and her staff prepare every day. Debbie also assembled the Dessert Pantry, which is filled with a pro's advice on ingredients, techniques, and tools.

Our longtime chef, J Kenyon, is the bedrock of Greens. His creativity, genuine love of work, and gift for organization keep the kitchen, and the entire restaurant, wired together and humming along during the most challenging of times. His incredible efforts made it possible for me to disappear and write this book.

Dinner chef Tai Do, our kitchen genie, introduced the flavors of Southeast Asia to Greens and worked closely with us in the test kitchen to develop the Asian recipes. Victoria Metzgar, our new chef, contributed recipes and fresh ideas and kept the kitchen running smoothly. Many thanks to Cristobal Cartagena for all of his efforts, as well as Ricardo Cartagena, Maria Moz, Alicia Ramirez, Yolanda Tillis, Ulysses Lowry, Dylan Lovett, Matt Enjem, and all the staff of Greens. And to Julie Swart, Chaylee Priete, Emily Birky, and Sarah Oliver, who manage the front of the house and Greens to Go seamlessly.

Very special thanks to Shirley Sarvis, our long-time friend, who contributed so much to the notes on Wines with Greens. We've benefited greatly over the years from her knowledge and passion for food and wine. Her unwavering friendship has truly stood the test of time. Thanks again to our dining room manager and wine buyer, Chaylee Priete, for shaping our extensive wine list and giving it new life. And to Rick Jones, our former general manager, who selected the wines for our list for many years, giving it amazing breadth and even notoriety.

To our growers, purveyors, and special friends: You're the best and you know who you are. I can't begin to thank all of you, except to say the restaurant wouldn't be what it is without you. Particular thanks go to those of you who shared your knowledge, love of work, and expertise for this book. There's a big pot of merit coming your way in this lifetime and the upcoming ones, too. And to the Water Street tasters, especially Evan, Lucy, Carol, and Zach, who tasted dutifully and supported me in every way. Big thanks to our publicist and friend Sally Shepard, who really understands what Greens is all about.

There must have been a lucky star shining over me when my editor, Fran McCullough, signed on for this book. She was the editor of *Fields of Greens,* published a decade ago and knew all too well how much help I would need. She gave me her crash course in writing in a late-night editing session. "Just write it the way you say it." From that moment on, the words came more easily and the work wasn't quite so weighty. She's a saint with a wicked sense of humor and a taste for chasing down new ideas and ingredients. And she's a great editor—she spirited me right through this book. At Scribner Beth Wareham and her associate Rica Allannic combed through the manuscript and brought a valuable fresh perspective to the project.

Our customers will recognize the gorgeous prints of Mayumi Oda, extraordinary artist and activist, which bring beauty and life to the jacket and pages of this book (and to the restaurant walls). And many thanks to Jenny Wunderly, for her skill and artistry in the design and work with Mayumi. Once again, my agent, Michael Katz, has pulled it off, creating the structure and fabric of yet another book and bringing an amazing cast of characters together. Thank you, Michael. And thanks to Michael Wenger, the Dean of Buddhist Studies at the Zen Center. His encouragement and unflagging support have been crucial to *Everyday Greens* and to the big work of opening our doors each day.

I deeply appreciate the tireless work of the Everyday Board of Directors who oversees our work at Greens, and especially to Karin Gjording, whose extraordinary commitment to the restaurant from the very first day has guided us all these years.

Finally, a deep bow of gratitude to Suzuki Roshi, the founding teacher of Zen Center, for his vision and the profound Buddhist teaching of bringing Zen practice and *everyday mind* to everyday life.

Index

aïoli, *see* basil aïoli; chipotle aïoli
All-Clad, Master Chef line from, 371
almond(s):
    brown butter cake with plums, 318–19
    -cherry couscous, 279
    chocolate mousse cakes, 338
    extract, 365
    macaroons, 309
    -nectarine upside-down cake, 320–21
    orecchiette with broccoli rabe, Manchego, and, 241–42
    paste, 365
    streusel, 325
    streusel, rhubarb tartlets with, 324–25
    toasted, dinosaur kale with, 301
    toasted, ice cream, 344
    warm spiced, 2
Anaheim chilies filled with corn, cheddar, and cilantro, 265–66
ancho chili puree, 147
ancho cress, 69
angel food cake, triple chocolate, 333–34
anise hyssop, 367
apple(s):
    -quince turnovers, 328–29
    romaine hearts and watercress with beets, Stilton, cider vinaigrette, and, 37–38
    in salads, 26
    types of, 38–39
    vinegar, 27
apricot:
    lattice tart, 326–27
    turnovers, 329

Arkansas Black apples, 38
artichoke(s):
    filo purses with mushrooms, Asiago, and, 133–34
    griddle cakes with Gruyère, 177–78
    grilled, with mint, 15
    marinade, 53–54
    panzanella with olives, Manchego, and, 50
    and portobello mushroom lasagne, 227–28
    prepping little, 178
    relish, 19
    and roasted shallot pizza, 169–70
    salad, simple, 53–54
    and spring onion tart, 139–40
    stuffed with garlic bread crumbs, lemon, and pine nuts, 269–70
    wine and, 352
arugula:
    corn and cherry tomato salad with, 56
    farro salad with roasted peppers and, 75
    linguine with sun-dried tomatoes, ricotta salata, and, 243
    pizza with portobello mushrooms, spring onions, and, 171
    sourdough baguette with goat cheese, tomatoes, and, 114
Asiago:
    in artichoke and portobello mushroom lasagne, 227–28
    artichoke and roasted shallot pizza with, 169–70

Asiago (*cont.*)
    filo purses with artichokes, mushrooms, and, 133–34
    focaccia with roasted eggplant, sun-dried tomatoes, and, 120
    Yellow Finn potato cakes with, 180–81
Asian-style dishes:
    condiments and seasonings for, 360–62
    dried, canned, and preserved vegetables for, 363
    fresh ingredients for, 358–60
    greens, spicy, 305
    kabocha squash soup with coconut milk and lime leaves, 90
    noodle salad with peanut sauce and lime, 82–84
    noodles and wrappers for, 362
    oils for, 353
    spring stir-fry with peanut sauce and Thai basil, 210–11
    stock, quick, 247–48
    udon with miso, shiitake mushrooms, and bok choy, 246–48
    wines to serve with, 351
    see also Southeast Asian–style dishes; Vietnamese-style dishes
asparagus:
    and beets with Meyer lemon vinaigrette, 48–49
    bread pudding, 216
    grilled, 14
    risotto with morels, Parmigiano-Reggiano, and, 249–50

avocado(s):
    butter lettuce with ruby grapefruit, grapefruit-chili vinaigrette, and, 30–31
    in guacamole, 13
    -mango salsa, 285
    in salads, 26
    and tomato sandwich with chipotle aïoli, 115–16

baguette:
    with grilled summer vegetables, fromage blanc, and basil, 125–26
    sourdough, with goat cheese, watercress, and tomatoes, 114
    with tapenade, grilled peppers, and Fontina, 117–18
baking dishes, 371
balsamic vinegar, reduced, 126
bamboo shoots, 363
basil:
    baguette with grilled summer vegetables, fromage blanc, and, 125–26
    and corn tart, 141
    crisp polenta triangles with Gorgonzola cream, walnuts, and, 281–82
    grilled tomato, and garlic sauce, 292
    Provençal tartlets with, 143
    roasted eggplant and cherry tomato pizza with, 164
    spinach tagliarini with corn, cherry tomatoes, and, 238
    summer risotto with tomatoes, mascarpone, and, 251–52
basil, Thai, 360
    corn soup with ginger and, 86
    spring stir-fry with peanut sauce and, 210–11
basil aïoli, 128
    focaccia with roasted eggplant, sun-dried tomatoes, Asiago, and, 120

basil aïoli (*cont.*)
    portobello sandwich with tomatoes, roasted onions, and, 127–28
basmati rice:
    pudding with mascarpone, 339–40
    with pumpkin seeds, 276
bean curd, *see* tofu
bean(s):
    big, preparing, 106–7
    borlotti, soup with roasted garlic and Parmesan croutons, 93–94
    soup, giant Peruvian lima, 105–6
    spicy rattlesnake, 272
    summer, linguine with gremolata, olives, and, 234–35
    white runner, with Champagne vinaigrette and tarragon, 61–62
    see also cannellini beans; chick-pea(s); fava bean(s); lentil(s)
beans, black:
    fermented, 363
    Mexican pizza with corn, tomatillos, chipotle chilies, and, 162–63
beans, green:
    and shelling beans with cherry tomatoes, 58
    Yellow Finn potato salad with tarragon and, 72–73
beans, shelling:
    general information about, 59
    and green beans with cherry tomatoes, 58
beans, white, 106
    fall vegetable ragoût with, 203–4
    and pasta with roasted garlic, rainbow chard, and olives, 239–40
    warm, 273–74
beer, 352

beet(s):
    and asparagus with Meyer lemon vinaigrette, 48–49
    general information about, 29
    green salad with fennel, walnuts, ricotta salata, and, 28–29
    romaine hearts and watercress with apples, Stilton, cider vinaigrette, and, 37–38
    salad, Moroccan, 51–52
    soup, chilled three, 87–88
    with tangerine-shallot vinaigrette, 52
Bellwether Farms, cheeses from, 354–55
beurre blanc, Meyer lemon, 296
Black Beluga lentils, 79
blackberry:
    -nectarine shortcake, 315
    sauce, 315
    sherbet, 346
    sorbet, 346
black fungus, 363
Black Jonathan apples, 38
blenders, 371
blueberry:
    -maple pecan spice muffins, 350
    -orange bread, 347
blue cheese:
    dressing, creamy, tomato salad with, 66
    source of, 357
bok choy:
    in spicy Asian greens, 305
    udon with miso, shiitake mushrooms, and, 246–48
borlotti bean(s), 106
    soup with roasted garlic and Parmesan croutons, 93–94
bowls, 371
braised French lentils, 275
bread crumbs:
    garlic, 219
    garlic, artichokes stuffed with lemon, pine nuts, and, 269–70

bread crumbs (*cont.*)
  Parmesan, 222
bread pudding, asparagus, 216
breakfast and brunch foods:
  blueberry-orange bread,
    347
  currant-pecan scones, 348
  maple-pecan spice muffins,
    349–50
Brennan, Georgeanne, 216
broccoli, Italian sprouting (*broccoli di ciccio*), 242
broccoli rabe:
  with hot pepper, 300
  orecchiette with almonds,
    Manchego, and, 241–42
  wilted, warm cannellini
    beans and, 22
brownies, Debbie's pecan, 312
brown lentils, 78
Bucharet, 356
buckwheat crêpes, 192
  with winter vegetables and
    caramelized onions,
    189–90
Buddhism, everyday mind and,
    xix
butter:
  herb, 268
  unsalted, 357
butter, brown, 245
  almond cake with plums,
    318–19
  penne with roasted butternut
    squash, sage, and,
    244–45
butter lettuce, *see* lettuce, butter
butternut squash:
  and chestnut soup, 95–96
  filo turnovers with Gruyère
    and, 135–36
  gratin, 222
  in New Mexican border stew,
    212–13
  risotto griddle cakes, 179
  soft tacos with plantain,
    poblano chilies, and,
    154–55

butternut squash, roasted:
  penne with brown butter,
    sage, and, 244–45
  risotto with kale and,
    253–54
  rounds with sage leaves,
    256

Cabecou, 356
cake flour, 364
cake(s), 314–21
  almond brown butter, with
    plums, 318–19
  chocolate chestnut mousse,
    338
  fromage blanc cheesecake
    with pistachio crust, 332
  ginger crunch, with poached
    pears, 316–17
  maple-pecan streusel, 350
  nectarine-almond upside-
    down, 320–21
  shortcake, 314
  shortcake, nectarine-
    blackberry, 315
  triple chocolate angel food,
    333–34
California crottin, 356
Camellia, 356
candied ginger shortbread, 310
cannellini beans, 106
  fall vegetable ragoût with,
    203–4
  warm, 273–74
  and wilted greens, warm, 22
canola oil, 353
capers:
  grilled pepper and fennel rel-
    ish with, 23
  roasted Japanese eggplant
    salad with pine nuts and,
    74
Capricious cheese, 358
carrot:
  –daikon radish pickles, 130
  -parsnip soup with orange
    crème fraîche, 97–98
cashews, jasmine rice with, 277

casseroles, 215–30
  asparagus bread pudding,
    216
  corn pudding, 217
  macaroni and cheese, 218–19
  see also gratin(s); lasagne
celery root:
  potato, and fennel soup,
    99–100
  tip for, 100
Champagne vinaigrette, 59
  green beans, shelling beans,
    and cherry tomatoes with,
    58
  mustard, 62
  white runner beans with tar-
    ragon and, 61–62
chanterelle tart with roasted gar-
    lic custard, 144–45
chard, in sautéed winter greens,
    304
chard, rainbow:
  general information about,
    303
  pasta and white beans with
    roasted garlic, olives, and,
    239–40
  with pumpkin seeds, 302–3
chard, wilted:
  fresh mozzarella sandwich
    with grilled onions and,
    121–22
  in rosemary crêpes with goat
    cheese and wilted greens,
    187–88
  warm cannellini beans and,
    22
charmoula, 293
cheddar:
  Anaheim chilies filled with
    corn, cilantro, and, 265–66
  in artichoke and spring onion
    tart, 139–40
  in corn and basil tart, 141
  in corn and scallion griddle
    cakes, 174
  in corn pudding, 217
  in corn quesadillas, 151

379

cheddar (*cont.*)
  grilled Mexican sandwich with
    poblano chilies and, 119
  macaroni and, 218–19
  masa harina crêpes with sum-
    mer vegetables, poblano
    chilies, and, 185–86
  Mexican pizza with corn,
    tomatillos, chipotle chilies,
    and, 162–63
  in Mexican tartlets with
    roasted winter vegetables,
    146–47
  in soft tacos with butternut
    squash, plantain, and
    poblano chilies, 154–55
  in soft tacos with grilled sum-
    mer vegetables, 152–53
  source of, 358
cheese:
  in artichoke and portobello
    mushroom lasagne,
    227–28
  macaroni and, 218–19
  pizza basics and, 160
  in roasted winter vegetable
    lasagne, 279–80
  in salads, 26
  Sonoma and West Marin
    counties' sources for,
    354–58
  Stilton, romaine hearts and
    watercress with apples,
    beets, cider vinaigrette,
    and, 37–38
  see also specific cheeses
cheesecake with pistachio crust,
  fromage blanc, 332
chef's chèvre, 114, 356
Chenel, Laura, 114, 355–56
cherry(ies):
  -almond couscous, 279
  dried, 367
  dried sour, quick bread, 347
  poached sour, 323
  sour, and quince compote, 16
cherry tomatoes, *see* tomato(es),
  cherry

chestnut:
  and butternut squash soup,
    95–96
  chocolate mousse cakes, 338
  puree, 96
chèvre (cheese), 356
Chèvre (company), 355–56
chick-pea(s):
  in hummous, 12
  soup, Moroccan, 101–2
  in spring vegetable tagine,
    207–9
chilies:
  Anaheim, filled with corn,
    cheddar, and cilantro,
    265–66
  ancho chili puree, 147
  chipotle, *see* chipotle aïoli;
    chipotle (chilies)
  jalapeño, *see* jalapeño (chilies)
  poblano, *see* poblano (chilies);
    poblano (chilies), fire-
    roasted
chili-grapefruit vinaigrette, 31
  butter lettuce with ruby
    grapefruit, avocado, and,
    30–31
chili-plantain sauce, 212
chilled soup(s):
  cucumber, with yogurt and
    mint, 89
  three beet, 87–88
chipotle (chilies):
  Mexican pizza with corn,
    tomatillos, and, 162–66
  puree, 163
chipotle aïoli, 115–16
  avocado and tomato sand-
    wich with, 115–16
chocolate:
  angel food cake, triple, 333–34
  bittersweet, 363–64
  chestnut mousse cakes, 338
  in Debbie's pecan brownies,
    312
  espresso bean shortbread,
    310
  glaze, 334

chocolate (*cont.*)
  mousse with filo crisps,
    335–36
  -rum steamed pudding, 337
  sauce, bittersweet, 342
  semisweet, 364
  unsweetened, 364
cider vinaigrette, 38
  romaine hearts and watercress
    with apples, beets, Stilton,
    and, 37–38
cilantro:
  Anaheim chilies filled with
    corn, cheddar, and, 265–66
  corn and fire-roasted poblano
    salad with, 63–64
cinnamon sugar, 129
citrus-honey vinaigrette, 33
  butter lettuce with blood
    oranges, tangerines, pista-
    chios, and, 32–33
citrus juice, fresh, in vinaigrettes,
    27
citrus shortbread, 311
  see also specific citrus fruits
cobbler, raspberry-plum, 313
cocoa powder, 364
coconut (milk), 360
  basmati rice pudding with
    mascarpone and, 340
  in Indian curry with tamarind
    and chilies, 194–95
  jasmine rice, 278
  kabocha squash soup with
    lime leaves and, 90
  in red curry with summer
    vegetables and Thai spices,
    196–99
  in Vietnamese yellow curry,
    200–202
compost, 109, 372–74
compote:
  cranberry, with tangerines, 341
  quince and sour cherry, 16
condiments and seasonings:
  for Asian dishes, 360–62
  cucumber raita, 284
  see also salsa

cookies, 308–11
  almond macaroons, 309
  candied ginger shortbread, 310
  chocolate espresso bean shortbread, 310
  citrus shortbread, 311
  ginger, 308
  pistachio shortbread, 311
  vanilla bean shortbread, 311
corn:
  Anaheim chilies filled with cheddar, cilantro, and, 265–66
  and basil tart, 141
  and cherry tomato salad with arugula, 56
  and fire-roasted poblano salad with cilantro, 63–64
  grilled fingerling potato salad with cherry tomatoes and, 70–71
  Mexican pizza with tomatillos, chipotle chilies, and, 162–63
  pudding, 217
  quesadillas, 151
  and scallion griddle cakes, 174
  soup with ginger and Thai basil, 86
  spinach tagliarini with cherry tomatoes, basil, and, 238
  stock, 111
  and tomatillo salsa, 286
  see also polenta
couscous:
  almond-cherry, 279
  salad with cherry tomatoes, lemon, and pine nuts, 60
Cowgirl Creamery, 98, 355
cranberry(ies):
  compote with tangerines, 341
  dried, quick bread, 347
cream:
  Gorgonzola, crisp polenta triangles with walnuts, basil, and, 281–82
  herb, 297

cream (cont.)
  lemon, pappardelle with spring vegetables and, 236–37
cream cheese:
  dough, 331
  natural, 365
  source of, 355
crème fraîche:
  general information about, 98
  orange, 98
  orange, carrot-parsnip soup with, 97–98
crêpes, 185–92
  batter for, 191–92
  buckwheat, 192
  buckwheat, with winter vegetables and caramelized onions, 189–90
  herb, 192
  masa harina, 192
  masa harina, with summer vegetables, poblano chilies, and cheddar, 185–86
  rosemary, 192
  rosemary, with goat cheese and wilted greens, 187–88
  scallion, 192
Crescenza, 354
cresses, types of, 69
  see also watercress
croutons, 26
  chunky sourdough, romaine hearts with sun-dried tomatoes, red wine vinaigrette, and, 40–41
  garlic, 17
  Parmesan, 94
  Parmesan, borlotti bean soup with roasted garlic and, 93–94
cucumber:
  raita, 284
  soup with yogurt and mint, chilled, 89
curly cress, 69
curly endive, 43
currant-pecan scones, 348

curry(ies), 194–202
  -laced lentil soup, 108
  spices, red, 198
  spices, yellow, 201
  with summer vegetables and Thai spices, red, 196–99
  with tamarind and chilies, Indian, 194–95
  Vietnamese yellow, 200–202
custard:
  cooling down of, 368
  roasted garlic, chanterelle tart with, 144–45

daikon radish, 358
  –carrot pickles, 130
  pickled, 4
dandelion greens, 44
Debbie's pecan brownies, 312
desserts, 307–50
  chocolate mousse with filo crisps, 335–36
  cranberry compote with tangerines, 341
  Debbie's pecan brownies, 312
  flavored sugars for, 366
  fresh herbs and their uses for, 366–67
  ingredients for, 363–67
  poached pears, 322
  poached sour cherries, 323
  raspberry-plum cobbler, 313
  tips and tools for, 367–69
  see also cakes; cookies; ice cream; pastry; pudding, sweet; sorbet
dough:
  cream cheese, 331
  masa harina, 149
  pizza, 172
  sweet tart, 326–27
  tart, 148
  yeasted tart, 150
dressing:
  creamy blue cheese, tomato salad with, 66
  creamy roasted garlic, 67
  see also vinaigrette(s)

eggplant, roasted:
    and cherry tomato pizza with
        basil, 164
    focaccia with sun-dried toma-
        toes, Asiago, and, 120
    Japanese, salad of pine nuts,
        capers, and, 74
eggs, hard-cooked, 41
egg wash, 143
    pastry, 327
El Asador, 64, 266, 371
enchiladas, roasted winter
    vegetable, 156–57
endive, 44
    curly, 43
    and fig salad, grilled, with
        watercress, 68
    and portobello mushroom
        salad, grilled, with shaved
        Parmesan, 80–81
English black peppermint, 367
escarole, 43
    in bitter greens, with Fuyu
        persimmons, Asian pears,
        and pecans, 35–36
    hearts and spinach, wilted,
        with portobello mush-
        rooms and Parmesan,
        42–43
espresso bean chocolate short-
    bread, 310
everyday mind, xix

fall vegetable ragoût with white
    beans, 203–4
farmers' markets, xvii, 352, 354,
    358
farro:
    -mushroom soup, 103–4
    salad with roasted peppers
        and arugula, 75
fava bean(s):
    about, 20–21
    puree, 20
fennel:
    garden lettuces with pears,
        pomegranates, pear vinai-
        grette, and, 34

fennel (cont.)
    green salad with beets, walnuts,
        ricotta salata, and, 28–29
    and parsley salad with Meyer
        lemon, 55
    and pepper relish, grilled,
        with capers, 23
    potato, and celery root soup,
        99–100
Ferry Plaza Farmers' Market, 352,
    354, 358
feta:
    in Santorini sandwich on a
        rosemary roll, 123–24
    and spinach griddle cakes,
        175–76
    tomato pizza with lemon,
        scallions, and, 161
fig and endive salad, grilled, with
    watercress, 68
filo, 132–38
    crisps, 336
    crisps, chocolate mousse with,
        335–36
    purses with artichokes, mush-
        rooms, and Asiago, 133–34
    turnover samosas, 10–11
    turnovers filled with goat
        cheese, leeks, and walnuts,
        137–38
    turnovers with butternut
        squash and Gruyère,
        135–36
fines herbes, gypsy peppers filled
    with fromage blanc and,
    267
flour, cake, 364
focaccia with roasted eggplant,
    sun-dried tomatoes, and
    Asiago, 120
Fontina:
    in asparagus bread pudding,
        216
    baguette with tapenade, grilled
        peppers, and, 117–18
    buckwheat crêpes with winter
        vegetables, caramelized
        onions, and, 189–90

Fontina (cont.)
    in butternut squash risotto
        griddle cakes, 179
    pizza with portobello mush-
        rooms, spring onions,
        arugula, and, 171
    potato pizza with roasted
        tomatoes, olives,
        Manchego, and, 165–66
    in Provençal tartlets, 142–43
    in risotto with roasted butter-
        nut squash and kale, 253–54
    roasted eggplant and cherry
        tomato pizza with basil
        and, 164
    roasted portobello mush-
        rooms filled with winter
        vegetables and, 263–64
    in winter root vegetable
        gratin, 225–26
food mills, 100, 371
food processors, 370–71
Fortuna Fontana, 353
French green lentils (lentilles
    du Puy), 79
French lentils, braised, 275
fromage blanc:
    baguette with grilled summer
        vegetables, basil, and,
        125–26
    cheesecake with pistachio
        crust, 332
    gypsy peppers filled with fines
        herbes and, 267
    pizza with wilted greens, hot
        pepper, and, 168
    sources of, 354, 355
fruit:
    dried, plumping of, 367
    vinegars, making of, 27
    see also specific fruits
Fuji apples, 39
fusilli col bucco with grilled
    tomatoes, Gorgonzola,
    and pine nuts, 232–33

Gala apples, 93
galangal, 358

garlic:
    bread crumbs, 219
    bread crumbs, artichokes
        stuffed with lemon, pine
        nuts, and, 269–70
    crisp sliced potatoes with
        fresh thyme and, 258
    croutons, 17
    grilled tomato, and basil
        sauce, 292
    oil, 14
    toasts, 17
garlic, green:
    gratin of potato and, 220–21
    mashed Yellow Finn potatoes
        with, 262
garlic, roasted:
    borlotti bean soup with
        Parmesan croutons and,
        93–94
    custard, chanterelle tart with,
        144–45
    dressing, creamy, 67
    mashed Yellow Finn potatoes
        with, 262
    pasta and white beans with
        rainbow chard, olives, and,
        239–40
    polenta gratin with fire-
        roasted poblano chilies
        and, 223–24
    and potato gratin, 221
    puree, 145
geranium, rose, *see* rose geranium
Giacomini family, 357
ginger(ed), 358–59
    cookies, 308
    corn soup with Thai basil and,
        86
    crunch cake with poached
        pears, 316–17
    -peanut sauce, 83
    -pecan streusel, 317
    shortbread, candied, 310
    yams, 259
glaze(d):
    chocolate, 334
    cipollini onions, 257

goat cheese:
    filo turnovers filled with leeks,
        walnuts, and, 137–38
    lentil salad with mint and,
        77–78
    pizza with wilted greens, hot
        pepper, and, 167–68
    rosemary crêpes with wilted
        greens and, 187–88
    sources of, 356, 358
    sourdough baguette with
        watercress, tomatoes, and,
        114
Goldstein, Joyce, 24
Gorgonzola:
    cream, crisp polenta triangles
        with walnuts, basil, and,
        281–82
    fusilli col bucco with grilled
        tomatoes, pine nuts, and,
        232–33
    wilted spinach salad with
        pears, toasted pecans, and,
        45
grains, *see* basmati rice; couscous;
    farro; jasmine rice;
    polenta; risotto
Granny Smith apples, 39
grapefruit:
    -chili vinaigrette, 31
    ruby, butter lettuce with avo-
        cado, grapefruit-chili
        vinaigrette, and, 30–31
gratin(s), 220 26
    butternut squash, 222
    polenta, with fire-roasted
        poblano chilies and
        roasted garlic, 223–24
    potato and green garlic,
        220–21
    winter root vegetable, 225–26
Gravenstein apples, 38
Greek-style dishes:
    Santorini sandwich on a rose-
        mary roll, 123–24
    spinach and feta griddle
        cakes, 175–76
Green, Connie, 354

Green Gulch, xvii
green papaya, *see* papaya, green
greens:
    sautéed winter, 304
    spicy Asian, 305
greens, bitter:
    with Fuyu persimmons, Asian
        pears, and pecans, 35–36
    types of, 43–44
    see also broccoli rabe; chard;
        chard, rainbow; kale;
        spinach
greens, wilted:
    pizza with goat cheese, hot
        pepper, and, 167–68
    rosemary crêpes with goat
        cheese and, 187–88
    warm cannellini beans and,
        22
    see also chard, wilted; kale,
        wilted; spinach, wilted
Greens (restaurant):
    changes at, xviii
    food sources of, xvii, 352–58
    spirit and continuity at, xix
    Tassajara Bread Bakery
        counter at, xviii
Greens to Go, xviii, 41, 82, 348,
    356
gremolata, 235
    linguine with summer beans,
        olives, and, 234–35
griddle cakes, 174–84
    artichoke, with Gruyère,
        177–78
    butternut squash risotto, 179
    corn and scallion, 174
    potato gordas, 184
    spinach and feta, 175–76
    two potato, 182–83
    Yellow Finn potato cakes with
        Asiago, 180–81
    see also crêpes
grilled:
    artichokes with mint, 15
    asparagus, 14
    fig and endive salad with
        watercress, 68

grilled (*cont.*)
  fingerling potato salad with corn and cherry tomatoes, 70–71
  Mexican sandwich with poblano chilies and cheddar, 119
  onions, fresh mozzarella sandwich with wilted chard and, 121–22
  pepper and fennel relish with capers, 23
  peppers, baguette with tapenade, Fontina, and, 117–18
  portobello mushroom and endive salad with shaved Parmesan, 80–81
  summer vegetables, baguette with fromage blanc, basil, and, 125–26
  summer vegetables, soft tacos with, 152–53
  tomatoes, *see* tomato(es), grilled
Gruyère:
  artichoke griddle cakes with, 177–78
  in chanterelle tart with roasted garlic custard, 144–45
  filo turnovers with butternut squash and, 135–36
  in potato and green garlic gratin, 220–21
  in roasted winter vegetable lasagne, 229–30
  in two potato griddle cakes, 182–83
guacamole, 13

herb(s):
  butter, 268
  cream, 297
  crêpes, 192
  fresh, desert uses for, 366–67
  fresh, using, 268

herb(s) (*cont.*)
  toasting and grinding of, 214
  wine and, 352
  see also fines herbes; *specific herbs*
Hoisin sauce, 361
  peanut-, Vietnamese spring rolls with, 7–9
honey-citrus vinaigrette, 33
  butter lettuce with blood oranges, tangerines, pistachios, and, 32–33
hot pepper:
  broccoli rabe with, 300
  pizza with wilted greens, goat cheese, and, 167–68
Hughes, Debbie, 312, 363
hummous, 12

ice cream:
  rose geranium, 343
  toasted almond, 344
Indian-style dishes:
  curry-laced lentil soup, 108
  curry with tamarind and chilies, 194–95
  filo turnover samosas, 10–11
  wines to serve with, 352
infused oils, 353

jalapeño (chilies):
  Indian curry with tamarind and, 194–95
  -lime vinaigrette, 71
jam, spicy tomato, 24
jasmine rice:
  with cashews, 277
  coconut, 278
juice, fresh citrus, in vinaigrettes, 27
juicers, 370

kabocha squash soup with coconut milk and lime leaves, 90
kaffir lime leaves, 359

kale:
  dinosaur, with toasted almonds, 301
  risotto with roasted butternut squash and, 253–54
  in sautéed winter greens, 304
kale, wilted:
  fresh mozzarella sandwich with grilled onions and, 122
  warm cannellini beans and, 22
knives, 369

lasagne:
  artichoke and portobello mushroom, 227–28
  roasted winter vegetable, 229–30
lavender, 366
leeks, filo turnovers filled with goat cheese, walnuts, and, 137–38
leftovers, for pizza, 160
lemon:
  artichokes stuffed with garlic bread crumbs, pine nuts, and, 269–70
  couscous salad with cherry tomatoes, pine nuts, and, 60
  cream, pappardelle with spring vegetables and, 236–37
  oil, 354
  tomato pizza with feta, scallions, and, 161
  vinaigrette, 78, 270
  vinaigrette, spicy, 124
lemon, Meyer:
  beurre blanc, 296
  fennel and parsley salad with, 55
  vinaigrette, 49
  vinaigrette, asparagus and beets with, 48–49
lemongrass, 359
  stock, 199

lemon verbena, 366
lentil(s), 78
    braised French, 275
    salad with goat cheese and
      mint, 77–78
    soup, curry-laced, 108
    types of, 78–79
lettuce, butter:
    with blood oranges, tanger-
      ines, pistachios, and
      citrus-honey vinaigrette,
      32–33
    in green salad with beets, fen-
      nel, walnuts, and ricotta
      salata, 28–29
    with ruby grapefruit, avocado,
      and grapefruit-chili vinai-
      grette, 30–31
lettuces, garden, with pears, fen-
    nel, pomegranates, and
    pear vinaigrette, 34
lima bean soup, giant Peruvian,
    105–6
lime:
    Asian noodle salad with
      peanut sauce and, 82–84
    -jalapeño vinaigrette, 71
    leaves, kabocha squash soup
      with coconut milk and, 90
linguine:
    with arugula, sun-dried
      tomatoes, and ricotta
      salata, 243
    with summer beans, gremo-
      lata, and olives, 234–35
lotus root, 359
    pickles, 3
Luchetti, Emily, 308

macaroni and cheese, 218–19
macaroons, almond, 309
Manchego:
    artichoke griddle cakes with,
      178
    orecchiette with broccoli rabe,
      almonds, and, 241–42
    panzanella with artichokes,
      olives, and, 50

Manchego (*cont.*)
    potato pizza with roasted
      tomatoes, olives, and,
      165–66
    shaved, heirloom tomato
      salad with, 65
mango:
    avocado salsa, 285
    tomatillo salsa, 285
maple-pecan spice muffins,
    349–50
marinade, artichoke, 53–54
Marsala olive oil, 352
masa harina:
    crêpes, 192
    crêpes with summer vegeta-
      bles, poblano chilies, and
      cheddar, 185–86
    dough, 149
    in potato gordas, 184
mascarpone:
    basmati rice pudding with,
      339–40
    summer risotto with toma-
      toes, basil, and, 251–52
mashed Yellow Finn potatoes, 262
Matos family, cheese from,
    357–58
Mediterranean-style dishes:
    grilled tomato, garlic, and
      basil sauce, 292
    spicy tomato jam, 24
    wines to serve with, 351
    see also Provençal-style dishes
Mexican-style dishes:
    corn quesadillas, 151
    grilled sandwich with
      poblano chilies and ched-
      dar, 119
    guacamole, 13
    masa harina crêpes with sum-
      mer vegetables, poblano
      chilies, and cheddar,
      185–86
    oils for, 353
    pizza with corn, tomatillos,
      and chipotle chilies,
      162–63

Mexican-style dishes (*cont.*)
    potato gordas, 184
    roasted winter vegetable
      enchiladas, 156–57
    soft tacos with butternut
      squash, plantain, and
      poblano chilies,
      154–55
    soft tacos with grilled
      summer vegetables,
      152–53
    tartlets with roasted winter
      vegetables, 146–47
    tomatillo sauce, 289
    wines served with, 352
    see also salsa
Mezzo Secco, 357
Middle Eastern–style dishes:
    cucumber raita, 284
    hummous, 12
    wines to serve with, 351
mint:
    chilled cucumber soup with
      yogurt and, 89
    grilled artichokes with, 15
    lentil salad with goat cheese
      and, 77–78
miso, 361
    udon with shiitake mush-
      rooms, bok choy and,
      246–48
mixers, standing, 368
morels, risotto with asparagus,
    Parmigiano-Reggiano,
    and, 249–50
Moroccan-style dishes:
    beet salad, 51–52
    charmoula, 293
    chick-pea soup, 101–2
    spring vegetable tagine,
      207–9
    vinaigrette, 51
Mt Tam, 355
mousse:
    cakes, chocolate chestnut,
      338
    chocolate, with filo crisps,
      335–36

mozzarella:
  fresh, sandwich with grilled
    onions, wilted chard, and,
    121–22
  pizza with wilted greens, goat
    cheese, hot pepper, and,
    167–68
muffins:
  blueberry maple-pecan spice,
    350
  maple-pecan spice, 349–50
mushroom(s):
  chanterelle tart with roasted
    garlic custard, 144–45
  -farro soup, 103–4
  morels, risotto with aspara-
    gus, Parmigiano-
    Reggiano, and, 249–50
  -sherry sauce, 294
  soy sauce, 361
  stock, 112
  white, filo purses with arti-
    chokes, Asiago, and,
    133–34
  see also portobello mush-
    rooms; shiitake mush-
    rooms
mustard:
  Champagne vinaigrette, 62
  red wine vinaigrette, 73
  vinaigrette basics and, 27
Mytime Ranch, cheese from,
  358

nectarine:
  -almond upside-down cake,
    320–21
  -blackberry shortcake, 315
New Mexican border stew,
  212–13
Nick Sciabica and Sons, 352
noodle(s):
  for Asian dishes, 362
  salad with peanut sauce and
    lime, Asian, 8–84
  udon with miso, shiitake
    mushrooms, and bok
    choy, 246–48

North African food:
  wines to serve with, 351
  see also Moroccan-style
    dishes
Northern Spy apples, 39
nut(s), 367
  cashews, jasmine rice with,
    277
  oils, 353
  toasting of, 26, 46–47
  see also specific nuts

oils, 352–54
  for vinaigrette, 27
olive oil:
  extra-virgin, 352
  garlic, 14
  pure, 353
olives:
  linguine with summer
    beans, gremolata, and,
    234–35
  panzanella with artichokes,
    Manchego, and, 50
  pasta and white beans with
    roasted garlic, rainbow
    chard, and, 239–40
  potato pizza with roasted
    tomatoes, Manchego,
    and, 165–66
  see also tapenade
onion(s):
  caramelized, buckwheat
    crêpes with winter vegeta-
    bles and, 189–90
  glazed cipollini, 257
  grilled, fresh mozzarella sand-
    wich with wilted chard
    and, 121–22
  roasted, portobello sandwich
    with tomatoes, basil aïoli,
    and, 127–28
onion(s), spring:
  and artichoke tart, 139–40
  pizza with portobello mush-
    rooms, arugula, and, 171
  potato, and sorrel soup,
    91–92

orange(s):
  blood, butter lettuce with tan-
    gerines, pistachios, citrus-
    honey vinaigrette, and,
    32–33
  -blueberry bread, 347
  crème fraîche, 98
  crème fraîche, carrot-parsnip
    soup with, 97–98
  zest threads, 88
orecchiette with broccoli rabe,
    almonds, and Manchego,
    241–42
Original Blue, 357
oven rack settings, 368

pak choi, in spicy Asian greens,
    305
pans, panning, 368–69, 371
  double, 367
panzanella with artichokes,
    olives, and Manchego,
    50
papaya, green, 359
  salad, 76
pappardelle with spring vegeta-
    bles and lemon cream,
    236–37
parchment paper, 368, 371
Pardina lentils, 79
Parmesan:
  in artichoke and portobello
    mushroom lasagne,
    227–28
  in asparagus bread pudding,
    216
  bread crumbs, 222
  croutons, 94
  croutons, borlotti bean soup
    with roasted garlic and,
    93–94
  in roasted winter vegetable
    lasagne, 229–30
  shaved, grilled portobello
    mushroom and endive
    salad with, 80–81
  summer risotto with toma-
    toes, basil, and, 252

386

Parmesan (*cont.*)
 wilted spinach and escarole
  hearts with portobello
  mushrooms and, 42–43
Parmigiano-Reggiano, risotto
  with asparagus, morels,
  and, 249–50
parsley and fennel salad with
  Meyer lemon, 55
parsnip-carrot soup with orange
  crème fraîche, 97–98
pasta, 232–48
 fusilli col bucco with grilled
  tomatoes, Gorgonzola, and
  pine nuts, 232–33
 orecchiette with broccoli rabe,
  almonds, and Manchego,
  241–42
 pappardelle with spring vegetables and lemon cream,
  236–37
 spinach tagliarini with corn,
  cherry tomatoes, and basil,
  238
 udon with miso, shiitake
  mushrooms, and bok
  choy, 246–48
 see also lasagne; linguine;
  penne
pastry:
 apple-quince turnovers,
  328–29
 apricot lattice tart, 326–27
 cream cheese dough for, 331
 egg wash, 327
 rhubarb tartlets with almond
  streusel, 324–25
 see also filo
pastry blenders, 369
pastry brushes, 368
peanut(s):
 allergies to, 353
 oil, 353
 spicy, 84
peanut sauce, 211
 Asian noodle salad with lime
  and, 82–84
 with ginger, 83

peanut sauce (*cont.*)
 Hoisin-, 8–9
 Hoisin-, Vietnamese spring
  rolls with, 7–9
 spring stir-fry with Thai basil
  and, 210–11
pear(s):
 Asian, bitter greens with Fuyu
  persimmons, pecans, and,
  35–36
 garden lettuces with fennel,
  pomegranates, pear vinaigrette, and, 34
 poached, 322
 poached, ginger crunch cake
  with, 316–17
 in salads, 26
 vinaigrette, 34
 vinegar, 27
 wilted spinach salad with
  Gorgonzola, toasted
  pecans, and, 45
pea shoots, 360
pecan(s):
 bitter greens with Fuyu persimmons, Asian pears,
  and, 35–36
 brownies, Debbie's, 312
 -currant scones, 347
 ginger streusel, 317
 -maple spice muffins, 349–50
 -maple streusel, 350
 -maple streusel cake, 350
 toasted, wilted spinach salad
  with pears, Gorgonzola,
  and, 45
pecorino pepato, 355
penne:
 with grilled tomatoes, Gorgonzola, and pine nuts,
  232–33
 with roasted butternut
  squash, brown butter, and
  sage, 244–45
 and white beans with roasted
  garlic, rainbow chard, and
  olives, 239–40
peppermint, English black, 367

pepper(s):
 and fennel relish, grilled, with
  capers, 23
 grilled, baguette with tapenade, Fontina, and, 117–18
 gypsy, filled with fromage
  blanc and fines herbes,
  267
 in New Mexican border stew,
  212–13
 sourdough baguette with goat
  cheese, watercress, and,
  114
 see also chilies; hot pepper
pepper(s), roasted:
 farro salad with arugula and,
  75
 general information for, 291
 sauce, 290
persimmons:
 Fuyu, bitter greens with Asian
  pears, pecans, and, 35–36
 general information about,
  36
Peruvian lima bean soup, giant,
  105–6
Phipps Ranch, 106
Picholine olive tapenade, 18
pickles, pickled:
 daikon radish, 4
 daikon radish–carrot, 130
 lotus root, 3
pine nuts:
 artichokes stuffed with garlic
  bread crumbs, lemon, and,
  269–70
 couscous salad with cherry
  tomatoes, lemon, and, 60
 fusilli col bucco with grilled
  tomatoes, Gorgonzola,
  and, 232–33
 linguine with arugula, sun-
  dried tomatoes, ricotta
  salata, and, 243
 roasted Japanese eggplant
  salad with capers and, 74
Pippin apples, 39
piquillo peppers, 114

pistachio(s):
  butter lettuce with blood
    oranges, tangerines,
    citrus-honey vinaigrette,
    and, 32–33
  crust, fromage blanc cheese-
    cake with, 332
  shortbread, 311
pizza, 159–72
  artichoke and roasted shallot,
    169–70
  with corn, tomatillos, and
    chipotle chilies, Mexican,
    162–63
  dough, 172
  with portobello mushrooms,
    spring onions, and
    arugula, 171
  potato, with roasted toma-
    toes, olives, and
    Manchego, 165–66
  roasted eggplant and
    cherry tomato, with
    basil, 164
  tomato, with feta, lemon, and
    scallions, 161
  with wilted greens, goat
    cheese, and hot pepper,
    167–68
plantain(s):
  -chili sauce, 212
  soft tacos with butternut
    squash, poblano chilies,
    and, 154–55
  tip for, 213
plum(s):
  almond brown butter cake
    with, 318–19
  -raspberry cobbler, 313
  sorbet, 345
poached:
  pears, 322
  pears, ginger crunch cake
    with, 316–17
  sour cherries, 323
poblano (chilies):
  grilled Mexican sandwich
    with cheddar and, 119

poblano (chilies) (cont.)
  masa harina crêpes with sum-
    mer vegetables, cheddar,
    and, 185–86
  soft tacos with butternut
    squash, plantain, and,
    154–55
poblano (chilies), fire-roasted, 64
  and corn salad with cilantro,
    63–64
  polenta gratin with roasted
    garlic and, 223–24
polenta, 280
  gratin with fire-roasted
    poblano chilies and
    roasted garlic, 223–24
  triangles, crisp, with Gor-
    gonzola cream, walnuts,
    and basil, 281–82
pomegranates, with garden let-
    tuces, pears, fennel, and
    pear vinaigrette, 34
porcini oil, 354
portobello mushroom(s):
  and artichoke lasagne, 227–28
  and endive salad, grilled, with
    shaved Parmesan, 80–81
  pizza with spring onions,
    arugula, and, 171
  roasted, 260
  roasted, filled with winter
    vegetables and Fontina,
    263–64
  sandwich with tomatoes,
    roasted onions, and basil
    aïoli, 127–28
  wilted spinach and escarole
    hearts with Parmesan and,
    42–43
  winter vegetable ragoût with,
    205–6
potato(es):
  cakes, Yellow Finn, with Asi-
    ago, 180–81
  fennel, and celery root soup,
    99–100
  filling, filo turnover samosas
    with, 10–11

potato(es) (cont.)
  with garlic and fresh thyme,
    crisp sliced, 258
  gordas, 184
  and green garlic gratin,
    220–21
  griddle cakes, two, 182–83
  mashed Yellow Finn, 262
  pizza with roasted tomatoes,
    olives, and Manchego,
    165–66
  purple, general information
    about, 73
  spring onion, and sorrel soup,
    91–92
potato salad:
  grilled fingerling, with corn
    and cherry tomatoes,
    70–71
  purple, 73
  Yellow Finn, with green beans
    and tarragon, 72–73
pots, 371
Provençal-style dishes:
  Picholine olive tapenade, 18
  tartlets, 142–43
pudding, savory:
  asparagus bread, 216
  corn, 217
pudding, sweet:
  chocolate-rum steamed, 337
  rice, with mascarpone,
    339–40
pumpkin seeds:
  basmati rice with, 276
  rainbow chard with, 302–3
puree:
  ancho chili, 147
  chestnut, 96
  chipotle, 163
  fava bean, 20
  roasted garlic, 145

quick bread(s):
  blueberry-orange, 347
  currant-pecan scones, 348
  maple-pecan spice muffins,
    349–50

quince:
-apple turnovers, 328–29
general information about,
330
and sour cherry compote,
16

radicchio:
in bitter greens, with Fuyu
persimmons, Asian
pears, and pecans,
35–36
types of, 43–55
radish, *see* daikon radish
ragoût(s), 203–6
fall vegetable, with white
beans, 203–4
winter vegetable, with
portobello mushrooms,
205–6
raita, cucumber, 284
Ras el Hanout, 209
raspberry-plum cobbler, 313
rattlesnake beans, spicy, 272
Red Chief lentils, 79
red curry:
spices, 198
with summer vegetables and
Thai spices, 196–99
Red Hawk cream cheese, 355
red wine vinaigrette, 41, 75
mustard, 73
romaine hearts with sun-
dried tomatoes, chunky
sourdough croutons,
and, 40–41
Redwood Hill Farm, cheeses
from, 356
relish:
artichoke, 19
grilled pepper and fennel,
with capers, 23
rhubarb tartlets with almond
streusel, 324–25
rice, *see* basmati rice; jasmine
rice; risotto
rice noodles, 362
rice vinegar, 361

rice wrappers, 362
handling tips for, 8
in Vietnamese spring rolls
with peanut-Hoisin sauce,
7–9
ricotta cheese, 355
in artichoke and portobello
mushroom lasagne,
227–28
in corn and scallion griddle
cakes, 174
in roasted winter vegetable
lasagne, 229–30
ricotta salata:
green salad with beets, fennel,
walnuts, and, 28–29
linguine with arugula, sun-
dried tomatoes, and, 243
risotto, 249–54
with asparagus, morels, and
Parmigiano-Reggiano,
249–50
butternut squash griddle
cakes, 179
the restaurant way, 250
with roasted butternut squash
and kale, 253–54
with tomatoes, mascarpone,
and basil, summer,
251–52
wine and, 352
romaine hearts:
with sun-dried tomatoes,
chunky sourdough crou-
tons, and red wine vinai-
grette, 40–41
and watercress with apples,
beets, Stilton, and cider
vinaigrette, 37–38
rose geranium, 366
ice cream, 343
sugar, 366
rosemary:
crêpes, 192
crêpes with goat cheese and
wilted greens, 187–88
roll, Santorini sandwich on a,
123–24

rum-chocolate steamed pudding,
337

Sagatelyan, Mihran, 132
sage:
leaves, roasted butternut
squash rounds with, 256
penne with roasted butternut
squash, brown butter, and,
244–45
Sahni, Julie, 108
Saint George cheddar, 141, 358
St Pats, 355
salad(s), 25–84
Asian noodle, with peanut
sauce and lime, 82–84
asparagus and beets with
Meyer lemon vinaigrette,
48–49
beets with tangerine-shallot
vinaigrette, 52
bitter greens with Fuyu persimmons, Asian pears, and
pecans, 35–36
corn and cherry tomato, with
arugula, 56
corn and fire-roasted
poblano, with cilantro,
63–64
couscous, with cherry tomatoes, lemon, and pine nuts,
60
farro, with roasted peppers
and arugula, 75
fennel and parsley, with
Meyer lemon, 55
garden lettuces with pears,
fennel, pomegranates, and
pear vinaigrette, 34
green, with beets, fennel, walnuts, and ricotta salata,
28–29
green beans and shelling
beans with cherry toma-
toes, 58–59
green papaya, 76
grilled fig and endive, with
watercress, 68

salad(s) (*cont.*)

grilled portobello mushroom and endive, with shaved Parmesan, 80–81

lentil, with goat cheese and mint, 77–78

make-ahead steps for, 26–27

Moroccan beet, 51–52

panzanella with artichokes, olives, and Manchego, 50

roasted Japanese eggplant, with pine nuts and capers, 74

simple artichoke, 53–54

simplifying of, 26–27

white runner beans with Champagne vinaigrette and tarragon, 61–62

see also lettuce, butter; potato salad; romaine hearts; spinach, wilted; tomato salad

salad spinners, 26

salsa, 285–88

avocado-mango, 285

corn and tomatillo, 286

fire-roasted, 287

mango-tomatillo, 285

negra, 288

salt, 81, 107

sambal, 361

samosas, filo turnover, 10–11

sandwich(es), 113–30

avocado and tomato, with chipotle aïoli, 115–16

baguette with grilled summer vegetables, fromage blanc, and basil, 125–26

baguette with tapenade, grilled peppers, and Fontina, 117–18

focaccia with roasted eggplant, sun-dried tomatoes, and Asiago, 120

fresh mozzarella, with grilled onions and wilted chard, 121–22

sandwich(es) (*cont.*)

with poblano chilies and cheddar, grilled Mexican, 119

portobello, with tomatoes, roasted onions, and basil aïoli, 127–28

on a rosemary roll, Santorini, 123–24

Santorini, on a rosemary roll, 123–24

sourdough baguette with goat cheese, watercress, and tomatoes, 114

Tai's Vietnamese tofu, 129–30

sauce(s):

charmoula, 293

cucumber raita, 284

grilled tomato, garlic, and basil, 292

herb cream, 297

Meyer lemon beurre blanc, 296

mushroom-sherry, 294

peanut, *see* peanut sauce

plantain-chili, 212

roasted pepper, 290

spicy dipping, 6

spicy dipping, crispy spring rolls with, 5–6

tomatillo, 289

tomato-Zinfandel, 295

see also salsa

sauce(s), dessert:

bittersweet chocolate, 342

blackberry, 315

Sausalito Springs, 69

sautéed winter greens, 304

savory bites, 1–24

artichoke relish, 19

crispy spring rolls with spicy dipping sauce, 5–6

fava bean puree, 20

filo turnover samosas, 10–11

garlic toasts for, 17

grilled artichokes with mint, 15

grilled asparagus, 14

grilled pepper and fennel relish with capers, 23

savory bites (*cont.*)

guacamole, 13

hummous, 12

lotus root pickles, 3

Picholine olive tapenade, 18

pickled daikon radish, 4

quince and sour cherry compote, 16

spicy tomato jam, 24

Vietnamese spring rolls with peanut-Hoisin sauce, 7–9

warm cannellini beans and wilted greens, 22

warm spiced almonds, 2

scallion(s):

and corn griddle cakes, 174

crêpes, 192

tomato pizza with feta, lemon, and, 161

scarlet runner beans, 106

Sciabica family, 354, 356

scones, currant-pecan, 348

seeds, toasting of, 46–47

see also pumpkin seeds

sesame oil, toasted, 353, 362

Sevillano olive oil, 352

Shaharazad Bakery, 132

shallot(s), 360

roasted, and artichoke pizza, 169–70

shallot-tangerine vinaigrette, 52

beets with, 52

sherbet, blackberry, 346

sherry:

mushroom sauce, 294

tangerine vinaigrette, 35–36

walnut vinaigrette, 29

shiitake mushrooms:

dried, 363

udon with miso, bok choy, and, 246–48

shortbread:

candied ginger, 310

chocolate espresso bean, 310

citrus, 311

pistachio, 311

vanilla bean, 311

shortcake, 314
  nectarine-blackberry, 315
Sierra Beauty apples, 39
sorbet:
  blackberry, 346
  plum, 345
sorrel, potato, and spring onion
  soup, 91–92
soup(s), 85–112
  borlotti bean, with roasted
    garlic and Parmesan crou-
    tons, 93–94
  butternut squash and chest-
    nut, 95–96
  carrot-parsnip, with orange
    crème fraîche, 97–98
  chilled cucumber, with yogurt
    and mint, 89
  chilled three-beet, 87–88
  corn, with ginger and Thai
    basil, 86
  curry-laced lentil, 108
  giant Peruvian lima bean,
    105–6
  kabocha squash, with
    coconut milk and lime
    leaves, 90
  Moroccan chick-pea, 101–2
  mushroom-farro, 103–4
  potato, fennel, and celery
    root, 99–100
  potato, spring onion, and sor-
    rel, 91–92
  see also stock
sourdough baguette with goat
  cheese, watercress, and
  tomatoes, 114
Southeast Asian–style dishes,
  xviii
  crispy spring rolls with spicy
    dipping sauce, 5–6
  green papaya salad, 76
  lotus root pickles, 3
  pickled daikon radish, 4
  see also Vietnamese-style
    dishes
soy milk, 365
soy sauce, 361

spice(s):
  mixture, 102
  muffins, blueberry maple-
    pecan, 350
  muffins, maple-pecan, 349–50
  Ras el Hanout, 209
  red curry, 198
  Thai, red curry with summer
    vegetables and, 196–99
  toasting and grinding of, 214
  yellow curry, 201
spiced, spicy:
  almonds, warm, 2
  Asian greens, 305
  dipping sauce, 6
  dipping sauce, crispy spring
    rolls with, 5–6
  lemon vinaigrette, 124
  peanuts, 84
  rattlesnake beans, 272
  tomato jam, 24
spice grinders, 370
spinach:
  and feta griddle cakes,
    175–76
  potato, and spring onion
    soup, 92
  tagliarini with corn, cherry
    tomatoes, and basil, 238
spinach, wilted:
  and escarole hearts with por-
    tobello mushrooms and
    Parmesan, 42–43
  in rosemary crêpes with goat
    cheese and wilted greens,
    187–88
  salad with pears, Gorgonzola,
    and toasted pecans, 45
spring onions, see onion(s),
  spring
spring rolls:
  crispy, with spicy dipping
    sauce, 5–6
  Vietnamese, with peanut-
    Hoisin sauce, 7–9
spring stir-fry with peanut sauce
  and Thai basil, 210–11
spring vegetable tagine, 207–9

squash:
  butternut, see butternut
    squash
  kabocha, soup with coconut
    milk and lime leaves, 90
standing mixers, 368
Star Route Farms, 69
stew(s):
  New Mexican border,
    212–13
  spring stir-fry with peanut
    sauce and Thai basil,
    210–11
  spring vegetable tagine, 207–9
  see also curry(ies); ragoût(s)
Stilton, romaine hearts and
  watercress with apples,
  beets, cider vinaigrette,
  and, 37–38
stir-fry with peanut sauce and
  Thai basil, spring,
  210–11
stock:
  corn, 111
  lemongrass, 199
  mushroom, 112
  quick Asian, 247–48
  vegetable, 109–10
strainers, 371
Straus Family Creamery, 89, 357
streusel:
  almond, 325
  almond, rhubarb tartlets with,
    324–25
  ginger-pecan, 317
  maple-pecan, 350
  maple-pecan, cake, 350
sugar:
  cinnamon, 329
  lavender, 366
  rose geranium, 366
  turbinado, 365
  vanilla, 366
summer risotto with tomatoes,
  mascarpone, and basil,
  251–52
sweet potato, in two potato
  griddle cakes, 182–83

tacos, soft:
with butternut squash, plantain, and poblano chilies, 154–55
with grilled summer vegetables, 152–53
tagine, spring vegetable, 207–9
tagliarini, spinach, with corn, cherry tomatoes, and basil, 238
tahini, in hummous, 12
Tai's Vietnamese tofu sandwich, 129–30
tamari, 361
tamarind, 362
Indian curry with chilies and, 194–95
tangerine(s):
butter lettuce with blood oranges, pistachios, citrus-honey vinaigrette, and, 32–33
cranberry compote with, 341
shallot vinaigrette, 52
shallot vinaigrette, beets with, 52
sherry vinaigrette, 35–36
tapenade, 118
baguette with grilled peppers, Fontina, and, 117–18
Picholine olive, 18
tapioca starch (tapioca flour), 365
tarragon:
white runner beans with Champagne vinaigrette and, 61–62
Yellow Finn potato salad with green beans and, 72–73
tart(s), tartlets, 139–50
artichoke and spring onion, 139–40
chanterelle, with roasted garlic custard, 144–45
corn and basil, 141
dough, 148
dough, yeasted, 150
masa harina dough for, 149

tart(s), tartlets (*cont.*)
Provençal, 142–43
with roasted winter vegetables, Mexican, 146–47
tart(s), tartlets, sweet:
apricot lattice, 326–27
dough, 326–27
rhubarb, with almond streusel, 324–25
Tassajara Bread Bakery counter, xviii
Thai basil, *see* basil, Thai
Thai-style dishes, xviii
spices, red curry with summer vegetables and, 196–99
thyme, fresh, crisp sliced potatoes with garlic and, 258
Tiger Brand olive oil, 353
toasted sesame oil, 353, 362
toasts, garlic, 17
tofu (bean curd), 360
in crispy spring rolls with spicy dipping sauce, 5–6
sandwich, Tai's Vietnamese, 129–30
in spring stir-fry with peanut sauce and Thai basil, 210–11
in Vietnamese spring rolls with peanut-Hoisin sauce, 7–9
tomatillo(s):
and corn salsa, 286
-mango salsa, 285
Mexican pizza with corn, chipotle chilies, and, 162–63
sauce, 289
tomato(es):
and avocado sandwich with chipotle aïoli, 115–16
jam, spicy, 24
pizza with feta, lemon, and scallions, 161
sourdough baguette with goat cheese, watercress, and, 114

tomato(es) (*cont.*)
summer risotto with mascarpone, basil, and, 251–52
-Zinfandel sauce, 295
tomato(es), cherry:
and corn salad with arugula, 56
couscous salad with lemon, pine nuts, and, 60
general information about, 57
green beans and shelling beans with, 58–59
grilled fingerling potato salad with corn and, 70–71
and roasted eggplant pizza with basil, 164
spinach tagliarini with corn, basil, and, 238
tomato(es), grilled, 233
fusilli col bucco with Gorgonzola, pine nuts, and, 232–33
garlic, and basil sauce, 292
tomatoes, roasted, 261
borlotti bean soup with roasted garlic and, 94
potato pizza with olives, Manchego, and, 165–66
tomatoes, sun-dried:
focaccia with roasted eggplant, Asiago, and, 120
linguine with arugula, ricotta salata, and, 243
romaine hearts with chunky sourdough croutons, red wine vinaigrette, and, 40–41
tomato salad:
with creamy blue cheese dressing, 66
heirloom, with shaved Manchego, 65
Tome, 356
tongs, spring-loaded, 370
Tropp, Barbara, 81
truffle oil, white, 354
turbinado sugar, 365

turnover(s):
    apple-quince, 328–29
    samosas, filo, 10–11

udon, 362
    with miso, shiitake mush-
        rooms, and bok choy,
        246–48
upside-down cake, nectarine-
    almond, 320–21

vanilla, vanilla bean(s), 364
    extract, 364
    shortbread, 311
    sugar, 366
vegetable peelers, 369
vegetable(s):
    dried, canned, and preserved,
        for Asian-style dishes, 363
    fall, ragoût with white beans
        and, 203–4
    tartlets, Provençal, 142–43
vegetable(s), spring:
    pappardelle with, 236–37
    tagine, 207–9
vegetable(s), summer:
    grilled, baguette with fromage
        blanc, basil, and, 125–26
    grilled, soft tacos with, 152–53
    masa harina crêpes with
        poblano chilies, cheddar,
        and, 185–86
    red curry with Thai spices
        and, 196–99
vegetable(s), winter:
    buckwheat crêpes with
        caramelized onions and,
        189–90
    ragoût with portobello mush-
        rooms and, 205–6
    roasted, enchiladas, 156–57
    roasted, lasagne, 229–30
    roasted, Mexican tartlets with,
        146–47
    roasted portobello mush-
        rooms filled with Fontina
        and, 263–64
    root, gratin, 225–26

vegetable slicers, 370
vegetable stock, 109–10
Vella Cheese Company, 357
Vella Dry jack, 357
Vietnamese-style dishes, xviii
    spring rolls with peanut-
        Hoisin sauce, 7–9
    Tai's tofu sandwich,
        129–30
    yellow curry, 200–202
vinaigrette(s), 26–27
    basic ingredients for, 27
    cider, 38
    cider, romaine hearts and
        watercress with apples,
        beets, Stilton, and,
        37–38
    citrus-honey, 33
    citrus-honey, butter lettuce
        with blood oranges, tan-
        gerines, pistachios, and,
        32–33
    grapefruit-chili, 31
    grapefruit-chili, butter
        lettuce with ruby grape-
        fruit, avocado, and,
        30–31
    jalapeño-lime, 71
    leftover, refreshing of, 27
    Moroccan, 51
    pear, 34
    pear, garden lettuces with
        pears, fennel, pomegran-
        ates, and, 34
    sherry-walnut, 29
    tangerine-shallot, 52
    tangerine-shallot, beets with,
        52
    tangerine-sherry, 35–36
vinaigrette(s), Champagne, 59
    mustard, 62
    white runner beans with tar-
        ragon and, 61–62
vinaigrette(s), lemon, 78, 270
    Meyer, 49
    Meyer, asparagus and beets
        with, 48–49
    spicy, 124

vinaigrette(s), red wine, 41, 75
    mustard, 73
    romaine hearts with sun-
        dried tomatoes, chunky
        sourdough croutons, and,
        40–41
vinegar(s), 27
    fruit, making of, 27
    reduced balsamic, 126
    rice, 361

walnut(s):
    crisp polenta triangles with
        Gorgonzola cream, basil,
        and, 281–82
    filo turnovers filled with
        goat cheese, leeks, and,
        137–38
    green salad with beets,
        fennel, ricotta salata,
        and, 28–29
    penne with roasted butternut
        squash, brown butter, sage,
        and, 244–45
    -sherry vinaigrette, 29
watercress, 69
    in bitter greens, with Fuyu
        persimmons, Asian pears,
        and pecans, 35–36
    grilled fig and endive salad
        with, 68
    and romaine hearts with
        apples, beets, Stilton, and
        cider vinaigrette, 37–38
    sourdough baguette with
        goat cheese, tomatoes,
        and, 114
whisks, 371
white lentils, 79
white truffle oil, 354
Wine Forest Wild Mushrooms,
    354
wines, 351–52
    see also red wine vinaigrette
winter vegetable ragoût with
    portobello mushrooms,
    205–6
Wolfert, Paula, 209

World of Food (Wolfert), 209
worm composting, 372–74
wrappers:
    for Asian dishes, 363
    egg roll, in crispy spring rolls
        with spicy dipping sauce,
        5–6
    rice, *see* rice wrappers

yam(s):
    gingered, 259

yam(s) (*cont.*)
    in two potato griddle cakes,
        182–83
yeasted tart dough, 150
yellow curry:
    spices, 201
    Vietnamese, 200–202
yellow lentils, 79
yogurt:
    chilled cucumber soup with
        mint and, 89

yogurt (*cont.*)
    in cucumber raita, 284
    nonfat, 357

Zen Center, xix
    farm of, *see* Green Gulch
zest, fruit:
    orange threads, 88
    in vinaigrette, 27
zesters, 370
Zinfandel-tomato sauce, 295

About the Author

Annie Somerville is the executive chef of Greens Restaurant and the author of the award-winning cookbook *Fields of Greens*. She came to Greens in 1981, trained under Deborah Madison, and has been the executive chef since 1985. Under her culinary guidance, Greens has flourished, expanding and adapting to a rapidly changing marketplace while leading the way with innovative vegetarian cuisine. Now in her twenty-second year at Greens, her commitment to using garden-fresh produce and cooking with the seasons remains stronger than ever. She's in close contact with the organic gardeners at Green Gulch Farm and local growers, cheese makers, and purveyors and works closely with the Greens chefs, planning menus and overseeing a talented kitchen staff.

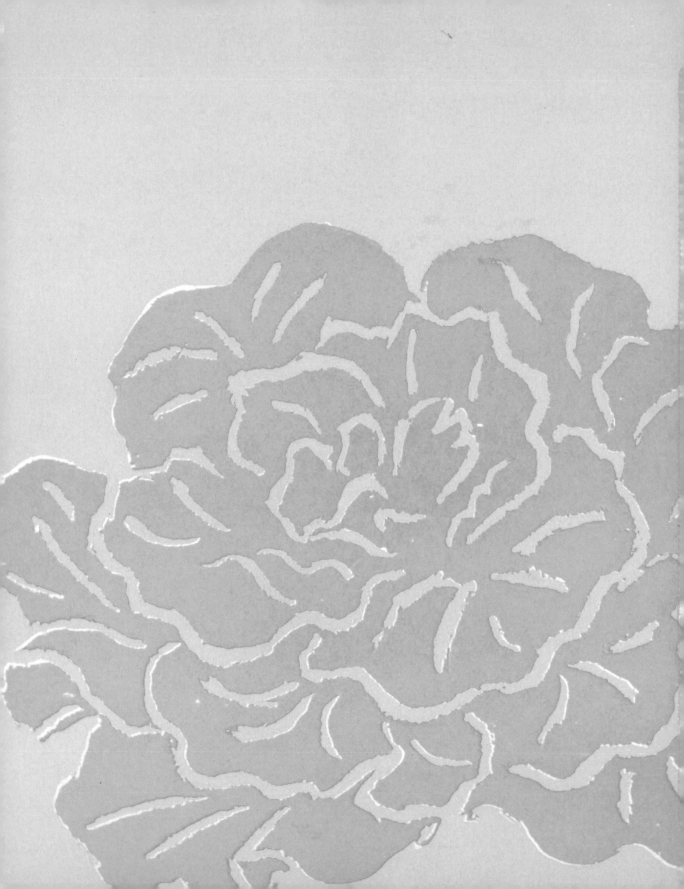